Military Aircraft Markings 1983

Peter R. March

LONDON

IAN ALLAN LTD

Note: Whilst every effort has been made to ensure the accuracy of this publication no part of the contents has been obtained from official or similar sources. The compiler will be pleased to receive readers' comments, corrections and further information for inclusion in subsequent editions of *Military Aircraft Markings*.

Cover: BAe Sea Harrier FRS1s seen aboard HMS *Hermes*.　　*Stephen W. D. Wolf/Flightlines International*

Photographs by Andrew March, Daniel March, and Peter R. March

This edition published 1983

ISBN 0 7110 1289 X

Published by Ian Allan Ltd, Shepperton, Surrey; and printed by Ian Allan Printing Ltd at their works at Coombelands in Runnymede, England

Introduction

This fourth edition of *Military Aircraft Markings*, a companion to *Civil Aircraft Markings*, sets out to list all current aircraft carrying service serial numbers in the British Isles. This includes all UK military aircraft, including those located overseas for operational reasons, USAF and USN machines based in the UK and the current Irish Army Air Corps fleet. Included in this edition there is an enlarged coverage of USAF aircraft normally based in north-west Europe and mainland USA, likely to be seen in the UK, visiting or taking part in exchanges, exercises or air shows. There is also an extended selection of aircraft from other overseas air arms which might be seen visiting the UK from time to time, and of historic aircraft which carry overseas military markings but are based in the UK.

The term aircraft used here covers powered, manned aeroplanes, helicopters and gliders. It does not include un-manned target drones. The serials listed are in the main those presently displayed on the aircraft, whether it is a primary or a secondary identity such as an RAF Support Command 'M' or Royal Navy 'A' maintenance number. Scrapped aeroplanes and those used as targets on MoD ranges are generally omitted.

UK serials are listed in strict alphabetical and numerical order with the manufacturer and type detailed and the owner, operator or location shown for each. If the aircraft has an alternative previous or current identifying serial or civil registration this is shown in brackets after the type. A cross reference to the many RAF 'M' and RN 'A' numbers is included.

All RAF, RN, Army Air Corps and Ministry of Defence (Procurement Executive) aircraft are listed if they remain current. For front-line RAF units the operating 'Group' or squadron number is shown while second-line squadrons and training units are detailed in full. Operational RN and Army aircraft have their normal location detailed and additional unit information is given for second-line squadrons.

Where a serial is omitted in a sequence this indicates that no aircraft is carrying that number at present, having been written off, scrapped, sold abroad or allocated an alternative marking.

Current USAF and USN aircraft based in the UK are listed by type. The full fiscal year serial is shown with the tail marking actually displayed following in brackets. Details of the operating wing, and the UK base are also provided. For European and mainland USA aircraft the full fiscal year serial is followed by the standard five-figure number in brackets. The serial numbers of overseas service aircraft are as usually presented on the individual machine or as they are normally identified. Likewise the listed historic aircraft show the number carried on the fuselage as principal means of identification.

New in this 1983 edition are entries in square brackets showing — where available — the code letters carried by Royal Air Force, Royal Navy and Army Air Corps aircraft, as recorded during 1982. It is hoped that coverage of these codes will be more universal in the next edition of *Military Aircraft Markings*. These unit markings are normally carried boldly on the sides of the fuselage or on the aircraft's fin. In the case of RAF and AAC machines currently in service they are usually a single letter or number, while the RN continues to use a well established system of three figure codes between 001 and 999 together with a fin letter code denoting the aircraft's operational base. RN squadrons, units and bases are allocated blocks of numbers from which individual aircraft codes are issued. Codes changes when aircraft move between units and therefore the markings shown in this edition might not be that currently painted on a particular aircraft, having been overtaken by events. This applies especially to RN aircraft involved in the Falklands conflict which, since their return have been re-allocated to different units after overhaul. To help identification of RN bases and landing platforms on ships a list of tail letter codes with their appropriate name, ship pennant number and type of vessel is included for the first time.

Information shown is believed to be correct at 1 January 1983 and the addendum carries any changes noted while the book was in production.

Acknowledgements

The compiler wishes to thank the many people who have taken trouble to send comments, criticism and other useful information following the publication of the first three editions of *Military Aircraft Markings*. In particular I would like to thank P. R. Arnold, R. Bonser, H. J. Curtis, P. Dopson, J. Jackson, K. Mason, D. Stephens, G. S. Taylor, G. Turner and A. J. Wright.

This compilation has relied heavily on information published by the following aviation groups and societies: British Aviation Research Group, Central Scotland Aviation Group, Cheshire Aviation Society, Humberside Aviation Society, Merseyside Aviation Society, Plymouth Aviation Research Society, South West Aviation Society, Stansted Aviation Society and the West of Scotland Aviation Group together with these publications: *British Military Aircraft Serials and Markings*, British Aviation Research Group; *A Directory of British Military Aviation*, by Paul S. Mercer, Jackson Publications; *French Military Aviation* (second edition) by Paul A. Jackson, Midland Counties Publications; *Foreign Military Air Arms to Europe* by S. M. Jessup and A. G. W. Mower, The Aviation Hobby Shop; *Militair 1982* by John Andrade, Aviation Press Ltd; *United States Military Aircraft to Europe* by S. M. Jessup and A. G. W. Mower, Seefive Publications; *United States Military Aviation: The Air Force* by Robert J. Archer, Midland Counties Publications; *Wrecks and Relics (8th Edition)* by Ken Ellis, Merseyside Aviation Society.

The new edition of *Military Aircraft Markings* would not have been possible without considerable research and checking by Andrew March and Wal Gandy, assisted by Alison & Daniel March and Brian Strickland.

PRM

Abbreviations

AAC	Army Air Corps
A&AEE	Aeroplane & Armament Experimental Establishment
ACCS	Airborne Command and Control Squadron
AEF	Air Experience Flight
AES	Air Engineering School
AETW	Air Engineering Training Wing
AEW	Airborne Early Warning
AIU	Accident Investigation Unit
ARRS	Aerospace Rescue and Recovery Squadron
ARWS	Advanced Rotary Wing Squadron
AS	Airspeed
AS&RU	Aircraft Salvage and Repair Unit
ATC	Air Training Corps
ATCC	Air Traffic Control Centre
ATS	Aircrewman Training Squadron
AW	Armstrong Whitworth Aircraft
BAC	British Aircraft Corporation
BAe	British Aerospace Company
BAOR	British Army of the Rhine
BAPC	British Aircraft Preservation Council
BATUS	British Army Training Unit Support
BDRF	Battle Damage Repair Flight
BHC	British Hovercraft Corporation
BP	Boulton & Paul
B-V	Boeing-Vertol
CATCS	Central Air Traffic Control School
CBAS	Commando Brigade Air Squadron
CCF	Combined Cadet Force
CFS	Central Flying School
CGS	Central Gliding School
CSDE	Central Servicing Development Establishment
CTE	Central Training Establishment
CTTS	Civilian Technical Training School
CV	Chance-Vought
D-BD	Dassault-Breguet Dornier
DH	De Havilland
DHC	De Havilland Canada
D&T	Demonstration & Trials
EE	English Electric
ETPS	Empire Test Pilots School
EWAU	Electronic Warfare Avionics Unit
FAA	Fleet Air Arm
FBW	Fly by wire
FF&SS	Fire Fighting & Safety School
Flt	Flight
FONAC	Flag Officer Naval Air Command
FRADU	Fleet Requirements and Direction Unit
FSS	Flying Selection School
FTS	Flying Training School
FW	Foster Wickner
GD	General Dynamics
GS	Gliding School
HAPS	Humberside Aircraft Preservation Society
HP	Handley-Page
HQ	Headquarters
HS	Hawker Siddeley
IAM	Institute of Aviation Medicine
IWM	Imperial War Museum
JSTU	Joint Services Trials Unit
LCF	Lynx Conversion Flight
LFV&HAC	Lincoln Field Vintage & Historic Aircraft Collection
LTF	Lightning Training Flight
McD	McDonnell Douglas
MGSP	Mobile Glider Servicing Party
MoD(PE)	Ministry of Defence (Procurement Executive)
Mod	Modified
MU	Maintenance Unit
NA	North American
NAHU	Naval Aircraft Holding Unit
NASU	Naval Air Support Unit
OCU	Operational Conversion Unit
PAX	Passenger procedural trainer
PRU	Photographic Reconnaissance Unit
RAE	Royal Aircraft Establishment
RAF	Royal Aircraft Factory
RAF	Royal Air Force
RAFA	Royal Air Force Association
RAFC	Royal Air Force College
RAFEF	Royal Air Force Exhibition Flight
RAFSKTF	Royal Air Force Sea King Training Flight
REME	Royal Electrical & Mechanical Engineers
RM	Royal Marines
RN	Royal Navy
RNAS	Royal Naval Air Station
RNAY	Royal Naval Aircraft Yard
RNEC	Royal Naval Engineering College
RNEFTS	Royal Naval Elementary Flying Training School
RR	Rolls-Royce
RS	Reid & Sigrist
RSRE	Royal Signals and Radar Establishment
SAH	School of Air Handling
SAL	Scottish Aviation Limited
SAR	Search and Rescue
SAREW	Search and Rescue Engineering Wing
SARTU	Search and Rescue Training Unit
SARO	Saunders-Roe
SoTT	School of Technical Training
Sqn	Squadron
SSTF	Sea Skua Trials Flight
SWWAPS	Second World War Aircraft Preservation Society
TFTAS	Tactical Fighter Training Aggressor Squadron
TFW	Tactical Fighter Wing
Trg	Training
TRS	Tactical Reconnaissance Squadron
TSF	Tornado Servicing Flight
TTTE	Tri-national Tornado Training Establishment
TWCU	Tornado Weapons Conversion Unit
TWU	Tactical Weapons Unit
UAS	University Air-Squadron
UK	United Kingdom
USAF	United States Air Force
USAREUR	US Army Europe
VS	Vickers-Supermarine
WS	Westland
WW2	World War II

British Military Aircraft Serials

The Committee of Imperial Defence through its Air Committee introduced a standardised system of numbering aircraft in November 1912. The Air Department of the Admiralty was allocated the first batch 1-200 and used these to cover aircraft already in use and those on order. The Army was issued with the next block from 201-800, which included the number 304 which was given to the Cody Biplane now preserved in the Science Museum. By the outbreak of World War 1 the Royal Navy was on its second batch of serials 801-1600 and this system continued with alternating allocations between the Army and Navy until 1916 when number 10000, a Royal Flying Corps BE2C, was reached.

It was decided not to continue with five digit numbers but instead to start again from 1, prefixing RFC aircraft with the letter A and RNAS aircraft with the prefix N. The RFC allocations commenced with A1 an FE2D and before the end of the year had reached A9999 an Armstrong Whitworth FK8. The next group commenced with B1 and continued in logical sequence through the C, D, E and F prefixes. G was used on a limited basis to identity captured German aircraft, while H was the last block of wartime ordered aircraft. To avoid confusion I was not used, so the new postwar machines were allocated serials in the J range. A further minor change was made in the serial numbering system in August 1929 when it was decided to maintain four numerals after the prefix letter, thus omitting numbers 1 to 999. The new K series therefore commenced at K1000, which was allocated to an AW Atlas.

The Naval N prefix was not used in such a logical way. Blocks of numbers were allocated for specific types of aircraft such as seaplanes or flying boats. By the late 1920s the sequence had largely been used up and a new series using the prefix S was commenced. In 1930 separate naval allocations were stopped and subsequent serials were issued in the 'military' range which had by this time reached the K series. A further change in the pattern of allocations came in the L range. Commencing with L7272 numbers were issued in blocks with smaller blocks of serials between not used. These were known as blackout blocks. As M had already been used as a suffix for Maintenance Command instructional airframes it was not used as a prefix. Although N had previously been used for naval aircraft it was used again for serials allocated from 1937.

With the build-up to World War 2 the rate of allocations quickly accelerated and the prefix R was being used when war was declared. The letters O and Q were not allotted, neither was S which had been used up to S1865 for naval aircraft before integration into the RAF series. By 1940 the serial Z9999 had been reached, as part of a blackout block, with the letters U and Y not used to avoid confusion. The option to recommence serial allocation at A1000 was not taken up, instead it was decided to use an alphabetical two letter prefix with three numerals running from 100 to 999. Thus AA100 was allocated to a Blenheim IV.

This two-letter, three-numeral serial system which started in 1940 continues today with the current issue being in the ZD range. The letters C, I, O, Q, U and Y were, with one or two exceptions, not used. For various reasons the following letter combinations were not issued: DA, DB, DH, EA, GA to GZ, HA, JE, JH, JJ, NZ and SA to SK. The first postwar serials issued were in the VP range while the end of the WZs had been reached by the Korean War. At the current rate of issue the Z range should last out the remainder of this century.

British Military Aircraft Markings

Serial	Type (alternative identity)	Owner, Operator or Location	Notes
164	Bleriot Type XI (BAPC 106)	RAF Museum, Hendon	
168	Sopwith Tabloid Replica (G-BFDE)	RAF Bomber Command Museum, Hendon	
304	Cody Biplane (BAPC 62)	Science Museum, South Kensington	
433	Bleriot Type XXVII (BAPC 107)	RAF Museum, Hendon	
2345	Vickers FB5 Gunbus Replica (G-ATVP)	RAF Museum, Hendon	
2699	RAF BE2C	Imperial War Museum, Duxford	
3066	Caudron GIII (G-AETA)	RAF Museum, Hendon	
5894	DH2 Replica (G-BFVH)	Leisure Sport, Thorpe Park	
5984	DH2 Replica (BAPC 112)	Leisure Sport, Thorpe Park	
6232	RAF BE2C Replica (BAPC 41)	RAF St Athan Museum	
8151	Sopwith Baby Replica (BAPC 137)	Leisure Sport, Thorpe Park	
8359	Short 184	FAA Museum, RNAS Yeovilton	
A1742	Scout D Replica (BAPC 38)	RAF St Athan Collection	
A2416	SE5A Replica	Privately owned, Powerscourt	
A3240	SE5A Replica	Privately owned, Powerscourt	
A5401	SE5A Replica (EI-ARK)	Privately owned, Powerscourt	
A6275	SE5A Replica	Privately owned, Powerscourt	
A8226	Sopwith 1½ Strutter (G-BIDW)	RAF Bomber Command Museum, Hendon	
B1807	Sopwith Pup (G-EAVX)	Privately owned, Bristol	
B4853	RAF SE5A Replica (BAPC 113)	Leisure Sport, Thorpe Park	
B7270	Sopwith Camel F1 Replica (G-BFCZ)	Leisure Sport, Thorpe Park	
C1701	Sopwith Camel F1 Replica (G-AWYY)	Leisure Sport, Thorpe Park	
C1904	RAF SE5A Replica (G-PFAP)	Privately owned, Bicester	
C4912	Bristol M1c Replica (BAPC 135)	Leisure Sport, Thorpe Park	
D3419	Sopwith Camel F1 Replica (BAPC 59)	RAF St Athan Museum	
D5329	Sopwith Dolphin	RAF Museum Store, Cardington	
D7560	Avro 504K	Science Museum, South Kensington	
D8096	Bristol Fighter (G-AEPH)	Shuttleworth Collection	
E449	Avro 504K (G-EBKN)	RAF Museum, Hendon	
E2581	Bristol Fighter	Imperial War Museum, Lambeth	
E3404	Avro 504K (G-ACNB, G-ADEV, H5199)	Shuttleworth Collection	
F344	Avro 504K Replica	RAF Museum Store, Henlow	
F373	Avro 504K Replica	RAF Museum Store, Henlow	
F904	RAF SE5A (G-EBIA)	Shuttleworth Collection	
F938	RAF SE5A (G-EBIC)	RAF Museum, Hendon	
F939	RAF SE5A (G-EBIB) [6]	Science Museum, South Kensington	
F943	SE5A Replica	Privately owned, Sherburn-in-Elmet	
F1010	DH9A	RAF Museum, Hendon	
F3556	RAF RE8	Imperial War Museum, Duxford	
F5459	RAF SE5A Replica	Cornwall Aero Park, Helston	
F6314	Sopwith Camel	RAF Museum, Hendon	
F8010	SE5A Replica (G-BDWJ)	Privately owned, Booker	
F8614	Vickers Vimy Replica (G-AWAU)	RAF Bomber Command Museum, Hendon	
H1968	Avro 504K Replica (BAPC 42)	RAF St Athan Museum	
H2311	Avro 504K (G-ABAA)	RAF Museum Store, Henlow	
J7326	DH Humming Bird (G-EBQP)	Russavia Collection, Duxford	
J8067	Pterodactyl 1a	Science Museum, South Kensington	
J9941	Hawker Hart (G-ABMR) [57]	RAF Museum, Abingdon	
K1786	Hawker Tomtit (G-AFTA)	Shuttleworth Collection	
K2567	DH Tiger Moth (G-MOTH)	Russavia Collection, Duxford	
K2568	DH Tiger Moth (G-APMM)	Russavia Collection, Duxford	
K2572	DH Tiger Moth	Privately owned, Castle Donington	

Notes	Serial	Type (alternative identity)	Owner, Operator or Location
	K2572	DH Tiger Moth (G-AOZH)	Privately owned, Shoreham
	K3215	Avro Tutor (G-AHSA)	Shuttleworth Collection
	K4232	Avro Rota (SE-AZB)	RAF Museum, Hendon
	K4235	Avro Rota (G-AHMJ)	Shuttleworth Collection
	K4972	Hawker Hart Trainer IIA (1746M)	RAF Museum, Hendon
	K6038	Westland Wallace II	RAF Museum Store, Cardington
	K7271	Hawker Fury II Replica (BAPC 148)	RAF Cosford Aerospace Museum
	K8042	Gloster Gladiator (8372M)	Battle of Britain Museum, Hendon
	K9942	VS Spitfire IA (8383M) [SD-V]	RAF Museum, Hendon
	L1592	Hawker Hurricane I	Science Museum, South Kensington
	L1592	Hawker Hurricane I Replica (BAPC 63) [KW-Z]	Torbay Aircraft Museum
	L2301	VS Walrus (G-AIZG)	FAA Museum, RNAS Yeovilton
	L2940	Blackburn Skua	FAA Museum, RNAS Yeovilton
	L5343	Fairey Battle I	RAF Museum Store, Cardington
	L6906	Miles Magister (BAPC 44)	Privately owned, Wroughton
	L8032	Gloster Gladiator (G-AMRK)	Shuttleworth Collection
	L8756	Bristol Bolingbroke (RCAF 10001) [XD-E]	Battle of Britain Museum, Hendon
	N248	Supermarine S6A	R. J. Mitchell Memorial, Soton
	N1671	Boulton Paul Defiant I (8370M) [EW-D]	Battle of Britain Museum, Hendon
	N1854	Fairey Fulmar II (G-AIBE)	FAA Museum, RNAS Yeovilton
	N2078	Sopwith Baby	FAA Museum, RNAS Yeovilton
	N3788	Miles Magister (G-AKPF)	Privately owned, Bassingbourn
	N4877	Avro Anson I (G-AMDA) [VX-F]	Skyfame Collection, Duxford
	N5180	Sopwith Pup (G-EBKY)	Shuttleworth Collection
	N5182	Sopwith Pup (G-APUP)	RAF Museum, Hendon
	N5430	Sopwith Triplane Replica (G-BHEW)	Privately owned, Booker
	N5492	Sopwith Triplane Replica (BAPC 111)	Leisure Sport, Thorpe Park
	N5628	Gloster Gladiator II	RAF Museum Store, Cardington
	N5903	Gloster Gladiator II	FAA Museum, RNAS Yeovilton
	N5912	Sopwith Triplane (8385M)	RAF Museum, Hendon
	N6720	DH Tiger Moth (7014M) [RUO-B]	No 493 Sqn ATC, Kings Heath
	N6812	Sopwith Camel	Imperial War Museum, Lambeth
	N6848	DH Tiger Moth (G-BALX)	Privately owned, Fairoaks
	N6985	DH Tiger Moth (G-AHMN)	Privately owned, Compton Abbas
	N8224	DH Tiger Moth (G-AHUR)	Privately owned, Blackbushe
	N9191	DH Tiger Moth (G-ALND)	Privately owned, Shipdham
	N9238	DH Tiger Moth (G-ANEL)	Privately owned, Catterick
	N9389	DH Tiger Moth (G-ANJA)	Privately owned, Seething
	N9510	DH Tiger Moth (G-AOEL)	Museum of Flight, East Fortune
	N9899	Supermarine Southampton	RAF Museum Store, Cardington
	P2183	Fairey Battle I	RAF St Athan Historic Aircraft Collection
	P2617	Hawker Hurricane I (8373M) [AF-F]	Battle of Britain Museum, Hendon
	P3308	Hawker Hurricane IIB (G-AWLW) [UP-A]	Davies Trust, Strathallan
	P6382	Miles Magister (G-AJRS)	Shuttleworth Collection
	P7350	VS Spitfire IIA (G-AWIJ) [SH-D]	RAF Battle of Britain Flight
	P7540	VS Spitfire IIA [DU-W]	Dumfries & Galloway Aviation Group
	P9390	VS Spitfire I Replica (BAPC 71) [KL-B]	Norfolk & Suffolk Aviation Museum
	P9444	VS Spitfire IA [RN-D]	Science Museum, South Kensington
	R1914	Miles Magister (G-AHUJ)	Strathallan Aircraft Collection
	R3950	Fairey Battle I	Strathallan Aircraft Collection
	R4907	DH Tiger Moth (G-ANCS)	Privately owned, Sywell
	R4959	DH Tiger Moth (G-ARAZ)	Privately owned, Goodwood
	R5086	DH Tiger Moth (G-APIH)	Privately owned, Little Gransden
	R5250	DH Tiger Moth (G-AODT)	Privately owned, Swanton Morley

Serial	Type (alternative identity)	Owner, Operator or Location	Notes
R5868	Avro Lancaster I (7325M)	RAF Bomber Command Museum, Hendon	
R6915	VS Spitfire I	Imperial War Museum, Lambeth	
R7524	Percival Proctor I (G-AIWA)	Privately owned, Redhill	
R9125	Westland Lysander III (8377M)	Battle of Britain Museum, Hendon	
S1287	Fairey Flycatcher Replica (G-BEYB)	Privately owned, Middle Wallop	
S1595	Supermarine S6B	Science Museum, South Kensington	
S1595	Supermarine S6B Replica (BAPC 156)	Leisure Sport, Thorpe Park	
T5424	DH Tiger Moth (G-AJOA)	Privately owned, Staverton	
T5493	DH Tiger Moth (G-ANEF)	Privately owned, Cranwell	
T5854	DH Tiger Moth (G-ANKK)	Privately owned, Halfpenny Green	
T5879	DH Tiger Moth (G-AXBW)	Privately owned, Tongham	
T6296	DH Tiger Moth (8387M)	RAF Museum, Hendon	
T6818	DH Tiger Moth (G-ANKT)	Shuttleworth Collection	
T7187	DH Tiger Moth (G-AOBX)	Privately owned, White Waltham	
T7281	DH Tiger Moth (G-ARTL)	Privately owned, Sunderland	
T7404	DH Tiger Moth (G-ANMV)	Privately owned, Compton Abbas	
T7909	DH Tiger Moth (G-ANON)	Privately owned, Sherburn	
T8191	DH Tiger Moth	RN Historic Flight, Yeovilton	
T9707	Miles Magister (G-AKKR/8378M)	Manchester Air & Space Museum	
T9738	Miles Magister (G-AKAT)	Newark Air Museum, Winthorpe	
V3388	Airspeed Oxford (G-AHTW)	Skyfame Collection, Duxford	
V7467	Hawker Hurricane Replica (BAPC 72)	Air Museum, North Weald	
V9281	Westland Lysander III (G-BCWL)	Warbirds of GB, Blackbushe	
V9441	Westland Lysander IIIA (RCAF2355/G-AZWT) [AR-A]	Strathallan Collection	
W1048	HP Halifax II (8465M)	RAF Bomber Command Museum, Hendon	
W4041	Gloster E28/39	Science Museum, South Kensington	
W4050	DH Mosquito	Mosquito Aircraft Museum	
W5856	Fairey Swordfish II	Strathallan Aircraft Collection	
W5984	Fairey Swordfish (HS618) [5H]	FAA Museum, RNAS Yeovilton	
X4590	VS Spitfire IA (8384M)	Battle of Britain Museum, Hendon	
Z2033	Fairey Firefly I (G-ASTL)	Skyfame Collection, Duxford	
Z7015	Sea Hurricane IB	Shuttleworth Collection, Duxford	
Z7197	Percival Proctor III (G-AKZN)	RAF St Athan, Historic Aircraft Collection	
Z7258	DH Dragon Rapide (G-AHGD)	Privately owned, Booker	
AB910	VS Spitfire VB (G-AISU) [XT-M]	RAF Battle of Britain Flight	
AL246	Grumman Martlet I	FAA Museum, RNAS Yeovilton	
AP507	Cierva C30a (G-ACWP) [KX-P]	Science Museum, South Kensington	
AR213	VS Spitfire IA (G-AIST) [QG-A]	Privately owned, Booker	
AR501	VS Spitfire VC (G-AWII) [NN-D]	Shuttleworth Collection, Duxford	
BB731	DH Tiger Moth (A2126)	RNAS Yeovilton, in store	
BB807	Tiger Moth (G-ADWO)	Wessex Aviation Society, Wimborne	
BB814	DH Tiger Moth (G-AFWI)	Privately owned, Yeovilton	
BL614	VS Spitfire VB (AB871) [ZD-F]	Manchester Air & Space Museum Museum	
BM597	VS Spitfire VB (5713M) [PR-O]	RAF Church Fenton, on gate	
BS676	Pfalzkuku/Spitfire Replica (G-KUKU)	Privately owned, Shoreham	
DE208	DH Tiger Moth (G-AGYU)	Privately owned, Nayland	
DE363	DH Tiger Moth (G-ANFC)	Mosquito Aircraft Museum	
DE623	DH Tiger Moth (G-ANFI)	Privately owned, Little Snoring	
DE673	DH Tiger Moth (G-ADNZ)	Privately owned, Walton-on-Thames	
DE992	DH Tiger Moth (G-AXXV)	Privately owned, Little Gransden	

Notes	Serial	Type (alternative identity)	Owner, Operator or Location
	DF130	DH Tiger Moth (G-BACK)	Privately owned, Laindon
	DF155	DH Tiger Moth (G-ANFV)	Privately owned, Dalcross
	DF198	DH Tiger Moth (G-BBRB)	Privately owned, Headcorn
	DG202	Gloster F9/40 Meteor (5758M)	RAF Cosford Aerospace Museum
	DG590	Miles Hawk Major (G-ADMW/8379M)	RAF Museum Store, Henlow
	DR613	FW Wicko GM1 (G-AFJB)	Privately owned, Berkswell
	DR628	Beech D.17s (N18V)	Privately owned, Duxford
	DV372	Avro Lancaster I	Imperial War Museum, Lambeth
	EE531	Gloster Meteor F4 (7090M)	Midland Air Museum, Coventry
	EE549	Gloster Meteor F4 (6372M)	RAF St Athan, Historic Aircraft Collection
	EJ693	Hawker Tempest V [SA-J]	RAF Museum Store, Henlow
	EM727	DH Tiger Moth (G-AOXN)	Leicester Aircraft Preservation Group
	EM903	DH Tiger Moth (G-APBI)	Privately owned, Audley End
	EP120	VS Spitfire VB (5377M) [QV-H]	RAF Wattisham
	EX976	NA Harvard III	FAA Museum, Yeovilton
	EZ259	NA Harvard III	Lincolnshire Aviation Museum
	EZ407	NA Harvard III	RN Historic Flight, Yeovilton
	FE992	NA Harvard IIB (G-BDAM)	Privately owned, Goodwood
	FH153	NA Harvard IIB (G-BBHK)	Privately owned, Long Marston
	FT229	NA Harvard IIB (G-AZKI)	Privately owned, Sandown
	FT323	NA Harvard IIB (G-AZSC)	Privately owned, Blackbushe
	FT375	NA Harvard !IB	MoD(PE) A&AEE Boscombe Down
	FT391	NA Harvard IIB (G-AZBN)	Colt Aviation, Staverton
	FX291	NA Harvard IIA (G-BGOV)	Aces High, Duxford
	FX301	NA Harvard IIB (G-JUDI) [FD-NQ]	Privately owned, Duxford
	FX442	NA Harvard IIB	Privately owned, Bournemouth
	HB751	Fairchild Argus III (G-BCBL)	Privately owned, Duxford
	HD368	NA B-25J Mitchell (N9089Z) [VO-A]	Historic Aircraft Museum
	HJ711	DH Mosquito NFII [VI-C]	Privately owned, York
	HM354	Percival Proctor III (G-ANPP)	Privately owned, Duxford
	HS503	Fairey Swordfish IV (BAPC 108)	RAF Museum Store, Henlow
	HS649	VS Spitfire XVIII	Privately owned, Hemel Hempstead
	HS877	VS Spitfire XIV	Warbirds of GB, Blackbushe
	HX922	DH Mosquito TT35 (G-AWJV) (really TA634)	Mosquito Aircraft Museum
	KB976	Avro Lancaster B10 (G-BCOH)	Strathallan Collection
	KD431	CV Corsair IV [EZ-M]	FAA Museum, RNAS Yeovilton
	KE209	Grumman Hellcat II	FAA Museum, RNAS Yeovilton
	KF183	NA Harvard IIB	MoD(PE) A&AEE Boscombe Down
	KG374	Douglas Dakota C4 (KN645/8355M)	RAF Cosford Aerospace Museum
	KH191	Consolidated Liberator [T-18]	Warbirds of GB, Blackbushe
	KK995	Sikorsky Hoverfly I (KL110)	RAF Museum, Hendon
	KN751	Consolidated Liberator VI	RAF Cosford Aerospace Museum
	KP208	Douglas Dakota C4 [75]	Airborne Forces Museum, Aldershot
	KX829	Hawker Hurricane IV [JV-I]	Birmingham Museum of Science
	LA198	VS Spitfire F21 (7118M) [JX-C]	RAF Locking, main gate
	LA226	VS Spitfire F21 (7119M)	VS South Marston, main gate
	LA255	VS Spitfire F21 (6490M) [JX-U]	RAF Wittering
	LA564	VS Seafire F46	Privately owned, Redbourn
	LA607	Hawker Tempest II [HF-T]	Skyfame Collection, Duxford
	LB312	Taylorcraft/D (G-AHXE)	Privately owned, Middle Wallop
	LF363	Hawker Hurricane IIC [GN-F]	RAF Battle of Britain Flight
	LF738	Hawker Hurricane IIC (5405M)	RAF Biggin Hill
	LF751	Hawker Hurricane IIC (5466M) [FB-B]	RAF Bentley Priory
	LS326	Fairey Swordfish II (G-AJVH) [5A]	RN Historic Flight, Yeovilton
	LZ551	DH Sea Vampire I	FAA Museum, RNAS Yeovilton
	LZ766	Percival Proctor III (G-ALCK)	Skyfame Collection, Duxford

Serial	Type (alternative identity)	Owner, Operator or Location	Notes
MC280	NA Harvard IIB (G-TEAC) [G]	Privately owned, Hurn	
MF628	Vickers Wellington T10	RAF Bomber Command Museum, Hendon	
MH434	VS Spitfire IX (G-ASJV) [AC-S]	Privately owned, Booker	
MJ627	VS Spitfire T9 (G-BMSB)	Privately owned, Kenilworth	
MJ730	VS Spitfire IX [66]	Privately owned, Hastings	
MK356	VS Spitfire IX (5690M) [21-V]	RAF St Athan Museum	
MK732	VS Spitfire IX (8633M)	RAF St Athan	
ML407	VS Spitfire T9 (G-LFIX)	Privately owned, St Merryn	
ML417	VS Spitfire IX (G-BJSG)	Privately owned, Booker	
ML427	VS Spitfire IX [IS-T]	Birmingham Museum of Science	
ML796	Short Sunderland V	Imperial War Museum, Duxford	
ML824	Short Sunderland V [NS-Z]	Battle of Britain Museum, Hendon	
MN235	Hawker Typhoon IB	RAF Museum, Hendon	
MP345	Airspeed Oxford (G-AITB/MP425)	RAF Museum Store, Cardington	
MT360	Auster 5 (G-AKWT)	Humberside Aircraft Preservation Society	
MT438	Auster III (G-AREI)	Privately owned, Bodmin	
MT818	VS Spitfire T8 (G-AIDN)	Privately owned, St Athan	
MT847	VS Spitfire XIV (6960M)	RAF Cosford Aerospace Museum	
MV154	VS Spitfire T.8	Privately owned, North London	
MV262	VS Spitfire XIV [42-G]	Warbirds of GB, Blackbushe	
MV293	VS Spitfire XIV (G-SPIT)	Warbirds of GB, Blackbushe	
MV370	VS Spitfire XIV (G-FXIV)	Privately owned, Hemel Hempstead	
MW100	Avro York C1 (G-AGNV/TS798)	RAF Cosford Aerospace Museum	
NF370	Fairey Swordfish III	Imperial War Museum, Lambeth	
NF389	Fairey Swordfish III [5B]	FAA Museum, Lee-on-Solent	
NF875	DH Dragon Rapide 6 (G-AGTM) [603/CH]	Privately owned, Old Warden	
NH238	VS Spitfire IX (N238V)	Warbirds of GB, Blackbushe	
NH749	VS Spitfire XIV (G-MXIV)	Privately owned, Cranfield	
NH799	VS Spitfire XIV	Warbirds of GB, Blackbushe	
NJ695	Auster 4 (G-AJXV)	Privately owned, Tollerton	
NJ703	Auster 5 (G-AKPI)	Privately owned, Sherburn	
NL750	DH Tiger Moth (A2123)	RNAS Yeovilton, in store	
NM181	DH Tiger Moth (G-AZGZ)	Privately owned, Little Gransden	
NP181	Percival Proctor IV	Lashenden Air Warfare Museum	
NP184	Percival Proctor IV (G-ANYP) [K]	Torbay Aircraft Museum	
NP294	Percival Proctor IV	Lincolnshire Aviation Museum	
NP303	Percival Proctor IV (G-ANZJ)	Historic Aircraft Museum	
NR747	DH Dragon Rapide (G-AJHO)	Privately owned, Bassingbourn	
NV778	Hawker Tempest V (8386M)	RAF Museum, Hendon	
NX611	Avro Lancaster VII (G-ASXX/8375M) [YF-C]	RAF Scampton, on gate	
PA474	Avro Lancaster I [AJ-G]	RAF Battle of Britain Flight	
PG617	DH Tiger Moth (G-AYVY)	Privately owned, Ronaldsway	
PG651	DH Tiger Moth (G-AYUX)	Privately owned, Booker	
PK624	VS Spitfire F22 (8072M)	RAF Abingdon, at main gate	
PK664	VS Spitfire F22 (7759M) (V6-B)	RAF Binbrook, at main gate	
PK683	VS Spitfire F24 (7150M)	R. J. Mitchell Hall, Southampton	
PK724	VS Spitfire F24 (7288M)	RAF Museum, Hendon	
PL983	VS Spitfire XI	Shuttleworth Collection, Duxford	
PM631	VS Spitfire XIX	RAF Battle of Britain Flight	
PM651	VS Spitfire XIX (7758M)	RAF Benson, at main gate	
PS853	VS Spitfire XIX	RAF Battle of Britain Flight	
PS915	VS Spitfire XIX (7711M)	RAF Brawdy, on display	
PV202	VS Spitfire T9	Privately owned, Hastings	
PZ865	Hawker Hurricane II (G-AMAU)	RAF Battle of Britain Flight	
RA848	Slingsby Cadet TXI	Privately owned, Harrogate	
RA854	Slingsby Cadet TXI	Privately owned, Wigan	
RD253	Beaufighter TFX (7931M)	RAF Museum, Hendon	
RF398	Avro Lincoln B2 (8376M)	RAF Cosford Aerospace Museum	
RG333	Miles Messenger IIA (G-AIEK)	Bristol Plane Preservation Unit, Felton	
RG333	Miles Messenger IIA (G-AKEZ)	Torbay Aircraft Museum	
RH377	Miles Messenger 4A (G-ALAH)	The Aeroplane Collection	
RH378	Miles Messenger IIA (G-AJOE)	Cotswold Aircraft Restoration Group	

11

Notes	Serial	Type (alternative identity)	Owner, Operator or Location
	RH746	Bristol Brigand TF1	North East Air Museum, Usworth
	RL962	DH Dragon Rapide (G-AHED)	RAF Museum Store, Cardington
	RM221	Percival Proctor IV (G-ANXR)	Privately owned, Southend
	RM619	VS Spitfire XIV (G-ALGT) [AP-D]	Rolls-Royce, East Midlands
	RR299	DH Mosquito T3 (G-ASKH) [HT-E]	British Aerospace, Hatfield
	RS709	DH Mosquito B35 (G-ASKA/ N9797)	Warbirds of GB, Blackbushe
	RW382	VS Spitfire XVIe (7245M)	RAF Uxbridge, at main gate
	RW386	VS Spitfire XVIe (6944M) [RAK-A]	Warbirds of GB, Blackbushe
	RW388	VS Spitfire XVIe (6947M) [U4-U]	R. J. Mitchell Memorial, Stoke
	RW393	VS Spitfire XVIe (7293M) [XT-A]	RAF Turnhouse, at main gate
	SL542	VS Spitfire XVIe (8390M)	RAF Coltishall, at main gate
	SL574	VS Spitfire XVIe (8391M)	RAF Bentley Priory
	SL674	VS Spitfire XVIe (8392M)	RAF Memorial Chapel, Biggin Hill
	SM832	VS Spitfire XIV (G-WWII)	Warbirds of GB, Blackbushe
	SM969	VS Spitfire XVIII (G-BRAF)	Warbirds of GB, Blackbushe
	SX137	VS Seafire XVII	FAA Museum, RNAS Yeovilton
	SX300	VS Seafire XVII	Midland Aircraft Museum, Coventry
	SX336	VS Seafire XVII (A2055)	Privately owned, Newark
	TA122	DH Mosquito FBVI [UP-G]	Mosquito Aircraft Museum
	TA634	DH Mosquito TT35 (G-AWJV) [EG-F]	Mosquito Aircraft Museum
	TA639	DH Mosquito TT35 (7806M)	RAF Cosford Aerospace Museum
	TA719	DH Mosquito TT35 (G-ASKC) [SY-G]	Skyfame Collection, Duxford
	TB252	VS Spitfire XVIe (7257M) [GW-H]	RAF Leuchars, at main gate
	TB382	VS Spitfire XVIe (7244M)	RAF Exhibition Flight, Abingdon
	TB752	VS Spitfire XVIe (7256M) [KH-7]	RAF Manston
	TB863	VS Spitfire XVIe [FB-Y]	Privately owned, Booker
	TD248	VS Spitfire XVIe (7246M) [DW-A]	RAF Sealand, at main gate
	TE184	VS Spitfire XVIe (6850M) [LA-A]	Ulster Folk and Transport Museum
	TE311	VS Spitfire XVIe (7241M) [AU-Y]	RAF Exhibition Flight, Abingdon
	TE356	VS Spitfire XVIe (6709M)	RAF Leeming
	TE392	VS Spitfire XVIe (7000M)	RAF Credenhill
	TE462	VS Spitfire XVIe (7243M)	Royal Scottish Museum of Flight
	TE476	VS Spitfire XVIe (7451M)	RAF Northolt at main gate
	TE517	VS Spitfire IX (G-BIXP)	Privately owned, Duxford
	TE566	VS Spitfire IX	EMK Aeroplane, Ware
	TF956	Hawker Sea Fury FB11 [123/T]	RN Historic Flight, Yeovilton
	TG263	Saro SRA1 (G-12-1)	Skyfame Collection, Duxford
	TG505	HP Hastings T5	RAF Leeming Fire Section
	TG511	HP Hastings T5 (8554M)	RAF Cosford Aerospace Museum
	TG517	HP Hastings T5 [517]	Newark Air Museum, Winthorpe
	TG528	HP Hastings C1A	Skyfame Collection, Duxford
	TG536	HP Hastings C1A (8405M)	RAF FF&SS Catterick
	TG568	HP Hastings C1A	RAE Bedford Fire Section
	TJ118	DH Mosquito B35	Mosquito Aircraft Museum
	TJ138	DH Mosquito B35 (7607M) [V-O]	RAF Museum Store, Swinderby
	TJ343	Auster 5 (G-AJXC)	Privately owned, Popham
	TJ472	Auster AOP5 (BAPC 70)	Royal Scottish Museum of Flight
	TJ569	Auster 5 (G-AKOW)	Museum of Army Flying, Middle Wallop
	TJ672	Auster 5 (G-ANIJ)	Privately owned, Thruxton
	TL659	Airspeed Horsa (BAPC 80)	Museum of Army Flying, Middle Wallop
	TS423	Douglas Dakota (G-DAKS, G-AGHY)	Aces High, Duxford
	TV959	DH Mosquito T3 [AF-V]	Imperial War Museum, Lambeth
	TW117	DH Mosquito T3 (7805M)	RAF Museum, Hendon
	TW439	Auster 5 (G-ANRP)	Warnham War Museum, Horsham
	TW536	Auster AOP6	Cotswold Aircraft Restoration Group

Serial	Type (alternative identity)	Owner, Operator or Location	Notes
TX183	Avro Anson C19	Shuttleworth Collection, Duxford	
TX192	Avro Anson C19	Privately owned, Guernsey	
TX213	Avro Anson C19 (G-AWRS)	North East Aircraft Museum	
TX214	Avro Anson C19 (7817M)	RAF Cosford Aerospace Museum	
TX226	Avro Anson C19 (7865M)	Privately owned, Little Staughton	
TX228	Avro Anson C19	Norwich Aviation Museum	
TX235	Avro Anson C19	Torbay Aircraft Museum	
VF301	DH Vampire F1 (7060M)	Midland Air Museum, Coventry	
VH127	Fairey Firefly TT4	FAA Museum, RNAS Yeovilton	
VL348	Avro Anson C19 (G-AVVO)	Newark Air Museum, Winthorpe	
VL349	Avro Anson C19 (G-AWSA)	Norfolk & Suffolk Av. Museum	
VM325	Avro Anson C19	Midland Air Museum, Coventry	
VM360	Avro Anson C19 (G-APHV)	Royal Scottish Museum of Flight	
VM791	Slingsby Cadet TX3 (really XA312)	RAF Support Command, 1 MGSP RAF Halton	
VN148	Grunau Baby	Russavia Collection, Duxford	
VP293	Avro Shackleton T4	Strathallan Aircraft Collection	
VP952	DH Devon C2	RAF Northolt, No 207 Sqn	
VP955	DH Devon C2	RAF Northolt, No 207 Sqn	
VP956	DH Devon C2	No 1404 Sqn ATC, RAF Manston	
VP957	DH Devon C2	RAF Northolt, No 207 Sqn	
VP958	DH Devon C2 [DC]	RAF Wyton, No 207 Sqn	
VP959	DH Devon C2 [L]	MoD(PE) RAE Farnborough	
VP960	DH Devon C2	CTE, RAF Manston	
VP962	DH Devon C2	RAF Northolt, No 207 Sqn	
VP963	DH Devon C2	CTE, RAF Manston	
VP965	DH Devon C2 [DE]	RAF Wyton, No 207 Sqn	
VP968	DH Devon C2	RAF Northolt, No 207 Sqn	
VP971	DH Devon C2	RAF Northolt, No 207 Sqn	
VP973	DH Devon C2 (8512M)	RAF Northolt, ground simulator	
VP975	DH Devon C2 [M]	MoD(PE) RAE Farnborough	
VP976	DH Devon C2	RAF Northolt, No 207 Sqn	
VP977	DH Devon C2 (G-ALTS)	RAF Northolt, No 207 Sqn	
VP981	DH Devon C2	RAF Northolt, No 207 Sqn	
VR137	Westland Wyvern TF1	FAA Museum, RNAS Yeovilton	
VR249	Percival Prentice T1 (G-APIY) [FA-EL]	Newark Air Museum, Winthorpe	
VR930	Hawker Sea Fury FB11 (8382M)	FAA Museum Store, RNAY Wroughton	
VS356	Percival Prentice T1 (G-AOLU)	Scottish Aircraft Collection Trust, Perth	
VS562	Avro Anson T21 (8012M)	No 2445 Sqn ATC at RAE Llanbedr	
VS610	Percival Prentice T1 (G-AOKL) [K-L]	Privately owned, Southend	
VS623	Percival Prentice T1 (G-AOKZ)	Midland Air Museum, Coventry	
VT229	Gloster Meteor F4 (7151M) [60]	Privately owned, Duxford	
VT260	Gloster Meteor F4 [67]	Defence School, Winterbourne Gunner	
VT409	Fairey Firefly AS5	North East Aircraft Museum	
VT812	DH Vampire F3 (7200M) [N]	RAF Museum, Hendon	
VT921	Grunau Baby	Midland Air Museum	
VT935	Boulton Paul P111A	Midland Air Museum, Coventry	
VV106	VS 510 (7175M)	RAF Cosford Aerospace Museum	
VV217	DH Vampire FB5 (7323M)	No 301 Sqn ATC, Bury St Edmunds	
VV901	Avro Anson T21	Pennine Aviation Museum, Bacup	
VW453	Gloster Meteor T7 (8703M)	Cotswold ARG, RAF Innsworth	
VX272	Hawker P1052 (7174M)	RAF Cosford Aerospace Museum	
VX275	Slingsby Sedbergh TX1	RAF Support Command, St Athan	
VX302	Hawker Sea Fury T20 (G-BCOV) [77/M]	Privately owned, Blackbushe	
VX461	DH Vampire FB5 (7646M)	RAF Museum Store, Henlow	
VX573	Vickers Valetta C2 (8389M)	RAF Cosford Aerospace Museum	
VX577	Vickers Valetta C2	North East Aircraft Museum	
VX580	Vickers Valetta C2	HQ Air Scouts, Norwich Airport	
VX595	Westland Dragonfly HR1 [29]	RAF Museum Store, Henlow	
VX653	Hawker Sea Fury FB11	RAF Museum, Hendon	
VZ304	DH Vampire FB5 (7630M) [S]	Privately owned, Duxford	
VZ345	Hawker Sea Fury T20	MoD(PE) A&AEE Boscombe Down	
VZ462	Gloster Meteor F8	Second World War Preservation Society	
VZ467	Gloster Meteor F8 [01]	RAF Leeming	
VZ608	Gloster Meteor FR9	Newark Air Museum, Winthorpe	

13

Notes	Serial	Type (alternative identity)	Owner, Operator or Location
	VZ634	Gloster Meteor T7 (8657M)	No 131 Sqn ATC, RAF Wattisham
	VZ638	Gloster Meteor T7 [X]	Historic Aircraft Museum, Southend
	VZ728	RS4 Desford Trainer (G-AGOS)	Scottish Aircraft Collection Trust, Perth
	VZ962	Westland Dragonfly HR5	Cornwall Aero Park, Helston
	VZ965	Westland Dragonfly HR5	FAA Museum, at RNAS Culdrose
	WA473	VS Attacker F1 [102/J]	FAA Museum, RNAS Yeovilton
	WA576	Bristol Sycamore 3 (G-ALSS/ 7900M)	Privately owned, East Fortune
	WA577	Bristol Sycamore 3 (G-ALST/ 7718M)	North East Aircraft Museum
	WA591	Gloster Meteor T7 (7917M) [W]	RAF Woodvale, on display
	WA634	Gloster Meteor T7/8	RAF St Athan Museum
	WA638	Gloster Meteor T7	Martin Baker Aircraft, Chalgrove
	WA662	Gloster Meteor T7	MoD(PE) RAE Llanbedr
	WA669	Gloster Meteor T7 [02]	RAF Leeming
	WA984	Gloster Meteor F8 [A]	Wessex Aviation Group, Wimborne
	WB188	Hawker Hunter F3 (7154M)	RAF St Athan Museum
	WB271	Fairey Firefly AS5 [204/R]	RN Historic Flight, Yeovilton
	WB491	Avro Ashton	Wales Air Museum, Cardiff
	WB530	DH Devon C2	RAF Northolt, No 207 Sqn
	WB531	DH Devon C2	RAF Northolt, No 207 Sqn
	WB533	DH Devon C2 [DA]	RAF Wyton, No 207 Sqn
	WB534	DH Devon C2 [DB]	RAF Wyton, No 207 Sqn
	WB535	DH Devon C2	JATE, Sennybridge
	WB550	DH Chipmunk T10 [F]	RAF Support Command, FSS Swinderby
	WB560	DH Chipmunk T10	RAF Support Command, 4 AEF
	WB565	DH Chipmunk T10 [X]	AAC, Middle Wallop
	WB567	DH Chipmunk T10	RAF Support Command, 12 AEF
	WB569	DH Chipmunk T10	RAF Support Command, 1 AEF
	WB575	DH Chipmunk T10 [907]	Britannia Royal Naval College AEF
	WB584	DH Chipmunk T10	RAF Support Command, 12 AEF, PAX
	WB586	DH Chipmunk T10 [A]	RAF Support Command, 6 AEF
	WB588	DH Chipmunk T10 (G-AOTD)	BAe Apprentice School, Kingston
	WB615	DH Chipmunk T10 [E]	AAC, Middle Wallop
	WB624	DH Chipmunk T10	Loughborough & Leics Aircraft Museum
	WB627	DH Chipmunk T10 [N]	RAF Support Command, 5 AEF
	WB630	DH Chipmunk T10	Britannia Royal Naval College AEF
	WB645	DH Chipmunk T10 (8218M)	RAFGSA Bicester
	WB647	DH Chipmunk T10 [R]	AAC, Middle Wallop
	WB652	DH Chipmunk T10 [V]	RAF Support Command, 5 AEF
	WB654	DH Chipmunk T10 [14]	RAF Support Command, 10 AEF
	WB657	DH Chipmunk T10 [908]	Britannia Royal Naval College AEF
	WB670	DH Chipmunk T10	Notts & Lincs Aviation Museum
	WB671	DH Chipmunk T10 [910]	Britannia Royal Naval College AEF
	WB685	DH Chipmunk T10	Privately owned, Harrogate PAX
	WB693	DH Chipmunk T10 [S]	AAC, Middle Wallop
	WB697	DH Chipmunk T10 [O]	RAF Support Command, 3 AEF
	WB739	DH Chipmunk T10 [8]	RAF Support Command, 8 AEF
	WB754	DH Chipmunk T10 [H]	AAC, Middle Wallop
	WB758	DH Chipmunk T10 (7729M) [P]	Torbay Aircraft Museum
	WB763	DH Chipmunk T10 (G-BBMR)	Southall Technical College
	WB847	Avro Shackleton T4 [B]	RAF Kinloss Fire Section
	WB919	Slingsby Sedbergh TXI (G-ALLH)	RAF Support Command 634 GS
	WB920	Slingsby Sedbergh TXI	RAF Support Command, 643 GS
	WB922	Slingsby Sedbergh TXI	RAF Support Command 1 MGSP
	WB923	Slingsby Sedbergh TXI	RAF Cranwell Gliding Club
	WB924	Slingsby Sedbergh TXI	RAF Support Command CGS/644 GS
	WB926	Slingsby Sedbergh TXI	RAF Support Command 634 GS
	WB927	Slingsby Sedbergh TXI	RAF Support Command 615 GS
	WB932	Slingsby Sedbergh TXI	RAF Support Command 615 GS
	WB934	Slingsby Sedbergh TXI	RAF Support Command 618 GS
	WB935	Slingsby Sedbergh TXI	RAF Support Command 631 GS
	WB937	Slingsby Sedbergh TXI	RAF Support Command GSS St Athan
	WB938	Slingsby Sedbergh TXI	RAF Support Command 1 SoTT Halton
	WB939	Slingsby Sedbergh TXI	RAF Support Command 663 GS

N5182 Sopwith Pup. *PRM*

P6382 Miles Magister. *APM*

FX301 NA Harvard IIB. *PRM*

WB271 Fairey Firefly AS5. *PRM*

WG655 Hawker Sea Fury T20. *PRM*

WK613 DH Chipmunk T10. *PRM*

Serial	Type (alternative identity)	Owner, Operator or Location	Notes
WB940	Slingsby Sedbergh TXI	RAF Support Command 615 GS	
WB941	Slingsby Sedbergh TXI	RAF Support Command 636 GS	
WB942	Slingsby Sedbergh TXI	RAF Support Command CGS	
WB943	Slingsby Sedbergh TXI	RAF Support Command 631 GS	
WB944	Slingsby Sedbergh TXI	RAF Support Command 622 GS	
WB946	Slingsby Sedbergh TXI	RAF Support Command 631 GS	
WB947	Slingsby Sedbergh TXI	RAF Support Command 634 GS	
WB958	Slingsby Sedbergh TXI	RAF Support Command 621 GS	
WB959	Slingsby Sedbergh TXI	RAF Support Command GSS St Athan	
WB960	Slingsby Sedbergh TXI	RAF Support Command 3 MGSP	
WB961	Slingsby Sedbergh TXI	RAF Support Command 661 GS	
WB962	Slingsby Sedbergh TXI	RAF Support Command CGS	
WB963	Slingsby Sedbergh TXI	RAF Support Command 618 GS	
WB971	Slingsby Sedbergh TXI	RAF Support Command 631 GS	
WB972	Slingsby Sedbergh TXI	RAF Support Command 626 GS	
WB973	Slingsby Sedbergh TXI	RAF Support Command 624 GS	
WB974	Slingsby Sedbergh TXI	RAF Support Command 643 GS	
WB975	Slingsby Sedbergh TXI	RAF Support Command 662 GS	
WB976	Slingsby Sedbergh TXI	RAF Support Command 661 GS	
WB978	Slingsby Sedbergh TXI	RAF Support Command 3 MGSP	
WB979	Slingsby Sedbergh TXI	RAF Support Command 645 GS	
WB980	Slingsby Sedbergh TXI	RAF Support Command 1 MGSP, RAF Halton	
WB981	Slingsby Sedbergh TXI	RAF Support Command 635 GS	
WB982	Slingsby Sedbergh TXI	RAF Support Command 3 MGSP	
WB983	Slingsby Sedbergh TXI	RAF Support Command 634 GS	
WB985	Slingsby Sedbergh TXI	RAF Support Command 645 GS	
WB986	Slingsby Sedbergh TXI	RAF Support Command 614 GS	
WB987	Slingsby Sedbergh TXI	RAF Support Command 662 GS	
WB988	Slingsby Sedbergh TXI	RAF Support Command 614 GS	
WB989	Slingsby Sedbergh TXI	RAF Support Command 635 GS	
WB990	Slingsby Sedbergh TXI	RAF Support Command 622 GS	
WB991	Slingsby Sedbergh TXI	RAF Support Command GSS St Athan	
WB992	Slingsby Sedbergh TXI	RAF Support Command 631 GS	
WB993	Slingsby Sedbergh TXI	RAF Support Command 631 GS	
WD289	DH Chipmunk T10	RAF Germany, Gatow Stn Flt	
WD310	DH Chipmunk T10	RAF Support Command, 5 MU store	
WD318	DH Chipmunk T10	No 145 Sqn ATC, Timperley (PAX)	
WD325	DH Chipmunk T10 [N]	AAC, Middle Wallop	
WD331	DH Chipmunk T10 [A]	RAF Support Command, FSS Swinderby	
WD356	DH Chipmunk T10 (7625M)	LFV&HAC, Bushey	
WD373	DH Chipmunk T10 [12]	RAF Support Command, 2 AEF	
WD374	DH Chipmunk T10 [903]	Britannia Royal Naval College, AEF	
WD390	DH Chipmunk T10 [H]	RAF Support Command, FSS Swinderby	
WD413	Avro Anson C 21 (G-BFIR)	Privately owned, Hurn	
WD480	HP Hastings C2	RAE Farnborough, Fire Section	
WD496	HP Hastings C2	A&AEE Boscombe Down Fire Section	
WD499	HP Hastings C2	RAF Honington Fire Section	
WD646	Gloster Meteor TT20 (8189M) [R]	No 2030 Sqn ATC, Sheldon	
WD686	Gloster Meteor NF11	Imperial War Museum, Duxford	
WD833	Fairey Firefly AS6 [910/NW]	Privately owned, St Merryn	
WD889	Fairey Firefly AS6	NorthEastAircraftMuseum,Sunderland	
WD935	EE Canberra B2 (8440M)	RAF St Athan Museum	
WD948	EE Canberra B2 (8530M) [R]	CTE Manston	
WD955	EE Canberra T17 [EM]	RAF Strike Command, No 360 Sqn	
WE113	EE Canberra B2 [BJ]	RAF Strike Command, 231 OCU	
WE122	EE Canberra TT18 [845/VL]	RN FRADU, RNAS Yeovilton	
WE139	EE Canberra PR3 (8369M)	RAF Museum, Hendon	
WE146	EE Canberra PR3	RAE Llanbedr Fire Section	
WE168	EE Canberra PR3 (8049M)	RAF Manston, on display	
WE173	EE Canberra PR3	RAF Coltishall, Fire Section	
WE188	EE Canberra T4	BAe Samlesbury, store	
WE192	EE Canberra T4 [92]	BAe Samlesbury, store	
WE569	Auster 7 (G-ASAJ)	Privately owned, Cambridge	
WE600	Auster T7 (mod) (7602M)	RAF St Athan Museum	
WE925	Gloster Meteor F8	Wales Air Museum, Cardiff	

Notes	Serial	Type (alternative identity)	Owner, Operator or Location
	WE982	Slingsby Prefect TX1	RAF Support Command CGS
	WF122	Sea Prince T1 (A2673) [575/CU]	Cornwell Aero Park, Helston
	WF125	Sea Prince T1 (A2674) [576/CU]	RN Fire School, Predannack
	WF128	Sea Prince T1 (8611M)	Norfolk & Suffolk Aviation Museum
	WF133	Sea Prince T1 (G-BIDN) [567/CW]	Privately owned, Staverton
	WF137	Sea Prince T1 [999/CU]	WW2 Aircraft Preservation Society, Lasham
	WF219	Hawker Sea Hawk F1 (A2439)	FAA Museum, RNAS Yeovilton
	WF225	Hawker Sea Hawk F1 (A2645)	RNAS Culdrose, at main gate
	WF259	Hawker Sea Hawk F1 (A2483) [171/A]	Royal Scottish Museum of Flight
	WF299	Hawker Sea Hawk F1 (A2509)	Midland Air Museum
	WF369	Vickers Varsity T1 [F]	Newark Air Museum, Winthorpe
	WF372	Vickers Varsity T1 [T]	Privately owned, Sibson
	WF376	Vickers Varsity T1	Bristol Airport Fire Section
	WF379	Vickers Varsity T1	RAE West Freugh, Fire Section
	WF408	Vickers Varsity T1 (8395M)	RAF Cosford Aerospace Museum
	WF410	Vickers Varsity T1 [F]	Brunel Technical College, Bristol
	WF413	Vickers Varsity T1 [V]	CTE, Manston
	WF425	Vickers Varsity T1	Imperial War Museum, Duxford
	WF643	Gloster Meteor F8 [X]	Norfolk & Suffolk Aviation Museum
	WF784	Gloster Meteor T7 (7895M)	RAF Quedgeley, at main gate
	WF791	Gloster Meteor T7	RAF Vintage Pair, Leeming
	WF825	Gloster Meteor T7 (8359M) [Z]	No 2491 Sqn ATC, RAF Lyneham
	WF877	Gloster Meteor T7	Torbay Aircraft Museum
	WF890	EE Canberra T17 [EJ]	RAF Strike Command, No 360 Sqn
	WF916	EE Canberra T17 [EL]	RAF Strike Command, No 360 Sqn
	WF922	EE Canberra PR3	Privately owned
	WG307	DH Chipmunk 22 (G-BCYJ)	Privately owned, Duxford
	WG308	DH Chipmunk T10	RAF Support Command, 7 AEF
	WG316	DH Chipmunk 22 (G-BCAH)	Privately owned, Cranfield
	WG321	DH Chipmunk T10 [G]	AAC, Middle Wallop
	WG323	DH Chipmunk T10 [F]	AAC, Middle Wallop
	WG348	DH Chipmunk 22 (G-BBMV)	Privately owned, Duxford
	WG350	DH Chipmunk 22 (G-BCYE)	Privately owned, Biggin Hill
	WG362	DH Chipmunk T10 (8630M)	RAF Support Command, FSS Swinderby (PAX)
	WG403	DH Chipmunk T10 [O]	AAC, Middle Wallop
	WG407	DH Chipmunk T10 [81]	RAF Support Command, 9 AEF
	WG418	DH Chipmunk T10 (8209M/ G-ATDY)	RAF Support Command, 10 AEF (PAX)
	WG419	DH Chipmunk T10 (8206M)	RAF Finningley (PAX)
	WG422	DH Chipmunk 22 (G-BFAX)	Privately owned, Sibson
	WG430	DH Chipmunk T10	RAF Support Command, 1AEF
	WG432	DH Chipmunk T10 [L]	AAC, Middle Wallop
	WG458	DH Chipmunk T10	RAF, 5 MU Store
	WG463	DH Chipmunk T10 (8363M)	No 188 Sqn ATC, Ipswich (PAX)
	WG464	DH Chipmunk T10 (8364M)	131 Sqn ATC, Newcastle (PAX)
	WG465	DH Chipmunk 22 (G-BCEY)	Privately owned, Debden
	WG466	DH Chipmunk T10	AAC, 5 MU Store
	WG469	DH Chipmunk T10	RAF Support Command, 7 AEF
	WG477	DH Chipmunk T10 (8362M)	No 281 Sqn ATC, Birkdale (PAX)
	WG478	DH Chipmunk T10 [J]	RAF Kemble, 5 MU store
	WG479	DH Chipmunk T10 [K]	RAF Support Command, FSS Swinderby
	WG480	DH Chipmunk T10 [K]	RAF Kemble, 5 MU store
	WG486	DH Chipmunk T10	AAC, 5 MU Store
	WG496	Slingsby Sedbergh TX1	RAF Support Command, Halton
	WG497	Slingsby Sedbergh TX1	RAF Support Command, 663 GS
	WG498	Slingsby Sedbergh TX1	RAF Cranwell Gliding Club
	WG499	Slingsby Sedbergh TX1	RAF Support Command 634 GS
	WG556	Avro Shackleton MR2 (8651M) [A]	RAF Lossiemouth Fire Section
	WG655	Hawker Sea Fury T20 [910]	RN Historic Flight, Yeovilton
	WG718	WS51 Dragonfly HR5 (A2531)	Wales Aircraft Museum, Cardiff
	WG719	WS51 Dragonfly HR5 (G-BRMA) [902]	British Rotorcraft Museum, Weston-super-Mare

Serial	Type (alternative identity)	Owner, Operator or Location	Notes
WG724	WS51 Dragonfly HR5 [932]	North East Aircraft Museum	
WG752	WS51 Dragonfly HR5 [901]	Alleyn's School CCF, Dulwich	
WG760	English Electric P1A (7755M)	RAF Binbrook, preserved	
WG763	English Electric P1A (7816M)	Manchester Air & Space Museum	
WG768	Short SB5 (8005M)	RAF Cosford Aerospace Museum	
WG774	BAC 221	Science Museum, RNAS Yeovilton	
WG777	Fairey FD2 (7986M)	RAF Cosford Aerospace Museum	
WG789	EE Canberra B2	MoD(PE) RAE Bedford	
WH132	Gloster Meteor T7 (7906M) [J]	No 276 Sqn ATC, Chelmsford	
WH166	Gloster Meteor T7 (8052M)	RAF Digby, at main gate	
WH291	Gloster Meteor F8	WW2 Aircraft Preservation Society	
WH301	Gloster Meteor F8 (7930M)	RAF Museum, Hendon	
WH364	Gloster Meteor F8 (8169M)	RAF Portreath, at main gate	
WH453	Gloster Meteor D16 [L]	MoD(PE) RAE Llanbedr	
WH589	Hawker Sea Fury (G-AGHB)	Privately owned, Cranfield	
WH646	EE Canberra T17 [EG]	RAF Strike Command, No 360 Sqn	
WH657	EE Canberra B2	RFD Ltd, Godalming	
WH664	EE Canberra T17 [EH]	RAF Strike Command, No 360 Sqn	
WH665	EE Canberra T17 [J]	RAF Wyton, store	
WH670	EE Canberra B2 [CB]	RAF Strike Command, No 100 Sqn	
WH703	EE Canberra B2 (8490M) [S]	RAF Marham for ground instruction	
WH718	EE Canberra TT18 [CW]	RAF Strike Command, No 100 Sqn	
WH725	EE Canberra B2	Imperial War Museum, Duxford	
WH734	EE Canberra TT2	Flight Refuelling Ltd, Hurn	
WH740	EE Canberra T17 [K]	RAF Wyton, store	
WH773	EE Canberra PR7 (8696M)	RAF Wyton, on gate	
WH774	EE Canberra PR7	MoD(PE) RAE Bedford	
WH775	EE Canberra PR7	RAF St Athan, in store	
WH777	EE Canberra PR7	BAe Samlesbury, store	
WH779	EE Canberra PR7 [CK]	RAF Strike Command, No 100 Sqn	
WH780	EE Canberra T22 [853]	RN FRADU, RNAS Yeovilton	
WH791	EE Canberra PR7 (8187M)	RAF Cottesmore, at main gate	
WH794	EE Canberra PR7 (8652M)	RAF Abingdon, BDRF	
WH796	EE Canberra PR7	BAe Samlesbury, store	
WH797	EE Canberra T22	RN FRADU, RNAS Yeovilton	
WH798	EE Canberra PR7	Wales Aircraft Museum, Cardiff	
WH801	EE Canberra T22 [850]	RN FRADU, RNAS Yeovilton	
WH803	EE Canberra T22 [856]	RN FRADU, RNAS Yeovilton	
WH840	EE Canberra T4 (8350M)	RAF Locking, at main gate	
WH844	EE Canberra T4	MoD(PE) RAE Farnborough	
WH846	EE Canberra T4	BAe Samlesbury, store	
WH848	EE Canberra T4 [BD]	RAF Strike Command, 231 OCU	
WH849	EE Canberra T4 [BE]	RAF Strike Command, 231 OCU	
WH850	EE Canberra T4	BAe Samlesbury, store	
WH856	EE Canberra TT18 (8742M)	RAF Abingdon, BDRF	
WH869	EE Canberra B2 (8515M)	RAF Abingdon, BDRF	
WH872	EE Canberra T17 [W]	RAE Bedford, Fire Section	
WH876	EE Canberra D14	MoD(PE) A&AEE Boscombe Down	
WH887	EE Canberra TT18 [847]	RN FRADU, RNAS Yeovilton	
WH902	EE Canberra T17 [EK]	RAF Strike Command, No 360 Sqn	
WH904	EE Canberra T19 [O4]	Marshalls, Cambridge in store	
WH911	EE Canberra E15	RAF St Athan, store	
WH914	EE Canberra B2 (G-27-373)	BAe Samlesbury, store	
WH919	EE Canberra B2	RAF St Athan, store	
WH946	EE Canberra B6 (Mod)	Army Training Area, Hereford	
WH952	EE Canberra B6	MoD(PE) RAE Bedford for ground instruction	
WH953	EE Canberra B6	MoD(PE) RAE Bedford	
WH957	EE Canberra E15 [V]	RAF St Athan, in store	
WH960	EE Canberra B15 (8344M) [A]	RAF Support Command, 2 SoTT, Cosford	
WH964	EE Canberra E15 [CX]	RAF St Athan, in store	
WH972	EE Canberra E15 [CM]	RAF Strike Command, No 100 Sqn	
WH981	EE Canberra E15 [CN]	RAF Strike Command, No 100 Sqn	
WH983	EE Canberra E15 [CP]	RAF Strike Command, No 100 Sqn	
WH984	EE Canberra B15 (8101M) [E]	RAF Support Command, 2 SoTT, Cosford	
WH991	WS51 Dragonfly HR5	Lincolnshire Aviation Museum	

Notes	Serial	Type (alternative identity)	Owner, Operator or Location
	WJ231	Hawker Sea Fury FB11 [115/O]	FAA Museum, RNAS Yeovilton
	WJ288	Hawker Sea Fury FB11 [029]	Historic Aircraft Museum, Southend
	WJ306	Slingsby Sedbergh TXI	RAF Support Command, 621 GS
	WJ349	Percival Sea Prince C2	No 11 Sqn ATC, Weybridge
	WJ350	Percival Sea Prince C2	Guernsey Airport Fire Section
	WJ358	Auster AOP6 (G-ARYD)	Museum of Army Flying, Middle Wallop
	WJ565	EE Canberra T17 [C]	RAF St Athan, in store
	WJ567	EE Canberra B2 [CC]	RAF Strike Command, No 100 Sqn
	WJ573	EE Canberra B2 (7656M)	RAF Museum Store, Henlow
	WJ574	EE Canberra TT18 [844]	RN FRADU, RNAS Yeovilton
	WJ576	EE Canberra T17	RAF St Athan, store
	WJ581	EE Canberra T17	RAF St Athan, store
	WJ603	EE Canberra B2 (8664M) [G]	RAF Wattisham, BDRF
	WJ607	EE Canberra T17 [EB]	RAF Strike Command, 360 Sqn
	WJ611	EE Canberra B2 (8451M)	Aldergrove Fire Section
	WJ614	EE Canberra TT18 [846]	RN FRADU, RNAS Yeovilton
	WJ625	EE Canberra T17 [EC]	RAF Strike Command, No 360 Sqn
	WJ627	EE Canberra B2	RAE Bedford Fire Section
	WJ629	EE Canberra TT18 (8747M)	RAF Chivenor, Battle Damage Trg
	WJ630	EE Canberra T17 [ED]	RAF Strike Command, No 360 Sqn
	WJ633	EE Canberra T17 [EF]	RAF Strike Command, No 360 Sqn
	WJ636	EE Canberra TT18 [842]	RN FRADU, RNAS Yeovilton
	WJ637	EE Canberra B2T	RAF College Eng Flt
	WJ639	EE Canberra TT18 [39]	BAe Samlesbury, store
	WJ640	EE Canberra B2 (8722M)	RAF Support Command, 2 SoTT, Cosford
	WJ676	EE Canberra B2 (7796M)	Princess Alexandra RAF Hospital Wroughton
	WJ678	EE Canberra B2 [CF]	RAF Strike Command, No 100 Sqn
	WJ680	EE Canberra TT18 [CT]	RAF Strike Command, No 100 Sqn
	WJ681	EE Canberra B2T (8735M)	RAF Brawdy, BDRF
	WJ682	EE Canberra TT18 [CU]	RAF Strike Command, No 100 Sqn
	WJ715	EE Canberra TT18 [CV]	RAF Strike Command, No 100 Sqn
	WJ717	EE Canberra TT18 [841]	RN FRADU, RNAS Yeovilton
	WJ721	EE Canberra TT18 [21]	BAe Samlesbury, store
	WJ722	EE Canberra B2	RAF Athan, store
	WJ728	EE Canberra B2 [R]	MoD(PE) Farnborough, ground instruction
	WJ731	EE Canberra B2 [BK]	RAF Strike Command, 231 OCU
	WJ756	EE Canberra E15 [CL]	RAF Strike Command, No 100 Sqn
	WJ775	EE Canberra B6 (8581M) [Z]	RAF CSDE, Swanton Morley
	WJ815	EE Canberra PR7 (8729M)	RAF Coningsby, Fire Section
	WJ817	EE Canberra PR7 (8695M)	RAF Wyton, BDRF
	WJ821	EE Canberra PR7 (8668M)	Bassingbourne, on display
	WJ825	EE Canberra PR7 (8697M)	RAF Abingdon, BDRF
	WJ861	EE Canberra T4 [BF]	RAF Strike Command, 231 OCU
	WJ865	EE Canberra T4	RAE Apprentice School, Farnborough
	WJ866	EE Canberra T4 (859)	RAF St Athan, store
	WJ867	EE Canberra T4 (8643M)	RAF Newton, Fire Section
	WJ870	EE Canberra T4 (8683M)	RAF St Mawgan, BDRF
	WJ874	EE Canberra T4 [858]	RN FRADU, RNAS Yeovilton
	WJ877	EE Canberra T4	RAF Strike Command, 231 OCU
	WJ879	EE Canberra T4 [BH]	RAF Strike Command, 231 OCU
	WJ880	EE Canberra T4 (8491M) [39]	RAF Abingdon
	WJ893	Vickers Varsity T1	RAE Aberporth Fire Section
	WJ897	Vickers Varsity T1 (G-BDFT) [E]	Privately owned, Leicester
	WJ898	Vickers Varsity T1	Aldergrove Fire Section
	WJ902	Vickers Varsity T1 [C]	RAF Wittering Fire Section
	WJ903	Vickers Varsity T1 [C]	Glasgow Airport Fire Section
	WJ907	Vickers Varsity T1 [G]	Norwich Airport Fire Section
	WJ909	Vickers Varsity T1 [A]	Privately owned, Sibson
	WJ916	Vickers Varsity T1	RAF Lyneham Fire Section
	WJ944	Vickers Varsity T1 [Y]	Wales Air Museum, Cardiff
	WJ945	Vickers Varsity T1 (G-BEDV) [21]	Duxford Aviation Society
	WJ975	EE Canberra T19 [S]	Marshalls (stored), Cambridge
	WJ977	EE Canberra T17 [R]	RAF Wyton, store

Serial	Type (alternative identity)	Owner, Operator or Location	Notes
WJ981	EE Canberra T17 [EN]	RAF Strike Command, No 360 Sqn	
WJ986	EE Canberra T17 [EP]	RAF Strike Command, No 360 Sqn	
WK102	EE Canberra T17 [EQ]	RAF Strike Command, No 360 Sqn	
WK111	EE Canberra T17 [EA]	RAF Strike Command, No 360 Sqn	
WK118	EE Canberra TT18 [CQ]	RAF Strike Command, No 100 Sqn	
WK122	EE Canberra TT18 [22]	BAe Samlesbury store	
WK123	EE Canberra TT18 [840]	RN FRADU, RNAS Yeovilton	
WK124	EE Canberra TT18 [CR]	RAF Strike Command, No 100 Sqn	
WK126	EE Canberra TT18 [843]	RN FRADU, RNAS Yeovilton	
WK127	EE Canberra TT18 [CS]	RAF Strike Command, No 100 Sqn	
WK128	EE Canberra B2	Flight Refuelling Ltd, Hurn	
WK142	EE Canberra TT18 [848]	RN FRADU, RNAS Yeovilton	
WK143	EE Canberra B2	Flight Refuelling Ltd, Hurn	
WK144	EE Canberra B2 (8689M)	RAF St Athan, Apprentice School	
WK162	EE Canberra B2 [CA]	RAF Strike Command, No 100 Sqn	
WK163	EE Canberra B6	MoD(PE) RAE Bedford	
WK164	EE Canberra B2 [CY]	RAF Strike Command, No 100 Sqn	
WK198	VS Swift F4	North East Air Museum, Usworth	
WK275	VS Swift F4	Privately owned, Leominster, Hereford	
WK277	VS Swift FR5 (7719M) [N]	Newark Air Museum, Winthorpe	
WK281	VS Swift FR5 (7712M) [S]	RAF St Athan Museum	
WK511	DH Chipmunk T10	RN, 5 MU, store	
WK512	DH Chipmunk T10 [A]	AAC, Middle Wallop	
WK517	DH Chipmunk T10 [84]	RAF Support Command, 11 AEF	
WK518	DH Chipmunk T10	RAF Support Command, 1 AEF	
WK549	DH Chipmunk T10	Privately owned, Currock Hill	
WK550	DH Chipmunk T10 [J]	RAF Support Command, FSS Swinderby	
WK554	DH Chipmunk T10	AAC, 5 MU store	
WK559	DH Chipmunk T10 [M]	AAC, Middle Wallop	
WK562	DH Chipmunk T10 [T]	RAF Support Command, 3 AEF	
WK570	DH Chipmunk T10 (8211M)	RAF Support Command 2 AEF (PAX)	
WK572	DH Chipmunk T10 [X]	RAF Support Command, 3 AEF	
WK574	DH Chipmunk T10 [738/VL]	RNAS Yeovilton Station Flight	
WK575	DH Chipmunk T10 [F]	No 301 Sqn ATC, Bury St Edmunds (PAX)	
WK576	DH Chipmunk T10 (8357M)	No 1206 Sqn ATC, Lichfield (PAX)	
WK585	DH Chipmunk T10	RAF Support Command, 12 AEF	
WK586	DH Chipmunk T10	RAF Support Command, 5 MU store	
WK587	DH Chipmunk T10 (8212M)	St Ignatius Coll, Enfield (PAX)	
WK589	DH Chipmunk T10 [C]	RAF Support Command, 6 AEF	
WK590	DH Chipmunk T10 [82]	RAF Support Command, 9 AEF	
WK608	DH Chipmunk T10 [906]	Britannia Royal Naval College AEF	
WK609	DH Chipmunk T10 [L]	RAF Support Command, 3 AEF	
WK613	DH Chipmunk T10 [P]	AAC, Middle Wallop	
WK620	DH Chipmunk T10 [T]	AAC, Middle Wallop	
WK624	DH Chipmunk T10 [12]	RAF Support Command, 10 AEF	
WK630	DH Chipmunk T10 [11]	RAF Support Command, 2 AEF	
WK633	DH Chipmunk T10 [B]	RAF Support Command, FSS Swinderby	
WK634	DH Chipmunk T10 [902]	Britannia Royal Naval College AEF	
WK635	DH Chipmunk T10	RNAS Yeovilton, station flight	
WK638	DH Chipmunk T10 [83]	RAF Support Command, 9 AEF	
WK639	DH Chipmunk T10 [10]	RAF Support Command, 10 AEF	
WK640	DH Chipmunk T10 [C]	RAF Support Command, FSS Swinderby	
WK642	DH Chipmunk T10	RAF Support Command, 7 AEF	
WK643	DH Chipmunk T10 [G]	RAF Support Command, FSS Swinderby	
WK654	Gloster Meteor F8 (8092M) [B]	RAF Neatishead, at main gate	
WK800	Gloster Meteor D16 [Z]	MoD(PE) RAE Llanbedr	
WK914	Gloster Meteor F8 [Y]	RAF Manston	
WK935	Gloster Meteor (Prone Pilot) (7869M)	RAF Cosford Aerospace Museum	
WK968	Gloster Meteor F8 (8053M) [A]	RAF Odiham, at main gate	
WK991	Gloster Meteor F8 (7825M)	Imperial War Museum, Duxford	
WL161	Gloster Meteor F8	Brunel Technical College, Bristol	
WL168	Gloster Meteor F8 (7750M) [A]	RAF St Athan Museum	
WL181	Gloster Meteor F8	North East Aircraft Museum	
WL332	Gloster Meteor T7	Wales Air Museum, Cardiff	
WL345	Gloster Meteor T7	Privately owned, Hastings	

Notes	Serial	Type (alternative identity)	Owner, Operator or Location
	WL349	Gloster Meteor T7 [Z]	Staverton Airport, on display
	WL360	Gloster Meteor T7 (7920M) [G]	RAF Locking, at main gate
	WL375	Gloster Meteor T7	Dumfries & Galloway Aviation Group
	WL405	Gloster Meteor T7	North East Air Museum
	WL419	Gloster Meteor T7	Martin Baker Aircraft, Chalgrove
	WL505	DH Vampire FB9 (7705M)	RAF St Athan Museum
	WL626	Vickers Varsity T1 (G-BHDD)	Loughborough & Leics Aviation Museum
	WL627	Vickers Varsity T1 [D]	RAF Newton Fire Section
	WL628	Vickers Varsity T1 [X]	RAF Wattisham Fire Section
	WL635	Vickers Varsity T1	RAF Machrihanish Police School
	WL678	Vickers Varsity T1 [C]	Leeds-Bradford Airport Fire Section
	WL679	Vickers Varsity T1	MoD(PE) RAE Farnborough
	WL732	BP Sea Balliol T21	RAF Cosford Aerospace Museum
	WL738	Avro Shackleton MR2C (8567M)	RAF Lossiemouth, at main gate
	WL747	Avro Shackleton AEW2	RAF Strike Command, No 8 Sqn
	WL754	Avro Shackleton AEW2 (8665M) [54]	RAF Valley, for preservation
✓	WL756	Avro Shackleton AEW2	RAF Lossiemouth, Fire Section
	WL757	Avro Shackleton AEW2	RAF Strike Command, No 8 Sqn
	WL790	Avro Shackleton AEW2	RAF Strike Command, No 8 Sqn
	WL793	Avro Shackleton AEW2 (8675M) [93]	RAF Lossiemouth, BDRF
	WL795	Avro Shackleton AEW2	RAF St Mawgan
	WL798	Avro Shackleton MR2C (8114M) [Z]	RAF Cosford
	WL801	Avro Shackleton MR2C (8629M) [01]	RAF Cosford
	WL925	Slingsby Cadet TX3 (really WV925)	Air Cadet Recruiting Team, Cosford
	WM167	AW Meteor TT20	Warbirds of GB, Blackbushe
	WM224	AW Meteor TT20 (8177M) [X]	Privately owned, North Weald
	WM292	AW Meteor TT20 [841]	FAA Museum, RNAS Yeovilton
	WM571	DH Sea Venom FAW 21 [742/VL]	Wessex Aviation Society, Wimborne
	WM913	Hawker Sea Hawk FB5 (A2510/8162M)	Sea Cadets, Fleetwood
	WM961	Hawker Sea Hawk FB5 (A2517)	Torbay Aircraft Museum
	WM969	Hawker Sea Hawk FB5 (A2530)	Imperial War Museum, Duxford
	WM983	Hawker Sea Hawk FB5 (A2511)	Cornwall Aero Park, Helston
	WM993	Hawker Sea Hawk FB5 (A2522)	RN HMS Royal Arthur, Corsham
	WM994	Hawker Sea Hawk FB5 (A2503)	Privately owned, Swansea
	WN108	Hawker Sea Hawk FB5 [033]	Shorts Apprentice School, Belfast
	WN464	Fairey Gannet AS6 (A2540)	Cornwall Aero Park, Helston
	WN493	WS51 Dragonfly HR5	FAA Museum, RNAS Yeovilton
	WN499	WS51 Dragonfly HR5 [Y]	Torbay Aircraft Museum
	WN516	EP Balliol T2	North East Aircraft Museum
	WN901	Hawker Hunter F2 (7543M)	RAF Newton
	WN904	Hawker Hunter F2 (7544M) [3]	Imperial War Museum, Duxford
	WN907	Hawker Hunter F2	Staravia, Ascot
	WP180	Hawker Hunter F5 (8473M) (really WP190)	RAF Stanbridge, at main gate
	WP185	Hawker Hunter F5 (7583M)	RAF Museum, Hendon
	WP270	EoN Eton TX1 (8598M)	Manchester Air & Space Museum
	WP271	EoN Eton TX1	Stored Keevil
	WP313	Percival Sea Prince T1 [568/CU]	RAE Farnborough
	WP314	Percival Sea Prince T1 (8634M) [579/CU]	RAF Police School, Syerston

Serial	Type (alternative identity)	Owner, Operator or Location	Notes
WP320	Percival Sea Prince T1 [573/CU]	RAF Leuchars, Fire Section	
WP321	Pervical Sea Prince T1 (G-BRFC) [570/CU]	Privately owned, Bourn	
WP497	Westland Dragonfly HR5	Privately owned, Uttoxeter	
WP503	Westland Dragonfly HR3 [901]	Humberside Aircraft Preservation Society, Cleethorpes	
WP515	EE Canberra B2 [CD]	RAF Strike Command, No 100 Sqn	
WP772	DH Chipmunk T10 [Q]	AAC, Middle Wallop	
WP776	DH Chipmunk T10	RNAS Culdrose, Station Flight	
WP786	DH Chipmunk T10 [D]	RAF Support Command, FSS Swinderby	
WP790	DH Chipmunk 22 (G-BBNC) [T]	Mosquito Aircraft Museum	
WP795	DH Chipmunk T10 [901]	Britannia Royal Naval College AEF	
WP801	DH Chipmunk T10 [911]	Britannia Royal Naval College AEF	
WP803	DH Chipmunk T10	RN, 5 MU store	
WP805	DH Chipmunk T10 [D]	RAF Support Command, 6 AEF	
WP808	DH Chipmunk 22 (G-BDEU)	Privately owned, Sibson	
WP809	DH Chipmunk T10 [912]	Britannia Royal Naval College AEF	
WP833	DH Chipmunk T10	RAF Support Command, 4 AEF	
WP837	DH Chipmunk T10 [L]	RAF Support Command, 5 AEF	
WP839	DH Chipmunk T10 [A]	RAF Support Command, 8 AEF	
WP840	DH Chipmunk T10 [09]	RAF Support Command, 2 AEF	
WP844	DH Chipmunk T10	RAF Support Command, FSS Swinderby	
WP851	DH Chipmunk 22 (G-BDET)	Privately owned, Popham	
WP855	DH Chipmunk T10	RAF Battle of Britain Flight	
WP856	DH Chipmunk T10 [904]	Britannia Royal Naval College AEF	
WP857	DH Chipmunk 22 (G-BDRJ)	Privately owned, Felthorpe	
WP859	DH Chipmunk T10 [E]	RAF Support Command, 8 AEF	
WP860	DH Chipmunk T10	RAF Support Command, 12 AEF	
WP869	DH Chipmunk T10	RAF Support Command, 8 AEF (PAX)	
WP871	DH Chipmunk T10	RAF, 5 MU, store	
WP872	DH Chipmunk T10	AAC, 5 MU, store	
WP896	DH Chipmunk T10 [11]	RAF Support Command, 10 AEF	
WP900	DH Chipmunk T10 [13]	RAF Support Command, 10 AEF	
WP901	DH Chipmunk T10 [B]	RAF Support Command, 6 AEF	
WP904	DH Chipmunk T10 [909]	Britannia Royal Naval College AEF	
WP906	DH Chipmunk T10 [739]	RNAS Lee-on-Solent Stn Flt	
WP912	DH Chipmunk T10 (8467M)	RAF Cosford Aerospace Museum	
WP914	DH Chipmunk T10 [E]	RAF Support Command, 6 AEF	
WP920	DH Chipmunk T10 [10]	RAF Support Command, 2 AEF	
WP925	DH Chipmunk T10 [C]	AAC, Middle Wallop	
WP927	DH Chipmunk T10 (8216M/G-ATJK)	No 1128 Sqn ATC, Woodvale (PAX)	
WP928	DH Chipmunk T10 [D]	AAC, 5 MU, store	
WP929	DH Chipmunk T10 [F]	RAF Support Command, 8 AEF	
WP930	DH Chipmunk T10 [J]	AAC, Middle Wallop	
WP962	DH Chipmunk T10 [V]	RAF Support Command, 3 AEF	
WP964	DH Chipmunk T10	AAC Middle Wallop	
WP967	DH Chipmunk T10	RAF Support Command, 12 AEF	
WP970	DH Chipmunk T10 [T]	RAF Support Command, 5 AEF	
WP974	DH Chipmunk T10 [N]	RAF Support Command, 3 AEF	
WP977	DH Chipmunk 22 (G-BHRD)	Privately owned, Oxford	
WP979	DH Chipmunk T10 [J]	CSDE Swanton Morley	
WP980	DH Chipmunk T10 [E]	RAF Support Command, FSS Swinderby	
WP981	DH Chipmunk T10	AAC, 5 MU, store	
WP983	DH Chipmunk T10 [B]	AAC, Middle Wallop	
WP984	DH Chipmunk T10	RAF Support Command, 7 AEF	
WR960	Avro Shackleton AEW2	Manchester Air & Space Museum	
WR963	Avro Shackleton AEW2	RAF Lossiemouth Fire Section	
WR965	Avro Shackleton AEW2	RAF Lossiemouth, spares	
WR967	Avro Shackleton MR2C (8398M)	RAF Lossiemouth as a simulator	
WR971	Avro Shackleton MR3 (8119M) [Q]	RAF Support Command, 2 SoTT, Cosford	
WR974	Avro Shackleton MR3 (8117M) [K]	RAF Cosford Aerospace Museum	
WR977	Avro Shackleton MR3 (8186M) [B]	Newark Air Museum, Winthorpe	
WR981	Avro Shackleton MR3 (8120M)	RAF Topcliffe Fire Section	

Notes	Serial	Type (alternative identity)	Owner, Operator or Location
	WR982	Avro Shackleton MR3 (8106M) [J]	RAF Support Command, 2 SoTT, Cosford
	WR985	Avro Shackleton MR3 (8103M) [H]	RAF Support Command, 2 SoTT, Cosford
	WS103	Gloster Meteor T7 [709/VL]	FAA Museum store, RNAY Wroughton
	WS692	Gloster Meteor NF12 (7605M)	Newark Air Museum, Winthorpe
	WS726	Gloster Meteor NF14 (7960M) [G]	No 1885 Sqn ATC, Royton
	WS739	Gloster Meteor NF14 (7961M)	Privately owned, Misson
	WS760	Gloster Meteor NF14 (7964M)	Privately owned, Duxford
	WS774	Gloster Meteor NF14 (7959M)	RAF Hospital Ely, at main gate
	WS776	Gloster Meteor NF14 (7716M) [K]	RAF North Luffenham, at main gate
	WS788	Gloster Meteor NF14 (7967M) [P]	RAF Leeming, at main gate
	WS792	Gloster Meteor NF14 (7965M) [K]	RAF Carlisle, at main gate
	WS807	Gloster Meteor NF14 (7973M) [N]	RAF Watton, at main gate
	WS832	Gloster Meteor NF14 [W]	Solway Aviation Society, Carlisle
	WS838	Gloster Meteor NF14	Manchester Air & Space Museum
	WS840	Gloster Meteor NF14 (7969M)	Aldergrove Fire Section
	WS843	Gloster Meteor NF14 (7937M) [Y]	RAF St Athan Museum
	WT121	Douglas Skyraider AEW1 [415/CU]	FAA Museum, RNAS Yeovilton
	WT301	EE Canberra B6 (Mod) [W]	Defence School, Chattenden
	WT305	EE Canberra B6 (8511M) [X]	RAF Wyton, on display
	WT308	EE Canberra B(I)6	MoD(PE) RAE Farnborough
	WT309	EE Canberra B(I)6	MoD(PE) RAE Farnborough
	WT327	EE Canberra B(I)8	Warbirds of GB, Blackbushe
	WT333	EE Canberra B(I)8	MoD(PE) RAE Bedford
	WT339	EE Canberra B(I)8 (8198M)	RAF College Cranwell Fire Section
	WT346	EE Canberra B(I)8 (8197M)	RAF Cosford Aerospace Museum
	WT478	EE Canberra T4 [BA]	RAF Strike Command, 231 OCU
	WT480	EE Canberra T4 [BC]	RAF Strike Command, 231 OCU
	WT483	EE Canberra T4	BAe Samlesbury store
	WT486	EE Canberra T4 (8102M)	RAF Support Command, Aldergrove
	WT488	EE Canberra T4	BAe Samlesbury store
	WT507	EE Canberra PR7 (8548M) [44]	RAF Support Command (nose only)
	WT509	EE Canberra PR7 [CG]	RAF Strike Command, No 100 Sqn
	WT510	EE Canberra T22 [854/VL]	RN FRADU, RNAS Yeovilton
	WT518	EE Canberra PR7 (8691M)	RAF St Athan, CTTS
	WT519	EE Canberra PR7 [CH]	RAF Strike Command, No 100 Sqn
	WT520	EE Canberra PR7 (8184M) [I]	RAF Swinderby, at main gate
	WT525	EE Canberra T22 [855/VL]	RN FRADU, RNAS Yeovilton
	WT532	EE Canberra PR7 (8728M)	MoD(PE) RAE Bedford
	WT534	EE Canberra PR7 (8549M) [43]	RAF Support Command (nose only)
	WT535	EE Canberra T22 [852/VL]	RN FRADU, RNAS Yeovilton
	WT536	EE Canberra PR7 (8063M) [F]	RAF Support Command, 2 SoTT, Cosford
	WT537	EE Canberra PR7	BAe Samlesbury store
	WT538	EE Canberra PR7 [CJ]	RAF Strike Command, No 100 Sqn
	WT555	Hawker Hunter F1 (7499M)	RAF Cosford Aerospace Museum
	WT569	Hawker Hunter F1 (7491M)	No 2117 Sqn ATC, West Glamorgan
	WT612	Hawker Hunter F1 (7496M)	RAF Credenhill, on display
	WT619	Hawker Hunter F1 (7525M)	RAF Museum Store, Henlow
	WT651	Hawker Hunter F1 (7532M) [C]	RAF Credenhill, on display
	WT660	Hawker Hunter F1 (7421M) [C]	RAF Carlisle, at main gate
	WT680	Hawker Hunter F1 (7533M)	No 1429 Sqn ATC at RAE Aberporth
	WT684	Hawker Hunter F1 (7422M)	RAF Brize Norton
	WT694	Hawker Hunter F1 (7510M) [Y]	RAF Newton, at main gate
	WT702	Hawker Hunter T8C [874/VL]	RN FRADU, RNAS Yeovilton
	WT711	Hawker Hunter GA11 [837/VL]	RN FRADU, RNAS Yeovilton
	WT722	Hawker Hunter T8C [878/VL]	RN FRADU, RNAS Yeovilton

Serial	Type (alternative identity)	Owner, Operator or Location	Notes
WT723	Hawker Hunter GA11 [866/VL]	RN FRADU, RNAS Yeovilton	
WT741	Hawker Hunter GA11	Humberside Aviation Museum	
WT744	Hawker Hunter GA11 [868/VL]	RN FRADU, RNAS Yeovilton	
WT746	Hawker Hunter F4 (7770M) [A]	RAF Support Command, 1 SoTT Halton	
WT778	Hawker Hunter F4 (7791M)	RAF Brize Norton, Air Movements School	
WT799	Hawker Hunter T8C [879/VL]	RAF Shawbury, store	
WT804	Hawker Hunter GA11 [831/VL]	RN FRADU, RNAS Yeovilton	
WT806	Hawker Hunter GA11 [838/VL]	RN FRADU, RNAS Yeovilton	
WT809	Hawker Hunter GA11 [867/VL]	RN FRADU, RNAS Yeovilton	
WT867	Slingsby Cadet TX3	RAF Support Command, 626 GS	
WT868	Slingsby Cadet TX3	RAF Support Command, 645 GS	
WT869	Slingsby Cadet TX3	RAF Support Command, 618 GS	
WT870	Slingsby Cadet TX3	RAF Support Command, 635 GS	
WT871	Slingsby Cadet TX3	RAF Support Command, 635 GS	
WT873	Slingsby Cadet TX3	RAF Support Command, GSS St Athan	
WT877	Slingsby Cadet TX3	RAF Support Command, 621 GS	
WT895	Slingsby Cadet TX3	RAF Support Command, GSS St Athan	
WT898	Slingsby Cadet TX3	RAF Support Command, 662 GS	
WT899	Slingsby Cadet TX3	RAF Support Command, 643 GS	
WT900	Slingsby Cadet TX3 [S]	RAF Support Command, CGS	
WT901	Slingsby Cadet TX3	RAF Support Command, 622 GS	
WT902	Slingsby Cadet TX3	RAF Support Command, 622 GS	
WT903	Slingsby Cadet TX3	RAF Support Command, GSS St Athan	
WT904	Slingsby Cadet TX3	RAF Support Command, 617 GS	
WT905	Slingsby Cadet TX3	RAF Support Command, 645 GS	
WT906	Slingsby Cadet TX3	RAF Support Command, 661 GS	
WT908	Slingsby Cadet TX3	RAF Support Command, 661 GS	
WT909	Slingsby Cadet TX3	RAF Support Command, 626 GS	
WT910	Slingsby Cadet TX3	RAF Support Command, 617 GS	
WT911	Slingsby Cadet TX3	RAF Support Command, 635 GS	
WT913	Slingsby Cadet TX3	RAF Support Command, 618 GS	
WT914	Slingsby Cadet TX3 [C]	RAF Support Command, 618 GS	
WT915	Slingsby Cadet TX3	RAF Support Command, 645 GS	
WT917	Slingsby Cadet TX3	RAF Support Command, 614 GS	
WT918	Slingsby Cadet TX3	RAF Support Command, 645 GS	
WT919	Slingsby Cadet TX3	RAF Support Command, 662 GS	
WT933	Bristol Sycamore 3 (G-ALSW/7709M)	Newark Air Museum, Winthorpe	
WV106	Douglas Skyraider AEW3 [427]	Cornwall Aero Park, Helston	
WV198	S.55 Whirlwind HAR21 (G-BJWY/A2576)	Privately owned, Heysham, Lancs	
WV256	Hawker Hunter GA11 [862/VL]	RN FRADU, RNAS Yeovilton	
WV267	Hawker Hunter GA11 [836/VL]	RN FRADU, RNAS Yeovilton	
WV276	Hawker Hunter F4 (7847M) [D]	RAF Support Command, 1 SoTT Halton	
WV318	Hawker Hunter T7B	RAF Laarbruch Station Flight/237 OCU	
WV322	Hawker Hunter T8B	RAF 5 MU store, Kemble	
WV363	Hawker Hunter T8 [872/VL]	RN FRADU, RNAS Yeovilton	
WV372	Hawker Hunter T7	RAF Strike Command, 208 Sqn	
WV381	Hawker Hunter GA11 [732/VL]	UKAEA, Culham, Oxon	
WV382	Hawker Hunter GA11 [830/VL]	RN 5 MU store, Kemble	
WV383	Hawker Hunter T7	MoD(PE) RAE Farnborough	
WV396	Hawker Hunter T8C [871/VL]	RN FRADU, RNAS Yeovilton	
WV483	Percival Provost T1 (7693M) [N-E]	Historic Aircraft Museum	
WV493	Percival Provost T1 (G-BDYG/7696M) [29]	Royal Scottish Museum of Flight	
WV495	Percival Provost T1 (7697M) [P-C]	Privately owned, Camberley	
WV499	Percival Provost T1 (7698M) [P-G]	RAF St Athan Historic Aircraft Collection	
WV562	Percival Provost T1 (7606M) [P-C]	RAF Cosford Aerospace Museum	
WV605	Percival Provost T1 [T-B]	Norfolk & Suffolk Av Museum	
WV606	Percival Provost T1 (7622M) [P-B]	Newark Air Museum, Winthorpe	

Notes	Serial	Type (alternative identity)	Owner, Operator or Location
	WV679	Percival Provost T1 (7615M) [O-J]	Torbay Aircraft Museum
	WV686	Percival Provost T1 (7621M) [O-P]	Privately owned, Blackbushe
	WV701	Percival Pembroke C1	RAF Germany, No 60 Sqn
	WV703	Percival Pembroke C1 (8108M)	RAF Coningsby Fire Section
	WV733	Percival Pembroke C1	Otterburn Training Area
	WV740	Percival Pembroke C1	RAF Germany, No 60 Sqn
	WV746	Percival Pembroke C1	RAF Germany, No 60 Sqn
	WV753	Percival Pembroke C1 (8113M)	Wales Air Museum, Cardiff
	WV781	Bristol Sycamore HC12 (G-ALTD/7839M)	RAF Odiham
	WV783	Bristol Sycamore HC12 (G-ALSP/7841M)	RAF Museum store, Henlow
	WV787	EE Canberra B2/8	MoD(PE) A&AEE Boscombe Down
	WV794	Hawker Sea Hawk FGA4 (A2634/8152M)	Air Service Training, Perth
	WV795	Hawker Sea Hawk FGA4 (A2661/8151M)	Privately owned, Bath, Avon
	WV797	Hawker Sea Hawk FGA4 (A2637/8155M)	Air Service Training, Perth
	WV798	Hawker Sea Hawk FGA4 (A2557) [028/CU]	SWWAPS Lasham
	WV826	Hawker Sea Hawk FGA6 (A2532) [147/CU]	Wales Air Museum, Cardiff
	WV856	Hawker Sea Hawk FGA6 [163]	FAA Museum, RNAS Yeovilton
	WV903	Hawker Sea Hawk FGA6 (A2632/8153M)	RNAS Culdrose, SAH
	WV908	Hawker Sea Hawk FGA6 (A2660/8154M) [188/A]	RN Historic Flight, RNAS Yeovilton
	WV911	Hawker Sea Hawk FGA4 (A2526) [115/C]	RN AES, RNAS Lee-on-Solent
	WW138	DH Sea Venom FAW21 [299/O]	FAA Museum, RNAS Yeovilton
	WW145	DH Sea Venom FAW21 [690/LM]	Royal Scottish Museum of Flight
	WW217	DH Sea Venom FAW22 [736/VL]	Ottershaw School CCF, Chertsey
	WW388	Percival Provost T1 (7616M)	Privately owned, Chertsey
	WW397	Percival Provost T1 (8060M/ G-BKHP) [N-E]	Privately owned, RAF Lyneham
	WW421	Percival Provost T1 (7688M)	Lincolnshire Aviation Museum
	WW442	Percival Provost T1 (7618M)	Privately owned, St Merryn
	WW444	Percival Provost T1 [D]	Privately owned, Coventry
	WW453	Percival Provost T1 [B-P]	Air Service Training, Perth
	WW654	Hawker Hunter GA11 [833/VL]	RN FRADU, RNAS Yeovilton
	WX788	DH Venom NF3	Wales Air Museum, Cardiff
	WX853	DH Venom NF3 (7443M)	Mosquito Aircraft Museum
	WX905	DH Venom NF3 (7458M)	RAF Museum Store, Henlow
	WZ425	DH Vampire T11 [22]	Wales Air Museum, Cardiff
	WZ450	DH Vampire T11 [23]	No 2371 Sqn ATC, Tile Cross
	WZ464	DH Vampire T11 (N62430) [40]	LFV&HAC, Bushey, Herts
	WZ514	DH Vampire T11	Privately owned, Irby Hall, Merseyside
	WZ515	DH Vampire T11 [60]	Skyfame Collection, Duxford
	WZ518	DH Vampire T11	North East Aviation Museum
	WZ549	DH Vampire T11 (8118M) [F]	Lincolnshire Aviation Museum
	WZ550	DH Vampire T11	Privately owned, Camberley
	WZ553	DH Vampire T11 [40]	Loughborough & Leics Air Museum,
	WZ557	DH Vampire T11 [47]	Privately owned, N York
	WZ576	DH Vampire T11 (8174M)	No 2192 Sqn ATC, Appleby
	WZ584	DH Vampire T11 [U]	St Albans College of FE
	WZ589	DH Vampire T11 [19]	Lashenden Air Warfare Museum
	WZ590	DH Vampire T11 [19]	Imperial War Museum, Duxford
	WZ662	Auster AOP9	Wales Air Museum, Swansea
	WZ670	Auster AOP9 (really WZ724)	AAC Middle Wallop, at main gate
	WZ679	Auster AOP9 (7863M)	No 2293 Sqn ATC, Marlborough
	WZ706	Auster AOP9	Royal Military College of Science

Serial	Type (alternative identity)	Owner, Operator or Location	Notes
WZ711	Auster 9/Beagle E3 (G-AVHT)	Privately owned, Middle Wallop	
WZ721	Auster AOP9	Museum of Army Flying,Middle Wallop	
WZ736	Avro 707A (7868M)	Manchester Air & Space Museum	
WZ744	Avro 707C (7932M)	RAF Cosford Aerospace Museum	
WZ753	Slingsby Grasshopper TX1	1 MGSP, RAF Halton	
WZ754	Slingsby Grasshopper TX1	Strathallan School CCF, Perth	
WZ755	Slingsby Grasshopper TX1	West Buckland School CCF, N. Devon	
WZ756	Slingsby Grasshopper TX1	2 MGSP, RAF Locking	
WZ757	Slingsby Grasshopper TX1	2 MGSP, RAF Locking	
WZ758	Slingsby Grasshopper TX1	King's School CCF, Grantham	
WZ760	Slingsby Grasshopper TX1	2 MGSP, RAF Locking	
WZ761	Slingsby Grasshopper TX1	1 MGSP, RAF Halton	
WZ762	Slingsby Grasshopper TX1	3 MGSP, RAF Cosford	
WZ764	Slingsby Grasshopper TX1	1 MGSP, RAF Halton	
WZ765	Slingsby Grasshopper TX1	2 MGSP, RAF Locking	
WZ767	Slingsby Grasshopper TX1	1 MGSP, RAF Halton	
WZ768	Slingsby Grasshopper TX1	Warwick School CCF, Warks	
WZ769	Slingsby Grasshopper TX1	Kingham Hill School CCF, Oxon	
WZ771	Slingsby Grasshopper TX1	14 MU, RAF Carlisle	
WZ772	Slingsby Grasshopper TX1	Brentwood School CCF, Essex	
WZ773	Slingsby Grasshopper TX1	Edinburgh Academy CCF, Lothian	
WZ774	Slingsby Grasshopper TX1	14 MU, RAF Carlisle	
WZ777	Slingsby Grasshopper TX1	14 MU, RAF Carlisle	
WZ778	Slingsby Grasshopper TX1	4 MGSP, RAF Dishforth	
WZ779	Slingsby Grasshopper TX1	Ratcliffe College CCF, Syerston	
WZ780	Slingsby Grasshopper TX1	Clifton College CCF, Bristol	
WZ781	Slingsby Grasshopper TX1	4 MGSP, RAF Dishforth	
WZ782	Slingsby Grasshopper TX1	Charterhouse School CCF, Godalming	
WZ783	Slingsby Grasshopper TX1	14 MU, RAF Carlisle	
WZ784	Slingsby Grasshopper TX1	4 MGSP, RAF Dishforth	
WZ785	Slingsby Grasshopper TX1	Wellingborough School CCF,Northants	
WZ786	Slingsby Grasshopper TX1	14 MU, RAF Carlisle	
WZ787	Slingsby Grasshopper TX1	4 MGSP, RAF Dishforth	
WZ789	Slingsby Grasshopper TX1	3 MGSP, RAF Cosford	
WZ791	Slingsby Grasshopper TX1	Royal Grammar School CCF, High Wycombe	
WZ792	Slingsby Grasshopper TX1	Barnard Castle School CCF,Co Durham	
WZ793	Slingsby Grasshopper TX1	Lord Wandsworth College CCF, Basingstoke	
WZ794	Slingsby Grasshopper TX1	Kings School CCF, Kent	
WZ795	Slingsby Grasshopper TX1	St Lawrence School CCF, Kent	
WZ796	Slingsby Grasshopper TX1	Eastbourne College CCF, East Sussex	
WZ797	Slingsby Grasshopper TX1	Canford School CCF, Dorset	
WZ798	Slingsby Grasshopper TX1	2 MGSP, RAF Locking	
WZ816	Slingsby Grasshopper TX1	2 MGSP, RAF Locking	
WZ817	Slingsby Grasshopper TX1	4 MGSP, RAF Dishforth	
WZ818	Slingsby Grasshopper TX1	Oakham School CCF, Leics	
WZ819	Slingsby Grasshopper TX1	4 MGSP RAF Dishforth	
WZ820	Slingsby Grasshopper TX1	Whitgift School CCF, Surrey	
WZ822	Slingsby Grasshopper TX1	Emmanuel School CCF, London	
WZ824	Slingsby Grasshopper TX1	St Bees School CCF, Cumbria	
WZ825	Slingsby Grasshopper TX1	Bradfield College CCF, Reading, Berks	
WZ826	Slingsby Grasshopper TX1	Dulwich College CCF, London	
WZ827	Slingsby Grasshopper TX1	RAF Support Command, CGS	
WZ828	Slingsby Grasshopper TX1	Heles School CCF, Exeter, Devon	
WZ829	Slingsby Grasshopper TX1	Launceston School CCF, Cornwall	
WZ830	Slingsby Grasshopper TX1	14 MU, RAF Carlisle	
WZ831	Slingsby Grasshopper TX1	Oratory School CCF, Reading	
WZ845	DH Chipmunk T10	RAF Support Command, 1 AEF	
WZ847	DH Chipmunk T10 [F]	RAF Support Command, 6 AEF	
WZ849	DH Chipmunk T10 (8439M)	No 1404 Sqn ATC, Chatham	
WZ856	DH Chipmunk T10	RAF Support Command, 7 AEF	
WZ858	DH Chipmunk T10	RAF Support Command, 1 AEF	
WZ862	DH Chipmunk T10	RAF Germany, Gatow Stn Flt	
WZ868	DH Chipmunk 22 (G-BCIW)	Privately owned, Bedford	
WZ869	DH Chipmunk T10 (8019M)	No 391 Sqn ATC, Handforth (PAX)	
WZ872	DH Chipmunk T10 [E]	RAF Support Command, 5 AEF	
WZ875	DH Chipmunk T10	RAF Support Command, 12 AEF	
WZ877	DH Chipmunk T10 [G]	RAF Support Command, 6 AEF	
WZ878	DH Chipmunk T10	RAF Support Command, 11 AEF	
WZ879	DH Chipmunk T10 [85]	RAF Support Command, 11 AEF	

Notes	Serial	Type (alternative identity)	Owner, Operator or Location
	WZ882	DH Chipmunk T10 [K]	AAC, Middle Wallop
	WZ884	DH Chipmunk T10	AAC, 5 MU, store
	XA109	DH Sea Vampire T22	Royal Scottish Museum of Flight
	XA129	DH Sea Vampire T22	FAA Museum, RNAS Yeovilton
	XA225	Slingsby Grasshopper TX1	Churchers College CCF, Petersfield
	XA226	Slingsby Grasshopper TX1	1 MGSP, RAF Halton
	XA227	Slingsby Grasshopper TX1	14 MU, RAF Carlisle
	XA228	Slingsby Grasshopper TX1	Glenalmond Trinity College CCF, Tayside
	XA229	Slingsby Grasshopper TX1	3 MGSP, RAF Cosford
	XA230	Slingsby Grasshopper TX1	Uppingham School CCFD, Leics
	XA231	Slingsby Grasshopper TX1	Kimbolton School CCF, Cambs
	XA233	Slingsby Grasshopper TX1	1 MGSP, RAF Halton
	XA236	Slingsby Grasshopper TX1	1 MGSP, RAF Halton
	XA237	Slingsby Grasshopper TX1	Queen Victory School CCF, Dunblane
	XA239	Slingsby Grasshopper TX1	Perse School CCF, Cambridge
	XA240	Slingsby Grasshopper TX1	Radley College CCF, Abingdon
	XA241	Slingsby Grasshopper TX1	Trinity School CCF, Croydon
	XA243	Slingsby Grasshopper TX1	Bournemouth School CCF, Dorset
	XA244	Slingsby Grasshopper TX1	3 MGSP, RAF Cosford
	XA282	Slingsby Cadet TX3	RAF Support Command, 635 GS
	XA284	Slingsby Cadet TX3	RAF Support Command, 636 GS
	XA286	Slingsby Cadet TX3	RAF Support Command, 615 GS
	XA287	Slingsby Cadet TX3	RAF Support Command, CGS
	XA288	Slingsby Cadet TX3	RAF Support Command, 624 GS
	XA289	Slingsby Cadet TX3	RAF Support Command, GSS St Athan
	XA290	Slingsby Cadet TX3	RAF Support Command, 643 GS
	XA292	Slingsby Cadet TX3	RAF Support Command, 615 GS
	XA293	Slingsby Cadet TX3 [I]	RAF Support Command, CGS
	XA294	Slingsby Cadet TX3	RAF Support Command, 622 GS
	XA295	Slingsby Cadet TX3 [D]	RAF Support Command, CGS
	XA302	Slingsby Cadet TX3	RAF Support Command, GSS St Athan
	XA306	Slingsby Cadet TX3	RAF Support Command, 618 GS
	XA308	Slingsby Cadet TX3	RAF Support Command, 621 GS
	XA309	Slingsby Cadet TX3	RAF Support Command, 618 GS
	XA310	Slingsby Cadet TX3	RAF Support Command, 621 GS
	XA311	Slingsby Cadet TX3	RAF Support Command, 615 GS
	XA363	Fairey Gannet AS1 (A2528)	RN Fire School, Predannack
	XA454	Fairey Gannet COD4	RNAS Yeovilton Fire Section
	XA456	Fairey Gannet AS4 (A2533)	RN Fire School, Predannack
	XA459	Fairey Gannet ECM6 (A2608)	Wales Air Museum, Cardiff
	XA460	Fairey Gannet ECM6 [768/BY]	Flint Technical College, Connah's Quay
	XA466	Fairey Gannet COD4 [777/LM]	FAA Museum, RNAS Yeovilton
	XA508	Fairey Gannet T2 (A2472) [627/GN]	Midland Air Museum, Coventry
	XA523	Fairey Gannet T2 (A2459)	RM Arbroath for ground instruction
	XA536	EE Canberra T19 (8605M)	RAF Abingdon, Fire Section
	XA549	Gloster Javelin FAW1 (7717M) [E]	RAF Museum store, Swinderby
	XA553	Gloster Javelin FAW1 (7470M)	RAF Stanmore Park
	XA564	Gloster Javelin FAW1 (7464M)	RAF Cosford Aerospace Museum
	XA634	Gloster Javelin FAW4 (7641M) [L]	RAF Leeming, at main gate
	XA699	Gloster Javelin FAW9 (7809M)	Midland Air Museum
	XA801	Gloster Javelin FAW2 (7739M)	RAF Stafford, at main gate
	XA847	English Electric P1B (8371M)	RAF Museum, Hendon
	XA862	Westland Whirlwind HAR1 (A2542/G-AMJT)	Midland Air Museum, Coventry
	XA864	Westland Whirlwind HAR1	FAA Museum, RNAS Yeovilton
	XA866	Westland Whirlwind HAR1 (A2550)	Donington Park, on display
	XA868	Westland Whirlwind HAR1 (A2551)	Privately owned, Horsham
	XA870	Westland Whirlwind HAR1 (A2543)	Cornwall Aero Park, Helston
	XA876	Slingsby Sky I	RAF GSA
	XA880	DH Devon C2	MoD(PE) RAE Llanbedr
	XA900	Avro Vulcan B1 (7896M)	RAF Cosford Aerospace Museum
	XA903	Avro Vulcan B1	RAE Farnborough Fire Section
	XA917	HP Victor B1 (7827M)	RAF Wyton, ground instruction
	XA923	HP Victor B1 (7850M) [N]	RAF Cosford Aerospace Museum

Serial	Type (alternative identity)	Owner, Operator or Location	Notes
XA932	HP Victor K1 (8517M)	RAF Museum, on display Marham	
XA939	HP Victor B(K)1A	RAF FF&SS Catterick	
XB259	Blackburn Beverley C1 (G-AOAI)	Privately owned, Hull-Paull	
XB261	Blackburn Beverley C1	Historic Aircraft Museum, Southend	
XB446	Grumman Avenger ECM6B [992-C]	FAA Museum, RNAS Yeovilton	
XB480	Hiller HT1 (A2577) [537]	FAA Museum, RNAS Yeovilton	
XD145	SARO SR53	RAF Cosford Aerospace Museum	
XD163	Westland Whirlwind HAR10 (8645M) [X]	British Rotorcraft Museum, Wroughton	
XD165	Westland Whirlwind HAR10 (8673M)	RAF Support Command, 1 SoTT Halton	
XD182	Westland Whirlwind HAR10 (8612M)	RAF Odiham, Fire Section	
XD184	Westland Whirlwind HAR10	RAF Strike Command, Cyprus	
XD186	Westland Whirlwind HAR10	RAF Chivenor, on display	
XD220	VS Scimitar F1	FAA Museum store, RNAY Wroughton	
XD317	VS Scimitar F1 [112/R]	FAA Museum, RNAS Yeovilton	
XD332	VS Scimitar F1 (A2574) [616]	Cornwall Aero Park, Helston	
XD375	DH Vampire T11 (7887M)	Humberside Aircraft Preservation Soc	
XD377	DH Vampire T11 (8203M)	No 487 Sqn ATC, Kingstanding	
XD382	DH Vampire T11 (8033M) [L]	RAF Shawbury, at main gate	
XD395	DH Vampire T11	BAe Apprentice School, Chadderton	
XD425	DH Vampire T11	Dumfries & Galloway Aviation Group	
XD429	DH Vampire T11 (7604M) (really XD542)	RAF Cranwell, at main gate	
XD434	DH Vampire T11	Manchester University, Barton	
XD435	DH Vampire T11 [26]	No 480 Sqn ATC, Studley, Warks	
XD445	DH Vampire T11	Bomber County Museum Cleethorpes	
XD447	DH Vampire T11 [33]	Lincolnshire Aviation Museum	
XD452	DH Vampire T11 (7990M) [66]	Mosquito Aircraft Museum	
XD453	DH Vampire T11 (7890M) [64]	No 1010 Sqn ATC, Salisbury	
XD463	DH Vampire T11 (8023M)	No 1360 Sqn ATC, Stapleford, Notts	
XD506	DH Vampire T11 (7983M) [E]	RAF Museum store, Swinderby	
XD511	DH Vampire T11 (7814M)	No 221 Sqn ATC, Gorleston, Norfolk	
XD515	DH Vampire T11 (7998M)	South Yorks APS, Misson	
XD527	DH Vampire T11	RAF Manston Fire Section	
XD528	DH Vampire T11 (8159M)	No 2415 Sqn ATC, Penkridge, Staffs	
XD534	DH Vampire T11	Military Aircraft Pres Grp Manchester	
XD535	DH Vampire T11	Preston Technical College	
XD536	DH Vampire T11 (7734M)	No 2287 Sqn ATC, Reading	
XD547	DH Vampire T11	Strathallan Collection	
XD593	DH Vampire T11 [50]	Newark Air Museum, Winthorpe	
XD595	DH Vampire T11	Moston Technical College, Gtr Manchester	
XD596	DH Vampire T11 (7939M) [VZ]	No 424 Sqn ATC, Calmore, Hants	
XD599	DH Vampire T11	Warbirds of GB, Blackbushe	
XD602	DH Vampire T11 (7737M)	No 495 Sqn ATC, Sutton Coldfield	
XD613	DH Vampire T11 (8122M) [M]	RAF Cosford, on parade ground	
XD616	DH Vampire T11 [56]	No 1239 Sqn ATC, Hoddesdon, Herts	
XD622	DH Vampire T11 (8160M)	No 2214 Sqn, ATC, Sunderland	
XD624	DH Vampire T11 [O]	Macclesfield Technical College	
XD626	DH Vampire T11 [Q]	Midland Air Museum, Coventry	
XD674	Hunting Jet Provost T1 (7570M) [T]	RAF St Athan Museum	
XD818	Vickers Valiant B(K)1 (7894M)	RAF Bomber Command Museum, Hendon	
XE317	Bristol Sycamore HR14 (G-AMWO) [S-N]	Newark Air Museum, Winthorpe	
XE327	Hawker Sea Hawk FGA6 (A2556) [644/LH]	RN Llangennech, Dyfed	
XE339	Hawker Sea Hawk FGA6 (8156M/A2635) [149]	RNAS Culdrose, SAH	
XE340	Hawker Sea Hawk FGA6 [131/Z]	FAA Museum store, RNAY Wroughton	

Notes	Serial	Type (alternative identity)	Owner, Operator or Location
	XE364	Hawker Sea Hawk FGA6 (really XE489) [485/J]	Historic Aircraft Museum, Southend
	XE368	Hawker Sea Hawk FGA6 (A2534) [200]	Cornwall Aero Park, Helston
	XE369	Hawker Sea Hawk FGA6 (A2580/8158M/A2633)	RNAS Culdrose, SAH
	XE390	Hawker Sea Hawk FGA6 (8157M/A2636)	RNAS Culdrose, SAH
	XE546	Hawker Hunter FGA9 [50]	RAF Strike Command, 1 TWU
	XE552	Hawker Hunter FGA9 [R]	RAF Strike Command, 1 TWU
	XE582	Hawker Hunter FGA9 [W]	RAF Strike Command, 1 TWU
	XE587	Hawker Hunter F6	RAF, 5MU store
	XE597	Hawker Hunter FGA9 [F]	RAF Strike Command, 1TWU
	XE601	Hawker Hunter FGA9	MoD(PE) ETPS Boscombe Down
	XE606	Hawker Hunter F6A [11]	RAF Strike Command, 1 TWU
	XE624	Hawker Hunter FGA9 [G]	RAF Strike Command, 1TWU
	XE627	Hawker Hunter F6A [10]	RAF Strike Command, 1 TWU
	XE643	Hawker Hunter FGA9 (8586M)	RAFEF, RAF Abingdon (nose only)
	XE653	Hawker Hunter F6A [14]	RAF Scampton, ground inst
	XE656	Hawker Hunter F6 (8678M) [35]	RAF Support Command, 1 SoTT Halton
	XE665	Hawker Hunter T8C	RAF Strike Command, 237 OCU
	XE668	Hawker Hunter GA11 [832/VL]	RN FRADU, RNAS Yeovilton
	XE670	Hawker Hunter F4 (8585M)	RAFEF, RAF Abingdon (nose only)
	XE677	Hawker Hunter F4	Loughborough University of Technology
	XE682	Hawker Hunter GA11 [835/VL]	RN FRADU, RAF Shawbury, store
	XE685	Hawker Hunter GA11 [861/VL]	RN FRADU, RNAS Yeovilton
	XE689	Hawker Hunter GA11 [864/VL]	RN FRADU, RNAS Yeovilton
	XE707	Hawker Hunter GA11 [865/—]	RN FRADU, RNAS Yeovilton
	XE712	Hawker Hunter GA11 [708/—]	RN, 5 MU store, Kemble
	XE716	Hawker Hunter GA11 [834/VL]	RN FRADU, RNAS Yeovilton
	XE785	Slingsby Cadet TX3	RAF Support Command 643 GS
	XE786	Slingsby Cadet TX3	RAF Support Command 662 GS
	XE789	Slingsby Cadet TX3	RAF Support Command 663 GS
	XE790	Slingsby Cadet TX3	RAF Support Command 614 GS
	XE791	Slingsby Cadet TX3	RAF Support Command 635 GS
	XE793	Slingsby Cadet TX3 (8666M)	RAF Support Command, St Athan
	XE794	Slingsby Cadet TX3	RAF Support Command 663 GS
	XE795	Slingsby Cadet TX3	RAF Support Command 663 GS
	XE798	Slingsby Cadet TX3 [E]	RAF Support Command CGS
	XE799	Slingsby Cadet TX3 [R]	RAF Support Command CGS
	XE800	Slingsby Cadet TX3	RAF Support Command 622 GS
	XE801	Slingsby Cadet TX3	RAF Support Command 617 GS
	XE802	Slingsby Cadet TX3	RAF Support Command 624 GS
	XE806	Slingsby Cadet TX3	RAF Support Command 622 GS
	XE807	Slingsby Cadet TX3	RAF Support Command 618 GS
	XE808	Slingsby Cadet TX3	RAF Support Command 645 GS
	XE810	Slingsby Cadet TX3	RAF Support Command 662 GS
	XE812	Slingsby Cadet TX3	RAF Support Command 1 MGSP RAF Halton
	XE849	DH Vampire T11 (7928M)	No 936 Sqn ATC, Ware, Herts
	XE852	DH Vampire T11 [60]	BAe Apprentice School, Hawarden
	XE855	DH Vampire T11	Upton School, Chester
	XE856	DH Vampire T11	SWWAPS, Lasham
	XE864	DH Vampire T11 [40]	No 480 Sqn ATC, Studley, Warks
	XE872	DH Vampire T11	Midland Air Museum, Coventry
	XE874	DH Vampire T11 (8582M)	RAF Valley, at main gate
	XE897	DH Vampire T11 (really XD403)	Strathallan Aircraft Collection
	XE920	DH Vampire T11 (8196M) [D]	RAF Museum store, Henlow
	XE935	DH Vampire T11	Nene Valley Aviation Society
	XE950	DH Vampire T11 (8175M)	CCF Gordon School, Chobham
	XE956	DH Vampire T11 [N]	St Albans College of FE
	XE979	DH Vampire T11 [54]	Privately owned, Badminton, Glos
	XE982	DH Vampire T11 (7564M)	No 124 Sqn ATC, Hereford
	XE993	DH Vampire T11 (8161M)	RAF Cosford Fire Section
	XE995	DH Vampire T11 [53]	Torbay Aircraft Museum
	XE998	DH Vampire T11 [36]	No 723 Sqn ATC Wigan
	XF114	VS Swift F7	Flint Tech Coll, Connah's Quay

Serial	Type (alternative identity)	Owner, Operator or Location	Notes
XF274	Gloster Meteor T7	RAE/AIU on display, Farnborough	
XF289	Hawker Hunter T8C [875/VL]	RN FRADU, RNAS Yeovilton	
XF300	Hawker Hunter GA11[860/VL]	RN FRADU, RNAS Yeovilton	
XF301	Hawker Hunter GA11[679/LM]	RN, 5 MU store, Kemble	
XF310	Hawker Hunter T7 [876/VL]	RN FRADU, RNAS Yeovilton	
XF319	Hawker Hunter F4 (7849M) [B]	RAF Support Command, 1 SoTT Halton	
XF321	Hawker Hunter T7	MoD(PE) RAE Farnborough	
XF357	Hawker Hunter T8C [877/VL]	RN FRADU, RNAS Yeovilton	
XF358	Hawker Hunter T8C [875/VL]	RN FRADU, RNAS Yeovilton	
XF368	Hawker Hunter GA11 [863/VL]	RN FRADU, RNAS Yeovilton	
XF375	Hawker Hunter F6	RAFC Cranwell, Engineering Wing	
XF376	Hawker Hunter FGA9 [D]	RAF Strike Command, 1 TWU	
XF382	Hawker Hunter F6A [15]	RAF Strike Command, 1 TWU	
XF383	Hawker Hunter F6A (8706M) [V]	RAF Wittering, BDRF	
XF386	Hawker Hunter F6A (8707M) [75]	RAF Coltishall, BDRF	
XF416	Hawker Hunter FGA9 [Z]	RAF Strike Command, 1 TWU	
XF418	Hawker Hunter F6A [16]	RAF Strike Command, 1 TWU	
XF419	Hawker Hunter FGA9 [C]	RAF Strike Command, 1 TWU	
XF431	Hawker Hunter FGA9 [O]	RAF Strike Command, 1 TWU	
XF435	Hawker Hunter FGA9 [52]	RAF Strike Command, 1 TWU	
XF439	Hawker Hunter F6A (8712M) [17]	RAF Abingdon BDRF	
XF442	Hawker Hunter FGA9 [V]	RAF Wittering, BDRF	
XF445	Hawker Hunter FGA9 [53]	RAF Strike Command, 1 TWU	
XF509	Hawker Hunter F6A (8708M) [73]	RAE Bedford Apprentice School	
XF511	Hawker Hunter FGA9 [A]	RAF Chivenor	
XF515	Hawker Hunter F6A [18]	RAF Scampton, ground inst	
XF516	Hawker Hunter F6A (8685M) [66]	RAF College Cranwell Eng Wing	
XF519	Hawker Hunter FGA9 [E]	RAF Strike Command, 1 TWU	
XF526	Hawker Hunter F6A (8679M) [78]	RAF Support Command, 1 SoTT Halton	
XF527	Hawker Hunter F6A (8680M) [70]	RAF Support Command, 1 SoTT Halton	
XF545	Percival Provost T1 (7957M) [13]	RAF Linton-on-Ouse, gate	
XF554	Percival Provost T1 (G-AWTD)	Privately owned, St Merryn	
XF597	Percival Provost T1 (G-BKFW) [G]	Privately owned, Speke	
XF603	Percival Provost T1 [H]	Rolls-Royce Tech Coll, Filton	
XF690	Percival Provost T1 (G-BGKA) (8041M)	Leics Aircraft Preservation Group	
XF708	Avro Shackleton MR3 [C]	Imperial War Museum, Duxford	
XF785	Bristol 173 (G-ALBN/7648M)	RAF Museum store, Henlow	
XF799	Percival Pembroke C1	RAF Germany, No 60 Sqn	
XF836	Percival Provost T1 (8043M) (G-AWRY)	Shuttleworth Collection	
XF844	Percival Provost T1	RAE Farnborough Apprentice School	
XF877	Percival Provost T1 (G-AWVF) [A]	Privately owned, Bourn	
XF898	Percival Provost T1 [08]	Privately owned, Chinnor	
XF914	Percival Provost T1 [P-V]	Loughborough and Leics Aviation Museum	
XF926	Bristol 188 (8368M)	RAF Cosford Aerospace Museum	
XF967	Hawker Hunter T8B	RAF Strike Command, 237 OCU	
XF974	Hawker Hunter F4 (7949M) [C]	RAF Support Command, 1 SoTT Halton	
XF985	Hawker Hunter T8C [873/VL]	RN FRADU, RNAS Yeovilton	
XF994	Hawker Hunter T8C [876/VL]	RN FRADU, RNAS Yeovilton	
XF995	Hawker Hunter T8B	RAF Strike Command, 237 OCU	
XG152	Hawker Hunter F6A [20]	RAF Strike Command, 1 TWU	
XG154	Hawker Hunter FGA9 [54]	RAF Strike Command, 1 TWU	
XG155	Hawker Hunter FGA9 [I]	RAF Strike Command, 1 TWU	
XG158	Hawker Hunter F6A (8686M) [21]	RAE Farnborough Apprentice School	
XG160	Hawker Hunter F6A [22]	RAF Support Command, 5 MU store	
XG164	Hawker Hunter F6A (8681M) [36]	RAF Support Command, 1 SoTT Halton	

Notes	Serial	Type (alternative identity)	Owner, Operator or Location
	XG172	Hawker Hunter F6A [23]	RAF Strike Command, 1 TWU
	XG194	Hawker Hunter FGA9 [55]	RAF Strike Command, 1 TWU
	XG196	Hawker Hunter F6A (8702M) [25]	RAF Bracknell, on gate
	XG207	Hawker Hunter FGA9 [T]	RAF Strike Command, 1 TWU
	XG209	Hawker Hunter F6A (8709M) [69]	RAF Support Command, 1 SoTT Halton
	XG210	Hawker Hunter F6	BAe, Hatfield/Dunsfold
	XG225	Hawker Hunter F6A (8713M) [S]	RAF Support Command, 2 SoTT Cosford
	XG226	Hawker Hunter F6A [28]	RAF Strike Command, 1 TWU
	XG228	Hawker Hunter FGA9 [56]	RAF Strike Command, 1 TWU
	XG252	Hawker Hunter FGA9	RAF Strike Command, 1 TWU
	XG254	Hawker Hunter FGA9 [57]	RAF Strike Command, 1 TWU
	XG264	Hawker Hunter FGA9 (8715M) [T]	RAF Brawdy, BDRF
	XG274	Hawker Hunter F6A (8710M) [71]	RAF Support Command, 1 SoTT Halton
	XG290	Hawker Hunter F6A (8711M) [74]	RAF Support Command, 1 SoTT Halton
	XG291	Hawker Hunter FGA9 [Y]	RAF Strike Command, 1 TWU
	XG327	EE Lightning F1 (8188M)	RAF Manston, on display
	XG329	EE Lightning F1 (8050M)	RAF College Cranwell Eng Wing
	XG337	EE Lightning F1 (8056M)	RAF Cosford Aerospace Museum
	XG452	Westland Belvedere HC1 (G-BRMB/7997M)	British Rotorcraft Museum
	XG454	Westland Belvedere HC1 (8366M)	Manchester Air & Space Museum
	XG474	Westland Belvedere HC1 (8367M) [O]	RAF Museum, Hendon
	XG496	DH Devon C2 (G-ANDX) [K]	MoD(PE) RAE Farnborough
	XG502	Bristol Sycamore HR14	Museum of Army Flying, Middle Wallop
	XG504	Bristol Sycamore HR14	Nostell Aviation Museum, Wakefield
	XG506	Bristol Sycamore HR14 (7852M)	South Yorks Aviation Museum
	XG518	Bristol Sycamore HR14 (8009M) [S-E]	Loch Lomond Bear Park
	XG544	Bristol Sycamore HR14	Torbay Aircraft Museum
	XG547	Bristol Sycamore HR14 (G-HAPR/8010M) [S-T]	British Rotorcraft Museum
	XG574	Westland Whirlwind HAR3 (A2575) [752/PO]	FAA Museum store, Wroughton
	XG577	Westland Whirlwind HAR3 (A2571)	Loughborough & Leics Air Museum
	XG592	Westland Whirlwind HAS7 [54]	Wales Air Museum, Cardiff
	XG594	Westland Whirlwind HAS7 [517/PO]	FAA Museum store, RNAY Wroughton
	XG596	Westland Whirlwind HAS7 (A2651)	British Rotorcraft Museum
	XG613	DH Sea Venom FAW21	Imperial War Museum, Duxford
	XG629	DH Sea Venom FAW21	Torbay Aircraft Museum
	XG680	DH Sea Venom FAW22 [735/VL]	North-East Aircraft Museum
	XG691	DH Sea Venom FAW22 [737/VL]	Sea Scouts, Chilton Cantelo
	XG692	DH Sea Venom FAW22 [668/LM]	Shorts Fire Section, Sydenham, NI
	XG730	DH Sea Venom FAW22 [499/A]	Mosquito Aircraft Museum
	XG734	DH Sea Venom FAW22 [669/LM]	Shorts Fire Section, Sydenham, NI
	XG736	DH Sea Venom FAW22 [012/VL]	Shorts Fire Section, Sydenham, NI
	XG737	DH Sea Venom FAW22 [438/BY]	Wales Air Museum, Cardiff
	XG743	DH Sea Vampire T22 [798/BY]	Imperial War Museum, Duxford
	XG797	Fairey Gannet ECM6 [766/BY]	Imperial War Museum, Duxford
	XG831	Fairey Gannet ECM6 (A2539)	Cornwall Aero Park, Helston
	XG882	Fairey Gannet T5 [771/LM]	RAF Lossiemouth on display
	XG883	Fairey Gannet T5 [773/BY]	FAA Museum, RNAS Yeovilton

Serial	Type (alternative identity)	Owner, Operator or Location	Notes
XG888	Fairey Gannet T5	RNAS Culdrose, stored	
XG900	Short SC1	Science Museum store	
XG905	Short SC1	Ulster Folk & Transport Museum	
XH124	Blackburn Beverley C1 (8025M)	RAF Museum, Hendon	
XH131	EE Canberra PR9	RAF St Athan, in store	
XH132	EE Canberra PR9 (SC9)	MoD(PE) RS&RE Bedford	
XH133	EE Canberra PR9	RAF St Athan, in store	
XH134	EE Canberra PR9	RAF Strike Command, No 1 PRU, Wyton	
XH135	EE Canberra PR9	RAF St Athan, in store	
XH136	EE Canberra PR9	RAF Strike Command, No 1 PRU, Wyton	
XH165	EE Canberra PR9	RAF Strike Command, No 1 PRU, Wyton	
XH166	EE Canberra PR9	RAF Strike Command, No 1 PRU, Wyton	
XH167	EE Canberra PR9	RAF Strike Command, No 1 PRU, Wyton	
XH168	EE Canberra PR9	RAF St Athan, in store	
XH169	EE Canberra PR9	RAF Strike Command	
XH170	EE Canberra PR9	RAF Wyton, on gate	
XH171	EE Canberra PR9	RAF Support Command, 2 SoTT Cosford	
XH173	EE Canberra PR9	RAF St Athan, in store	
XH174	EE Canberra PR9	RAF Strike Command, No 1 PRU, Wyton	
XH175	EE Canberra PR9	RAF Strike Command	
XH228	EE Canberra B(1)8 [B]	RAF FF&SS Catterick	
XH278	DH Vampire T11 (8595M/7866M)	No 2482 Sqn ATC, RAF Henlow	
XH304	DH Vampire T11	RAF *Vintage Pair* CFS, Leeming	
XH312	DH Vampire T11 [18]	No 2056 Sqn ATC, Knutsford	
XH313	DH Vampire T11 [E]	St Albans College of FE	
XH318	DH Vampire T11 (7761M) [68]	No 424 Sqn ATC, Southampton	
XX330	DH Vampire T11 [40]	LFV&HAC, Bushey, Herts	
XH537	Avro Vulcan B2 MRR	RAF Abingdon, BDRF	
XH539	Avro Vulcan B2	RAF Waddington, rescue trg	
XH554	Avro Vulcan B2 (8694M)	RAF FF&SS Catterick	
XH557	Avro Vulcan B2	RAF Waddington	
XH558	Avro Vulcan K2	RAF Strike Command, No 50 Sqn	
XH560	Avro Vulcan K2	RAF Strike Command, No 50 Sqn	
XH561	Avro Vulcan K2	RAF Strike Command, No 50 Sqn	
XH562	Avro Vulcan B2	RAF FF&SS Catterick	
XH563	Avro Vulcan B2 MRR	RAF Scampton, preserved	
XH567	EE Canberra B6(mod)	MoD(PE) RAE Bedford	
XH568	EE Canberra B6(mod)	MoD(PE) RAE Bedford	
XH583	EE Canberra T4 (G-9-374)	BAe Samlesbury	
XH588	HP Victor K1A	RAF Machrihanish, Fire Section	
XH590	HP Victor K1A	CTE RAF Manston	
XH592	HP Victor B1A (8429M) [L]	RAF Support Command, 2 SoTT Cosford	
XH593	HP Victor B1A (8428M) [T]	RAF Support Command, 2 SoTT Cosford	
XH616	HP Victor K1A	CTE RAF Manston	
XH647	HP Victor B1A	RAF FF&SS, Catterick	
XH648	HP Victor K1A	Imperial War Museum, Duxford	
XH669	HP Victor K2	RAF Strike Command, No 57 Sqn	
XH670	HP Victor SR2	RAF stored at Woodford	
XH671	HP Victor K2	RAF Strike Command, No 55 Sqn	
XH672	HP Victor K2	RAF Strike Command, No 57 Sqn	
XH673	HP Victor K2	RAF Strike Command, No 57 Sqn	
XH675	HP Victor K2	RAF Strike Command, No 55 Sqn	
XH764	Gloster Javelin FAW9 (7972M)	RAF Manston on display	
XH767	Gloster Javelin FAW9 (7955M) [E]	No 187 Sqn ATC, Worcester	
XH768	Gloster Javelin FAW9 (7929M) [E]	Historic Aircraft Museum, Southend	
XH892	Gloster Javelin FAW9 (7982M) [B]	Privately owned, Duxford	
XH897	Gloster Javelin FAW9	Imperial War Museum, Duxford	
XH903	Gloster Javelin FAW9 (7938M)	RAF Innsworth, at main gate	
XH980	Gloster Javelin FAW9 (7867M) [A]	RAF West Raynham, at main gate	
XH992	Gloster Javelin FAW9 (7829M) [P]	Newark Air Museum, Winthorpe	

Notes	Serial	Type (alternative identity)	Owner, Operator or Location
	XJ314	RR Thrust Measuring Rig	Science Museum, Strathallan
	XJ319	DH Sea Devon C20 (G-AMXP)	RNAS Culdrose Station Flight
	XJ322	DH Sea Devon C20 (G-AMYP)	Privately owned, Biggin Hill
	XJ324	DH Sea Devon C20 (G-AMXZ)	RN 5 MU Kemble
	XJ348	DH Sea Devon C20 (G-AMXX/ G-NAVY)	Privately owned, Shoreham
	XJ380	Bristol Sycamore HR14 (8628M)	RAF Finningley, on display
	XJ385	Bristol Sycamore HR14 (7899M/8345M) (really XG540) [S-J]	RAF Shawbury main gate
	XJ389	Fairey Jet Gyrodyne (G-AJJP)	RAF Cosford, Aerospace Museum
	XJ393	Westland Whirlwind HAR3 (A2538)	Torbay Aircraft Museum
	XJ402	Westland Whirlwind HAR3 (A2572) [61]	FAA Museum store, RNAS Yeovilton
	XJ407	Westland Whirlwind HAR10 (G-BKHB)	Privately owned, Tattershall Thorpe
	XJ409	Westland Whirlwind HAR10	Wales Aircraft Museum, Cardiff
	XJ411	Westland Whirlwind HAR10 [Z]	RAE Farnborough, Fire Section
	XJ430	Westland Whirlwind HAR10	RAF Manston
	XJ435	Westland Whirlwind HAR10 (8671M) [V]	RAF Support Command, 1 SoTT Halton
	XJ437	Westland Whirlwind HAR10	RAF Strike Command, Cyprus
	XJ445	Westland Whirlwind HAR5	MRE Porton Down
	XJ477	DH Sea Vixen FAW1 (A2601) [714/AB]	RN, Arbroath
	XJ481	DH Sea Vixen FAW1 [VL]	FAA Museum, RNAS Yeovilton
	XJ482	DH Sea Vixen FAW1 (A2598) [713/VL]	Norfolk & Suffolk Aviation Museum, Flixton
	XJ490	DH Sea Vixen FAW2	Flight Refuelling Ltd, Hurn
	XJ494	DH Sea Vixen FAW2	MoD(PE) RAE Farnborough, stored
	XJ524	DH Sea Vixen FAW (TT) 2 [E]	Flight Refuelling Ltd
	XJ526	DH Sea Vixen FAW2 (8145M) [38]	RAF Halton Fire Section
	XJ560	DH Sea Vixen FAW2 (8142M)	MoD(PE) RAE Bedford
	XJ565	DH Sea Vixen FAW2 [127/E]	Mosquito Aircraft Museum
	XJ571	DH Sea Vixen FAW2 (8140M) [133/E]	RAF Support Command, 2 SoTT Cosford
	XJ572	DH Sea Vixen FAW2	MoD(PE) RAE Farnborough, stored
	XJ575	DH Sea Vixen FAW2 (A2611)	RNAS Culdrose Fire School
	XJ577	DH Sea Vixen FAW2	Flight Refuelling Ltd, Hurn
	XJ579	DH Sea Vixen FAW2	MoD(PE) RAE Farnborough, stored
	XJ580	DH Sea Vixen FAW2 [131/E]	Flight Refuelling Ltd, Hurn
	XJ582	DH Sea Vixen FAW2 (8139M)	RAF Cottesmore Fire Section
	XJ584	DH Sea Vixen FAW2 (A2621)	RNAS Culdrose Fire School
	XJ602	DH Sea Vixen FAW2 (A2622) [E]	Flight Refuelling Ltd, Hurn
	XJ604	DH Sea Vixen FAW2 (8222M)	RAF Support Command 1 SoTT Halton
	XJ607	DH Sea Vixen FAW2 (8171M) [701]	RAF Support Command, 2 SoTT Cosford
	XJ608	DH Sea Vixen FAW2	MoD(PE) RAE Llanbedr
	XJ634	Hawker Hunter F6A (8684M) [29]	RAFC Cranwell Engineering Wing
	XJ639	Hawker Hunter F6A (8687M) [31]	RAFC Cranwell Engineering Wing
	XJ676	Hawker Hunter F6A [32]	RAF Strike Command, 1 TWU
	XJ683	Hawker Hunter FGA9 [X]	RAF 5 MU store, Kemble
	XJ686	Hawker Hunter FGA9 [L]	RAF Strike Command, 1 TWU
	XJ687	Hawker Hunter FGA9 [58]	RAF Strike Command, 1 TWU
	XJ688	Hawker Hunter FGA9 [59]	RAF Strike Command, 1 TWU
	XJ695	Hawker Hunter FGA9 (8677M) [J]	RAF Manston, Fire School
	XJ723	Westland Whirlwind HAR10	PITB Montrose
	XJ724	Westland Whirlwind HAR10 (8613M)	RAF FF&SS Catterick
	XJ726	Westland Whirlwind HAR10 [Q]	Nene Valley Aviation Society, Sywell
	XJ727	Westland Whirlwind HAR10 (8661M) [L]	RAF Support Command, 1 SoTT Halton
	XJ729	Westland Whirlwind HAR10	RAF Finningley, SAREW

Serial	Type (alternative identity)	Owner, Operator or Location	Notes
XJ763	Westland Whirlwind HAR10 (G-BKHA)	Privately owned, Tattershall Thorpe	
XJ772	DH Vampire T11 [H]	Brooklands Technical College	
XJ782	Avro Vulcan B2 MRR	RAF Finningley	
XJ823	Avro Vulcan B2	RAF Strike Command, No 50 Sqn	
XJ824	Avro Vulcan B2	Imperial War Museum, Duxford	
XJ825	Avro Vulcan K2	RAF Strike Command, No 50 Sqn	
XJ917	Bristol Sycamore HR14 [S-H]	Cornwall Aero Park, Helston	
XJ918	Bristol Sycamore HR14 (8190M)	Cosford Aerospace Museum	
XK137	Hawker Hunter FGA9 [M]	RAF Strike Command, 1 TWU	
XK138	Hawker Hunter FGA9 [S]	RAF Strike Command, 1 TWU	
XK141	Hawker Hunter F6A [33]	RAF Strike Command, 1 TWU	
XK149	Hawker Hunter F6A (8714M) [34]	RAFC Cranwell Engineering Wing	
XK151	Hawker Hunter FGA9 [Z]	RAF Strike Command, 1 TWU	
XK406	Auster AOP9	Privately owned, Saffron Walden	
XK412	Auster AOP9	Privately owned, Swindon	
XK416	Auster AOP9 (G-AYUA/ 7855M)	LFV&HAC, Bushey	
XK417	Auster AOP9 (G-AVXY)	Privately owned, Leicester	
XK418	Auster AOP9 (7976M)	WW2 Aircraft Preservation Soc, Lasham	
XK421	Auster AOP9 (8365M)	Brunel Technical College, Bristol	
XK482	Saro Skeeter AOP12 (7840M) [C]	Privately owned, Carnforth	
XK488	Blackburn Buccaneer S1	FAA Museum, RNAS Yeovilton	
XK526	Blackburn Buccaneer S2 (8648M)	RAF Honington	
XK527	Blackburn Buccaneer S2D	MoD(PE) A&AEE Boscombe Down	
XK530	Blackburn Buccaneer S1	RAE Bedford Fire Section	
XK531	Blackburn Buccaneer S1 (8403M)	RAF Honington, at main gate	
XK532	Blackburn Buccaneer S1 (A2581) [632/LM]	RNEC Manadon, for instructional use	
XK590	DH Vampire T11 [V]	West Oxfordshire Tech Coll, Witney	
XK623	DH Vampire T11	Moston Tech College, Manchester	
XK624	DH Vampire T11	Norfolk & Suffolk Aviation Museum	
XK625	DH Vampire T11 [12]	Historic Aircraft Museum, Southend	
XK627	DH Vampire T11	Pennine Aviation Museum, Bacup	
XK637	DH Vampire T11 [56]	No 1885 Sqn ATC, Royton, Manchester	
XK655	DH Comet 2R (G-AMXA)	Strathallan Aircraft Collection	
XK695	DH Comet 2R (G-AMXH)	Imperial War Museum, Duxford	
XK697	DH Comet 2R (G-AMXJ) [D]	Air Scouts, RAF Wyton	
XK699	DH Comet C2 (G-AMXM/ 7971M)	RAF Museum store, Henlow	
XK724	Folland Gnat F1 (7715M)	RAF College Cranwell Eng Flight	
XK740	Folland Gnat F1 (8396M)	RAF Cosford Aerospace Museum	
XK749	Folland Gnat F1 (really XK741)	Midland Air Museum, Coventry	
XK776	ML Utility I	RAF Museum, loaned AAC Middle Wallop	
XK788	Slingsby Grasshopper TX1	1 MGSP, RAF Halton	
XK789	Slingsby Grasshopper TX1	Stamford School CCF, Lincs	
XK790	Slingsby Grasshopper TX1	1 MGSP, RAF Halton	
XK791	Slingsby Grasshopper TX1	14 MU, RAF Carlisle	
XK819	Slingsby Grasshopper TX1	Malvern College CCF, Grt Malvern	
XK820	Slingsby Grasshopper TX1	2 MGSP, RAF Locking	
XK822	Slingsby Grasshopper TX1	Kings College School CCF, London	
XK824	Slingsby Grasshopper TX1	Wycliffe School CCF	
XK862	Percival Pembroke C1 (8194M)	St Athan Fire Section	
XK884	Percival Pembroke C1	RAF Germany, No 60 Sqn	
XK885	Percival Pembroke C1 (8452M)	RAF St Athan, CTTS	
XK895	DH Sea Devon C20	RNAS Culdrose Station Flight	
XK896	DH Sea Devon C20	RN, 5 MU Kemble	
XK906	WS55 Whirlwind HAS7	Fire Section, Netheravon	
XK907	WS55 Whirlwind HAS7 [9]	Midland Air Museum, Coventry	
XK911	WS55 Whirlwind HAS7 (A2603) [519/PO]	RNAY Wroughton store	
XK912	WS55 Whirlwind HAS7 [60/CU]	Privately owned, Swindon	

Notes	Serial	Type (alternative identity)	Owner, Operator or Location
	XK936	WS55 Whirlwind HAS7 [62]	Imperial War Museum, Duxford
	XK940	WS55 Whirlwind HAS7 (G-AYXT)	Stored at Panshanger
	XK943	WS55 Whirlwind HAS7 [57]	RNAS Lee-on-Solent, dumped
	XK944	WS55 Whirlwind HAS7 (A2607)	Brunel Technical College, Bristol
	XK968	WS55 Whirlwind HAR10 (8445M) [E]	RAF Manston, on display
	XK969	WS55 Whirlwind HAR10 (8646M)	RAF Abingdon, BDRF
	XK970	WS55 Whirlwind HAR10 [P]	RAF Strike Command, Cyprus
	XK986	WS55 Whirlwind HAR10	RAF Strike Command, Cyprus
	XK987	WS55 Whirlwind HAR10 (8393M)	RAF Stafford
	XK988	WS55 Whirlwind HAR10 (A2646) [D]	Museum of Army Flying Middle Wallop
	XL158	HP Victor K2	RAF Marham, ground inst
	XL160	HP Victor K2	RAF Strike Command, No 57 Sqn
	XL161	HP Victor K2	RAF Strike Command, No 55 Sqn
	XL162	HP Victor K2	RAF Strike Command, No 55 Sqn
	XL163	HP Victor K2	RAF Strike Command, No 57 Sqn
	XL164	HP Victor K2	RAF Strike Command, No 57 Sqn
	XL188	HP Victor K2	RAF Strike Command, No 55 Sqn
	XL189	HP Victor K2	RAF Strike Command, No 55 Sqn
	XL190	HP Victor K2	RAF Strike Command, No 50 Sqn
	XL191	HP Victor K2	RAF Strike Command, No 55 Sqn
	XL192	HP Victor K2	RAF Strike Command, No 57 Sqn
	XL231	HP Victor K2	RAF Strike Command, No 57 Sqn
	XL233	HP Victor K2	RAF Strike Command, No 55 Sqn
	XL318	Avro Vulcan B2	RAF Bomber Command Museum, Hendon
	XL319	Avro Vulcan B2	RAF Strike Command, No 44 Sqn
	XL321	Avro Vulcan B2	RAF FF&SS Catterick
	XL360	Avro Vulcan B2	RAF Waddington
	XL386	Avro Vulcan B2	RAF Waddington
	XL387	Avro Vulcan B2	RAF St Athan
	XL388	Avro Vulcan B2	RAF Honington, Fire Section
	XL391	Avro Vulcan B2	RAF Strike Command, No 44 Sqn
	XL392	Avro Vulcan B2	RAF Valley, Fire Section
	XL426	Avro Vulcan B2	RAF Strike Command, No 50 Sqn
	XL427	Avro Vulcan B2	RAF Machrihanish, Fire Section
	XL444	Avro Vulcan B2	RAF Waddington
	XL445	Avro Vulcan K2	RAF Strike Command, No 50 Sqn
	XL449	Fairey Gannet AEW3	Wales Air Museum, Cardiff
	XL471	Fairey Gannet AEW3 [043/R]	MoD(PE) RAE Farnborough
	XL472	Fairey Gannet AEW3 [044/R]	Apprentice School, Boscombe Down
	XL497	Fairey Gannet AEW3 [041/R]	HMS Gannet, Prestwick, at gate
	XL500	Fairey Gannet AEW3 (A2701)	SAH, RNAS Culdrose
	XL502	Fairey Gannet AEW3 (8610M)	RAF Leuchars BDRF
	XL503	Fairey Gannet AEW3 [070/E]	FAA Museum, RNAS Yeovilton
	XL511	HP Victor K2	RAF Strike Command, No 55 Sqn
	XL512	HP Victor K2	RAF Strike Command, No 57 Sqn
	XL563	Hawker Hunter T7	MoD(PE) RAE/IAM Farnborough
	XL564	Hawker Hunter T7 [4]	MoD(PE) ETPS Boscombe Down
	XL565	Hawker Hunter T7 [89]	RAF Kemble, 5 MU
	XL566	Hawker Hunter T7 [86]	RAF Germany, No 15 Sqn
	XL567	Hawker Hunter T7 (8723M) [84]	RAF Chivenor Fire Section
	XL568	Hawker Hunter T7B	RAF Strike Command, No 12 Sqn
	XL569	Hawker Hunter T7 [80]	RAF Strike Command, 1 TWU
	XL572	Hawker Hunter T7 [83]	RAF Kemble, 5 MU
	XL573	Hawker Hunter T7	RAF Germany, 237 OCU
	XL576	Hawker Hunter T7 [81]	RAF Strike Command, 1 TWU
	XL577	Hawker Hunter T7 (8676M) [01]	RAF College Cranwell, Engineering Wing
	XL578	Hawker Hunter T7 [89]	RAF 5 MU, Kemble
	XL580	Hawker Hunter T8M [717/VL]	RN, No 899 Sqn, RNAS Yeovilton
	XL584	Hawker Hunter T8C [871/VL]	RAF Chivenor, Fire Section
	XL586	Hawker Hunter T7 [85]	RAF Strike Command, 1 TWU
	XL587	Hawker Hunter T7	RAF Laarbruch, Stn Flt

WT525 EE Canberra T22. *APM*

WV908 Hawker Sea Hawk FGA6. *APM*

XD145 SARO SR53. *PRM*

XD674 Hunting Jet Provost T1. *PRM*

XL580 Hawker Hunter T8M. *PRM*

XL728 Westland Wessex HAS1. *APM*

Serial	Type (alternative identity)	Owner, Operator or Location	Notes
XL591	Hawker Hunter T7	RAF Strike Command, 208 Sqn	
XL592	Hawker Hunter T7 [87]	RAF Strike Command, 1 TWU	
XL595	Hawker Hunter T7 [98]	RAF 5 MU, Kemble	
XL598	Hawker Hunter T8C [870/VL]	RN FRADU, RNAS Yeovilton	
XL600	Hawker Hunter T7	RAF Germany, No 15 Sqn	
XL601	Hawker Hunter T7	RAF Strike Command, 237 OCU	
XL602	Hawker Hunter T8M	MoD(PE\BAe Holme-on-Spalding Moor	
XL603	Hawker Hunter T8M	MoD(PE) RAE Bedford/BAe	
XL609	Hawker Hunter T7 [80]	RAF Strike Command, 1 TWU	
XL612	Hawker Hunter T7	MoD(PE) ETPS Boscombe Down	
XL613	Hawker Hunter T7	RAF Germany/237 OCU	
XL614	Hawker Hunter T7B	RAF Strike Command, 237 OCU	
XL616	Hawker Hunter T7	RAF Kemble, 5 MU	
XL617	Hawker Hunter T7 [89]	RAF Strike Command, 1 TWU	
XL618	Hawker Hunter T7 [87]	RAF Kemble, 5 MU	
XL621	Hawker Hunter T7	MoD(PE)/BAe, Warton	
XL623	Hawker Hunter T7 [90]	RAF Strike Command, 1 TWU	
XL629	EE Lightning T4	A&AEE Boscombe Down, at main gate	
XL703	SAL Pioneer CC1 (8034M)	Manchester Air & Space Museum	
XL714	DH Tiger Moth (G-AOGR)	Privately owned, Shipdham	
XL717	DH Tiger Moth (G-AOXG) [LM]	FAA Museum, RNAS Yeovilton	
XL728	Westland Wessex HAS1	MoD(PE) RAE Farnborough	
XL735	Saro Skeeter AOP12	No 1404 Sqn ATC, Manston	
XL738	Saro Skeeter AOP12	Museum of Army Flying, Middle Wallop	
XL762	Saro Skeeter AOP12 (8017M)	Royal Scottish Museum of Flight	
XL763	Saro Skeeter AOP12	Southall Technical College	
XL764	Saro Skeeter AOP12 (7940M)	Newark Air Museum	
XL770	Saro Skeeter AOP12 (8046M)	Royal Military College of Science, Shrivenham	
XL811	Saro Skeeter AOP12 [157]	Historic Aircraft Museum, Southend	
XL812	Saro Skeeter AOP12(G-SARO)	Privately owned, Dalcross	
XL813	Saro Skeeter AOP12	Museum of Army Flying, Middle Wallop	
XL814	Saro Skeeter AOP12	AAC Historic Aircraft Flt, Middle Wallop	
XL824	Bristol Sycamore HR14 (8021M)	RAF Museum store, Henlow	
XL829	Bristol Sycamore HR14	Bristol Industrial Museum	
XL836	WS55 Whirlwind HAS7 (A2642)	Fareham Technical College	
XL839	WS55 Whirlwind HAR9 (A2665) [588/CU]	RNAY Fleetlands	
XL840	WS55 Whirlwind HAS7 [56]	Nene Valley Aviation Society, Sywell	
XL847	WS55 Whirlwind HAS7 (A2626)	AAC, AETW Middle Wallop	
XL853	WS55 Whirlwind HAS7 (A2630)	Museum of Army Flying, Andover store	
XL867	WS55 Whirlwind HAS7 [59]	Cliff Holiday Centre, Trearddur Bay	
XL875	WS55 Whirlwind HAR9 [12]	Air Service Training, Perth	
XL880	WS55 Whirlwind HAR9 [443/ED]	RNAY Fleetlands Apprentice School	
XL898	WS55 Whirlwind HAR9 (8654M) [330/ED]	Boscombe Down, Fire Section	
XL899	WS55 Whirlwind HAR9 [587/CU]	RN Predannack Fire Section	
XL929	Percival Pembroke C1	RAF Germany, No 60 Sqn	
XL954	Percival Pembroke C1	RAF Germany, No 60 Sqn	
XL993	SAL Twin Pioneer CC1 (8388M)	RAF Cosford Aerospace Museum	
XM135	BAC Lightning F1 [135]	Imperial War Museum, Duxford	
XM139	BAC Lightning F1 (8411M) [F]	RAF Wattisham	
XM144	BAC Lightning F1 (8417M) [J]	RAF Leuchars, at main gate	
XM147	BAC Lightning F1 (8412M) [J]	RAF Wattisham	
XM169	BAC Lightning F1A (8422M) [W]	RAF Leuchars	
XM172	BAC Lightning F1A (8427M) [B]	RAF Coltishall, at main gate	
XM173	BAC Lightning F1A (8414M) [C]	RAF Bentley Priory, at main gate	

Notes	Serial	Type (alternative identity)	Owner, Operator or Location
	XM178	BAC Lightning F1A (8418M) [Y]	RAF Leuchars
	XM181	BAC Lightning F1A (8415M)	RAF Binbrook
	XM183	BAC Lightning F1A (8416M)	RAF Binbrook
	XM191	BAC Lightning F1A (8590M)	RAF Exhibition Flight
	XM192	BAC Lightning F1A (8413M) [K]	RAF Wattisham, at main gate
	XM223	DH Devon C2 [J]	MoD(PE) RAE Farnborough
	XM275	EE Canberra B(I)8	RAF Wattisham, Fire Section
	XM296	DH Heron C4	RN FONAC, RNAS Yeovilton
	XM300	Westland Wessex HAS1	MoD(PE) RAE Farnborough
	XM326	Westland Wessex HAS1 [515/PO]	RNAS Portland, Fire Section
	XM327	Westland Wessex HAS3 [410/KE]	RNAY Wroughton, store
	XM328	Westland Wessex HAS3 [406/AN]	RN No 737 Sqn RNAS Portland
	XM329	Westland Wessex HAS1 (A2609) [533/PO]	RN AES Lee-on-Solent
	XM330	Westland Wessex HAS1	MoD(PE) RAE Farnborough
	XM331	Westland Wessex HAS3 [653/PO]	RNAY Fleetlands, store
	XM349	Hunting Jet Provost T3A [H]	RAF Support Command, CFS
	XM350	Hunting Jet Provost T3A [89]	RAF Support Command, 7 FTS
	XM351	Hunting Jet Provost T3 (8078M) [05]	RAF Support Command, 1 SoTT Halton
	XM352	Hunting Jet Provost T3A [92]	RAF Support Command, 7 FTS
	XM355	Hunting Jet Provost T3 (8229M) [G]	RAF Support Command, 1 SoTT Halton
	XM357	Hunting Jet Provost T3A	RAF St Athan, hack
	XM358	Hunting Jet Provost T3A [J]	RAF Support Command, CFS
	XM362	Hunting Jet Provost T3 (8230M) [S]	RAF Support Command, 1 SoTT Halton
	XM365	Hunting Jet Provost T3A [37]	RAF Support Command, 1 FTS
	XM367	Hunting Jet Provost T3 (8083M) [04]	RAF Support Command, 1 SoTT Halton
	XM369	Hunting Jet Provost T3 (8084M) [07]	RAF Support Command, 1 SoTT Halton
	XM370	Hunting Jet Provost T3A [93]	RAF Support Command, 7 FTS
	XM371	Hunting Jet Provost T3A [K]	RAF Support Command, CFS
	XM372	Hunting Jet Provost T3A [55]	RAF Support Command, 1 FTS
	XM374	Hunting Jet Provost T3A [83]	RAF Support Command, 7 FTS
	XM375	Hunting Jet Provost T3 (8231M) [B]	RAF Support Command, 1 SoTT Halton
	XM376	Hunting Jet Provost T3A [97]	RAF Support Command, 7 FTS
	XM378	Hunting Jet Provost T3A	RAF St Athan, hack
	XM381	Hunting Jet Provost T3 (8232M) [O]	RAF Support Command, 1 SoTT Halton
	XM383	Hunting Jet Provost T3A [90]	RAF Support Command, 7 FTS
	XM386	Hunting Jet Provost T3 (8076M) [08]	RAF Support Command, 1 SoTT Halton
	XM387	Hunting Jet Provost T3A [I]	RAF Support Command, CFS
	XM401	Hunting Jet Provost T3A [17]	RAF Support Command, 1 FTS
	XM402	Hunting Jet Provost T3 (8055AM) [J]	RAF Support Command, 1 SoTT Halton
	XM403	Hunting Jet Provost T3A [M]	RAF Support Command, CFS
	XM404	Hunting Jet Provost T3 (8055BM) [24]	RAF Support Command, 1 SoTT Halton
	XM405	Hunting Jet Provost T3A [42]	RAF Support Command, 1 FTS
	XM408	Hunting Jet Provost T3 (8233M) [P]	RAF Support Command, 1 SoTT Halton
	XM409	Hunting Jet Provost T3 (8082M) [A]	RAF Support Command, 1 SoTT Halton
	XM410	Hunting Jet Provost T3 (8054AM) [C]	RAF Support Command, 1 SoTT Halton
	XM411	Hunting Jet Provost T3 (8434M) [L]	RAF Support Command, 1 SoTT Halton
	XM412	Hunting Jet Provost T3A [41]	RAF Support Command, 1 FTS
	XM414	Hunting Jet Provost T3A [101]	RAF Support Command, 7 FTS
	XM417	Hunting Jet Provost T3A (8054BM) [D]	RAF Support Command, 1 SoTT Halton
	XM419	Hunting Jet Provost T3A [N]	RAF Support Command, CFS
	XM424	Hunting Jet Provost T3A	RAF Support Command

Serial	Type (alternative identity)	Owner, Operator or Location	Notes
XM425	Hunting Jet Provost T3A [88]	RAF Support Command, 7 FTS	
XM453	Hunting Jet Provost T3A [G]	RAF Support Command, CFS	
XM455	Hunting Jet Provost T3A [F]	RAF Support Command, CFS	
XM458	Hunting Jet Provost T3A [P]	RAF Support Command, CFS	
XM459	Hunting Jet Provost T3A [20]	RAF Support Command, 5 MU	
XM461	Hunting Jet Provost T3A [11]	RAF Support Command, 1 FTS	
XM463	Hunting Jet Provost T3A [38]	RAF Support Command, 1 FTS	
XM464	Hunting Jet Provost T3A [23]	RAF Support Command, 1 FTS	
XM465	Hunting Jet Provost T3A [85]	RAF Support Command, 7 FTS	
XM466	Hunting Jet Provost T3A [105]	RAF Support Command, 7 FTS	
XM467	Hunting Jet Provost T3 (8085M) [06]	RAF Support Command, 1 SoTT Halton	
XM468	Hunting Jet Provost T3 (8081M) [B]	RAF Support Command, 1 SoTT Halton	
XM470	Hunting Jet Provost T3A	RAF Shawbury, store	
XM471	Hunting Jet Provost T3A [10]	RAF Support Command, 1 FTS	
XM472	Hunting Jet Provost T3A [22]	RAF Support Command, 1 FTS	
XM473	Hunting Jet Provost T3A [19]	RAF Support Command, 1 FTS	
XM474	Hunting Jet Provost T3 (8121M) [17]	Shrewsbury School	
XM475	Hunting Jet Provost T3A [96]	RAF Support Command, 7 FTS	
XM478	Hunting Jet Provost T3A [104]	RAF Support Command, 7 FTS	
XM479	Hunting Jet Provost T3A [54]	RAF Support Command, 1 FTS	
XM480	Hunting Jet Provost T3 (8080M)	RAF Support Command, 1 SoTT Halton	
XM527	Saro Skeeter AOP12 (7820M)	AETW Middle Wallop	
XM553	Saro Skeeter AOP12 (G-AWSV)	Privately owned, Middle Wallop	
XM555	Saro Skeeter AOP12 (8027M)	RAF Shawbury, at main gate	
XM556	Saro Skeeter AOP12 (G-HELI/7870M) [V]	British Rotorcraft Museum	
XM561	Saro Skeeter AOP12 (7980M)	Moston Tech Coll Manchester	
XM564	Saro Skeeter AOP12	AETW Middle Wallop	
XM569	Avro Vulcan B2	RAF Strike Command, No 44 Sqn	
XM571	Avro Vulcan K2	RAF Strike Command, No 50 Sqn	
XM575	Avro Vulcan B2	RAF Strike Command, No 44 Sqn	
XM594	Avro Vulcan B2	RAF Strike Command, No 44 Sqn	
XM597	Avro Vulcan B2	RAF Strike Command, No 44 Sqn	
XM598	Avro Vulcan B2	RAF Strike Command, No 44 Sqn	
XM603	Avro Vulcan B2	BAe Woodford	
XM606	Avro Vulcan B2	RAF Strike Command	
XM607	Avro Vulcan B2	RAF Strike Command, No 44 Sqn	
XM612	Avro Vulcan B2	RAF Strike Command	
XM646	Avro Vulcan B2	RAF St Athan	
XM648	Avro Vulcan B2	RAF Waddington	
XM652	Avro Vulcan B2	RAF Strike Command, No 50 Sqn	
XM654	Avro Vulcan B2	RAF Strike Command, No 50 Sqn	
XM655	Avro Vulcan B2	RAF Strike Command, No 44 Sqn	
XM656	Avro Vulcan B2	RAF Cottesmore, Fire Section	
XM657	Avro Vulcan B2	RAF Manston, Fire School	
XM660	WS55 Whirlwind HAS7 [78]	RNAW Almond Bank, Perth	
XM665	WS55 Whirlwind HAS7	Privately owned, Warwick	
XM667	WS55 Whirlwind HAS7 (A2629) [556/CU]	RN store, RNAY Wroughton	
XM685	WS55 Whirlwind HAS7 (G-AYZJ) [518/PO]	Newark Air Museum, Winthrope	
XM693	HS Gnat T1 (7891M)	Privately owned, Hamble	
XM694	HS Gnat T1	RAE Bedford Apprentice School	
XM697	HS Gnat T1	No 1349 Sqn ATC, Woking	
XM698	HS Gnat T1 (8090M/8497M)	RAF Leeming, preserved	
XM706	HS Gnat T1 (8572M) [12]	RAF Support Command, 1 SoTT Halton	
XM708	HS Gnat T1 (8573M) [18]	RAF Support Command, 1 SoTT Halton	
XM709	HS Gnat T1 (8617M) [67]	RAF Support Command, 1 SoTT Halton	
XM715	HP Victor K2	RAF Strike Command, No 55 Sqn	
XM717	HP Victor K2	RAF Strike Command, No 55 Sqn	
XM832	Westland Wessex HAS1	RN NASU, RNAS Yeovilton	
XM833	Westland Wessex HAS3	RN No 737 Sqn RNAS Portland	
XM836	Westland Wessex HAS3 [651/PO]	RN No 737 Sqn RNAS Portland	
XM838	Westland Wessex HAS3	RNAS Portland, stored	

Notes	Serial	Type (alternative identity)	Owner, Operator or Location
	XM843	Westland Wessex HAS1 (A2693) [527/CU]	RN AES Lee-on-Solent
	XM845	Westland Wessex HAS1 (A2682) [530/CU]	RN AES Lee-on-Solent
	XM868	Westland Wessex HAS1 [517/PO]	RN AES Lee-on-Solent
	XM870	Westland Wessex HAS3 [652/PO]	RN No 737 Sqn RNAS Portland
	XM874	Westland Wessex HAS1 (A2689) [521/CU]	RNAS Culdrose, SAH
	XM916	Westland Wessex HAS3 [666/PO]	RN No 737 Sqn, RNAS Portland
	XM917	Westland Wessex HAS1 (A2692) [528/CU]	RN AES Lee-on-Solent
	XM919	Westland Wessex HAS3 [55]	RNAS Yeovilton, Fire Section
	XM923	Westland Wessex HAS3	RNAS Portland, stored
	XM926	Westland Wessex HAS1	MoD(PE) RAE Farnborough
	XM927	Westland Wessex HAS3 [660/PO]	RN No 737 Sqn RNAS Portland
	XM969	BAC Lightning T4 (8592M)	RAF Binbrook, Fire Section
	XM972	BAC Lightning T4	RAF Waddington Fire Section
	XM987	BAC Lightning T4	RAF Coningsby, BDRF
	XN126	WS55 Whirlwind HAR10 (8655M) [S]	RAF Support Command, 1 SoTT, Halton
	XN132	Sud Alouette AH2	AAC Cyprus
	XN148	Slingsby Sedburgh TX1	RAF Support Command CGS
	XN150	Slingsby Sedburgh TX1	RAF Support Command 614 GS
	XN151	Slingsby Sedburgh TX1	RAF Support Command CGS
	XN155	Slingsby Sedburgh TX1	RAF Support Command 617 GS
	XN156	Slingsby Sedburgh TX1	RAF Support Command 3 MGSP
	XN157	Slingsby Sedburgh TX1	RAF Support Command 631 GS
	XN185	Slingsby Sedburgh TX1	RAF Support Command 635 GS
	XN186	Slingsby Sedburgh TX1	RAF Support Command 618 GS
	XN187	Slingsby Sedburgh TX1	RAF Support Command 662 GS
	XN198	Slingsby Cadet TX3	RAF Support Command 661 GS
	XN238	Slingsby Cadet TX3	RAF Support Command GSS St Athan
	XN239	Slingsby Cadet TX3 [G]	RAF Support Command CGS
	XN240	Slingsby Cadet TX3	RAF Support Command 621 GS
	XN241	Slingsby Cadet TX3	RAF Support Command 643 GS
	XN243	Slingsby Cadet TX3	RAF Support Command 624 GS
	XN244	Slingsby Cadet TX3	RAF Support Command 626 GS
	XN246	Slingsby Cadet TX3	RAF Support Command 617 GS
	XN251	Slingsby Cadet TX3	RAF Support Command GSS St Athan
	XN252	Slingsby Cadet TX3	RAF Support Command 661 GS
	XN253	Slingsby Cadet TX3 [L]	RAF Support Command, CGS
	XN258	WS55 Whirlwind HAR9 [589/PV]	Cornwall Aero Park, Helston
	XN261	WS55 Whirlwind HAS7 (A2652) [61]	RNAS Lee-on-Solent, dumped
	XN263	WS55 Whirlwind HAS7	RMC of S at Wroughton
	XN264	WS55 Whirlwind HAS7	Lydiard Park, Swindon
	XN297	WS Whirlwind HAR9 (really XN311) (A2643)	RNAY Fleetlands Apprentice Trg School
	XN298	WS55 Whirlwind HAR9 [810/LS]	RNAS Yeovilton
	XN299	WS55 Whirlwind HAS7 [758/—]	Torbay Aircraft Museum
	XN302	WS55 Whirlwind HAS7 (A2654)	RNAS Fire Section, Lee-on-Solent
	XN304	WS55 Whirlwind HAS7 [64]	Norfolk & Suffolk Aviation Museum, Flixton
	XN306	WS55 Whirlwind HAR9 [434/ED]	RNAS Portland Fire Section
	XN308	WS55 Whirlwind HAS7 (A2605) [510/PO]	RN store, RNAY Wroughton
	XN309	WS55 Whirlwind HAR9 (A2663) [590/CU]	SWWAPS, Lasham
	XN314	WS55 Whirlwind HAS7 (A2614)	RN store, RNAY Wroughton
	XN332	Saro P531 (G-APNV/A2579) [759]	FAA Museum, RNAS Yeovilton

Serial	Type (alternative identity)	Owner, Operator or Location	Notes
XN334	Saro P531 (Ä2525)	FAA Museum store, RNAS Yeovilton	
XN341	Saro Skeeter AOP12 (8022M)	RAF St Athan Museum	
XN344	Saro Skeeter AOP12 (8018M)	Science Museum, South Kensington	
XN351	Saro Skeeter AOP12	Wales Air Museum, Cardiff	
XN359	WS55 Whirlwind HAR9 [434/ED]	RN Store, RNAY Wroughton	
XN380	WS55 Whirlwind HAS7 [67]	Lashenden Air Warfare Museum	
XN382	WS55 Whirlwind HAS7	Museum of Army Flying, Andover store	
XN385	WS55 Whirlwind HAS7	RN Historic Flight, RNAY Wroughton	
XN386	WS55 Whirlwind HAR9 [425/ED]	RN store, RNAY Wroughton	
XN387	WS55 Whirlwind HAR9 (8564M)	RAF Odiham, BDRF	
XN435	Auster AOP9 (G-BGBU)	Privately owned, Chesham	
XN437	Auster AOP9 (G-AXWA)	Privately owned, Luton	
XN441	Auster AOP9 (G-BGKT)	Privately owned, Reymerston Hall	
XN453	DH Comet 2e	RAE Farnborough Fire Section	
XN458	Hunting Jet Provost T3 (8234M) [H]	RAF Support Command, 1 SoTT Halton	
XN459	Hunting Jet Provost T3A [20]	RAF Support Command, 1 FTS	
XN461	Hunting Jet Provost T3A [28]	RAF Support Command, 1 FTS	
XN462	Hunting Jet Provost T3A [E]	RAF Support Command, CFS	
XN465	Hunting Jet Provost T3A [30]	RAF Support Command, 1 FTS	
XN466	Hunting Jet Provost T3A [29]	RAF Support Command, 1 FTS	
XN467	Hunting Jet Provost T3 (8559M) [F]	RAF Support Command, 1 SoTT Halton	
XN470	Hunting Jet Provost T3A [86]	RAF Shawbury, store	
XN471	Hunting Jet Provost T3A [24]	RAF Support Command, 1 FTS	
XN472	Hunting Jet Provost T3A [84]	RAF Support Command, 7 FTS	
XN473	Hunting Jet Provost T3A [98]	RAF Support Command, 7 FTS	
XN492	Hunting Jet Provost T3 (8079M) [08]	RAF Support Command, 1 SoTT Halton	
XN494	Hunting Jet Provost T3A [43]	RAF Support Command, 1 FTS	
XN495	Hunting Jet Provost T3A [102]	RAF Support Command, 7 FTS	
XN497	Hunting Jet Provost T3A [52]	RAF Support Command, 1 FTS	
XN498	Hunting Jet Provost T3A [16]	RAF Support Command, 1 FTS	
XN499	Hunting Jet Provost T3A [L]	RAF Support Command, CFS	
XN500	Hunting Jet Provost T3A [80]	RAF Support Command, 7 FTS	
XN501	Hunting Jet Provost T3A [S]	RAF Support Command, CFS	
XN502	Hunting Jet Provost T3A	RAF Fire School, Manston	
XN505	Hunting Jet Provost T3A [25]	RAF Support Command, 1 FTS	
XN506	Hunting Jet Provost T3A	RAF Support Command, 7 FTS	
XN508	Hunting Jet Provost T3A [U]	RAF Support Command, CFS	
XN509	Hunting Jet Provost T3A [50]	RAF Support Command, 1 FTS	
XN510	Hunting Jet Provost T3A [40]	RAF Support Command, 1 FTS	
XN512	Hunting Jet Provost T3 (8435M) [E]	RAF Support Command, 1 SoTT Halton	
XN547	Hunting Jet Provost T3A [48]	RAF Support Command, 1 FTS	
XN548	Hunting Jet Provost T3A [103]	MoD(PE) BAe Warton	
XN549	Hunting Jet Provost T3 (8235M) [R]	RAF Support Command, 1 SoTT Halton	
XN551	Hunting Jet Provost T3A [100]	RAF Support Command, 7 FTS	
XN552	Hunting Jet Provost T3A [86]	RAF Support Command, 7 FTS	
XN553	Hunting Jet Provost T3A [34]	RAF Support Command, 1 FTS	
XN554	Hunting Jet Provost T3 (8436M) [K]	RAF Support Command, 1 SoTT Halton	
XN574	Hunting Jet Provost T3A [21]	RAF Support Command, 1 FTS	
XN577	Hunting Jet Provost T3A [18]	RAF Support Command, 1 FTS	
XN579	Hunting Jet Provost T3A [14]	RAF Support Command, 1 FTS	
XN581	Hunting Jet Provost T3A [Q]	RAF Support Command, CFS	
XN582	Hunting Jet Provost T3A [95]	RAF Support Command, 7 FTS	
XN584	Hunting Jet Provost T3A [R]	RAF Support Command, CFS	
XN585	Hunting Jet Provost T3A	RAF Linton-on-Ouse, Fire Section	
XN586	Hunting Jet Provost T3A [91]	RAF Support Command, 7 FTS	
XN589	Hunting Jet Provost T3A [46]	RAF Support Command, 1 FTS	
XN593	Hunting Jet Provost T3A [27]	RAF Support Command, 1 FTS	
XN594	Hunting Jet Provost T3 (8077M) [09]	RAF Support Command, 1 SoTT Halton	
XN595	Hunting Jet Provost T3A [82]	RAF Support Command, 7 FTS	
XN602	Hunting Jet Provost T3 (8088M)	RAF Manston, Fire Section	

Notes	Serial	Type (alternative identity)	Owner, Operator or Location
	XN605	Hunting Jet Provost T3A [T]	RAF Support Command, CFS
	XN606	Hunting Jet Provost T3A [36]	RAF Support Command, 1 FTS
	XN629	Hunting Jet Provost T3A [39]	RAF Support Command, 1 FTS
	XN632	Hunting Jet Provost T3 (8352M)	CTTS, RAF St Athan
	XN634	Hunting Jet Provost T3A [94]	RAF Support Command, 7 FTS
	XN636	Hunting Jet Provost T3A [15]	RAF Support Command, 1 FTS
	XN637	Hunting Jet Provost T3	Privately owned, Duxford
	XN640	Hunting Jet Provost T3A [99]	RAF Support Command, 7 FTS
	XN641	Hunting Jet Provost T3A [47]	RAF Support Command, 1 FTS
	XN643	Hunting Jet Provost T3A (8704M) [26]	RAF Abingdon, BDRF
	XN647	DH Sea Vixen FAW2 (A2610)	Cornwall Aero Park, Helston
	XN649	DH Sea Vixen FAW2	MoD(PE) RAE Farnborough
	XN650	DH Sea Vixen FAW2 (A2639)	Wales Air Museum, Cardiff
	XN651	DH Sea Vixen FAW2 (A2616) [705/VL]	RN Predannack Fire Section
	XN652	DH Sea Vixen FAW2	Flight Refuelling Ltd, Hurn
	XN653	DH Sea Vixen FAW2	MoD(PE) RAE Farnborough
	XN657	DH Sea Vixen D3 [TR-1]	Flight Refuelling Ltd, Hurn/Llanbedr
	XN658	DH Sea Vixen FAW2 (8223M)	MoD(PE) RAE Farnborough, stored
	XN685	DH Sea Vixen FAW2 (8173M) [703]	RAF Support Command, 2 SoTT Cosford
	XN688	DH Sea Vixen FAW2 (8141M)	MoD(PE) RAE Farnborough, stored
	XN691	DH Sea Vixen FAW2 (8143M)	RAF Support Command, 2 SoTT Cosford
	XN692	DH Sea Vixen FAW2 (A2624) [254/H]	RNAS Culdrose, SAH
	XN694	DH Sea Vixen FAW2	Flight Refuelling Ltd, Hurn
	XN696	DH Sea Vixen FAW2	MoD(PE) RAE Farnborough, stored
	XN697	DH Sea Vixen FAW2 (A2623) [234/H]	Flight Refuelling Ltd, Hurn
	XN699	DH Sea Vixen FAW2 (8224M)	RAF Support Command, 1 SoTT Halton
	XN700	DH Sea Vixen FAW2 (8138M)	MoD(PE) RAE Farnborough, stored
	XN705	DH Sea Vixen FAW2 (8225M)	MoD(PE) RAE Farnborough, stored
	XN706	DH Sea Vixen FAW2 (A2613)	MoD(PE) RAE Farnborough, stored
	XN707	DH Sea Vixen FAW2 (8144M)	Flight Refuelling Ltd, Hurn
	XN714	Hunting H126	RAF Cosford Aerospace Museum
	XN728	BAC Lightning F2A (8546M) [V]	RAF Coningsby
	XN734	BAC Lightning F2 (8346M)	BAe Warton (G27-239)
	XN769	BAC Lightning F2 (8402M) [Z]	London ATCC, West Drayton gate
	XN774	BAC Lightning F2A (8551M) [F]	RAF Coningsby
	XN778	BAC Lightning F2A (8537M) [A]	Royal Scottish Museum of Flight
	XN781	BAC Lightning F2A (8538M) [B]	RAF Leuchars
	XN816	AW Argosy E1 (8489M) [G]	RAF Support Command, 2 SoTT Cosford
	XN817	AW Argosy C1	MoD(PE) A&AEE/ETPS Boscombe Down
	XN819	AW Argosy C1 (8205M)	RAF Finningley Fire Section
	XN855	AW Argosy E1 (8556M)	CTE Manston
	XN923	HS Buccaneer S1	MoD(PE) A&AEE Boscombe Down
	XN925	HS Buccaneer S1 (8087M) (A2602)	RAF FF&SS Catterick
	XN928	HS Buccaneer S1 (8179M)	Wales Air Museum, Cardiff
	XN930	HS Buccaneer S1 (8180M) [632/LM]	RAF Honington ground instruction
	XN934	HS Buccaneer S1 (A2600) [631/LS]	RNAS Culdrose, Fire Section
	XN953	HS Buccaneer S1 (A2655/8182M)	RNAS Culdrose, SAH
	XN956	HS Buccaneer S1 (8059M)	MoD(PE) RAE Farnborough stored
	XN957	HS Buccaneer S1 [636/LM]	FAA Museum, RNAS Yeovilton
	XN962	HS Buccaneer S1 (8183M)	RAFEF, RAF Abingdon (nose only)

Serial	Type (alternative identity)	Owner, Operator or Location	Notes
XN964	HS Buccaneer S1 [613]	BAe Apprentice School, Brough	
XN965	HS Buccaneer S1 [636]	MoD(PE) RAE Farnborough	
XN967	HS Buccaneer S1 (A2627)	Cornwall Aero Park, Helston	
XN974	HS Buccaneer S2A	MoD(PE) RAE/BAe Holme-on-Spalding Moor	
XN976	HS Buccaneer S2B	RAF Strike Command, 1 Group	
XN977	HS Buccaneer S2B [G]	RAF Germany	
XN981	HS Buccaneer S2B [J]	RAF Strike Command, 1 Group	
XN982	HS Buccaneer S2A	MoD(PE)/BAe Holme-on-Spalding Moor	
XN983	HS Buccaneer S2B [K]	RAF Strike Command, 1 Group	
XP000	DHC Beaver AL1 (7735M) really XP812	Army Apprentice College, Arborfield	
XP105	Westland Wessex HAS3 (A2698) [03/CU]	RNAES Lee-on-Solent	
XP110	Westland Wessex HAS3 [655/PO]	RN No 737 Sqn, RNAS Portland	
XP116	Westland Wessex HAS3 (A2618) [520/CU]	RN AES Lee-on-Solent	
XP117	Westland Wessex HAS1 (A2681) [521/PO]	RNAS Culdrose, SAH	
XP118	Westland Wessex HAS3 [664/PO]	RN Predannack Fire Section	
XP137	Westland Wessex HAS3 [665/PO]	RN No 737 Sqn RNAS Portland	
XP139	Westland Wessex HAS3	RNAY Fleetlands	
XP140	Westland Wessex HAS3 [654/PO]	RN No 737 Sqn RNAS Portland	
XP142	Westland Wessex HAS3	Fleet Air Arm Museum, Yeovilton	
XP143	Westland Wessex HAS3	RN AES Lee-on-Solent	
XP149	Westland Wessex HAS1 (A2669) [574/PO]	RNEC Manadon	
XP150	Westland Wessex HAS3	RN No 737 Sqn RNAS Portland	
XP151	Westland Wessex HAS1 (A2684) [047/R]	RN AES Lee-on-Solent	
XP157	Westland Wessex HAS1 (A2680)	RN AES Lee-on-Solent	
XP158	Westland Wessex HAS1 (A2688) [522/CU]	RNAS Culdrose, SAH	
XP159	Westland Wessex HAS1 [521/CU]	Electrical Research Association, Leatherhead	
XP160	Westland Wessex HAS1 (A2650) [521/CU]	RNAS Culdrose, SAH	
XP165	Westland Scout AH1	Historic Aircraft Museum, Southend	
XP166	Westland Scout AH1 (G-APVL)	MoD(PE) RAE Farnborough, in store	
XP189	Westland Scout AH1 (G-ARGI)	MoD(PE) RAE Farnborough	
XP190	Westland Scout AH1	Army Apprentice College, Arborfield	
XP191	Westland Scout AH1	AAC, RNAY Wroughton store	
XP226	Fairey Gannet AEW3 (A2667) [070/E]	Newark Air Museum, Winthrope	
XP241	Auster AOP9	Tagmore Nurseries, Stevenage	
XP242	Auster AOP9	Museum of Army Flying Middle Wallop	
XP248	Auster AOP9 (7822M)	Army Apprentice College, Arborfield	
XP279	Auster AOP9 (G-BWKK)	Privately owned, RAF Wyton	
XP280	Auster AOP9	Leicester Museum of Technology	
XP281	Auster AOP9	Imperial War Museum, Duxford	
XP282	Auster AOP9 (G-BGTC)	Privately owned, Swanton Morley	
XP283	Auster AOP9 (7859M)	Privately owned, Shoreham	
XP286	Auster AOP9 (8044M)	No 152 Sqn ATC, Hull	
XP299	WS55 Whirlwind HAR10 (8726M)	RAF Cosford Aerospace Museum	
XP300	WS55 Whirlwind HAR10 [S]	RAF, stored RNAY Wroughton	
XP328	WS55 Whirlwind HAR10 (G-BKHC)	Privately owned, Tattershall Thorpe	
XP329	WS55 Whirlwind HAR10	RAF Strike Command, Cyprus	
XP330	WS55 Whirlwind HAR10	CAA Fire School, Teeside	
XP331	WS55 Whirlwind HAR10 (8649M) [T]	RN AES Lee-on-Solent	
XP333	WS55 Whirlwind HAR10 (8650M) [G]	RAF Odiham Fire Section	
XP338	WS55 Whirlwind HAR10 (8647M) [N]	RAF Shawbury, ground inst	

Notes	Serial	Type (alternative identity)	Owner, Operator or Location
	XP339	WS55 Whirlwind HAR10	Privately owned, Hadfield, Derby
	XP341	WS55 Whirlwind HAR10 (8340M) [E]	RAF Barkston Heath Fire Section
	XP344	WS55 Whirlwind HAR10 [X]	RAF Chivenor, stored
	XP345	WS55 Whirlwind HAR10	RAF Strike Command, Cyprus
	XP350	WS55 Whirlwind HAR10	Cornwall Aero Park, Helston
	XP351	WS55 Whirlwind HAR10 (8672M) [Z]	RAF Shawbury, BDRF
	XP352	WS55 Whirlwind HAR10 (8701M)	RAF Abingdon, BDRF
	XP353	WS55 Whirlwind HAR10 (8720M)	RAF FF&SS, Catterick
	XP354	WS55 Whirlwind HAR10 (8721M)	RAF Support Command, 1 SoTT Halton
	XP355	WS55 Whirlwind HAR10 (8463M/G-BEBC) [A]	Aircraft Museum Norwich
	XP356	WS55 Whirlwind HAR10	MoD(PE) RAE Farnborough, Fire Section
	XP357	WS55 Whirlwind HAR10	RAF Manston Fire Section
	XP359	WS55 Whirlwind HAR10 (8447M)	RAF Exhibition Flight, Abingdon
	XP360	WS55 Whirlwind HAR10 [V]	Second World War APS, Lasham
	XP361	WS55 Whirlwind HAR10 (8731M)	RAF Chivenor, fire section
	XP393	WS55 Whirlwind HAR10 [U]	RAE Farnborough Fire Section
	XP394	WS55 Whirlwind HAR10 [C]	RAF Manston Fire Section
	XP395	WS55 Whirlwind HAR10 (8674M)	RAF Support Command, 1 SoTT Halton
	XP398	WS55 Whirlwind HAR10	RAF Strike Command, Cyprus
	XP399	WS55 Whirlwind HAR10	Privately owned, Glastonbury, Som
	XP400	WS55 Whirlwind HAR10 (8444M) [N]	RAF Manston Fire Section
	XP404	WS55 Whirlwind HAR10 (8682M)	RAF Benson, BDRF
	XP405	WS55 Whirlwind HAR10 (8656M) [Y]	RAF Support Command, 1 SoTT, Halton
	XP409	AW Argosy C1 (8221M)	NB&CD Centre Winterbourne Gunner
	XP411	AW Argosy C1 (8442M) [C]	RAF Support Command, 2 SoTT Cosford
	XP439	AW Argosy C1 (8558M)	RAF Lossiemouth Fire Section
	XP442	AW Argosy T2 (8454M) [10]	RAF Support Command, 1 SoTT Halton
	XP444	AW Argosy C1 (8455M) [D]	RAF Support Command, 2 SoTT Cosford
	XP454	Slingsby Grasshopper TX1	3 MGSP, RAF Cosford
	XP455	Slingsby Grasshopper TX1	1 MGSP, RAF Halton
	XP458	Slingsby Grasshopper TX1	1 MGSP, RAF Halton
	XP459	Slingsby Grasshopper TX1	Woodbridge School CCF, Suffolk
	XP462	Slingsby Grasshopper TX1	Felstead School CCF, Essex
	XP463	Slingsby Grasshopper TX1	William Parker School CCF, Sussex
	XP464	Slingsby Grasshopper TX1	Sherborne School CCF, Dorset
	XP487	Slingsby Grasshopper TX1	Hampton School CCF, Middlesex
	XP488	Slingsby Grasshopper TX1	Sevenoaks Grammar School CCF, Kent
	XP489	Slingsby Grasshopper TX1	Tonbridge School CCF, Kent
	XP490	Slingsby Grasshopper TX1	RAF CGS, Syerston
	XP492	Slingsby Grasshopper TX1	King's College CCF, Taunton
	XP493	Slingsby Grasshopper TX1	RAF CGS, Syerston
	XP494	Slingsby Grasshopper TX1	3 MGSP, RAF Cosford
	XP502	HS Gnat T1 (8576M) [02]	RAF St Athan, CTTS
	XP503	HS Gnat T1 (8568M) [03]	RAF Support Command, 1 SoTT Halton
	XP504	HS Gnat T1 (8618M) [68]	RAF Support Command, 1 SoTT Halton
	XP505	HS Gnat T1 [05]	MoD(PE) RAE Bedford
	XP506	HS Gnat T1 [06]	RPEE Spadeadam on gate
	XP511	HS Gnat T1 (8619M) [65]	RAF Support Command, 1 SoTT Halton
	XP513	HS Gnat T1 [13]	MoD(PE) A&AEE Boscombe Down
	XP514	HS Gnat T1 (8635M)	RAF Support Command, 2 SoTT Cosford
	XP515	HS Gnat T1 (8614M) [59]	RAF Wattisham, BDRF
	XP516	HS Gnat T1 (8580M) [16]	MoD(PE) RAE Farnborough
	XP530	HS Gnat T1 (8606M) [60]	RAF Support Command, 1 SoTT Halton
	XP531	HS Gnat T1	RAF Coltishall, BDRF
	XP532	HS Gnat T1 (8577M) [33]	MoD(PE) RAE Farnborough
	XP533	HS Gnat T1 (8632M) [33]	RAF Support Command, 2 SoTT Cosford
	XP534	HS Gnat T1 (8620M) [64]	RAF Support Command, 1 SoTT Halton
	XP535	HS Gnat T1 (A2679) [SAH-1]	RNAS Culdrose, SAH

XR244 Auster AOP9. *PRM*

XR520 Westland Wessex HC2. *APM*

XR759 EE Lightning F6. *PRM*

XS101 HS Gnat T1. *PRM*

48

Serial	Type (alternative identity)	Owner, Operator or Location	Notes
XP538	HS Gnat T1 (8607M) [61]	RAF Support Command, 1 SoTT Halton	
XP540	HS Gnat T1 (8608M) [62]	RAF Support Command, 1 SoTT Halton	
XP541	HS Gnat T1 (8616M) [41]	RAF Abingdon, BDRF,	
XP542	HS Gnat T1 (8575M) [42]	RAF St Athan, CTTS	
XP547	Hunting Jet Provost T4 [03]	RAF Strike Command, 1 TWU/79 Sqn	
XP556	Hunting Jet Provost T4 [B]	RAF Support Command, CATCS	
XP557	Hunting Jet Provost T4 (8494M)	RAF Support Command, 1 SoTT Halton	
XP558	Hunting Jet Provost T4 (8627M) [20]	RAF St Athan, CTTS	
XP563	Hunting Jet Provost T4 [C]	RAF Support Command, CATCS	
XP564	Hunting Jet Provost T4 [04]	RAF Brawdy (wreck)	
XP567	Hunting Jet Provost T4 (8510M) [23]	RAF Support Command, 1 SoTT Halton	
XP573	Hunting Jet Provost T4 (8236M) [19]	RAF Support Command, 1 SoTT Halton	
XP583	Hunting Jet Provost T4 (8400M)	CTE, RAF Manston	
XP585	Hunting Jet Provost T4 (8407M) [24]	RAF Support Command, 1 SoTT Halton	
XP627	Hunting Jet Provost T4	North East Aircraft Museum	
XP629	Hunting Jet Provost T4	RAF Support Command, CATCS	
XP638	Hunting Jet Provost T4 [A]	RAF Support Command, CATCS	
XP640	Hunting Jet Provost T4 (8501M) [E]	RAF Support Command, 1 SoTT Halton	
XP669	Hunting Jet Provost T4	RAF St Athan, CTTS	
XP672	Hunting Jet Provost T4 (8458M) [C]	RAF Support Command, 1 SoTT Halton	
XP680	Hunting Jet Provost T4 (8460M)	RAF St Athan, CTTS	
XP686	Hunting Jet Provost T4 (8401M/8502M) [D]	RAF Support Command, 1 SoTT Halton	
XP688	Hunting Jet Provost T4 [E]	RAF Support Command, CATCS	
XP693	BAC Lightning F6 [M]	MoD(PE) BAe Warton	
XP694	BAC Lightning F3 [BO]	RAF Strike Command, 11 Group	
XP695	BAC Lightning F3 [M]	RAF Strike Command, 11 Group	
XP697	BAC Lightning F6	MoD(PE) BAe Warton (static test)	
XP701	BAC Lightning F3 [BN]	RAF Strike Command, 11 Group	
XP702	BAC Lightning F3 [BO]	RAF Strike Command, 11 Group	
XP703	BAC Lightning F3	MoD(PE) BAe Warton (static test)	
XP706	BAC Lightning F3 [BM]	RAF Strike Command, 11 Group	
XP707	BAC Lightning F3 [BM]	RAF Strike Command, 11 Group	
XP741	BAC Lightning F3 [DD]	RAF Strike Command, 11 Group, LTF	
XP745	BAC Lightning F3 (8453M) [H]	RAF Boulmer, at main gate	
XP748	BAC Lightning F3 (8446M) [M]	RAF Binbrook, at main gate	
XP749	BAC Lightning F3 [DB]	RAF Strike Command, 11 Group, LTF	
XP750	BAC Lightning F3	RAF Strike Command, 11 Group	
XP751	BAC Lightning F3 [AQ]	RAF Strike Command, 11 Group	
XP753	BAC Lightning F3 [DC]	RAF Strike Command, 11 Group, LTF	
XP761	BAC Lightning F3 (8438M) [N]	RAF Binbrook, ground instruction	
XP764	BAC Lightning F3	RAF Strike Command, 11 Group, LTF	
XP769	DHC Beaver AL1	AAC, Aldergrove	
XP771	DHC Beaver AL1	AAC, Aldergrove	
XP772	DHC Beaver AL1	Museum of Army Flying, Middle Wallop	
XP774	DHC Beaver AL1	AAC, 5 MU Kemble	
XP775	DHC Beaver AL1	AAC, 5 MU Kemble	
XP778	DHC Beaver AL1	AAC, Middle Wallop	
XP779	DHC Beaver AL1	AAC, 5 MU Kemble	
XP780	DHC Beaver AL1	AAC, 5 MU Kemble	
XP804	DHC Beaver AL1	AAC, 5 MU Kemble	
XP806	DHC Beaver AL1	Army Apprentice Coll, Arborfield	
XP808	DHC Beaver AL1	AAC, 5 MU Kemble	
XP810	DHC Beaver AL1	AAC, 5 MU Kemble	
XP811	DHC Beaver AL1	AAC, 5 MU Kemble	
XP814	DHC Beaver AL1	AAC, 5 MU Kemble	
XP816	DHC Beaver AL1	AAC, 5 MU Kemble	
XP817	DHC Beaver AL1	AAC, 5 MU Kemble	
XP818	DHC Beaver AL1	AAC, 5 MU Kemble	
XP820	DHC Beaver AL1	AAC, Middle Wallop	

Notes	Serial	Type (alternative identity)	Owner, Operator or Location
	XP821	DHC Beaver AL1	AAC, 5 MU Kemble
	XP822	DHC Beaver AL1	AAC, 5 MU Kemble
	XP823	DHC Beaver AL1	AAC, 5 MU Kemble
	XP825	DHC Beaver AL1	AAC, Aldergrove
	XP826	DHC Beaver AL1	AAC, BATUS, Alberta, Canada
	XP827	DHC Beaver AL1	AAC, 5 MU Kemble
	XP831	Hawker P1127 (8406M)	RAF Museum, Hendon
	XP841	Handley Page HP115	FAA Museum, Yeovilton
	XP846	Westland Scout AH1 [Y]	AAC, Hong Kong
	XP847	Westland Scout AH1	AETW, Middle Wallop
	XP848	Westland Scout AH1	AETW, Middle Wallop
	XP849	Westland Scout AH1	MoD(PE) ETPS Boscombe Down
	XP850	Westland Scout AH1	AAC, RNAY Wroughton store
	XP852	Westland Scout AH1	RNAY Wroughton, store
	XP853	Westland Scout AH1	AAC, UK
	XP854	Westland Scout AH1 (7898M)	AETW Middle Wallop
	XP855	Westland Scout AH1	AAC, RNAY Wroughton Store
	XP856	Westland Scout AH1	AETW Middle Wallop
	XP857	Westland Scout AH1 [H]	AAC, Hong Kong
	XP883	Westland Scout AH1	AAC, RNAY Wroughton, store
	XP884	Westland Scout AH1	AAC, AETW Middle Wallop
	XP885	Westland Scout AH1 [Y]	AAC, ATS Middle Wallop
	XP886	Westland Scout AH1	AAC, RNAY Wroughton, store
	XP887	Westland Scout AH1 [C]	AAC, Hong Kong
	XP888	Westland Scout AH1	AETW, Middle Wallop
	XP891	Westland Scout AH1	AAC, UK
	XP893	Westland Scout AH1 [S]	Royal Marines, 3 CBAS
	XP894	Westland Scout AH1 [D]	AAC, Hong Kong
	XP897	Westland Scout AH1	AAC, RNAY Wroughton, store
	XP898	Westland Scout AH1	AAC, RNAY Wroughton, store
	XP899	Westland Scout AH1 [D]	Army Apprentice College, Arborfield
	XP900	Westland Scout AH1 [Z]	AAC, ATS Middle Wallop
	XP901	Westland Scout AH1 [E]	AAC, Hong Kong
	XP902	Westland Scout AH1 [T]	Royal Marines, 3 CBAS
	XP903	Westland Scout AH1 [C]	AAC, RNAY Wroughton, store
	XP905	Westland Scout AH1	AAC, UK
	XP906	Westland Scout AH1 [F]	AAC, Hong Kong
	XP907	Westland Scout AH1 [U]	Royal Marines, 3 CBAS
	XP909	Westland Scout AH1	AETW Middle Wallop
	XP910	Westland Scout AH1	AAC, RNAY Wroughton, store
	XP919	DH Sea Vixen FAW2 (8163M) [706]	Norwich Air Museum
	XP920	DH Sea Vixen FAW2	MoD(PE) RAE Farnborough, stored
	XP921	DH Sea Vixen FAW2 (8226M)	RAF Support Command, 1 SoTT Halton
	XP924	DH Sea Vixen D3	Flight Refuelling Ltd, Hurn
	XP925	DH Sea Vixen FAW2	MoD(PE) RAE Farnborough, stored
	XP956	DH Sea Vixen FAW2	MoD(PE) RAE Farnborough, stored
	XP967	Sud Alouette AH2	AAC, Cyprus
	XP976	Hawker Kestrel FGA1	RAF Wittering for instruction
	XP980	Hawker Kestrel FGA1 (A2700)	RNAS Culdrose, SAH
	XP984	Hawker Kestrel FGA1 (A2658)	RNEC Manadon for instruction
	XR107	AW Argosy T2 (8441M) [D]	RAF Support Command, 2 SoTT Cosford
	XR137	AW Argosy E1	RAF Northolt Fire Section
	XR140	AW Argosy E1 (8579M) [56]	RAF Support Command, 1 SoTT Halton
	XR220	BAC TSR2 (7933M)	RAF Cosford Aerospace Museum
	XR222	BAC TSR2	Imperial War Museum, Duxford
	XR232	Sud Alouette AH1 (F-WEIP)	AAC, RNAY Wroughton
	XR240	Auster AOP9 (G-BDFH)	Privately owned, Booker
	XR241	Auster AOP9 (G-AXRR)	Shuttleworth Trust, Old Warden
	XR243	Auster AOP9 (8057M)	RAF St Athan, museum
	XR244	Auster AOP9	AAC Historic Aircraft Flight, Middle Wallop
	XR246	Auster AOP9 (7862M/ G-AZBU)	Privately owned, Reymerston Hall, Norfolk
	XR267	Auster AOP9	Cotswold Aircraft Restoration Group
	XR269	Auster AOP9 (G-BDXY)	Privately owned, Leicester
	XR271	Auster AOP9	Museum of Artillery, Woolwich
	XR371	Short Belfast C1	RAF Cosford Aerospace Museum
	XR376	Sud Alouette AH2	AAC, Cyprus
	XR378	Sud Alouette AH2	AAC, Cyprus

Serial	Type (alternative identity)	Owner, Operator or Location	Notes
XR379	Sud Alouette AH2	AAC, Cyprus	
XR380	Sud Alouette AH2	AAC, Cyprus	
XR382	Sud Alouette AH2	AAC, Cyprus	
XR385	Sud Alouette AH2	AAC, Cyprus	
XR386	Sud Alouette AH2	AAC, Cyprus	
XR436	SARO P531/2	Museum of Army Flying, Andover store	
XR441	DH Sea Heron C1 (G-AORG)	RNAS Yeovilton Station Flight	
XR442	DH Sea Heron C1 (G-AORH)	RN 5 MU Kemble	
XR443	DH Sea Heron C1 (G-ARKU)	RNAS Yeovilton Station Flight	
XR445	DH Sea Heron C1 (G-ARKW)	RNAS Yeovilton Station Flight	
XR455	WS55 Whirlwind HAR10 (8219M) [J]	RAF Support Command, 1 SoTT Halton	
XR457	WS55 Whirlwind HAR10 (8644M)	RAF Netheravon	
XR458	WS55 Whirlwind HAR10 (8662M) [H]	RAF Support Command, 1 SoTT Halton	
XR478	WS55 Whirlwind HAR10 [P]	Defence School, Winterbourne Gunner	
XR479	WS55 Whirlwind HAR10 [A]	RAE Farnborough Fire Section	
XR481	WS55 Whirlwind HAR10	RAF Store, RNAY Wroughton	
XR482	WS55 Whirlwind HAR10	Defence School, Winterbourne Gunner	
XR483	WS55 Whirlwind HAR10	RAF store, RNAY Wroughton	
XR485	WS55 Whirlwind HAR10 [Q]	Norfolk & Suffolk Aviation Museum	
XR486	WS55 Whirlwind HCC12 (8727M)	RAF St Athan Historic Aircraft Collection	
XR493	Westland Scout AH1 (G-APVM/8040M)	MoD(PE) Farnborough	
XR497	Westland Wessex HAR2	RAF Strike Command, No 22 Sqn	
XR498	Westland Wessex HC2 [X]	RAF Strike Command, No 72 Sqn	
XR499	Westland Wessex HC2 [W]	RAF Strike Command, No 72 Sqn	
XR501	Westland Wessex HAR2	RAF Strike Command, No 22 Sqn	
XR502	Westland Wessex HC2 [Z]	RAF Strike Command, No 72 Sqn	
XR503	Westland Wessex HC2	MoD(PE) RAE Bedford	
XR504	Westland Wessex HAR2	RAF SupportCommand,No22 Sqn/SARTU	
XR505	Westland Wessex HC2 [WA]	RAF Support Command, 2 FTS	
XR506	Westland Wessex HC2 [V]	RAF Strike Command, No 72 Sqn	
XR507	Westland Wessex HC2	RAF Valley, No 22 Sqn/SARTU	
XR508	Westland Wessex HC2 [D]	RAF Strike Command, Hong Kong	
XR509	Westland Wessex HC2 [BM]	RAF Strike Command, WCF	
XR511	Westland Wessex HC2 [L]	RAF Strike Command, No 72 Sqn	
XR515	Westland Wessex HC2 [B]	RAF Strike Command, Hong Kong	
XR516	Westland Wessex HC2 [WB]	RAF Support Command, 2 FTS	
XR517	Westland Wessex HC2 [N]	RAF Strike Command, No 72 Sqn	
XR518	Westland Wessex HAR2	RAF Support Command,No 22Sqn/SARTU	
XR519	Westland Wessex HC2 [WC]	RAF Support Command, 2 FTS	
XR520	Westland Wessex HAR2	RAF Strike Command, SAREW	
XR521	Westland Wessex HC2 [WD]	RAF Support Command, 2 FTS	
XR522	Westland Wessex HAR2	RAF Strike Command, No 84 Sqn	
XR523	Westland Wessex HC2 [M]	RAF Strike Command, No 72 Sqn	
XR524	Westland Wessex HAR2	RAF Vallley, No 22 Sqn/SARTU	
XR525	Westland Wessex HAR2	RAF Strike Command, No 84 Sqn	
XR527	Westland Wessex HC2 [C]	RAF Strike Command, Hong Kong	
XR528	Westland Wessex HC2 [A]	RAF Strike Command, Hong Kong	
XR529	Westland Wessex HC2 [E]	RAF Strike Command, No 72 Sqn	
XR534	HS Gnat T1 (8578M) [65]	RAF Valley,.on display	
XR535	HS Gnat T1 (8569M)	RAF Support Command, 1 SoTT Halton	
XR537	HS Gnat T1 (8642M)	RAF Support Command, 2 SoTT Cosford	
XR538	HS Gnat T1 (8621M) [69]	RAF Support Command, 1 SoTT Halton	
XR540	HS Gnat T1 (8636M)	RNAS Culdrose, SAH	
XR541	HS Gnat T1 (8602M)	CTTS, RAF St Athan	
XR568	HS Gnat T1 (7874M)	RAF Support Command, Abingdon	
XR569	HS Gnat T1 (8560M)	RAF Support Command, 1 SoTT Halton	
XR571	HS Gnat T1 (8493M) [23]	RAF Cosford Aerospace Museum	
XR572	HS Gnat T1 (A2676)	RNAS Culdrose, SAH	
XR574	HS Gnat T1 (8631M) [24]	RAF Support Command, 2 SoTT Cosford	
XR588	Westland Wessex HAR2	RAF Strike Command, No 22 Sqn	
XR595	Westland Scout AH1	AAC, RNAY store, Wroughton	
XR597	Westland Scout AH1	AAC Exhibition Unit	
XR600	Westland Scout AH1 [B]	AAC, RNAY Wroughton store	
XR601	Westland Scout AH1	Army Apprentice College Arborfield	
XR602	Westland Scout AH1	AAC, RNAY store, Wroughton	
XR603	Westland Scout AH1 [A]	AAC, UK	

Notes	Serial	Type (alternative identity)	Owner, Operator or Location
	XR604	Westland Scout AH1	AAC, RNAY store, Wroughton
	XR625	Westland Scout AH1 (really XT625)	St Georges Barracks, Sutton Coldfield
	XR627	Westland Scout AH1 [G]	Royal Marines, 3 CBAS
	XR629	Westland Scout AH1	AAC, UK
	XR630	Westland Scout AH1	AAC, UK
	XR632	Westland Scout AH1	AAC, RNAY store, Wroughton
	XR635	Westland Scout AH1	AAC, AETW Middle Wallop
	XR637	Westland Scout AH1	AAC, UK
	XR639	Westland Scout AH1	AAC, RNAY store, Wroughton
	XR643	Hunting Jet Provost T4 (8516M) [26]	RAF Support Command, 1 SoTT Halton
	XR650	Hunting Jet Provost T4 (8459M) [28]	RAF Support Command, 1 SoTT Halton
	XR651	Hunting Jet Provost T4 (8431M) [A]	RAF Support Command, 1 SoTT Halton
	XR653	Hunting Jet Provost T4 [H]	RAF Support Command, CATCS
	XR654	Hunting Jet Provost T4	Aircraft Radio Museum, Coventry
	XR658	Hunting Jet Provost T4 (8192M) [Y]	RAF Exhibition Flt, Abingdon
	XR662	Hunting Jet Provost T4 (8410M) [25]	RAF Support Command, 1 SoTT Halton
	XR669	Hunting Jet Provost T4 (8062M) [02]	RAF Support Command, 1 SoTT Halton
	XR670	Hunting Jet Provost T4 (8498M)	RAF Support Command, 1 SoTT Halton
	XR672	Hunting Jet Provost T4 (8495M) [C]	RAF Support Command, 1 SoTT Halton
	XR673	Hunting Jet Provost T4 [L]	RAF Support Command, CATCS
	XR674	Hunting Jet Provost T4 [D]	RAF Support Command, CATCS
	XR679	Hunting Jet Provost T4 [04]	RAF Strike Command, 1 TWU
	XR701	Hunting Jet Provost T4 [K]	RAF Support Command, CATCS
	XR704	Hunting Jet Provost T4 (8506M) [30]	RAF Support Command, 1 SoTT Halton
	XR713	EE Lightning F3 [AR]	RAF Strike Command, 11 Group
	XR716	EE Lightning F3 [AS]	RAF Strike Command, 11 Group
	XR717	EE Lightning F3	A&AEE Boscombe Down Fire Section
	XR718	EE Lightning F3 [DC]	RAF Strike Command, LTF
	XR720	EE Lightning F3 [DA]	RAF Strike Command, LTF
	XR724	EE Lightning F6	RAF Strike Command, 11 Group
	XR725	EE Lightning F6	RAF Strike Command, 11 Group
	XR726	EE Lightning F6	RAF Strike Command, 11 Group
	XR727	EE Lightning F6	RAF Strike Command, 11 Group
	XR728	EE Lightning F6 [BA]	RAF Strike Command, 11 Group
	XR747	EE Lightning F6 [BF]	RAF Strike Command, 11 Group
	XR749	EE Lightning F3	RAF Strike Command, 11 Group
	XR751	EE Lightning F3	RAF Strike Command, 11 Group
	XR752	EE Lightning F6 [BH]	RAF Strike Command, 11 Group
	XR753	EE Lightning F6	RAF Strike Command, 11 Group
	XR754	EE Lightning F6 [AE]	RAF Strike Command, 11 Group
	XR755	EE Lightning F6 [BJ]	RAF Strike Command, 11 Group
	XR756	EE Lightning F6 [F]	RAF Strike Command, 11 Group
	XR757	EE Lightning F6 [BE]	RAF Strike Command, 11 Group
	XR758	EE Lightning F6 [AF]	RAF Strike Command, 11 Group
	XR759	EE Lightning F6 [AH]	RAF Strike Command, 11 Group
	XR760	EE Lightning F6	RAF Strike Command, 11 Group
	XR761	EE Lightning F6 [AC]	RAF Strike Command, 11 Group
	XR763	EE Lightning F6	RAF Strike Command, 11 Group
	XR769	EE Lightning F6 [BD]	RAF Strike Command, 11 Group
	XR770	EE Lightning F6	RAF Strike Command, 11 Group
	XR771	EE Lightning F6	RAF Strike Command, 11 Group
	XR772	EE Lightning F6 [BB]	RAF Strike Command, 11 Group
	XR773	EE Lightning F6	RAF Strike Command, 11 Group
	XR806	BAC VC10 C1	RAF Strike Command, No 10 Sqn
	XR807	BAC VC10 C1	RAF Strike Command, No 10 Sqn
	XR808	BAC VC10 C1	RAF Strike Command, No 10 Sqn
	XR810	BAC VC10 C1	RAF Strike Command, No 10 Sqn
	XR951	HS Gnat T1 (8603M) [26]	RAF Support Command, 1 SoTT Halton
	XR953	HS Gnat T1 (8609M) [63]	RAF Support Command, 1 SoTT Halton
	XR954	HS Gnat T1 (8570M) [30]	RAF Support Command, 1 SoTT Halton
	XR955	HS Gnat T1 (A2678)	RNAS Culdrose, SAH
	XR977	HS Gnat T1 (8640M)	RAF Cosford Aerospace Museum

Serial	Type (alternative identity)	Owner, Operator or Location	Notes
XR980	HS Gnat T1 (8622M) [70]	RAF Support Command, 1 SoTT Halton	
XR984	HS Gnat T1 (8571M) [52]	RAF Support Command, 1 SoTT Halton	
XR987	HS Gnat T1 (8641M)	RAF Support Command, 2 SoTT Cosford	
XR991	HS Gnat T1 (8637M)	RNAS Culdrose, SAH	
XR993	HS Gnat T1 (A2677)	RNAS Culdrose, SAH	
XR998	HS Gnat T1 (8623M) [71]	RAF Support Command, 1 SoTT Halton	
XS100	HS Gnat T1 (8561M) [57]	RAF Support Command, 1 SoTT Halton	
XS101	HS Gnat T1 (8638M) (G-GNAT)	Privately owned, Stansted	
XS102	HS Gnat T1 (8624M) [66]	RAF Support Command, 1 SoTT Halton	
XS104	HS Gnat T1 (8604M) [44]	RAF Support Command, 2 SoTT Cosford	
XS105	HS Gnat T1 (8625M) [35]	RAF Support Command, 2 SoTT Cosford	
XS107	HS Gnat T1 (8639M)	RAF Support Command, 2 SoTT Cosford	
XS109	HS Gnat T1 (8626M) [63]	RAF Support Command, 2 SoTT Cosford	
XS110	HS Gnat T1 (8562M) [20]	RAF Support Command, 1 SoTT Halton	
XS119	Westland Wessex HAS3	RN No 737 Sqn RNAS Portland	
XS120	Westland Wessex HAS1 (8653M) [520/CU]	RAF Abingdon, BDRF	
XS122	Westland Wessex HAS3	RNEC, Manadon	
XS125	Westland Wessex HAS1 (A2648) [517/PO]	RN AES Lee-on-Solent	
XS127	Westland Wessex HAS3	RNAY Wroughton, store	
XS128	Westland Wessex HAS1 (A2670) [437/PO]	RNEC Manadon	
XS149	Westland Wessex HAS3 [661/PO]	RNAY Wroughton, store	
XS150	Westland Wessex HAS1	RN AES Lee-on-Solent	
XS153	Westland Wessex HAS3 [662/PO]	RN No 737 Sqn, RNAS Portland	
XS175	Hunting Jet Provost T4	Technical College, Preston	
XS176	Hunting Jet Provost T4 (8514M) [N]	RAF Support Command, 1 SoTT Halton	
XS177	Hunting Jet Provost T4 [N]	RAF Support Command, CATCS	
XS178	Hunting Jet Provost T4 [05]	RAF Strike Command, 1 TWU No 79 Sqn	
XS179	Hunting Jet Provost T4 (8237M) [20]	RAF Support Command, 1 SoTT Halton	
XS180	Hunting Jet Provost T4 (8238M) [21]	RAF Support Command, 1 SoTT Halton	
XS181	Hunting Jet Provost T4 [F]	RAF Support Command, CATCS	
XS186	Hunting Jet Provost T4 (8408M) [M]	RAF Support Command, 1 SoTT Halton	
XS209	Hunting Jet Provost T4 (8409M) [29]	RAF Support Command, 1 SoTT Halton	
XS210	Hunting Jet Provost T4 (8239M) [22]	RAF Support Command, 1 SoTT Halton	
XS215	Hunting Jet Provost T4 (8507M) [17]	RAF Support Command, 1 SoTT Halton	
XS216	Hunting Jet Provost T4	RAF Support Command, Finningley	
XS217	Hunting Jet Provost T4 [O]	RAF Support Command, CATCS	
XS218	Hunting Jet Provost T4 (8508M) [18]	RAF Support Command, 1 SoTT Halton	
XS219	Hunting Jet Provost T4 [06]	RAF Strike Command, 1 TWU	
XS230	BAC Jet Provost T5	MoD(PE) A&AEE/ETPS Boscombe Down	
XS231	BAC Jet Provost T5 (G-ATAJ)	RAF Kemble, 5 MU	
XS235	HS Comet 4C	MoD(PE) A&AEE Boscombe Down	
XS241	Westland Wessex HU5	MoD(PE) RAE Farnborough	
XS416	EE Lightning T5 [DU]	RAF Strike Command, 11 Group LTF	
XS417	EE Lightning T5 [BT]	RAF Strike Command, 11 Group	
XS418	EE Lightning T5 (8531M)	RAF Binbrook	
XS419	EE Lightning T5	RAF Strike Command, 11 Group LTF	
XS420	EE Lightning T5 [DV]	RAF Strike Command, 11 Group LTF	
XS422	EE Lightning T5	MoD(PE) ETPS Boscombe Down	
XS423	EE Lightning T5 (8532M)	RAF Binbrook	
XS449	EE Lightning T5 (8533M)	RAF Binbrook	
XS450	EE Lightning T5 (8534M) [X]	RAF Binbrook	
XS451	EE Lightning T5 (8503M)	RAF Newton for ground instruction	
XS452	EE Lightning T5 [DZ]	RAF Strike Command, 11 Group LTF	
XS454	EE Lightning T5 (8535M) [Y]	RAF Binbrook	
XS456	EE Lightning T5 [DT]	RAF Strike Command 11 Group LTF	
XS457	EE Lightning T5 [AT]	RAF Strike Command, 11 Group	

Notes	Serial	Type (alternative identity)	Owner, Operator or Location
	XS458	EE Lightning T5	RAF Strike Command, 11 Group
	XS459	EE Lightning T5 [DX]	RAF Strike Command, 11 Group LTF
	XS463	Westland Wasp HAS1 (A2647)	British Rotorcraft Museum, RNAY Fleetlands
	XS479	Westland Wessex HU5 [XF]	RN No 847 Sqn, RNAS Yeovilton
	XS481	Westland Wessex HU5 [522/CU]	RNAS Yeovilton
	XS482	Westland Wessex HU5 [A-D]	MoD(PE) A&AEE Boscombe Down
	XS483	Westland Wessex HU5 [T]	RN No 845 Sqn RNAS Yeovilton
	XS484	Westland Wessex HU5	No 771 Sqn RNAS Culdrose
	XS485	Westland Wessex HU5 [ZD]	RN No 707 Sqn RNAS Yeovilton
	XS486	Westland Wessex HU5 [WW]	RN NASU RNAS Yeovilton
	XS488	Westland Wessex HU5 [XK]	RN No 771 Sqn RNAS Culdrose
	XS489	Westland Wessex HU5 [WY]	RN NASU RNAS Yeovilton
	XS491	Westland Wessex HU5 [XL]	RN NASU RNAS Yeovilton
	XS492	Westland Wessex HU5 [B]	RN NASU RNAS Yeovilton
	XS493	Westland Wessex HU5 [VE]	RNAY Fleetlands
	XS496	Westland Wessex HU5	RN No 772 Sqn, RNAS Portland
	XS498	Westland Wessex HU5 [ZK]	RN No 707 Sqn RNAS Yeovilton
	XS506	Westland Wessex HU5 [XE]	RN NASU RNAS Yeovilton
	XS507	Westland Wessex HU5 [XU]	RN NASU RNAS Yeovilton
	XS508	Westland Wessex HU5 [ZE] [627/PO]	RN No 707 Sqn RNAS Yeovilton
	XS509	Westland Wessex HU5 (A2597)	MoD(PE) A&AEE Boscombe Down
	XS510	Westland Wessex HU5 [814/PO]	RN No 772 Sqn, RNAS Portland
	XS511	Westland Wessex HU5 [D]	RN RNAY Fleetlands store
	XS513	Westland Wessex HU5	RN NASU RNAS Yeovilton
	XS514	Westland Wessex HU5 [XA]	RN NASU Sqn RNAS Yeovilton
	XS515	Westland Wessex HU5	RN No 845 Sqn RNAS Yeovilton
	XS516	Westland Wessex HU5 [XD]	RN NASU RNAS Yeovilton
	XS517	Westland Wessex HU5 [ZC]	RN No 707 Sqn RNAS Yeovilton
	XS518	Westland Wessex HU5 [XP]	RN RNAY Fleetlands
	XS520	Westland Wessex HU5 [WZ]	RN NASU RNAS Yeovilton
	XS521	Westland Wessex HU5 [621/PO]	RN No 772 Sqn RNAS Portland
	XS522	Westland Wessex HU5 [635/PO]	RN No 772 Sqn RNAS Portland
	XS523	Westland Wessex HU5 [XJ]	RN NASU RNAS Yeovilton
	XS527	Westland Wasp HAS1 [434/ED]	RN No 829 Sqn RNAS Portland
	XS528	Westland Wasp HAS1 [423/—]	FAA Museum, RNAS Yeovilton
	XS529	Westland Wasp HAS1 [360/—]	RN No 829 Sqn RNAS Portland
	XS532	Westland Wasp HAS1	RNAY Wroughton, store
	XS535	Westland Wasp HAS1	RNAY Wroughton, store
	XS536	Westland Wasp HAS1	RNAY Wroughton, store
	XS537	Westland Wasp HAS1 (A2672) [582/—]	RNAS Portland for instruction
	XS538	Westland Wasp HAS1 [425/—]	RN No 829 Sqn RNAS Portland
	XS539	Westland Wasp HAS1 [435/—]	RN No 829 Sqn RNAS Portland
	XS541	Westland Wasp HAS1 [95/DM]	BRNC Dartmouth
	XS543	Westland Wasp HAS1 [602/—]	RN No 829 Sqn, RNAS Portland
	XS545	Westland Wasp HAS1 (A2702) [635/PO]	RN AES Lee-on-Solent
	XS562	Westland Wasp HAS1 [371/—]	RN No 829 Sqn, RNAS Portland
	XS565	Westland Wasp HAS1	RNAY Wroughton, store
	XS566	Westland Wasp HAS1 [607/—]	RN No 829 Sqn RNAS Portland
	XS567	Westland Wasp HAS1 [470/AP]	RN No 829 Sqn RNAS Portland
	XS568	Westland Wasp HAS1 [441/—]	RN No 829 Sqn RNAS Portland
	XS569	Westland Wasp HAS1	RNAY Wroughton, store
	XS570	Westland Wasp HAS1 (A2699)	RN AES Lee-on-Solent
	XS571	Westland Wasp HAS1	RNAY Wroughton, store
	XS572	Westland Wasp HAS1 [610/—]	RN No 829 Sqn RNAS Portland
	XS576	DH Sea Vixen FAW2 [125/E]	Imperial War Museum, Duxford
	XS577	DH Sea Vixen D3	Flight Refuelling Ltd, Hurn
	XS580	DH Sea Vixen FAW2	MoD(PE) RAE Farnborough, stored
	XS587	DH Sea Vixen D3	Flight Refuelling Ltd, Hurn
	XS590	DH Sea Vixen FAW2 [131/E]	FAA Museum, RNAS Yeovilton
	XS595	HS Andover C1 [A]	RAF Brize Norton Fire Section
	XS596	HS Andover C1	RAF Strike Command, No 115 Sqn
	XS597	HS Andover C1	RAF Northolt, No 32 Sqn

XS484 Westland Wessex HU5. *PRM*

XS605 HS Andover E3. *PRM*

56

Serial	Type (alternative identity)	Owner, Operator or Location	Notes
XS598	HS Andover C1 [E]	RAF Brize Norton for instruction	
XS603	HS Andover E3	RAF Strike Command, No 115 Sqn	
XS605	HS Andover E3	RAF Strike Command, No 115 Sqn	
XS606	HS Andover C1	MoD(PE) A&AEE/ETPS Boscombe Down	
XS607	HS Andover C1	MoD(PE) RAE, West Freugh	
XS610	HS Andover E3	RAF Strike Command, No 115 Sqn	
XS637	HS Andover C1	RAF CinC AFNORTH, Oslo	
XS639	HS Andover E3A	RAF Strike Command, No 115 Sqn	
XS640	HS Andover E3	RAF Strike Command, No 115 Sqn	
XS641	HS Andover E3A	RAF Strike Command, No 115 Sqn	
XS642	HS Andover C1 [C]	RAF Benson Fire Section	
XS643	HS Andover E3A	RAF Strike Command, No 115 Sqn	
XS644	HS Andover C1 (Mod)	RAF Strike Command, EWAU	
XS646	HS Andover C1	MoD(PE) RAE Farnborough	
XS647	HS Andover C1	British Aerospace, Woodford	
XS650	Slingsby Swallow TX1	RAF Support Command, CGS	
XS651	Slingsby Swallow TX1	RAF Support Command, CGS	
XS652	Slingsby Swallow TX1 (BGA 1107)	RAF Support Command, 662 GS	
XS674	Westland Wessex HC2 [AH]	RAF Strike Command, No 72 Sqn	
XS675	Westland Wessex HAR2	RAF Strike Command, No 22 Sqn	
XS676	Westland Wessex HC2 [WJ]	RAF Support Command, 2 FTS	
XS677	Westland Wessex HC2 [WK]	RAF Support Command, 2 FTS	
XS679	Westland Wessex HC2 [WG]	RAF Support Command, 2 FTS	
XS695	HS Kestrel FGA1 (A2619)	RNAS Culdrose, SAH	
XS709	HS Dominie T1 [M]	RAF Support Command, 6 FTS	
XS710	HS Dominie T1 [O]	RAF Support Command, 6 FTS	
XS711	HS Dominie T1 [L]	RAF Support Command, 6 FTS	
XS712	HS Dominie T1 [A]	RAF Support Command, 6 FTS	
XS713	HS Dominie T1 [C]	RAF Support Command, 6 FTS	
XS714	HS Dominie T1 [P]	RAF Support Command, 6 FTS	
XS726	HS Dominie T1 [T]	RAF Support Command, 6 FTS	
XS727	HS Dominie T1 [D]	RAF Support Command, 6 FTS	
XS728	HS Dominie T1 [E]	RAF Support Command, 6 FTS	
XS729	HS Dominie T1 [G]	RAF Support Command, 6 FTS	
XS730	HS Dominie T1 [H]	RAF Support Command, 6 FTS	
XS731	HS Dominie T1 [J]	RAF Support Command, 6 FTS	
XS732	HS Dominie T1 [B]	RAF Support Command, 6 FTS	
XS733	HS Dominie T1 [Q]	RAF Support Command, 6 FTS	
XS734	HS Dominie T1 [N]	RAF Support Command, 6 FTS	
XS735	HS Dominie T1 [R]	RAF Support Command, 6 FTS	
XS736	HS Dominie T1 [S]	RAF Support Command, 6 FTS	
XS737	HS Dominie T1 [K]	RAF Support Command, 6 FTS	
XS738	HS Dominie T1 [U]	RAF Support Command, 6 FTS	
XS739	HS Dominie T1 [F]	RAF Support Command, 6 FTS	
XS743	Beagle Basset CC1	MoD(PE) ETPS Boscombe Down	
XS765	Beagle Basset CC1	MoD(PE) A&AEE/ETPS Boscombe Down	
XS770	Beagle Basset CC1	MoD(PE) A&AEE/ Boscombe Down	
XS789	HS Andover CC2	RAF, Queen's Flight, Benson	
XS790	HS Andover CC2	RAF, Queen's Flight, Benson	
XS791	HS Andover CC2	RAF Northolt, No 32 Sqn	
XS792	HS Andover CC2	RAF Northolt, No 32 Sqn	
XS793	HS Andover CC2	RAF, Queen's Flight, Benson	
XS794	HS Andover CC2	RAF Northolt, No 32 Sqn	
XS859	Slingsby Swallow TX1	RAF Support Command, CGS	
XS862	Westland Wessex HAS3 [650/PO]	RN No 737 Sqn, RNAS Portland	
XS863	Westland Wessex HAS1	Imperial War Museum, Duxford	
XS865	Westland Wessex HAS1 (A2694) [529/CU]	RN AES Lee-on-Solent	
XS866	Westland Wessex HAS1 [520/CU]	RNAY Wroughton store	
XS867	Westland Wessex HAS1 (A2671)	RNAS Lee-on-Solent	
XS868	Westland Wessex HAS1 (A2691) [526/CU]	RNAY Fleetlands on gate	
XS869	Westland Wessex HAS1 (A2649) [508/PO]	Seafield Park rescue training	
XS870	Westland Wessex HAS1 (A2697) [—/PO]	RN AES Lee-on-Solent	
XS871	Westland Wessex HAS1 (8457M) [AI]	RAF Odiham Fire Section	

Notes	Serial	Type (alternative identity)	Owner, Operator or Location
	XS872	Westland Wessex HAS1 (A2666) [572/CU]	Apprentice School, RNAY Fleetlands
	XS873	Westland Wessex HAS1 (A2686) [525/PO]	RN AES Lee-on-Solent
	XS876	Westland Wessex HAS1 (A2695) [523/PO]	RN AES Lee-on-Solent
	XS877	Westland Wessex HAS1 (A2687) [516/PO]	RNAS Culdrose, SAH
	XS878	Westland Wessex HAS1 (A2683) [—/PO]	RN AES Lee-on-Solent
	XS880	Westland Wessex HAS1	RNAY Fleetlands
	XS881	Westland Wessex HAS1 (A2675) [046/CU]	FAA Museum, RNAS Yeovilton
	XS882	Westland Wessex HAS1 (A2696) [524/CU]	RN AES Lee-on-Solent
	XS885	Westland Wessex HAS1 (A2668) [512/PO]	RNAS Culdrose, SAH
	XS886	Westland Wessex HAS1 (A2685) [527/CU]	RN AES Lee-on-Solent
	XS887	Westland Wessex HAS1 (A2690) [514/PO]	RNAS Culdrose, SAH
	XS888	Westland Wessex HAS1 [521/CU]	RN Exhibition unit, Yeovilton
	XS895	EE Lightning F6 [AK]	RAF Strike Command, 11 Group
	XS897	EE Lightning F6	RAF Strike Command, 11 Group
	XS898	EE Lightning F6 [J]	RAF Strike Command, 11 Group
	XS899	EE Lightning F6 [AA]	RAF Strike Command, 11 Group
	XS901	EE Lightning F6 [BJ]	RAF Strike Command, 11 Group
	XS903	EE Lightning F6	RAF Strike Command, 11 Group
	XS904	EE Lightning F6 [BD]	RAF Strike Command, 11 Group
	XS919	EE Lightning F6 [AD]	RAF Strike Command, 11 Group
	XS920	EE Lightning F6 [BB]	RAF Strike Command, 11 Group
	XS921	EE Lightning F6 [AB]	RAF Strike Command, 11 Group
	XS922	EE Lightning F6 [AC]	RAF Strike Command, 11 Group
	XS923	EE Lightning F6 [BG]	RAF Strike Command, 11 Group
	XS925	EE Lightning F6	RAF Strike Command, 11 Group
	XS927	EE Lightning F6 [BH]	RAF Strike Command, 11 Group
	XS928	EE Lightning F6 [AJ]	RAF Strike Command, 11 Group
	XS929	EE Lightning F6 [BC]	RAF Strike Command, 11 Group
	XS932	EE Lightning F6 [F]	RAF Strike Command, 11 Group
	XS933	EE Lightning F6 [G]	MoD(PE) BAe Warton
	XS935	EE Lightning F6	RAF Strike Command, 11 Group
	XS936	EE Lightning F6 [DF]	RAF Strike Command, 11 Group LTF
	XT108	Agusta-Bell Sioux AH1 [U]	Museum of Army Flying Middle Wallop
	XT131	Agusta-Bell Sioux AH1 [B]	AAC Historic Aircraft Flight, Middle Wallop
	XT133	Agusta-Bell Sioux AH1 (7923M)	Army Apprentice Coll Arborfield
	XT140	Agusta-Bell Sioux AH1	Air Service Training, Perth
	XT141	Agusta-Bell Sioux AH1 (8509M)	Air Movements Sqn Brize Norton
	XT150	Agusta-Bell Sioux AH1 [R]	Museum of Army Flying, in store, Andover
	XT151	Westland Sioux AH1	AAC, RNAY Wroughton, store
	XT175	Westland Sioux AH1	CSE Oxford for ground instruction
	XT176	Westland Sioux AH1	Royal Marines, for display, Coypool
	XT190	Westland Sioux AH1	Museum of Army Flying, in store, Andover
	XT200	Westland Sioux AH1 [F]	Newark Air Museum, Winthorpe
	XT242	Westland Sioux AH1	Wessex Aviation Society, Stapehill
	XT248	Westland Sioux AH1	Privately owned, Ripon
	XT255	Westland Wessex HAS3	MoD(PE) ETPS Boscombe Down
	XT256	Westland Wessex HAS3 (A2615)	RN AES Lee-on-Solent
	XT257	Westland Wessex HAS3 (8719M)	RAF Support Command, 1 SoTT Halton
	XT270	HS Buccaneer S2B	RAF St Athan, store
	XT271	HS Buccaneer S2A [C]	RAF Strike Command, 237 OCU
	XT272	HS Buccaneer S2	MoD(PE), RAE Farnborough
	XT273	HS Buccaneer S2A [D]	RAF Strike Command, 237 OCU
	XT274	HS Buccaneer S2A [E]	RAF Strike Command, 237 OCU
	XT275	HS Buccaneer S2B [A]	RAF St Athan, store

Serial	Type (alternative identity)	Owner, Operator or Location	Notes
XT276	HS Buccaneer S2B [S]	RAF St Athan, store	
XT277	HS Buccaneer S2A [F]	RAF Strike Command, 237 OCU	
XT278	HS Buccaneer S2A	RAF St Athan, store	
XT279	HS Buccaneer S2B [C]	RAF Germany	
XT280	HS Buccaneer S2A [Q]	RAF Germany	
XT281	HS Buccaneer S2B (8705M)	RAF Lossiemouth, ground instruction	
XT283	HS Buccaneer S2A [G]	RAF Strike Command, 237 OCU	
XT284	HS Buccaneer S2A [H]	RAF Strike Command, 237 OCU	
XT286	HS Buccaneer S2B [W]	RAF Germany	
XT287	HS Buccaneer S2B [F]	RAF Germany	
XT288	HS Buccaneer S2B [Q]	MoD(PE)BAe Holme-on-Spalding Moor	
XT415	Westland Wasp HAS1 [476/—]	RN No 829 Sqn, RNAS Portland	
XT416	Westland Wasp HAS1 [442/—]	RNAY Fleetlands	
XT420	Westland Wasp HAS1 [604/—]	RN No 829 Sqn, RNAS Portland	
XT421	Westland Wasp HAS1 [433/EU]	RN No 829 Sqn, RNAS Portland	
XT422	Westland Wasp HAS1	RNAY Wroughton, store	
XT423	Westland Wasp HAS1 [451/—]	RN No 829 Sqn, RNAS Portland	
XT426	Westland Wasp HAS1 [455/AE]	RN No 829 Sqn, RNAS Portland	
XT427	Westland Wasp HAS1 [606/—]	RN No 829 Sqn, RNAS Portland	
XT428	Westland Wasp HAS1	RNAY Wroughton, store	
XT429	Westland Wasp HAS1	RN No 829 Sqn, RNAS Portland	
XT430	Westland Wasp HAS1 [611/PO]	RN No 829 Sqn, RNAS Portland	
XT431	Westland Wasp HAS1 [462/—]	RN No 829 Sqn, RNAS Portland	
XT432	Westland Wasp HAS1 [414/HT]	RN No 829 Sqn, RNAS Portland	
XT434	Westland Wasp HAS1 [600/—]	RN No 829 Sqn, RNAS Portland	
XT435	Westland Wasp HAS1	RNAY Wroughton, store	
XT436	Westland Wasp HAS1 [461/—]	RN No 829 Sqn, RNAS Portland	
XT437	Westland Wasp HAS1 [426/—]	RN No 829 Sqn, RNAS Portland	
XT438	Westland Wasp HAS1 [465/—]	RNAY Wroughton store	
XT439	Westland Wasp HAS1 [605/—]	RN No 829 Sqn, RNAS Portland	
XT441	Westland Wasp HAS1 [337/—]	RNAY Wroughton, store	
XT443	Westland Wasp HAS1 [422/—]	RN No 829 Sqn, RNAS Portland	
XT449	Westland Wessex HU5 [C]	RN No 845 Sqn, RNAS Yeovilton	
XT450	Westland Wessex HU5 [V]	RN No 845 Sqn, RNAS Yeovilton	
XT451	Westland Wessex HU5 [J]	RN No 845 Sqn, RNAS Yeovilton	
XT453	Westland Wessex HU5	RN No 707 Sqn, RNAS Yeovilton	
XT455	Westland Wessex HU5 [ZB]	RN No 707 Sqn, RNAS Yeovilton	
XT456	Westland Wessex HU5 [XZ]	RN NASU RNAS Yeovilton	
XT458	Westland Wessex HU5 [315/PO]	RNAS Portland, No 772 Sqn	
XT459	Westland Wessex HU5 [B]	RN No 845 Sqn, RNAS Yeovilton	
XT460	Westland Wessex HU5 [K]	RN No 845 Sqn, RNAS Yeovilton	
XT461	Westland Wessex HU5 [W]	RN No 845 Sqn, RNAS Yeovilton	
XT463	Westland Wessex HU5	RNAY Fleetlands	
XT466	Westland Wessex HU5	RN NASU RNAS Yeovilton	
XT467	Westland Wessex HU5 [525/CU]	RN No 771 Sqn, RNAS Culdrose	
XT468	Westland Wessex HU5 [D]	RN No 845 Sqn, RNAS Yeovilton	
XT469	Westland Wessex HU5 [XN]	RN No 771 Sqn, RNAS Culdrose	
XT470	Westland Wessex HU5 [A]	RN No 845 Sqn, RNAS Yeovilton	
XT471	Westland Wessex HU5 [XW]	RN NASU RNAS Yeovilton	
XT472	Westland Wessex HU5 [XC]	RN NASU RNAS Yeovilton	
XT474	Westland Wessex HU5 [520/CU]	RN No 771 Sqn, RNAS Culdrose	
XT475	Westland Wessex HU5 [XG]	RN NASU RNAS Yeovilton	

Notes	Serial	Type (alternative identity)	Owner, Operator or Location
	XT479	Westland Wessex HU5 [ZA]	RN No 707 Sqn, RNAS Yeovilton
	XT480	Westland Wessex HU5 [XQ]	RN No 771 Sqn, RNAS Culdrose
	XT481	Westland Wessex HU5	RN No 771 Sqn, RNAS Culdrose
	XT482	Westland Wessex HU5	RN NASU RNAS Yeovilton
	XT484	Westland Wessex HU5 [H]	RN No 845 Sqn, RNAS Yeovilton
	XT485	Westland Wessex HU5 [314/PO]	RN No 772 Sqn, RNAS Portland
	XT486	Westland Wessex HU5 [XR]	RN No 771 Sqn, RNAS Culdrose
	XT487	Westland Wessex HU5 [815/LS]	RNAY Wroughton, store
	XT548	Westland Sioux AH1 [D]	Army Apprentice Coll, Arborfield
	XT550	Westland Sioux AH1 [D]	Museum of Army Flying Middle Wallop
	XT575	Vickers Viscount (OE-LAG)	MoD(PE) RSRE Bedford
	XT596	McD Phantom FG1	BAe Holme-on-Spalding Moor
	XT597	McD Phantom FG1	MoD(PE) A&AEE Boscombe Down
	XT601	Westland Wessex HAR2	RAF Strike Command, No 22 Sqn
	XT602	Westland Wessex HAR2	RAF Strike Command, No 22 Sqn/SARTU
	XT603	Westland Wessex HC2 [WF]	RAF Support Command, 2 FTS
	XT604	Westland Wessex HAR2	RAF Strike Command, No 22 Sqn/SARTU
	XT605	Westland Wessex HC2 [E]	RAF Strike Command, Hong Kong
	XT606	Westland Wessex HAR2	RAF Strike Command, No 84 Sqn
	XT607	Westland Wessex HC2 [P]	RAF Strike Command, No 72 Sqn
	XT614	Westland Scout AH1 [G]	AAC, Hong Kong
	XT616	Westland Scout AH1	AAC, Hong Kong
	XT617	Westland Scout AH1	AAC, RNAY Wroughton, store
	XT618	Westland Scout AH1 [K]	AAC, Hong Kong
	XT620	Westland Scout AH1 [B]	AAC, RNAY Wroughton, store
	XT621	Westland Scout AH1	AAC, UK
	XT623	Westland Scout AH1	AAC, UK
	XT624	Westland Scout AH1 [W]	AAC, ATS Middle Wallop
	XT626	Westland Scout AH1	AAC, Hong Kong
	XT627	Westland Scout AH1 [A]	AAC, Hong Kong
	XT628	Westland Scout AH1 [J]	AAC, Hong Kong
	XT630	Westland Scout AH1 [F]	AAC, UK
	XT631	Westland Scout AH1	AAC, UK
	XT632	Westland Scout AH1	AAC, Dem & Trials Sqn, Middle Wallop
	XT633	Westland Scout AH1	AAC, RNAY Wroughton, store
	XT634	Westland Scout AH1	AAC, RNAY Wroughton, store
	XT636	Westland Scout AH1 [X]	AAC, RCS Middle Wallop
	XT637	Westland Scout AH1	AAC, RNAY, Wroughton, store
	XT638	Westland Scout AH1	AAC, UK
	XT639	Westland Scout AH1	AAC, UK
	XT640	Westland Scout AH1 [D]	AAC, AETW Middle Wallop
	XT642	Westland Scout AH1 [A]	AAC, UK
	XT643	Westland Scout AH1 [B]	AAC, Hong Kong
	XT644	Westland Scout AH1 [B]	AAC, UK
	XT645	Westland Scout AH1	AAC, UK
	XT646	Westland Scout AH1	AAC, UK
	XT648	Westland Scout AH1	AAC, RNAY Wroughton, store
	XT649	Westland Scout AH1	AAC, RNAY Wroughton, store
	XT653	Slingsby Swallow TX1	RAF Support Command, GSS St Athan
	XT657	BHC SR.N6 Winchester 5	British Hovercraft Corpn
	XT661	Vickers Viscount (9G-AAV)	MoD(PE) RSRE Bedford
	XT667	Westland Wessex HC2 [F]	RAF Strike Command, Hong Kong
	XT668	Westland Wessex HC2 [S]	RAF Strike Command, No 72 Sqn
	XT669	Westland Wessex HC2 [T]	RAF Strike Command, No 72 Sqn
	XT670	Westland Wessex HC2 [U]	RAF Strike Command, No 72 Sqn
	XT671	Westland Wessex HC2 [D]	RAF Strike Command, No 72 Sqn
	XT672	Westland Wessex HC2 [WE]	RAF Support Command, 2 FTS
	XT673	Westland Wessex HC2 [G]	RAF Strike Command, Hong Kong
	XT674	Westland Wessex HAR2	RAF Strike Command, No 22 Sqn
	XT675	Westland Wessex HC2	RAF Strike Command, No 84 Sqn
	XT676	Westland Wessex HC2 [I]	RAF Strike Command, No 72 Sqn
	XT678	Westland Wessex HC2 [H]	RAF Strike Command, Hong Kong
	XT680	Westland Wessex HAR2	RAF Strike Command, No 22 Sqn/SARTU
	XT681	Westland Wessex HC2 [U]	RAF Strike Command, No 72 Sqn
	XT752	Fairey Gannet T5 (G-APYO/WN365)	RN NASU store RNAS Culdrose
	XT755	Westland Wessex HU5 [XX]	RN NASU RNAS Yeovilton
	XT756	Westland Wessex HU5 [WM]	RN NASU RNAS Yeovilton
	XT757	Westland Wessex HU5 [XH]	RN NASU RNAS Yeovilton

Serial	Type (alternative identity)	Owner, Operator or Location	Notes
XT759	Westland Wessex HU5 [XY]	RN NASU RNAS Yeovilton	
XT760	Westland Wessex HU5 [WV]	RN NASU RNAS Yeovilton	
XT761	Westland Wessex HU5	RN No 845 Sqn, RNAS Yeovilton	
XT762	Westland Wessex HU5	MoD(PE) RS&RE Bedford	
XT763	Westland Wessex HU5 [515]	RNAS Portland Fire Section	
XT764	Westland Wessex HU5 [XM]	RN NASU RNAS Yeovilton	
XT765	Westland Wessex HU5	RNAY Fleetlands	
XT766	Westland Wessex HU5 [XS]	RN No 771 Sqn RNAS Culdrose	
XT767	Westland Wessex HU5 [814/—]	RN No 772 Sqn, RNAS Portland	
XT768	Westland Wessex HU5	MoD(PE) A&AEE Boscombe Down	
XT769	Westland Wessex HU5 [530/CU]	RN No 771 Sqn, RNAS Culdrose	
XT770	Westland Wessex HU5	RN No 707 Sqn, RNAS Yeovilton	
XT771	Westland Wessex HU5 [WR]	RN No 772 Sqn, RNAS Portland	
XT772	Westland Wessex HU5	RNAY Wroughton, store	
XT773	Westland Wessex HU5 [XT]	RN NASU RNAS Yeovilton	
XT778	Westland Wasp HAS1	RNAY Wroughton, store	
XT779	Westland Wasp HAS1 [322/—]	RN No 829 Sqn, RNAS Portland	
XT780	Westland Wasp HAS1	RNAY Wroughton, store	
XT781	Westland Wasp HAS1 [444/GU]	RNAY Wroughton, store	
XT782	Westland Wasp HAS1 [324/NA]	RN No 829 Sqn, RNAS Portland	
XT783	Westland Wasp HAS1 [442/—]	RN No 829 Sqn, RNAS Portland	
XT784	Westland Wasp HAS1 [600/—]	RN No 829 Sqn, RNAS Portland	
XT785	Westland Wasp HAS1	RN No 829 Sqn, RNAS Portland	
XT786	Westland Wasp HAS1	RN No 829 Sqn, RNAS Portland	
XT787	Westland Wasp HAS1	RN No 829 Sqn, RNAS Portland	
XT788	Westland Wasp HAS1	RNAY Wroughton, store	
XT790	Westland Wasp HAS1 [603/—]	RN No 829 Sqn, RNAS Portland	
XT791	Westland Wasp HAS1	RN No 829 Sqn, RNAS Portland	
XT793	Westland Wasp HAS1 [440/—]	RN No 829 Sqn, RNAS Portland	
XT794	Westland Wasp HAS1	RN No 829 Sqn, RNAS Portland	
XT795	Westland Wasp HAS1 [373/—]	RN No 829 Sqn, RNAS Portland	
XT803	Westland Sioux AH1 [Y]	Privately owned, High Melton	
XT827	Westland Sioux AH1 [D]	Army Apprentice Coll Arborfield	
XT852	McD Phantom FGR2	MoD(PE) BAe Holme-on-Spalding Moor	
XT853	McD Phantom FGR2	MoD(PE) BAe Holme-on-Spalding Moor	
XT857	McD Phantom FG1 [C]	RAF Strike Command, 11 Group	
XT858	McD Phantom FG1	MoD(PE) BAe Brough (structures test)	
XT859	McD Phantom FG1 [K]	RAF Strike Command, 11 Group	
XT861	McD Phantom FG1	RAF Strike Command, 11 Group	
XT863	McD Phantom FG1	RAF Strike Command, 11 Group	
XT864	McD Phantom FG1 [J]	RAF Strike Command, 11 Group	
XT865	McD Phantom FG1	RAF Strike Command, 11 Group	
XT867	McD Phantom FG1 [H]	RAF Strike Command, 11 Group	
XT870	McD Phantom FG1	RAF Strike Command, 11 Group	
XT872	McD Phantom FG1	RAF Strike Command, 11 Group	
XT873	McD Phantom FG1	RAF Strike Command, 11 Group	
XT874	McD Phantom FG1 [E]	RAF Strike Command, 11 Group	
XT875	McD Phantom FG1 [K]	RAF Strike Command, 11 Group	
XT891	McD Phantom FGR2 [Z]	RAF Strike Command, 228 OCU	
XT892	McD Phantom FGR2 [V]	RAF Strike Command, 228 OCU	
XT893	McD Phantom FGR2	RAF Strike Command, 228 OCU	
XT894	McD Phantom FGR2 [P]	RAF Strike Command, 228 OCU	
XT895	McD Phantom FGR2 [T]	RAF Germany	
XT896	McD Phantom FGR2 [T]	RAF Strike Command, 11 Group	
XT897	McD Phantom FGR2 [M]	RAF Strike Command, 228 OCU	
XT898	McD Phantom FGR2 [E]	RAF Strike Command, 228 OCU	
XT899	McD Phantom FGR2 [X]	RAF Strike Command, 11 Group	
XT900	McD Phantom FGR2 [O]	RAF Strike Command, 228 OCU	
XT901	McD Phantom FGR2 [D]	RAF Strike Command, 228 OCU	
XT902	McD Phantom FGR2 [I]	RAF Strike Command, 228 OCU	
XT903	McD Phantom FGR2 [X]	RAF Strike Command, 11 Group	
XT905	McD Phantom FGR2 [L]	RAF Strike Command, 228 OCU	

Notes	Serial	Type (alternative identity)	Owner, Operator or Location
	XT906	McD Phantom FGR2 [S]	RAF Strike Command, 228 OCU
	XT907	McD Phantom FGR2 [T]	RAF Strike Command, 228 OCU
	XT908	McD Phantom FGR2 [Y]	RAF Strike Command, 11 Group
	XT909	McD Phantom FGR2 [M]	RAF Strike Command, 11 Group
	XT910	McD Phantom FGR2	RAF Strike Command, 228 OCU
	XT911	McD Phantom FGR2 [K]	RAF Germany
	XT914	McD Phantom FGR2	RAF Germany
	XV101	BAC VC10 C1	RAF Strike Command, No 10 Sqn
	XV102	BAC VC10 C1	RAF Strike Command, No 10 Sqn
	XV103	BAC VC10 C1	RAF Strike Command, No 10 Sqn
	XV104	BAC VC10 C1	RAF Strike Command, No 10 Sqn
	XV105	BAC VC10 C1	RAF Strike Command, No 10 Sqn
	XV106	BAC VC10 C1	RAF Strike Command, No 10 Sqn
	XV107	BAC VC10 C1	RAF Strike Command, No 10 Sqn
	XV108	BAC VC10 C1	RAF Strike Command, No 10 Sqn
	XV109	BAC VC10 C1	RAF Strike Command, No 10 Sqn
	XV118	Westland Scout AH1	AAC, RNAY Wroughton, store
	XV119	Westland Scout AH1	AAC, RNAY Wroughton, store
	XV121	Westland Scout AH1	AAC, RNAY Wroughton, store
	XV122	Westland Scout AH1	AAC, RNAY Wroughton, store
	XV123	Westland Scout AH1	AAC, RNAY Wroughton, store
	XV124	Westland Scout AH1	AAC, RNAY Wroughton, store
	XV125	Westland Scout AH1	RAF Fire School, Manston
	XV126	Westland Scout AH1	AAC, UK
	XV128	Westland Scout AH1	AAC, UK
	XV129	Westland Scout AH1	AAC, RNAY Wroughton, store
	XV130	Westland Scout AH1	AAC, UK
	XV131	Westland Scout AH1 [X]	AAC, Brunei
	XV134	Westland Scout AH1	AAC, RNAY Wroughton, store
	XV135	Westland Scout AH1	AAC, RNAY Wroughton, store
	XV136	Westland Scout AH1	AAC, RNAY Wroughton, store
	XV137	Westland Scout AH1	AAC, RNAY Wroughton, store
	XV138	Westland Scout AH1	AAC, UK
	XV139	Westland Scout AH1	AAC, RNAY Wroughton, store
	XV140	Westland Scout AH1	AAC, RNAY Wroughton, store
	XV141	Westland Scout AH1	AAC, RNAY Wroughton, store
	XV147	HS Nimrod MR1 (Mod)	MoD(PE) RAE Farnborough
	XV148	HS Nimrod MR1 (Mod)	MoD(PE) RAE/BAe Woodford
	XV152	HS Buccaneer S2A [A]	RAF St Athan, store
	XV154	HS Buccaneer S2A [A]	RAF Strike Command, 237 OCU
	XV155	HS Buccaneer S2B (8716M)	BAe Brough
	XV156	HS Buccaneer S2A	RAF St Athan, store
	XV157	HS Buccaneer S2B	RAF St Athan, store
	XV161	HS Buccaneer S2B	RAF Strike Command, 1 Group
	XV163	HS Buccaneer S2A [B]	RAF Strike Command, 237 OCU
	XV165	HS Buccaneer S2B	RAF Strike Command, 1 Group
	XV168	HS Buccaneer S2B	RAF Strike Command, 1 Group
	XV176	Lockheed Hercules C3	RAF Strike Command, 38 Group
	XV177	Lockheed Hercules C1	RAF Strike Command, 38 Group
	XV178	Lockheed Hercules C1	RAF Strike Command, 38 Group
	XV179	Lockheed Hercules C1	RAF Strike Command, 38 Group
	XV181	Lockheed Hercules C1	RAF Strike Command, 38 Group
	XV182	Lockheed Hercules C1	RAF Strike Command, 38 Group
	XV183	Lockheed Hercules C3	RAF Strike Command, 38 Group
	XV184	Lockheed Hercules C3	RAF Strike Command, 38 Group
	XV185	Lockheed Hercules C1	RAF Strike Command, 38 Group
	XV186	Lockheed Hercules C1	RAF Strike Command, 38 Group
	XV187	Lockheed Hercules C1	RAF Strike Command, 38 Group
	XV188	Lockheed Hercules C3	RAF Strike Command, 38 Group
	XV189	Lockheed Hercules C3	RAF Strike Command, 38 Group
	XV190	Lockheed Hercules C1	RAF Strike Command, 38 Group
	XV191	Lockheed Hercules C1	RAF Strike Command, 38 Group
	XV192	Lockheed Hercules K1	RAF Strike Command, 38 Group
	XV193	Lockheed Hercules C1	RAF Strike Command, 38 Group
	XV195	Lockheed Hercules C1	RAF Strike Command, 38 Group
	XV196	Lockheed Hercules C1	RAF Strike Command, 38 Group
	XV197	Lockheed Hercules C3	RAF Strike Command, 38 Group
	XV199	Lockheed Hercules C1	RAF Strike Command, 38 Group
	XV200	Lockheed Hercules C3	RAF Strike Command, 38 Group
	XV201	Lockheed Hercules K1	RAF Strike Command, 38 Group

XS731 HS Dominie T1. *APM*

XV178 Lockheed Hercules C1. *PRM*

Serial	Type (alternative identity)	Owner, Operator or Location	Notes
XV202	Lockheed Hercules C3	RAF Strike Command, 38 Group	
XV203	Lockheed Hercules C3	RAF Strike Command, 38 Group	
XV204	Lockheed Hercules K1	RAF Strike Command, 38 Group	
XV205	Lockheed Hercules C1	RAF Strike Command, 38 Group	
XV206	Lockheed Hercules C1	RAF Strike Command, 38 Group	
XV207	Lockheed Hercules C3	RAF Strike Command, 38 Group	
XV208	Lockheed Hercules W2	MoD(PE) RAE Farnborough	
XV209	Lockheed Hercules C1	RAF Strike Command, 38 Group	
XV210	Lockheed Hercules C1	RAF Strike Command, 38 Group	
XV211	Lockheed Hercules C1	RAF Strike Command, 38 Group	
XV212	Lockheed Hercules C3	RAF Strike Command, 38 Group	
XV213	Lockheed Hercules C1	RAF Strike Command, 38 Group	
XV214	Lockheed Hercules C1	RAF Strike Command, 38 Group	
XV215	Lockheed Hercules C1	RAF Strike Command, 38 Group	
XV217	Lockheed Hercules C1	RAF Strike Command, 38 Group	
XV218	Lockheed Hercules C1	RAF Strike Command, 38 Group	
XV219	Lockheed Hercules C3	RAF Strike Command, 38 Group	
XV220	Lockheed Hercules C3	RAF Strike Command, 38 Group	
XV221	Lockheed Hercules C3	RAF Strike Command, 38 Group	
XV222	Lockheed Hercules C1	RAF Strike Command, 38 Group	
XV223	Lockheed Hercules C3	RAF Strike Command, 38 Group	
XV226	HS Nimrod MR1	RAF Strike Command, 18 Group	
XV227	HS Nimrod MR2	RAF Strike Command, 18 Group	
XV228	HS Nimrod MR2	RAF Strike Command, 18 Group	
XV229	HS Nimrod MR2	RAF Strike Command, 18 Group	
XV230	HS Nimrod MR2	RAF Strike Command, 18 Group	
XV231	HS Nimrod MR1	RAF Strike Command, 18 Group	
XV232	HS Nimrod MR2	RAF Strike Command, 18 Group	
XV233	HS Nimrod MR1	RAF Strike Command, 18 Group	
XV234	HS Nimrod MR2	RAF Strike Command, 18 Group	
XV235	HS Nimrod MR1	RAF Strike Command, 18 Group	
XV236	HS Nimrod MR2	RAF Strike Command, 18 Group	
XV237	HS Nimrod MR2	RAF Strike Command, 18 Group	
XV238	HS Nimrod MR2	RAF Strike Command, 18 Group	
XV239	HS Nimrod MR2	RAF Strike Command, 18 Group	
XV240	HS Nimrod MR1	RAF Strike Command, 18 Group	
XV241	HS Nimrod MR2	RAF Strike Command, 18 Group	
XV242	HS Nimrod MR1	RAF Strike Command, 18 Group	
XV243	HS Nimrod MR2	RAF Strike Command, 18 Group	
XV244	HS Nimrod MR1	RAF Strike Command, 18 Group	
XV245	HS Nimrod MR1	RAF Strike Command, 18 Group	
XV246	HS Nimrod MR1	RAF Strike Command, 18 Group	
XV247	HS Nimrod MR1	RAF Strike Command, 18 Group	
XV248	HS Nimrod MR1	RAF Strike Command, 18 Group	
XV249	HS Nimrod MR1	RAF Strike Command, 18 Group	
XV250	HS Nimrod MR1	RAF Strike Command, 18 Group	
XV251	HS Nimrod MR1	RAF Strike Command, 18 Group	
XV252	HS Nimrod MR1	RAF Strike Command, 18 Group	
XV253	HS Nimrod MR2	RAF Strike Command, 18 Group	
XV254	HS Nimrod MR2	RAF Strike Command, 18 Group	
XV255	HS Nimrod MR2	RAF Strike Command, 18 Group	
XV257	HS Nimrod MR1	RAF Strike Command, 18 Group	
XV258	HS Nimrod MR1	RAF Strike Command, 18 Group	
XV259	BAe Nimrod AEW3	MoD(PE) BAe Woodford	
XV260	HS Nimrod MR1	RAF Strike Command, 18 Group	
XV261	BAe Nimrod AEW3	MoD(PE) BAe Woodford	
XV262	BAe Nimrod AEW3	MoD(PE) BAe Woodford	
XV263	BAe Nimrod AEW3	MoD(PE) BAe Woodford	
XV268	DHC Beaver AL1	AAC, stored at 5 MU Kemble	
XV269	DHC Beaver AL1 (8011M)	AAC, AETW Middle Wallop	
XV270	DHC Beaver AL1	AAC, Aldergrove	
XV271	DHC Beaver AL1	AAC, Aldergrove	
XV272	DHC Beaver AL1	AAC, Aldergrove	
XV277	HS Harrier GR1	MoD(PE) Rolls-Royce, Filton	
XV278	HS Harrier GR1	MoD(PE) Rolls-Royce, Filton	
XV279	HS Harrier GR1 (8566M)	RAF Wittering, ground instruction	
XV281	HS Harrier GR1	MoD(PE) A&AEE Boscombe Down	
XV290	Lockheed Hercules C3	RAF Strike Command, 38 Group	
XV291	Lockheed Hercules C1	RAF Strike Command, 38 Group	
XV292	Lockheed Hercules C1	RAF Strike Command, 38 Group	
XV293	Lockheed Hercules C1	RAF Strike Command, 38 Group	

Notes	Serial	Type (alternative identity)	Owner, Operator or Location
	XV294	Lockheed Hercules C3	RAF Strike Command, 38 Group
	XV295	Lockheed Hercules C1	RAF Strike Command, 38 Group
	XV296	Lockheed Hercules K1	RAF Strike Command, 38 Group
	XV297	Lockheed Hercules C1	RAF Strike Command, 38 Group
	XV298	Lockheed Hercules C1	RAF Strike Command, 38 Group
	XV299	Lockheed Hercules C1	RAF Strike Command, 38 Group
	XV300	Lockheed Hercules C1	RAF Strike Command, 38 Group
	XV301	Lockheed Hercules C1	RAF Strike Command, 38 Group
	XV302	Lockheed Hercules C1	RAF Strike Command, 38 Group
	XV303	Lockheed Hercules C3	RAF Strike Command, 38 Group
	XV304	Lockheed Hercules C1	RAF Strike Command, 38 Group
	XV305	Lockheed Hercules C3	RAF Strike Command, 38 Group
	XV306	Lockheed Hercules C1	RAF Strike Command, 38 Group
	XV307	Lockheed Hercules C3	RAF Strike Command, 38 Group
	XV328	EE Lightning T5 [DY]	RAF Strike Command, 11 Group, LTF
	XV332	HS Buccaneer S2B	RAF Strike Command, 1 Group
	XV333	HS Buccaneer S2B	RAF Strike Command, 1 Group
	XV334	HS Buccaneer S2B [D]	RAF St Athan, store
	XV336	HS Buccaneer S2A	RAF St Athan, store
	XV337	HS Buccaneer S2C	MoD(PE) A&AEE Boscombe Down
	XV338	HS Buccaneer S2A	RAF St Athan, store
	XV340	HS Buccaneer S2B (8659M) [F]	RAF Honington, ground instruction
	XV341	HS Buccaneer S2B [D]	RAF Germany
	XV342	HS Buccaneer S2B [W]	RAF Germany
	XV344	HS Buccaneer S2C	MoD(PE) RAE Farnborough
	XV349	HS Buccaneer S2B	RAF St Athan, store
	XV350	HS Buccaneer S2B	BAe Holme-on-Spalding Moor
	XV352	HS Buccaneer S2B	RAF Strike Command, 1 Group
	XV353	HS Buccaneer S2B	RAF Strike Command, 1 Group
	XV354	HS Buccaneer S2A	RAF St Athan, store
	XV355	HS Buccaneer S2A [I]	RAF Strike Command, 237 OCU
	XV356	HS Buccaneer S2A [B]	RAF St Athan, store
	XV357	HS Buccaneer S2A	RAF St Athan, store
	XV359	HS Buccaneer S2C	RAF Strike Command, 1 Group
	XV361	HS Buccaneer S2C [E]	RAF Germany
	XV370	Sikorsky SH-3D (G-ATYU)	MoD(PE) ETPS Boscombe Down
	XV371	Westland Sea King HAS1	MoD(PE) RAE Farnborough
	XV372	Westland Sea King HAS1	Westland Helicopters, Yeovil
	XV373	Westland Sea King HAS1	MoD(PE) A&AEE Boscombe Down
	XV393	McD Phantom FGR2 [A]	RAF Strike Command, 228 OCU
	XV394	McD Phantom FGR2 [C]	RAF Strike Command, 228 OCU
	XV396	McD Phantom FGR2	RAF Strike Command, 228 OCU
	XV398	McD Phantom FGR2 [H]	RAF Strike Command, 228 OCU
	XV399	McD Phantom FGR2 [L]	RAF Strike Command, 11 Group
	XV400	McD Phantom FGR2 [F]	RAF Germany
	XV401	McD Phantom FGR2 [B]	RAF Strike Command, 228 OCU
	XV402	McD Phantom FGR2 [G]	RAF Strike Command, 228 OCU
	XV404	McD Phantom FGR2 [B]	RAF Strike Command, 11 Group
	XV406	McD Phantom FGR2 [A]	RAF Strike Command, 11 Group
	XV407	McD Phantom FGR2 [O]	RAF Strike Command, 11 Group
	XV408	McD Phantom FGR2 [N]	RAF Strike Command, 11 Group
	XV409	McD Phantom FGR2	RAF Strike Command, 228 OCU
	XV410	McD Phantom FGR2 [E]	RAF Strike Command, 11 Group
	XV411	McD Phantom FGR2	RAF Germany
	XV412	McD Phantom FGR2 [F]	RAF Strike Command, 11 Group
	XV415	McD Phantom FGR2 [P]	RAF Germany
	XV419	McD Phantom FGR2	RAF Strike Command, 11 Group
	XV420	McD Phantom FGR2 [W]	RAF Strike Command, 11 Group
	XV421	McD Phantom FGR2 [Q]	RAF Strike Command, 228 OCU
	XV422	McD Phantom FGR2	RAF Strike Command, 11 Group
	XV423	McD Phantom FGR2 [D]	RAF Strike Command, 11 Group
	XV424	McD Phantom FGR2 [I]	RAF Strike Command, 11 Group
	XV425	McD Phantom FGR2 [D]	RAF Strike Command, 11 Group
	XV426	McD Phantom FGR2	RAF Strike Command, 228 OCU
	XV428	McD Phantom FGR2 [I]	RAF Strike Command, 11 Group
	XV429	McD Phantom FGR2 [K]	RAF Strike Command, 11 Group
	XV430	McD Phantom FGR2 [C]	RAF Germany
	XV432	McD Phantom FGR2	RAF Strike Command, 11 Group
	XV433	McD Phantom FGR2 [F]	RAF Strike Command, 228 OCU
	XV434	McD Phantom FGR2 [J]	RAF Strike Command, 228 OCU

XV234 HS Nimrod MR2. *PRM*

67

XV407 McD Phantom FGR2. *APM*

Serial	Type (alternative identity)	Owner, Operator or Location	Notes
XV435	McD Phantom FGR2 [X]	RAF Germany	
XV437	McD Phantom FGR2	RAF Strike Command, 11 Group	
XV438	McD Phantom FGR2 [Y]	RAF Strike Command, 228 OCU	
XV439	McD Phantom FGR2 [D]	RAF Germany	
XV442	McD Phantom FGR2 [H]	RAF Strike Command, 11 Group	
XV460	McD Phantom FGR2 [W]	RAF Germany	
XV461	McD Phantom FGR2 [G]	RAF Strike Command, 11 Group	
XV462	McD Phantom FGR2 [U]	RAF Germany	
XV464	McD Phantom FGR2 [U]	RAF Strike Command, 228 OCU	
XV465	McD Phantom FGR2 [Z]	RAF Germany	
XV466	McD Phantom FGR2 [E]	RAF Strike Command, 11 Group	
XV467	McD Phantom FGR2 [Q]	RAF Germany	
XV468	McD Phantom FGR2	RAF Strike Command, Falkland-Det	
XV469	McD Phantom FGR2 [T]	RAF Strike Command, 11 Group	
XV470	McD Phantom FGR2 [W]	RAF Strike Command, 228 OCU	
XV471	McD Phantom FGR2 [V]	RAF Germany	
XV472	McD Phantom FGR2 [E]	RAF Germany	
XV473	McD Phantom FGR2 [L]	RAF Strike Command, 228 OCU	
XV474	McD Phantom FGR2	RAF Strike Command, 11 Group	
XV475	McD Phantom FGR2 [S]	RAF Germany	
XV476	McD Phantom FGR2 [L]	RAF Germany	
XV478	McD Phantom FGR2 [Q]	RAF Strike Command, 11 Group	
XV480	McD Phantom FGR2 [B]	RAF Germany	
XV481	McD Phantom FGR2 [G]	RAF Germany	
XV482	McD Phantom FGR2 [C]	RAF Strike Command, 11 Group	
XV484	McD Phantom FGR2 [C]	RAF Strike Command, 11 Group	
XV485	McD Phantom FGR2 [P]	RAF Strike Command, 11 Group	
XV486	McD Phantom FGR2 [X]	RAF Strike Command, 228 OCU	
XV487	McD Phantom FGR2	RAF Strike Command, 11 Group	
XV488	McD Phantom FGR2 [R]	RAF Strike Command, 228 OCU	
XV489	McD Phantom FGR2 [A]	RAF Strike Command, 11 Group	
XV490	McD Phantom FGR2 [H]	RAF Strike Command, 11 Group	
XV492	McD Phantom FGR2 [U]	RAF Strike Command, 11 Group	
XV494	McD Phantom FGR2 [M]	RAF Strike Command, 11 Group	
XV495	McD Phantom FGR2 [N]	RAF Strike Command, 11 Group	
XV496	McD Phantom FGR2 [J]	RAF Germany	
XV497	McD Phantom FGR2 [A]	RAF Germany	
XV498	McD Phantom FGR2	RAF Germany	
XV499	McD Phantom FGR2 [R]	RAF Strike Command, 228 OCU	
XV500	McD Phantom FGR2 [S]	RAF Strike Command, 11 Group	
XV501	McD Phantom FGR2 [T]	RAF Strike Command, 11 Group	
XV567	McD Phantom FG1	RAF Strike Command, 11 Group	
XV568	McD Phantom FG1 [T]	RAF Strike Command, 11 Group	
XV569	McD Phantom FG1 [Q]	RAF Strike Command, 11 Group	
XV570	McD Phantom FG1 [N]	RAF Strike Command, 11 Group	
XV571	McD Phantom FG1 [A]	RAF Strike Command, 11 Group	
XV572	McD Phantom FG1 [N]	RAF Strike Command, 11 Group	
XV573	McD Phantom FG1 [D]	RAF Strike Command, 11 Group	
XV574	McD Phantom FG1 [Z]	RAF Strike Command, 11 Group	
XV575	McD Phantom FG1 [S]	RAF Strike Command, 11 Group	
XV576	McD Phantom FG1 [D]	RAF Strike Command, 11 Group	
XV577	McD Phantom FG1 [M]	RAF Strike Command, 11 Group	
XV579	McD Phantom FG1 [R]	RAF Strike Command, 11 Group	
XV581	McD Phantom FG1 [E]	RAF Strike Command, 11 Group	
XV582	McD Phantom FG1 [F]	RAF Strike Command, 11 Group	
XV583	McD Phantom FG1 [B]	RAF Strike Command, 11 Group	
XV584	McD Phantom FG1 [F]	RAF Strike Command, 11 Group	
XV585	McD Phantom FG1 [P]	RAF Strike Command, 11 Group	
XV586	McD Phantom FG1	RAF Strike Command, 11 Group	
XV587	McD Phantom FG1 [G]	RAF Strike Command, 11 Group	
XV590	McD Phantom FG1 [X]	RAF Strike Command, 11 Group	
XV591	McD Phantom FG1 [M]	RAF Strike Command, 11 Group	
XV592	McD Phantom FG1 [L]	RAF Strike Command, 11 Group	
XV615	BHC SR.N6 Winchester 2	RN Hong Kong	
XV622	Westland Wasp HAS1 [634/—]	RNAY Wroughton, store	
XV623	Westland Wasp HAS1 [601/—]	RN No 829 Sqn, RNAS Portland	
XV624	Westland Wasp HAS1 [456/—]	RN No 829 Sqn, RNAS Portland	
XV625	Westland Wasp HAS1 [471/PB]	RNEC Manadon, for instruction	

Notes	Serial	Type (alternative identity)	Owner, Operator or Location
	XV626	Westland Wasp HAS1 [601/—]	RN No 829 Sqn, RNAS Portland
	XV627	Westland Wasp HAS1	RNAY Wroughton, store
	XV629	Westland Wasp HAS1	RNAY Wroughton, store
	XV631	Westland Wasp HAS1 [617/—]	RNAY Wroughton, store
	XV632	Westland Wasp HAS1	RNAY Wroughton, store
	XV634	Westland Wasp HAS1 [423/—]	RN No 829 Sqn, RNAS Portland
	XV636	Westland Wasp HAS1 [607/—]	RN No 829 Sqn, RNAS Portland
	XV638	Westland Wasp HAS1 [430/AC]	RN No 829 Sqn, RNAS Portland
	XV639	Westland Wasp HAS1 [612/—]	RN No 829 Sqn, RNAS Portland
	XV642	Westland Sea King HAS2A	MoD(PE) A&AEE Boscombe Down
	XV643	Westland Sea King HAS2A [705/PW]	RN No 819 Sqn, Prestwick
	XV644	Westland Sea King HAS1 (A2664)	RN AES Lee-on-Solent
	XV647	Westland Sea King HAS5 [147/H]	RN No 826 Sqn, RNAS Culdrose
	XV648	Westland Sea King HAS2A [597/—]	RN No 825 Sqn, RNAS Culdrose
	XV649	Westland Sea King HAS2A [355/CU]	RN No 824 Sqn, RNAS Culdrose
	XV650	Westland Sea King AEW5 [588/L]	RN No 824 Sqn, RNAS Culdrose
	XV651	Westland Sea King HAS5 [266/—]	RN No 814 Sqn, RNAS Culdrose
	XV652	Westland Sea King HAS5 [270/—]	RN No 814 Sqn, RNAS Culdrose
	XV653	Westland Sea King HAS2A [598/CU]	RN No 706 Sqn, RNAS Culdrose
	XV654	Westland Sea King HAS2A [585/—]	RN No 825 Sqn, RNAS Culdrose
	XV655	Westland Sea King HAS5 [265/—]	RN No 814 Sqn, RNAS Culdrose
	XV656	Westland Sea King HAS2A	RN No 825 Sqn, RNAS Culdrose
	XV657	Westland Sea King HAS2A [350/CU]	RN No 824 Sqn, RNAS Culdrose
	XV658	Westland Sea King HAS5	RN No 706 Sqn, RNAS Culdrose
	XV659	Westland Sea King HAS2A [584/—]	RN No 825 Sqn, RNAS Culdrose
	XV660	Westland Sea King HAS2A	RN NASU RNAS Culdrose
	XV661	Westland Sea King HAS5 [274/—]	RN No 814 Sqn, RNAS Culdrose
	XV663	Westland Sea King HAS2A [581/—]	RN No 825 Sqn, RNAS Culdrose
	XV664	Westland Sea King HAS2A [704/PW]	RN No 819 Sqn, Prestwick
	XV665	Westland Sea King HAS2A [535/—]	RNAY Fleetlands, on rebuild
	XV666	Westland Sea King HAS2A [591/CU]	RN No 706 Sqn, RNAS Culdrose
	XV668	Westland Sea King HAS2A [592/CU]	RN No 706 Sqn, RNAS Culdrose
	XV669	Westland Sea King HAS1 (A2659) [410/BL]	RNAS Culdrose Engineering Training School
	XV670	Westland Sea King HAS2A [590/CU]	RN No 706 Sqn, RNAS Culdrose
	XV671	Westland Sea King HAS2A [597/CU]	RN No 706 Sqn, RNAS Culdrose
	XV672	Westland Sea King HAS2A [145/H]	RN No 826 Sqn, RNAS Culdrose
	XV673	Westland Sea King HAS2A [583/CU]	RN No 706 Sqn, RNAS Culdrose
	XV674	Westland Sea King HAS2A [706/PW]	RN No 819 Sqn, Prestwick
	XV675	Westland Sea King HAS5 [264/—]	RN No 814 Sqn, RNAS Culdrose
	XV676	Westland Sea King HAS2A [587/CU]	RN No 706 Sqn, RNAS Culdrose

Serial	Type (alternative identity)	Owner, Operator or Location	Notes
XV677	Westland Sea King HAS2A [595/—]	RN No 706 Sqn, RNAS Culdrose	
XV696	Westland Sea King HAS2A [268/—]	RN No 825 Sqn, RNAS Culdrose	
XV697	Westland Sea King HAS2A [354/CU]	RN No 824 Sqn, RNAS Culdrose	
XV699	Westland Sea King HAS5 [143/H]	RN No 826 Sqn, RNAS Culdrose	
XV700	Westland Sea King HAS2A [264/—]	RN No 825 Sqn, RNAS Culdrose	
XV701	Westland Sea King HAS2A [589/—]	RN No 706 Sqn, RNAS Culdrose	
XV703	Westland Sea King HAS5 [596/CU]	RN No 706 Sqn, RNAS Culdrose	
XV704	Westland Sea King HAS AEW5	RN No 824 Sqn, RNAS Culdrose	
XV705	Westland Sea King HAS2A [703/—]	RN No 819 Sqn, Prestwick	
XV706	Westland Sea King HAS5 [594/CU]	RN No 706 Sqn, RNAS Culdrose	
XV707	Westland Sea King HAS2A [707/PW]	RN No 819 Sqn, Prestwick	
XV708	Westland Sea King HAS2A [702/PW]	RN No 819 Sqn, Prestwick	
XV709	Westland Sea King HAS2A [144/H]	RN No 826 Sqn, RNAS Culdrose	
XV710	Westland Sea King HAS2A [701/PW]	RN No 819 Sqn, Prestwick	
XV711	Westland Sea King HAS5 [581/—]	RN No 706 Sqn, RNAS Culdrose	
XV712	Westland Sea King HAS5 [591/CU]	RN No 706 Sqn, RNAS Culdrose	
XV713	Westland Sea King HAS5 [267/H]	RN No 814 Sqn, RNAS Culdrose	
XV714	Westland Sea King HAS2A [586/—]	RN No 825 Sqn, RNAS Culdrose	
XV719	Westland Wessex HC2	RAF Strike Command, No 84 Sqn	
XV720	Westland Wessex HAR	RAF Strike Command, No 22 Sqn	
XV721	Westland Wessex HC2	RAF Strike Command, No 84 Sqn	
XV722	Westland Wessex HC2 [BH]	RAF Strike Command, WCF Benson	
XV723	Westland Wessex HC2 [Q]	RAF Strike Command, No 72 Sqn	
XV724	Westland Wessex HAR	RAF Strike Command, No 22 Sqn	
XV725	Westland Wessex HC2 [C]	RAF Strike Command, No 72 Sqn	
XV726	Westland Wessex HC2 [J]	RAF Strike Command, No 72 Sqn	
XV728	Westland Wessex HC2 [A]	RAF Strike Command, No 72 Sqn	
XV729	Westland Wessex HAR	RAF Strike Command, No 22 Sqn	
XV730	Westland Wessex HAR	RAF Strike Command, No 22 Sqn	
XV731	Westland Wessex HC2 [BX]	RAF Strike Command, WCF Benson	
XV732	Westland Wessex HCC4	RAF Queens Flight, Benson	
XV733	Westland Wessex HCC4	RAF Queens Flight, Benson	
XV738	HS Harrier GR3 [AB]	RAF Germany	
XV740	HS Harrier GR3 [A]	RAF Germany	
XV741	HS Harrier GR3 [AA]	RAF Germany	
XV742	HS Harrier GR3 (G-VSTO) [11]	RAF Strike Command, No 1 Sqn	
XV744	HS Harrier GR3 [D]	RAF Strike Command, 233 OCU	
XV747	HS Harrier GR3 [G]	RAF Germany	
XV748	HS Harrier GR3 [B]	RAF Strike Command, 233 OCU	
XV751	HS Harrier GR3 [08]	RAF Strike Command, No 1 Sqn	
XV752	HS Harrier GR3 [04]	RAF Strike Command, No 1 Sqn	
XV753	HS Harrier GR3 [M]	RAF Strike Command, 233 OCU	
XV755	HS Harrier GR3 [20]	RAF Strike Command, No 1 Sqn	
XV758	HS Harrier GR3 [AV]	RAF Germany	
XV759	HS Harrier GR3 [E]	RAF Strike Command, 233 OCU	
XV760	HS Harrier GR3 [F]	RAF Strike Command, 233 OCU	
XV762	HS Harrier GR3 [37]	RAF Strike Command, No 1 Sqn	
XV778	HS Harrier GR3 [16]	RAF Strike Command, No 1 Sqn	
XV779	HS Harrier GR3 [AP]	RAF Germany	
XV782	HS Harrier GR3 [C]	RAF Germany	
XV783	HS Harrier GR3 [O]	RAF Strike Command, 1417 Flt	
XV784	HS Harrier GR3 [D]	RAF Germany	
XV786	HS Harrier GR3 [V]	RAF Germany	

Notes	Serial	Type (alternative identity)	Owner, Operator or Location
	XV787	HS Harrier GR3 [02]	RAF Strike Command, No 1 Sqn
	XV789	HS Harrier GR3	RAF Strike Command, No 1 Sqn
	XV790	HS Harrier GR3 [S]	RAF Germany
	XV793	HS Harrier GR3 [L]	RAF Germany
	XV795	HS Harrier GR3 [AF]	RAF Germany
	XV804	HS Harrier GR3 [O]	RAF Strike Command, 233 OCU
	XV806	HS Harrier GR3 [B]	RAF Germany
	XV808	HS Harrier GR3 [AW]	RAF Germany
	XV809	HS Harrier GR3 [J]	RAF Germany
	XV810	HS Harrier GR3 [X]	RAF Germany
	XV814	HS Comet 4C (G-APDF)	MoD(PE) RAE Farnborough
	XV859	BHC SR.N6 Winchester 6	RN NHTU Lee-on-Solent
	XV863	HS Buccaneer S2B [U]	RAF Germany
	XV864	HS Buccaneer S2B [S]	RAF Germany
	XV865	HS Buccaneer S2B	RAF Strike Command, 1 Group
	XV866	HS Buccaneer S2B [Y]	RAF St Athan, store
	XV867	HS Buccaneer S2B [K]	RAF Strike Command, 237 OCU
	XV868	HS Buccaneer S2B	RAF Strike Command, 1 Group
	XV869	HS Buccaneer S2B	RAF Strike Command, 1 Group
	XW175	HS Harrier T4	MoD(PE) RAE Bedford
	XW179	Westland Sioux AH1	AAC, RNAY Wroughton, store
	XW198	Westland Puma HC1 [DL]	RAF Germany, No 230 Sqn
	XW199	Westland Puma HC1 [DU]	RAF Germany, No 230 Sqn
	XW200	Westland Puma HC1 [FA]	RAF Strike Command, 240 OCU
	XW201	Westland Puma HC1 [FB]	RAF Strike Command, 240 OCU
	XW202	Westland Puma HC1 [FC]	RAF Strike Command, 240 OCU
	XW204	Westland Puma HC1 [CA]	RAF Strike Command, No 33 Sqn
	XW206	Westland Puma HC1 [CC]	RAF Strike Command, No 33 Sqn
	XW207	Westland Puma HC1 [CD]	RAF Strike Command, No 33 Sqn
	XW208	Westland Puma HC1 [CE]	RAF Strike Command, No 33 Sqn
	XW209	Westland Puma HC1 (F-YEFA) [CF]	RAF Strike Command, No 33 Sqn
	XW210	Westland Puma HC1 [CG]	RAF Strike Command, No 33 Sqn
	XW211	Westland Puma HC1 [CH]	RAF Strike Command, No 33 Sqn
	XW212	Westland Puma HC1 [FD]	RAF Strike Command, 240 OCU
	XW213	Westland Puma HC1 [CJ]	RAF Strike Command, No 33 Sqn
	XW214	Westland Puma HC1 [CK]	RAF Strike Command, No 33 Sqn
	XW215	Westland Puma HC1 [DM]	RAF Germany, No 230 Sqn
	XW216	Westland Puma HC1 [CL]	RAF Strike Command, No 33 Sqn
	XW217	Westland Puma HC1 [DA]	RAF Germany, No 230 Sqn
	XW218	Westland Puma HC1 [DT]	RAF Germany, No 230 Sqn
	XW219	Westland Puma HC1 [DC]	RAF Germany, No 230 Sqn
	XW220	Westland Puma HC1 [DD]	RAF Germany, No 230 Sqn
	XW221	Westland Puma HC1 [DE]	RAF Germany, No 230 Sqn
	XW222	Westland Puma HC1 [DF]	RAF Germany, No 230 Sqn
	XW223	Westland Puma HC1 [DG]	RAF Germany, No 230 Sqn
	XW224	Westland Puma HC1 [DH]	RAF Germany, No 230 Sqn
	XW225	Westland Puma HC1 [FE]	RAF Strike Command, 240 OCU
	XW226	Westland Puma HC1 [DK]	RAF Germany, No 230 Sqn
	XW227	Westland Puma HC1 [DN]	RAF Germany, No 230 Sqn
	XW229	Westland Puma HC1 [DB]	RAF Germany, No 230 Sqn
	XW231	Westland Puma HC1 [CM]	RAF Strike Command, No 33 Sqn
	XW232	Westland Puma HC1	RAF Germany, No 230 Sqn
	XW233	Westland Puma HC1 [CN]	RAF Strike Command, No 33 Sqn
	XW234	Westland Puma HC1 [CO]	RAF Strike Command, No 33 Sqn
	XW235	Westland Puma HC1 [CP]	RAF Strike Command, No 33 Sqn
	XW236	Westland Puma HC1 [CQ]	RAF Strike Command, No 33 Sqn
	XW237	Westland Puma HC1 [CR]	RAF Strike Command, No 33 Sqn
	XW241	Aerospatiale SA330 (F-ZJUX)	MoD(PE) RAE Bedford
	XW249	Cushioncraft CC7	Cornwall Aero Park, Helston
	XW255	BHC BH-7 Wellington	RN NHTU Lee-on-Solent
	XW265	HS Harrier T4	MoD(PE) BAe Holme-on-Spalding Moor
	XW266	HS Harrier T4 [S]	RAF Strike Command, 233 OCU
	XW267	HS Harrier T4 [T]	RAF Strike Command, 233 OCU
	XW268	HS Harrier T4 [U]	RAF Strike Command, 233 OCU
	XW269	HS Harrier T4 [06]	RAF Strike Command, No 1 Sqn
	XW270	HS Harrier T4 [V]	RAF Strike Command, 233 OCU
	XW271	HS Harrier T4 [R]	RAF Strike Command, 233 OCU
	XW276	Aerospatiale SA341 (F-ZWRI)	Museum of Army Flying, Andover store
	XW280	Westland Scout AH1	AAC, UK
	XW281	Westland Scout AH1	AAC, RNAY Wroughton, store

Serial	Type (alternative identity)	Owner, Operator or Location	Notes
XW282	Westland Scout AH1	AAC, RNAY Wroughton, store	
XW283	Westland Scout AH1	AAC, RNAY Wroughton, store	
XW284	Westland Scout AH1 [A]	AAC, RNAY Wroughton store	
XW287	BAC Jet Provost T5 [P]	RAF Support Command, 6 FTS	
XW289	BAC Jet Provost T5A [31]	RAF Support Command, RAFC	
XW290	BAC Jet Provost T5A [41]	RAF Support Command, RAFC	
XW291	BAC Jet Provost T5 [N]	RAF Support Command, 6 FTS	
XW292	BAC Jet Provost T5A [32]	RAF Support Command, RAFC	
XW293	BAC Jet Provost T5 [Z]	RAF Support Command, 6 FTS	
XW294	BAC Jet Provost T5A [45]	RAF Support Command, RAFC	
XW295	BAC Jet Provost T5A [67]	RAF Support Command, 1FTS	
XW296	BAC Jet Provost T5 [Q]	RAF Support Command, 6 FTS	
XW298	BAC Jet Provost T5 [O]	RAF Support Command, 6 FTS	
XW299	BAC Jet Provost T5A [40]	RAF Support Command, RAFC	
XW301	BAC Jet Provost T5A [63]	RAF Support Command, 1 FTS	
XW302	BAC Jet Provost T5 [T]	RAF Support Command, 6 FTS	
XW303	BAC Jet Provost T5A [127]	RAF Support Command, 7 FTS	
XW304	BAC Jet Provost T5 [X]	RAF Support Command, 6 FTS	
XW305	BAC Jet Provost T5A [42]	RAF Support Command, RAFC	
XW306	BAC Jet Provost T5 [Y]	RAF Support Command, 6 FTS	
XW307	BAC Jet Provost T5 [S]	RAF Support Command, 6 FTS	
XW309	BAC Jet Provost T5 [V]	RAF Support Command, 6 FTS	
XW310	BAC Jet Provost T5A	RAF Support Command, RAFC	
XW311	BAC Jet Provost T5 [W]	RAF Support Command, 6 FTS	
XW312	BAC Jet Provost T5A [64]	RAF Support Command, 1 FTS	
XW313	BAC Jet Provost T5A [30]	RAF Support Command, RAFC	
XW315	BAC Jet Provost T5A [63]	RAF Support Command, 3FTS/CFS	
XW316	BAC Jet Provost T5A [64]	RAF Support Command, 3 FTS/CFS	
XW317	BAC Jet Provost T5A [25]	RAF Support Command, RAFC	
XW318	BAC Jet Provost T5A [12]	RAF Support Command, RAFC	
XW319	BAC Jet Provost T5A [67]	RAF Support Command, 3 FTS/CFS	
XW320	BAC Jet Provost T5A [71]	RAF Support Command, 1 FTS	
XW321	BAC Jet Provost T5A [29]	RAF Support Command, RAFC	
XW322	BAC Jet Provost T5A [43]	RAF Support Command, RAFC	
XW323	BAC Jet Provost T5A [44]	RAF Support Command, RAFC	
XW324	BAC Jet Provost T5 [U]	RAF Support Command, 6 FTS	
XW325	BAC Jet Provost T5A	RAF Support Command, RAFC	
XW326	BAC Jet Provost T5A [120]	RAF Support Command, 7 FTS	
XW327	BAC Jet Provost T5A [62]	RAF Support Command, 1 FTS	
XW328	BAC Jet Provost T5A [22]	RAF Support Command, RAFC	
XW329	BAC Jet Provost T5A [48]	RAF Church Fenton, Fire Section	
XW330	BAC Jet Provost T5A [65]	RAF Support Command, 3 FTS/CFS	
XW332	BAC Jet Provost T5A [34]	RAF Support Command, RAFC	
XW333	BAC Jet Provost T5A [36]	RAF Support Command, RAFC	
XW334	BAC Jet Provost T5A [39]	RAF Support Command, RAFC	
XW335	BAC Jet Provost T5A [27]	RAF Support Command, RAFC	
XW336	BAC Jet Provost T5A [6]	RAF Support Command, RAFC	
XW351	BAC Jet Provost T5A [74]	RAF Support Command, 1 FTS	
XW352	BAC Jet Provost T5 [R]	RAF Support Command, 6 FTS	
XW353	BAC Jet Provost T5A [51]	RAF Support Command, 3 FTS/CFS	
XW354	BAC Jet Provost T5A [7]	RAF Support Command, RAFC	
XW355	BAC Jet Provost T5A [20]	RAF Support Command, RAFC	
XW357	BAC Jet Provost T5A [5]	RAF Support Command, RAFC	
XW358	BAC Jet Provost T5A [18]	RAF Support Command, RAFC	
XW359	BAC Jet Provost T5A [128]	RAF Support Command, 7 FTS	
XW360	BAC Jet Provost T5A [129]	RAF Support Command, 7 FTS	
XW361	BAC Jet Provost T5A [21]	RAF Support Command, RAFC	
XW362	BAC Jet Provost T5A [17]	RAF Support Command, RAFC	
XW363	BAC Jet Provost T5A [68]	RAF Support Command, 1 FTS	
XW364	BAC Jet Provost T5A [35]	RAF Support Command, RAFC	
XW365	BAC Jet Provost T5A [73]	RAF Support Command, 1 FTS	
XW366	BAC Jet Provost T5A [75]	RAF Support Command, 1 FTS	
XW367	BAC Jet Provost T5A [26]	RAF Support Command, RAFC	
XW368	BAC Jet Provost T5A [66]	RAF Support Command, 3 FTS/CFS	
XW369	BAC Jet Provost T5A [9]	RAF Support Command, RAFC	
XW370	BAC Jet Provost T5A [72]	RAF Support Command, 1 FTS	
XW372	BAC Jet Provost T5A [121]	RAF Support Command, 7 FTS	
XW373	BAC Jet Provost T5A [11]	RAF Support Command, RAFC	
XW374	BAC Jet Provost T5A [38]	RAF Support Command, RAFC	
XW375	BAC Jet Provost T5A [10]	RAF Support Command, RAFC	
XW404	BAC Jet Provost T5A [77]	RAF Support Command, 1 FTS	

Notes	Serial	Type (alternative identity)	Owner, Operator or Location
	XW405	BAC Jet Provost T5A [61]	RAF Support Command, 1 FTS
	XW406	BAC Jet Provost T5A [23]	RAF Support Command, RAFC
	XW407	BAC Jet Provost T5A [122]	RAF Support Command, 7 FTS
	XW408	BAC Jet Provost T5A [24]	RAF Support Command, RAFC
	XW409	BAC Jet Provost T5A [123]	RAF Support Command, 7 FTS
	XW410	BAC Jet Provost T5A [14]	RAF Support Command, RAFC
	XW411	BAC Jet Provost T5A [16]	RAF Support Command, RAFC
	XW412	BAC Jet Provost T5A [15]	RAF Support Command, RAFC
	XW413	BAC Jet Provost T5A [69]	RAF Support Command, 1 FTS
	XW415	BAC Jet Provost T5A [53]	RAF Support Command, 3 FTS/CFS
	XW416	BAC Jet Provost T5A [19]	RAF Support Command, RAFC
	XW417	BAC Jet Provost T5A [124]	RAF Support Command, 7 FTS
	XW418	BAC Jet Provost T5A [54]	RAF Support Command, 3 FTS/CFS
	XW419	BAC Jet Provost T5A [125]	RAF Support Command, 7 FTS
	XW420	BAC Jet Provost T5A [8]	RAF Support Command, RAFC
	XW421	BAC Jet Provost T5A [68]	RAF Support Command, 3 FTS/CFS
	XW422	BAC Jet Provost T5A [3]	RAF Support Command, RAFC
	XW423	BAC Jet Provost T5A [78]	RAF Support Command, 1 FTS
	XW424	BAC Jet Provost T5A [62]	Privately owned, Misson, Notts
	XW425	BAC Jet Provost T5A [69]	RAF Support Command, 3 FTS/CFS
	XW427	BAC Jet Provost T5A [56]	RAF Support Command, 3 FTS/CFS
	XW428	BAC Jet Provost T5A [70]	RAF Support Command, 1 FTS
	XW429	BAC Jet Provost T5A [28]	RAF Support Command, RAFC
	XW430	BAC Jet Provost T5A [58]	RAF Support Command, 3 FTS/CFS
	XW431	BAC Jet Provost T5A [59]	RAF Support Command, 3 FTS/CFS
	XW432	BAC Jet Provost T5A [76]	RAF Support Command, 1 FTS
	XW433	BAC Jet Provost T5A [61]	RAF Support Command, 3 FTS/CFS
	XW434	BAC Jet Provost T5A [126]	RAF Support Command, 7 FTS
	XW435	BAC Jet Provost T5A [4]	RAF Support Command, RAFC
	XW436	BAC Jet Provost T5A [62]	RAF Support Command, 3 FTS/CFS
	XW437	BAC Jet Provost T5A [1]	RAF Support Command, RAFC
	XW438	BAC Jet Provost T5A [2]	RAF Support Command, RAFC
	XW527	HS Buccaneer S2B	RAF Strike Command, 1 Group
	XW528	HS Buccaneer S2B [C]	RAF St Athan, store
	XW529	HS Buccaneer S2B	MoD(PE) A&AEE Boscombe Down
	XW530	HS Buccaneer S2B	RAF Strike Command, 1 Group
	XW533	HS Buccaneer S2B [K]	RAF Germany
	XW534	HS Buccaneer S2B [Z]	RAF Germany
	XW538	HS Buccaneer S2B (8660M) [T]	RAF Lossiemouth, Fire Section
	XW540	HS Buccaneer S2B	RAF Strike Command, 1 Group
	XW541	HS Buccaneer S2B	RAF St Athan, store
	XW542	HS Buccaneer S2B	RAF Strike Command, 1 Group
	XW543	HS Buccaneer S2B [Y]	RAF Germany
	XW544	HS Buccaneer S2B [O]	RAF Germany
	XW545	HS Buccaneer S2B [L]	RAF St Athan, store
	XW546	HS Buccaneer S2B [L]	RAF Germany
	XW547	HS Buccaneer S2B	RAF Strike Command, 1 Group
	XW549	HS Buccaneer S2B	RAF St Athan, store
	XW550	HS Buccaneer S2B [X]	RAF St Athan, store
	XW566	SEPECAT Jaguar T2	MoD(PE) RAE Farnborough
	XW612	Westland Scout AH1	AAC, BAOR
	XW613	Westland Scout AH1 [V]	AAC, RCS Middle Wallop
	XW614	Westland Scout AH1	AAC, UK
	XW615	Westland Scout AH1	AAC, UK
	XW616	Westland Scout AH1	Royal Marines, 3 CBAS
	XW626	HS Comet 4AEW (G-APDS)	MoD(PE) RAE Bedford
	XW630	HS Harrier GR3 [AG]	RAF Germany
	XW635	Beagle D5/180 (G-AWSW)	RAF Support Command, 5 AEF
	XW664	HS Nimrod R1	RAF Strike Command, No 51 Sqn
	XW665	HS Nimrod R1	RAF Strike Command, No 51 Sqn
	XW666	HS Nimrod R1	RAF Strike Command, No 51 Sqn
	XW750	HS748 Series 107 (G-ASJT)	MoD(PE) RAE Bedford
	XW763	HS Harrier GR3 [N]	RAF Germany
	XW764	HS Harrier GR3 [AC]	RAF Germany
	XW767	HS Harrier GR3 [06]	RAF Strike Command, No 1 Sqn
	XW768	HS Harrier GR3 [O]	RAF Germany
	XW769	HS Harrier GR3 [24]	RAF Strike Command, No 1 Sqn
	XW788	HS125 CC1	RAF Northolt, No 32 Sqn
	XW789	HS125 CC1	RAF Northolt, No 32 Sqn
	XW790	HS125 CC1	RAF Northolt, No 32 Sqn

Serial	Type (alternative identity)	Owner, Operator or Location	Notes
XW791	HS125 CC1	RAF Northolt, No 32 Sqn	
XW795	Westland Scout AH1	AAC, RNAY Wroughton, store	
XW796	Westland Scout AH1 [W]	AAC, Hong Kong	
XW797	Westland Scout AH1	AAC, RNAY Wroughton, store	
XW798	Westland Scout AH1 [H]	AAC, RNAY Wroughton, store	
XW799	Westland Scout AH1	AAC, UK	
XW836	Westland Lynx	Westland store, Sherborne	
XW837	Westland Lynx	MoD(PE) A&AEE Boscombe Down	
XW838	Westland Lynx	AAC, AETW, Middle Wallop	
XW839	Westland Lynx	Rolls-Royce, Filton	
XW842	Westland Gazelle AH1	AAC, AETW, Middle Wallop	
XW843	Westland Gazelle AH1	AAC, UK	
XW844	Westland Gazelle AH1 (F-ZKCW)	AAC, BAOR	
XW845	Westland Gazelle HT2	RNAY Wroughton, store	
XW846	Westland Gazelle AH1	MoD(PE) A&AEE Boscombe Down	
XW847	Westland Gazelle AH1	AAC Dem & Trials Sqn, Middle Wallop	
XW848	Westland Gazelle AH1	AAC, AETW, Middle Wallop	
XW849	Westland Gazelle AH1	AAC, UK	
XW851	Westland Gazelle AH1	AAC, Andover	
XW852	Westland Gazelle HT3	RAF Northolt, No 32 Sqn	
XW853	Westland Gazelle HT2	RNAY Wroughton, store	
XW854	Westland Gazelle HT2 [546/CU]	RN No 705 Sqn, RNAS Culdrose	
XW855	Westland Gazelle HCC4	RAF Northolt, No 32 Sqn	
XW856	Westland Gazelle HT2 [547/CU]	RN No 705 Sqn, RNAS Culdrose	
XW857	Westland Gazelle HT2 [555/CU]	RN No 705 Sqn, RNAS Culdrose	
XW858	Westland Gazelle HT3	RAF Support Command, CFS	
XW859	Westland Gazelle HT2	RN No 705 Sqn, RNAS Culdrose	
XW860	Westland Gazelle HT2 [544/CU]	RN No 705 Sqn, RNAS Culdrose	
XW861	Westland Gazelle HT2 [559/CU]	RN No 705 Sqn, RNAS Culdrose	
XW862	Westland Gazelle HT3 [D]	RAF Support Command, CFS	
XW863	Westland Gazelle HT2 [542/CU]	RN No 705 Sqn, RNAS Culdrose	
XW864	Westland Gazelle HT2 [554/CU]	RN No 705 Sqn, RNAS Culdrose	
XW865	Westland Gazelle AH1	AAC, AETW Middle Wallop	
XW866	Westland Gazelle HT3 [E]	RAF Support Command, CFS	
XW868	Westland Gazelle HT2 [550/CU]	RN No 705 Sqn, RNAS Culdrose	
XW870	Westland Gazelle HT3 [F]	RAF Support Command, CFS	
XW871	Westland Gazelle HT2 [549/CU]	RNAY Wroughton, store	
XW884	Westland Gazelle HT2 [541/CU]	RN No 705 Sqn, RNAS Culdrose	
XW885	Westland Gazelle AH1 [B]	AAC, ARWS Middle Wallop	
XW886	Westland Gazelle HT2 [548/CU]	RN No 705 Sqn, RNAS Culdrose	
XW887	Westland Gazelle HT2 [557/CU]	RN No 705 Sqn, RNAS Culdrose	
XW888	Westland Gazelle AH1 [C]	AAC, ARWS Middle Wallop	
XW889	Westland Gazelle AH1 [D]	AAC, ARWS Middle Wallop	
XW890	Westland Gazelle HT2 [553/CU]	RN No 705 Sqn, RNAS Culdrose	
XW891	Westland Gazelle HT2 [549/CU]	RN No 705 Sqn, RNAS Culdrose	
XW892	Westland Gazelle AH1	AAC, BAOR	
XW893	Westland Gazelle AH1	AAC, UK	
XW894	Westland Gazelle HT2 [552/CU]	RN No 705 Sqn, RNAS Culdrose	
XW895	Westland Gazelle HT2 [551/CU]	RN No 705 Sqn, RNAS Culdrose	
XW896	Westland Gazelle AH1	AAC, BAOR	
XW897	Westland Gazelle AH1	AAC, BAOR	
XW898	Westland Gazelle HT3 [G]	RAF Support Command, CFS	
XW899	Westland Gazelle AH1	AAC, BAOR	
XW900	Westland Gazelle AH1	AETW Middle Wallop	
XW902	Westland Gazelle HT3 [H]	RAF Support Command, CFS	

Notes	Serial	Type (alternative identity)	Owner, Operator or Location
	XW903	Westland Gazelle AH1 [E]	AAC, ARWS Middle Wallop
	XW904	Westland Gazelle AH1	AAC, BAOR
	XW905	Westland Gazelle AH1	AAC, UK
	XW906	Westland Gazelle HT3 [J]	RAF Support Command, CFS
	XW907	Westland Gazelle HT2 [540/CU]	RN No 705 Sqn, RNAS Culdrose
	XW908	Westland Gazelle AH1	AAC, UK
	XW909	Westland Gazelle AH1	AAC, BAOR
	XW910	Westland Gazelle HT3 [K]	RAF Support Command, CFS
	XW911	Westland Gazelle AH1 [I]	AAC, ARWS Middle Wallop
	XW912	Westland Gazelle AH1	AAC, UK
	XW913	Westland Gazelle AH1	AAC, BAOR
	XW916	HS Harrier GR3 [W]	RAF Germany
	XW917	HS Harrier GR3 [F]	RAF Germany
	XW919	HS Harrier GR3 [03]	RAF Strike Command, No 1 Sqn
	XW921	HS Harrier GR3	RAF Strike Command, 1417 Flt
	XW922	HS Harrier GR3 [49]	RAF Strike Command, No 1 Sqn
	XW924	HS Harrier GR3 [35]	RAF Strike Command, No 1 Sqn
	XW925	HS Harrier T4 [17]	RAF Strike Command, No 1 Sqn
	XW926	HS Harrier T4 [X]	RAF Strike Command, 233 OCU
	XW927	HS Harrier T4 [Y]	RN No 899 Sqn, RNAS Yeovilton
	XW930	HS125 (G-ATPC)	MoD(PE) RAE Bedford
	XW933	HS Harrier T4 [AQ]	RAF Germany
	XW934	HS Harrier T4 [W]	RAF Strike Command, 233 OCU
	XW986	HS Buccaneer S2	MoD(PE) RAE Farnborough
	XW987	HS Buccaneer S2	MoD(PE) RAE West Freugh
	XW988	HS Buccaneer S2	MoD(PE) RAE Farnborough
	XX101	Cushioncraft CC7	FAA Museum, Yeovilton
	XX105	BAC 1-11/201 (G-ASJD)	MoD(PE) RAE Bedford
	XX108	SEPECAT Jaguar GR1 (G27-313)	MoD(PE) BAe Warton
	XX109	SEPECAT Jaguar GR1	MoD(PE) BAe/A&AEE
	XX110	SEPECAT Jaguar GR1 [EP]	RAF Strike Command, 38 Group
	XX110	SEPECAT Jaguar Replica (BAPC 169)	RAF Support Command, 1 SoTT Halton
	XX112	SEPECAT Jaguar GR1 [EA]	RAF Strike Command, 38 Group
	XX114	SEPECAT Jaguar GR1 [02]	RAF Strike Command, 226 OCU
	XX115	SEPECAT Jaguar GR1 (JI005)	RAF Strike Command, St Athan
	XX118	SEPECAT Jaguar GR1 (JI018)	RAF Strike Command, St Athan
	XX119	SEPECAT Jaguar GR1 [GC]	RAF Strike Command, 38 Group
	XX121	SEPECAT Jaguar GR1 [GB]	RAF Strike Command, 38 Group
	XX139	SEPECAT Jaguar T2 [C]	RAF Strike Command, 226 OCU
	XX140	SEPECAT Jaguar T2 [D]	RAF Strike Command, 226 OCU
	XX141	SEPECAT Jaguar T2 [E]	RAF Strike Command, 226 OCU
	XX143	SEPECAT Jaguar T2 (J1002)	RAF Strike Command, Abingdon
	XX144	SEPECAT Jaguar T2 [ET]	RAF Strike Command, 38 Group
	XX145	SEPECAT Jaguar T2 [H]	RAF Strike Command, 226 OCU
	XX146	SEPECAT Jaguar T2 [S]	RAF Strike Command, 38 Group
	XX150	SEPECAT Jaguar T2 [DY]	RAF Germany
	XX153	Westland Lynx	MoD(PE) Westland, Yeovil
	XX154	HS Hawk T1	MoD(PE) RAE Llanbedr
	XX156	HS Hawk T1	MoD(PE) A&AEE Boscombe Down
	XX157	HS Hawk T1	RAF Strike Command, 2 TWU/63 Sqn
	XX158	HS Hawk T1	RAF Strike Command, 2TWU/63 Sqn
	XX159	HS Hawk T1	RAF Strike Command, 1 TWU
	XX160	HS Hawk T1	MoD(PE) A&AEE Boscombe Down
	XX161	HS Hawk T1	RAF Support Command, CFS
	XX162	HS Hawk T1	RAF Support Command, CFS
	XX162	HS Hawk T1 replica (BAPC 152)	RAF Exhibition Flight, Abingdon
	XX163	HS Hawk T1	RAF Support Command, CFS
	XX164	HS Hawk T1	RAF Support Command, CFS
	XX165	HS Hawk T1	RAF Support Command, CFS
	XX166	HS Hawk T1	RAF Support Command, 4 FTS
	XX167	HS Hawk T1	RAF Support Command, 4 FTS
	XX168	HS Hawk T1	RAF Support Command, 4 FTS
	XX169	HS Hawk T1	RAF Support Command, 4 FTS
	XX170	HS Hawk T1	RAF Support Command, 4 FTS
	XX171	HS Hawk T1	RAF Support Command, 4 FTS
	XX172	HS Hawk T1	RAF Support Command, 4 FTS

Serial	Type (alternative identity)	Owner, Operator or Location	Notes
XX173	HS Hawk T1	RAF Support Command, 4 FTS	
XX174	HS Hawk T1	RAF Support Command, 4 FTS	
XX175	HS Hawk T1	RAF Support Command, 4 FTS	
XX176	HS Hawk T1	RAF Support Command, 4 FTS	
XX177	HS Hawk T1	RAF Support Command, CFS	
XX178	HS Hawk T1	RAF Support Command, 4 FTS	
XX179	HS Hawk T1	RAF Support Command, 4 FTS	
XX180	HS Hawk T1	RAF Support Command, 4 FTS	
XX181	HS Hawk T1	RAF Support Command, CFS	
XX182	HS Hawk T1	RAF Support Command, 4 FTS	
XX183	HS Hawk T1	RAF Support Command, 4 FTS	
XX184	HS Hawk T1	RAF Support Command, 4 FTS	
XX185	HS Hawk T1	RAF Support Command, 4 FTS	
XX186	HS Hawk T1	RAF Strike Command, 2 TWU/63 Sqn	
XX187	HS Hawk T1 [L]	RAF Strike Command, 2 TWU/151 Sqn	
XX188	HS Hawk T1	RAF Strike Command, 1 TWU	
XX189	HS Hawk T1	RAF Strike Command, 2 TWU/63 Sqn	
XX190	HS Hawk T1	RAF Strike Command, 2 TWU/63 Sqn	
XX191	HS Hawk T1	RAF Strike Command, 1 TWU	
XX192	HS Hawk T1	RAF Strike Command, 1 TWU	
XX193	HS Hawk T1	RAF Strike Command, 1 TWU	
XX194	HS Hawk T1	RAF Strike Command, 1 TWU	
XX195	HS Hawk T1	RAF Strike Command, 2 TWU/63 Sqn	
XX196	HS Hawk T1 [N]	RAF Strike Command, 2 TWU/151 Sqn	
XX197	HS Hawk T1	RAF Strike Command, 1 TWU	
XX198	HS Hawk T1	RAF Strike Command, 2 TWU/63 Sqn	
XX199	HS Hawk T1	RAF Strike Command, 1 TWU	
XX200	HS Hawk T1 [O]	RAF Strike Command, 2 TWU/151 Sqn	
XX201	HS Hawk T1	RAF Strike Command, 2 TWU/63 Sqn	
XX202	HS Hawk T1 [P]	RAF Strike Command, 2 TWU/151 Sqn	
XX203	HS Hawk T1	RAF Strike Command, 2 TWU/63 Sqn	
XX204	HS Hawk T1	RAF Strike Command, 2 TWU/63 Sqn	
XX205	HS Hawk T1	RAF Strike Command, 2 TWU/63 Sqn	
XX217	HS Hawk T1	RAF Strike Command, 2 TWU/63 Sqn	
XX218	HS Hawk T1	RAF Strike Command, 1 TWU	
XX219	HS Hawk T1	RAF Strike Command, 2 TWU/63 Sqn	
XX220	HS Hawk T1	RAF Strike Command, 1 TWU	
XX221	HS Hawk T1	RAF Strike Command, 1 TWU	
XX222	HS Hawk T1	RAF Strike Command, 1 TWU	
XX223	HS Hawk T1	RAF Support Command, CFS	
XX224	HS Hawk T1	RAF Support Command, CFS	
XX225	HS Hawk T1	RAF Support Command, 4 FTS	
XX226	HS Hawk T1	RAF Support Command, 4 FTS	
XX227	HS Hawk T1	RAF Support Command, Red Arrows	
XX228	HS Hawk T1 [Q]	RAF Strike Command, 2 TWU/151 Sqn	
XX229	HS Hawk T1	RAF Strike Command, 1 TWU	
XX230	HS Hawk T1	RAF Strike Command, 2 TWU/63 Sqn	
XX231	HS Hawk T1	RAF Support Command, 4 FTS	
XX232	HS Hawk T1	RAF Support Command, 4 FTS	
XX233	HS Hawk T1	RAF Support Command, 4 FTS	
XX234	HS Hawk T1	RAF Support Command, CFS	
XX235	HS Hawk T1	RAF Support Command, 4 FTS	
XX236	HS Hawk T1	RAF Support Command, 4 FTS	
XX237	HS Hawk T1	RAF Support Command, 4 FTS	
XX238	HS Hawk T1	RAF Support Command, 4 FTS	
XX239	HS Hawk T1	RAF Support Command, 4 FTS	
XX240	HS Hawk T1	RAF Support Command, 4 FTS	
XX241	HS Hawk T1	RAF Support Command, 4 FTS	
XX242	HS Hawk T1	RAF Support Command, 4 FTS	
XX244	HS Hawk T1	RAF Support Command, 4 FTS	
XX245	HS Hawk T1	RAF Support Command, 4 FTS	
XX246	HS Hawk T1	RAF Strike Command, 2 TWU/63 Sqn	
XX247	HS Hawk T1	RAF Strike Command, 2 TWU/63 Sqn	
XX248	HS Hawk T1	RAF Strike Command, 2 TWU/63 Sqn	
XX249	HS Hawk T1	RAF Support Command, 4 FTS	
XX250	HS Hawk T1	RAF Support Command, CFS	
XX251	HS Hawk T1	RAF Support Command, Red Arrows	
XX252	HS Hawk T1	RAF Support Command, Red Arrows	
XX253	HS Hawk T1	RAF Support Command, Red Arrows	
XX254	HS Hawk T1	RAF Strike Command, 2 TWU/63 Sqn	
XX255	HS Hawk T1	RAF Strike Command, 2 TWU/63 Sqn	

Notes	Serial	Type (alternative identity)	Owner, Operator or Location
	XX256	HS Hawk T1	RAF Strike Command, 2 TWU/63 Sqn
	XX257	HS Hawk T1	RAF Support Command, Red Arrows
	XX258	HS Hawk T1	RAF Strike Command, 1 TWU
	XX259	HS Hawk T1	RAF Support Command, Red Arrows
	XX260	HS Hawk T1	RAF Support Command, Red Arrows
	XX261	HS Hawk T1	RAF Strike Command, 1 TWU
	XX262	HS Hawk T1 replica	RAF Exhibition Flight, Abingdon
	XX263	HS Hawk T1	RAF Strike Command, 2 TWU/63 Sqn
	XX264	HS Hawk T1	RAF Support Command, Red Arrows
	XX265	HS Hawk T1 [U]	RAF Strike Command, 2 TWU/151 Sqn
	XX266	HS Hawk T1	RAF Support Command, Red Arrows
	XX278	HS Hawk T1	RAF Strike Command, 2 TWU/63 Sqn
	XX279	HS Hawk T1	RAF Strike Command, 2 TWU/63 Sqn
	XX280	HS Hawk T1	RAF Strike Command, 1 TWU
	XX281	HS Hawk T1	RAF Strike Command, 1 TWU
	XX282	HS Hawk T1	RAF Strike Command, 2 TWU/63 Sqn
	XX283	HS Hawk T1	RAF Strike Command, 2 TWU/63 Sqn
	XX284	HS Hawk T1	RAF Strike Command, 2 TWU/63 Sqn
	XX285	HS Hawk T1 [R]	RAF Strike Command, 2 TWU/151 Sqn
	XX286	HS Hawk T1	RAF Strike Command, 1 TWU
	XX287	HS Hawk T1	RAF Strike Command, 2 TWU/63 Sqn
	XX288	HS Hawk T1	RAF Strike Command, 2 TWU/63 Sqn
	XX289	HS Hawk T1	RAF Strike Command, 2 TWU/63 Sqn
	XX290	HS Hawk T1	RAF Support Command, 4 FTS
	XX291	HS Hawk T1	RAF Support Command, 4 FTS
	XX292	HS Hawk T1	RAF Support Command, 4 FTS
	XX293	HS Hawk T1	RAF Support Command, 4 FTS
	XX294	HS Hawk T1	RAF Support Command, 4 FTS
	XX295	HS Hawk T1	RAF Support Command, 4 FTS
	XX296	HS Hawk T1	RAF Support Command, 4 FTS
	XX297	HS Hawk T1	RAF Support Command, 4 FTS
	XX298	HS Hawk T1	RAF Support Command, 4 FTS
	XX299	HS Hawk T1	RAF Support Command, 4 FTS
	XX300	HS Hawk T1 [S]	RAF Strike Command, 2 TWU/151 Sqn
	XX301	HS Hawk T1	RAF Strike Command, 1 TWU
	XX302	HS Hawk T1	RAF Strike Command, 1 TWU
	XX303	HS Hawk T1	RAF Strike Command, 1 TWU
	XX304	HS Hawk T1	RAF Support Command, Red Arrows
	XX305	HS Hawk T1	RAF Support Command, 4 FTS
	XX306	HS Hawk T1	RAF Support Command, Red Arrows
	XX307	HS Hawk T1	RAF Support Command, 4 FTS
	XX308	HS Hawk T1	RAF Support Command, 4 FTS
	XX309	HS Hawk T1	RAF Support Command, 4 FTS
	XX310	HS Hawk T1	RAF Support Command, 4 FTS
	XX311	HS Hawk T1	RAF Support Command, 4 FTS
	XX312	HS Hawk T1	RAF Support Command, CFS
	XX313	HS Hawk T1	RAF Support Command, 4 FTS
	XX314	HS Hawk T1	RAF Support Command, 4 FTS
	XX315	HS Hawk T1	RAF Strike Command, 1 TWU
	XX316	HS Hawk T1	RAF Strike Command, 1 TWU
	XX317	HS Hawk T1	RAF Strike Command, 1 TWU
	XX318	HS Hawk T1	RAF Strike Command, 1 TWU
	XX319	HS Hawk T1	RAF Strike Command, 1 TWU
	XX320	HS Hawk T1 [V]	RAF Strike Command, 2 TWU/151 Sqn
	XX321	HS Hawk T1	RAF Strike Command, 1 TWU
	XX322	HS Hawk T1 [W]	RAF Strike Command, 2 TWU/151 Sqn
	XX323	HS Hawk T1	RAF Strike Command, 1 TWU
	XX324	HS Hawk T1	RAF Strike Command, 1 TWU
	XX325	HS Hawk T1 [X]	RAF Strike Command, 2 TWU/151 Sqn
	XX326	HS Hawk T1 [A]	RAF Strike Command, 2 TWU/151 Sqn
	XX327	HS Hawk T1 [B]	RAF Strike Command, 2 TWU/151 Sqn
	XX329	HS Hawk T1 [C]	RAF Strike Command, 2 TWU/151 Sqn
	XX330	HS Hawk T1 [D]	RAF Strike Command, 2 TWU/151 Sqn
	XX331	HS Hawk T1 [E]	RAF Strike Command, 2 TWU/151 Sqn
	XX332	HS Hawk T1 [F]	RAF Strike Command, 2 TWU/151 Sqn
	XX333	HS Hawk T1 [G]	RAF Strike Command, 2 TWU/151 Sqn
	XX334	HS Hawk T1 [H]	RAF Strike Command, 2 TWU/151 Sqn
	XX335	HS Hawk T1 [I]	RAF Strike Command, 2 TWU/151 Sqn
	XX336	HS Hawk T1 [J]	RAF Strike Command, 2 TWU/151 Sqn
	XX337	HS Hawk T1 [K]	RAF Strike Command, 2 TWU/151 Sqn
	XX338	HS Hawk T1	MoD(PE) BAe Dunsfold

Serial	Type (alternative identity)	Owner, Operator or Location	Notes
XX339	HS Hawk T1	MoD(PE) BAe Dunsfold	
XX340	HS Hawk T1 [Z]	RAF Strike Command, 2 TWU/151 Sqn	
XX341	HS Hawk T1	MoD(PE) ETPS Boscombe Down	
XX342	HS Hawk T1	MoD(PE) ETPS Boscombe Down	
XX343	HS Hawk T1	MoD(PE) ETPS Boscombe Down	
XX345	HS Hawk T1 [Y]	RAF Strike Command, 2 TWU/151 Sqn	
XX346	HS Hawk T1 [T]	RAF Strike Command, 2 TWU/151 Sqn	
XX347	HS Hawk T1	RAF Support Command, 4 FTS	
XX348	HS Hawk T1 [M]	RAF Strike Command, 2 TWU/151 Sqn	
XX349	HS Hawk T1	RAF Support Command, 4 FTS	
XX350	HS Hawk T1	RAF Strike Command, 1 TWU	
XX351	HS Hawk T1	RAF Strike Command, 1 TWU	
XX352	HS Hawk T1	RAF Strike Command, 2 TWU/63 Sqn	
XX353	HS Hawk T1	RAF Strike Command, 2 TWU/63 Sqn	
XX367	Bristol Britannia 312F (G-AOVM)	MoD(PE) A&AEE Boscombe Down	
XX370	Westland Gazelle AH1	AAC, UK	
XX371	Westland Gazelle AH1	AAC, BAOR	
XX372	Westland Gazelle AH1	AAC, UK	
XX374	Westland Gazelle HT3 [L]	RAF Support Command, CFS	
XX375	Westland Gazelle AH1	AAC, UK	
XX376	Westland Gazelle AH1 [K]	Royal Marines, 3 CBAS	
XX377	Westland Gazelle AH1 [L]	Royal Marines, 3 CBAS	
XX378	Westland Gazelle AH1	AAC, UK	
XX379	Westland Gazelle AH1	AAC, UK	
XX380	Westland Gazelle AH1 [M]	Royal Marines, 3 CBAS	
XX381	Westland Gazelle AH1 [Y]	AAC, UK	
XX382	Westland Gazelle HT3 [M]	RAF Support Command, CFS	
XX383	Westland Gazelle AH1	AAC, UK	
XX384	Westland Gazelle AH1	AAC, UK	
XX385	Westland Gazelle AH1	AAC, BAOR	
XX386	Westland Gazelle AH1	AAC, BAOR	
XX387	Westland Gazelle AH1	AAC, UK	
XX388	Westland Gazelle AH1	AAC, UK	
XX389	Westland Gazelle AH1	AAC, BAOR	
XX391	Westland Gazelle HT2 [556/CU]	RN No 705 Sqn RNAS Culdrose	
XX392	Westland Gazelle AH1 [W]	AAC, ARWS Middle Wallop	
XX393	Westland Gazelle AH1	AAC, UK	
XX394	Westland Gazelle AH1	AAC, UK	
XX395	Westland Gazelle AH1	AAC, BAOR	
XX396	Westland Gazelle HT3 (8718M) [N]	RAF Exhibition Flight, Abingdon	
XX398	Westland Gazelle AH1	AAC, UK	
XX399	Westland Gazelle AH1 [E]	Royal Marines, 3 CBAS	
XX400	Westland Gazelle AH1	AAC, UK	
XX403	Westland Gazelle AH1 [Y]	AAC, ARWS Middle Wallop	
XX405	Westland Gazelle AH1	AAC, BAOR	
XX406	Westland Gazelle HT3 [P]	RAF Support Command, CFS	
XX407	Westland Gazelle AH1	AAC, UK	
XX408	Westland Gazelle AH1	AAC, UK	
XX409	Westland Gazelle AH1 [AA]	AAC, ARWS, Middle Wallop	
XX410	Westland Gazelle HT2 [558/CU]	RN AES Lee-on-Solent	
XX412	Westland Gazelle AH1 [Y]	Royal Marines, 3 CBAS	
XX413	Westland Gazelle AH1 [Z]	Royal Marines, 3 CBAS	
XX414	Westland Gazelle AH1	AAC, BAOR	
XX416	Westland Gazelle AH1	AAC, BAOR	
XX417	Westland Gazelle AH1	AAC, BAOR	
XX418	Westland Gazelle AH1	AAC, BAOR	
XX419	Westland Gazelle AH1	AAC, BAOR	
XX431	Westland Gazelle HT2 [543/CU]	RN No 705 Sqn RNAS Culdrose	
XX432	Westland Gazelle AH1	AAC, BAOR	
XX433	Westland Gazelle AH1	AAC, BAOR	
XX435	Westland Gazelle AH1	AAC, BAOR	
XX436	Westland Gazelle HT2 [539/CU]	RN No 705 Sqn RNAS Culdrose	
XX437	Westland Gazelle AH1	AAC, BAOR	
XX438	Westland Gazelle AH1	AAC, BAOR	
XX439	Westland Gazelle AH1	AAC, BAOR	

Notes	Serial	Type (alternative identity)	Owner, Operator or Location
	XX440	Westland Gazelle AH1 (G-BCHN)	AAC, BAOR
	XX441	Westland Gazelle HT2	RNAY Wroughton
	XX442	Westland Gazelle AH1	AAC, BAOR
	XX443	Westland Gazelle AH1	AAC, BAOR
	XX444	Westland Gazelle AH1	AAC, ARWS Middle Wallop
	XX445	Westland Gazelle AH1	AAC, BAOR
	XX446	Westland Gazelle HT2	RN, RNAY Wroughton
	XX447	Westland Gazelle AH1	AAC, BAOR
	XX448	Westland Gazelle AH1	AAC, BAOR
	XX449	Westland Gazelle AH1	AAC, BAOR
	XX450	Westland Gazelle AH1	RM 3CBAS, RNAS Yeovilton
	XX451	Westland Gazelle HT2 [558/CU]	RN No 705 Sqn RNAS Culdrose
	XX452	Westland Gazelle AH1 [G]	AAC, ARWS Middle Wallop
	XX453	Westland Gazelle AH1	AAC, BAOR
	XX454	Westland Gazelle AH1	AAC, BAOR
	XX455	Westland Gazelle AH1	AAC, BAOR
	XX456	Westland Gazelle AH1	AAC, BAOR
	XX457	Westland Gazelle AH1 [H]	AAC, ARWS Middle Wallop
	XX458	Westland Gazelle AH1	AAC, BAOR
	XX459	Westland Gazelle AH1	AAC, BAOR
	XX460	Westland Gazelle AH1	AAC, BAOR
	XX462	Westland Gazelle AH1	AAC, BAOR
	XX466	HS Hunter T66B/T7 [79]	RAF Strike Command, 1 TWU
	XX467	HS Hunter T66B/T7 [86]	RAF Strike Command, 1 TWU
	XX469	Westland Lynx HAS2	Westland Training School, Sherborne
	XX475	SA Jetstream T2 (N1036S) [572/CU]	RN No 750 Sqn RNAS Culdrose
	XX476	SA Jetstream T2 (N1037S) [561/CU]	RN No 750 Sqn RNAS Culdrose
	XX478	SA Jetstream T2 (G-AXXT) [564/CU]	RN No 750 Sqn RNAS Culdrose
	XX479	SA Jetstream T2 (G-AXUR) [563/CU]	RN No 750 Sqn RNAS Culdrose
	XX480	SA Jetstream T2 (G-AXXU) [565/CU]	RN No 750 Sqn RNAS Culdrose
	XX481	SA Jetstream T2 (G-AXUP) [560/CU]	RN No 750 Sqn RNAS Culdrose
	XX482	SA Jetstream T1 [J]	RAF Support Command, 6 FTS
	XX483	SA Jetstream T2 [562/CU]	RN No 750 Sqn RNAS Culdrose
	XX484	SA Jetstream T2 [566/CU]	RN No 750 Sqn RNAS Culdrose
	XX485	SA Jetstream T2 [567/CU]	RN No 750 Sqn RNAS Culdrose
	XX486	SA Jetstream T2 [569/CU]	RN No 750 Sqn RNAS Culdrose
	XX487	SA Jetstream T2 [568/CU]	RN No 750 Sqn RNAS Culdrose
	XX488	SA Jetstream T2 [571/CU]	RN No 750 Sqn RNAS Culdrose
	XX489	SA Jetstream T2	MoD(PE) BAe Prestwick/A&AEE
	XX490	SA Jetstream T2 [570/CU]	RN No 750 Sqn RNAS Culdrose
	XX491	SA Jetstream T1 [K]	RAF Support Command, 6 FTS
	XX492	SA Jetstream T1 [A]	RAF Support Command, 6 FTS
	XX493	SA Jetstream T1 [L]	RAF Support Command, 6 FTS
	XX494	SA Jetstream T1 [B]	RAF Support Command, 6 FTS
	XX495	SA Jetstream T1 [C]	RAF Support Command, 6 FTS
	XX496	SA Jetstream T1 [D]	RAF Support Command, 6 FTS
	XX497	SA Jetstream T1 [E]	RAF Support Command, 6 FTS
	XX498	SA Jetstream T1 [F]	RAF Support Command, 6 FTS
	XX499	SA Jetstream T1 [G]	RAF Support Command, 6 FTS
	XX500	SA Jetstream T1 [H]	RAF Support Command, 6 FTS
	XX507	HS125 CC2	RAF Northolt, No 32 Sqn
	XX508	HS125 CC2	RAF Northolt, No 32 Sqn
	XX510	Westland Lynx	MoD(PE) A&AEE/ETPS, Boscombe Down
	XX513	SA Bulldog T1 [31]	RAF Support Command, RNEFTS
	XX514	SA Bulldog T1 [25]	RAF Support Command, CFS
	XX515	SA Bulldog T1 [7]	RAF Support Command, RNEFTS
	XX516	SA Bulldog T1 [10]	RAF Support Command, RNEFTS
	XX517	SA Bulldog T1 [23]	RAF Support Command, CFS
	XX518	SA Bulldog T1 [24]	RAF Support Command, CFS
	XX519	SA Bulldog T1 [1]	RAF Support Command, RNEFTS
	XX520	SA Bulldog T1 [2]	RAF Support Command, RNEFTS
	XX521	SA Bulldog T1 [01]	RAF, East Lowlands UAS
	XX522	SA Bulldog T1 [4]	RAF Support Command, RNEFTS

Serial	Type (alternative identity)	Owner, Operator or Location	Notes
XX523	SA Bulldog T1 [5]	RAF Support Command, RNEFTS	
XX524	SA Bulldog T1 [04]	RAF, London UAS	
XX525	SA Bulldog T1 [03]	RAF, East Lowlands UAS	
XX526	SA Bulldog T1 [C]	RAF, Oxford UAS	
XX527	SA Bulldog T1 [9]	RAF Support Command, RNEFTS	
XX528	SA Bulldog T1 [D]	RAF, Oxford UAS	
XX529	SA Bulldog T1 [11]	RAF Support Command, RNEFTS	
XX530	SA Bulldog T1 [12]	CTE Manston	
XX531	SA Bulldog T1 [14]	RAF Support Command, RNEFTS	
XX532	SA Bulldog T1 [15]	RAF Support Command, RNEFTS	
XX533	SA Bulldog T1 [16]	RAF Support Command, RNEFTS	
XX534	SA Bulldog T1 [04]	RAF, East Lowlands UAS	
XX535	SA Bulldog T1 [18]	RAF Support Command, RNEFTS	
XX536	SA Bulldog T1 [19]	RAF Support Command, RNEFTS	
XX537	SA Bulldog T1 [02]	RAF, East Lowlands UAS	
XX538	SA Bulldog T1 [E]	RAF, East Midlands UAS	
XX539	SA Bulldog T1 [12]	RAF Support Command, RNEFTS	
XX540	SA Bulldog T1 [28]	RAF Support Command, CFS	
XX541	SA Bulldog T1 [29]	RAF Support Command, CFS	
XX543	SA Bulldog T1 [F]	RAF, Yorkshire UAS	
XX544	SA Bulldog T1 [01]	RAF, London UAS	
XX545	SA Bulldog T1 [02]	RAF East Lowlands UAS (PAX)	
XX546	SA Bulldog T1 [03]	RAF, London UAS	
XX547	SA Bulldog T1 [05]	RAF, London UAS	
XX548	SA Bulldog T1 [06]	RAF, London UAS	
XX549	SA Bulldog T1 [5]	RAF, Manchester UAS	
XX550	SA Bulldog T1 [8]	RAF SupportCommand,Shawbury, store	
XX551	SA Bulldog T1 [32]	RAF Support Command, CFS	
XX552	SA Bulldog T1 [08]	RAF, London UAS	
XX553	SA Bulldog T1 [07]	RAF, London UAS	
XX554	SA Bulldog T1 [09]	RAF, London UAS	
XX555	SA Bulldog T1 [20]	RAF Support Command, RNEFTS	
XX556	SA Bulldog T1 [S]	RAF, East Midlands UAS	
XX557	SA Bulldog T1	RAF Topcliffe (ground inst)	
XX558	SA Bulldog T1 [A]	RAF, Birmingham UAS	
XX559	SA Bulldog T1 [01]	RAF, Glasgow & Strathclyde UAS	
XX560	SA Bulldog T1 [02]	RAF, Glasgow & Strathclyde UAS	
XX561	SA Bulldog T1 [A]	RAF, Aberdeen, Dundee & St Andrews UAS	
XX562	SA Bulldog T1 [S]	RAF, Queens UAS	
XX611	SA Bulldog T1 [04]	RAF, Glasgow & Strathclyde UAS	
XX612	SA Bulldog T1 [05]	RAF, University of Wales AS	
XX613	SA Bulldog T1 [A]	RAF, Queens UAS	
XX614	SA Bulldog T1 [1]	RAF, Manchester UAS	
XX615	SA Bulldog T1 [2]	RAF, Manchester UAS	
XX616	SA Bulldog T1 [3]	RAF, Manchester UAS	
XX617	SA Bulldog T1 [4]	RAF, Manchester UAS	
XX619	SA Bulldog T1 [B]	RAF, Yorkshire UAS	
XX620	SA Bulldog T1 [C]	RAF, Yorkshire UAS	
XX621	SA Bulldog T1 [D]	RAF, Yorkshire UAS	
XX622	SA Bulldog T1 [E]	RAF, Yorkshire UAS	
XX623	SA Bulldog T1 [M]	RAF, East Midlands UAS	
XX624	SA Bulldog T1 [G]	RAF, Yorkshire UAS	
XX625	SA Bulldog T1 [01]	RAF, University of Wales AS	
XX626	SA Bulldog T1 [02]	RAF, University of Wales AS	
XX627	SA Bulldog T1 [03]	RAF, University of Wales AS	
XX628	SA Bulldog T1 [04]	RAF, University of Wales AS	
XX629	SA Bulldog T1 [V]	RAF, Northumbrian UAS	
XX630	SA Bulldog T1 [A]	RAF, Liverpool UAS	
XX631	SA Bulldog T1 [W]	RAF, Northumbrian UAS	
XX632	SA Bulldog T1 [D]	RAF, Bristol UAS	
XX633	SA Bulldog T1 [X]	RAF, Northumbrian UAS	
XX634	SA Bulldog T1 [C]	RAF, Cambridge UAS	
XX635	SA Bulldog T1 [S]	RAF, East Midlands UAS	
XX636	SA Bulldog T1 [Y]	RAF, Northumbrian UAS	
XX637	SA Bulldog T1 [Z]	RAF, Northumbrian UAS	
XX638	SA Bulldog T1 [21]	RAF Support Command, RNEFTS	
XX639	SA Bulldog T1 [02]	RAF, London UAS	
XX640	SA Bulldog T1 [U]	RAF, Queens UAS	
XX653	SA Bulldog T1 [E]	RAF, Bristol UAS	
XX654	SA Bulldog T1 [A]	RAF, Bristol UAS	

Notes	Serial	Type (alternative identity)	Owner, Operator or Location
	XX655	SA Bulldog T1 [B]	RAF, Bristol UAS
	XX656	SA Bulldog T1 [C]	RAF, Bristol UAS
	XX657	SA Bulldog T1 [U]	RAF, Cambridge UAS
	XX658	SA Bulldog T1 [A]	RAF, Cambridge UAS
	XX659	SA Bulldog T1 [S]	RAF, Cambridge UAS
	XX660	SA Bulldog T1 [A]	RAF, Oxford UAS
	XX661	SA Bulldog T1 [B]	RAF, Oxford UAS
	XX663	SA Bulldog T1 [B]	RAF, Aberdeen, Dundee & St Andrews UAS
	XX664	SA Bulldog T1 [05]	RAF, East Lowlands UAS
	XX665	SA Bulldog T1 [E]	RAF, Aberdeen, Dundee & St Andrews UAS
	XX666	SA Bulldog T1 [C]	RAF, Aberdeen, Dundee & St Andrews UAS
	XX667	SA Bulldog T1 [D]	RAF, Aberdeen, Dundee & St Andrews UAS
	XX668	SA Bulldog T1 [26]	RAF Support Command, CFS
	XX669	SA Bulldog T1 [B]	RAF, Birmingham UAS
	XX670	SA Bulldog T1 [C]	RAF, Birmingham UAS
	XX671	SA Bulldog T1 [D]	RAF, Birmingham UAS
	XX672	SA Bulldog T1 [E]	RAF, Birmingham UAS
	XX685	SA Bulldog T1 [L]	RAF, Liverpool UAS
	XX686	SA Bulldog T1 [U]	RAF, Liverpool UAS
	XX687	SA Bulldog T1 [A]	RAF, East Midlands UAS
	XX688	SA Bulldog T1 [S]	RAF, Liverpool UAS
	XX689	SA Bulldog T1 [3]	RAF Support Command, RNEFTS
	XX690	SA Bulldog T1 [A]	RAF, Yorkshire UAS
	XX691	SA Bulldog T1	RAF Support Command, 5 MU
	XX692	SA Bulldog T1	RAF Support Command, 5 MU
	XX693	SA Bulldog T1	RAF Support Command, 5 MU
	XX694	SA Bulldog T1 [E]	RAF, East Midlands UAS
	XX695	SA Bulldog T1	RAF Support Command, 5 MU
	XX696	SA Bulldog T1	RAF Support Command, 5 MU
	XX697	SA Bulldog T1 [Q]	RAF, Queens UAS
	XX698	SA Bulldog T1	MoD(PE) A&AEE Boscombe Down
	XX699	SA Bulldog T1 [30]	RAF Support Command, RNEFTS
	XX700	SA Bulldog T1 [27]	RAF Support Command, CFS
	XX701	SA Bulldog T1 [02]	RAF, Southampton UAS
	XX702	SA Bulldog T1 [03]	RAF, Glasgow & Strathclyde UAS
	XX704	SA Bulldog T1 [U]	RAF, East Midlands UAS
	XX705	SA Bulldog T1 [05]	RAF, Southampton UAS
	XX706	SA Bulldog T1 [01]	RAF, Southampton UAS
	XX707	SA Bulldog T1 [04]	RAF, Southampton UAS
	XX708	SA Bulldog T1 [03]	RAF, Southampton UAS
	XX709	SA Bulldog T1 [33]	RAF Support Command, RNEFTS
	XX710	SA Bulldog T1 [34]	RAF Support Command, RNEFTS
	XX711	SA Bulldog T1 [E]	RAF Support Command, 13 AEF
	XX712	SA Bulldog T1 [6]	RAF Support Command, RNEFTS
	XX713	SA Bulldog T1 [22]	RAF Support Command, RNEFTS
	XX714	SA Bulldog T1	MoD(PE) A&AEE Boscombe Down
	XX718	SEPECAT Jaguar Replica (BAPC150)	RAF Exhibition Flight, Abingdon
	XX719	SEPECAT Jaguar GR1 [GD]	RAF Strike Command, 38 Group
	XX721	SEPECAT Jaguar GR1 [GE]	RAF Strike Command, 38 Group
	XX722	SEPECAT Jaguar GR1 [GF]	RAF Strike Command, 38 Group
	XX723	SEPECAT Jaguar GR1 [GG]	RAF Strike Command, 38 Group
	XX724	SEPECAT Jaguar GR1 [GH]	RAF Strike Command, 38 Group
	XX726	SEPECAT Jaguar GR1 [EB]	RAF Strike Command, 38 Group
	XX727	SEPECAT Jaguar GR1 [GJ]	RAF Strike Command, 38 Group
	XX728	SEPECAT Jaguar GR1 (JIO09)	RAF Strike Command, St Athan
	XX729	SEPECAT Jaguar GR1 (JIO12)	RAF Strike Command, St Athan
	XX730	SEPECAT Jaguar GR1 [EC]	RAF Strike Command, 38 Group
	XX731	SEPECAT Jaguar GR1 [GK]	RAF Strike Command, 38 Group
	XX732	SEPECAT Jaguar GR1 [GL]	RAF Strike Command, 38 Group
	XX733	SEPECAT Jaguar GR1 [ED]	RAF Strike Command, 38 Group
	XX734	SEPECAT Jaguar GR1 (JIO14)	RAF Strike Command, St Athan
	XX737	SEPECAT Jaguar GR1 (JIO15)	RAF Strike Command, St Athan
	XX739	SEPECAT Jaguar GR1 [EE]	RAF Strike Command, 38 Group
	XX741	SEPECAT Jaguar GR1 [GM]	RAF Strike Command, 38 Group
	XX742	SEPECAT Jaguar GR1 [EF]	RAF Strike Command, 38 Group
	XX743	SEPECAT Jaguar GR1 [EG]	RAF Strike Command, 38 Group

Serial	Type (alternative identity)	Owner, Operator or Location	Notes
XX744	SEPECAT Jaguar GR1 [DG]	RAF Germany	
XX745	SEPECAT Jaguar GR1 [EJ]	RAF Strike Command, 38 Group	
XX746	SEPECAT Jaguar GR1 [BD]	RAF Germany	
XX747	SEPECAT Jaguar GR1 [17]	RAF Strike Command, 226 OCU	
XX748	SEPECAT Jaguar GR1 [20]	RAF Strike Command, 226 OCU	
XX750	SEPECAT Jaguar GR1 [22]	RAF Strike Command, 226 OCU	
XX751	SEPECAT Jaguar GR1 [10]	RAF Strike Command, 226 OCU	
XX752	SEPECAT Jaguar GR1 [06]	RAF Strike Command, 226 OCU	
XX753	SEPECAT Jaguar GR1 [05]	RAF Strike Command, 226 OCU	
XX754	SEPECAT Jaguar GR1 [23]	RAF Strike Command, 226 OCU	
XX756	SEPECAT Jaguar GR1 [07]	RAF Strike Command, 226 OCU	
XX757	SEPECAT Jaguar GR1 [CU]	RAF Germany	
XX763	SEPECAT Jaguar GR1 [24]	RAF Strike Command, 226 OCU	
XX764	SEPECAT Jaguar GR1 [13]	RAF Strike Command, 226 OCU	
XX765	SEPECAT Jaguar GR1	MoD(PE) BAe Warton	
XX766	SEPECAT Jaguar GR1 [14]	RAF Strike Command, 226 OCU	
XX767	SEPECAT Jaguar GR1 [AN]	RAF Germany	
XX818	SEPECAT Jaguar GR1 [CC]	RAF Germany	
XX819	SEPECAT Jaguar GR1 [CE]	RAF Germany	
XX821	SEPECAT Jaguar GR1 [BF]	RAF Germany	
XX824	SEPECAT Jaguar GR1 [BH]	RAF Germany	
XX824	SEPECAT Jaguar Replica (BAPC 151)	RAF Exhibition Flight, Abingdon	
XX825	SEPECAT Jaguar GR1 [AC]	RAF Germany	
XX826	SEPECAT Jaguar GR1 [AD]	RAF Germany	
XX829	SEPECAT Jaguar T2 [GT]	RAF Strike Command, 38 Group	
XX830	SEPECAT Jaguar T2 [R]	RAF Strike Command, 226 OCU	
XX832	SEPECAT Jaguar T2 [S]	RAF Strike Command, 226 OCU	
XX833	SEPECAT Jaguar T2 [CZ]	RAF Germany	
XX834	SEPECAT Jaguar T2 [U]	RAF Strike Command, 226 OCU	
XX835	SEPECAT Jaguar T2 [V]	RAF Strike Command, 226 OCU	
XX836	SEPECAT Jaguar T2 [BZ]	RAF Germany	
XX837	SEPECAT Jaguar T2 [Z]	RAF Strike Command, 226 OCU	
XX838	SEPECAT Jaguar T2 [X]	RAF Strike Command, 226 OCU	
XX839	SEPECAT Jaguar T2 [Y]	RAF Strike Command, 226 OCU	
XX840	SEPECAT Jaguar T2 [T]	RAF Strike Command, 226 OCU	
XX841	SEPECAT Jaguar T2 [K]	RAF Strike Command, 226 OCU	
XX842	SEPECAT Jaguar T2 [T]	RAF Strike Command, 38 Group	
XX843	SEPECAT Jaguar T2 [33]	RAF Germany	
XX844	SEPECAT Jaguar T2 [DZ]	RAF Germany	
XX845	SEPECAT Jaguar T2 [BY]	RAF Germany	
XX846	SEPECAT Jaguar T2 [A]	RAF Strike Command, 226 OCU	
XX847	SEPECAT Jaguar T2 [AY]	RAF Germany	
XX885	HS Buccaneer S2B	RAF Strike Command, 1 Group	
XX886	HS Buccaneer S2B	RAE Honington, ground instruction	
XX888	HS Buccaneer S2B [Z]	RAF St Athan, store	
XX889	HS Buccaneer S2B [P]	RAF Strike Command, 1 Group	
XX891	HS Buccaneer S2B [J]	RAF Germany	
XX892	HS Buccaneer S2B [R]	RAF Germany	
XX893	HS Buccaneer S2B [H]	RAF Germany	
XX894	HS Buccaneer S2B	MoD(PE) A&AEE Boscombe Down	
XX895	HS Buccaneer S2B [B]	RAF Germany	
XX896	HS Buccaneer S2B	RAF St Athan, store	
XX897	HS Buccaneer S2B	MoD(PE) RS&RE Bedford	
XX899	HS Buccaneer S2B [A]	RAF Germany	
XX900	HS Buccaneer S2B	RAF Strike Command, 1 Group	
XX901	HS Buccaneer S2B	RAF Strike Command, 1 Group	
XX910	Westland Lynx HAS2	MoD(PE) RAE, Farnborough	
XX914	BAC VC10 srs 1103 (G-ATDJ)	MoD(PE) RAE, Bedford	
XX915	SEPECAT Jaguar T2	MoD(PE) A&AEE/ETPS, Boscombe Down	
XX919	BAC 1-11/402 (PI-C 1121)	MoD(PE) RAE, Farnborough	
XX944	HS Comet 4 (G-APDP)	RAE Apprentice School, Farnborough	
XX946	Panavia Tornado (P02)	MoD(PE) BAe Warton	
XX947	Panavia Tornado (P03)	MoD(PE) BAe Warton	
XX948	Panavia Tornado (P06)	MoD(PE) BAe Warton	
XX955	SEPECAT Jaguar GR1 [AF]	RAF Germany	
XX956	SEPECAT Jaguar GR1 [AB]	RAF Germany	
XX958	SEPECAT Jaguar GR1 [AH]	RAF Germany	
XX959	SEPECAT Jaguar GR1 [CJ]	RAF Germany	
XX962	SEPECAT Jaguar GR1 [CK]	RAF Germany	
XX965	SEPECAT Jaguar GR1	RAF Germany	

Notes	Serial	Type (alternative identity)	Owner, Operator or Location
	XX966	SEPECAT Jaguar GR1 [CD]	RAF Germany
	XX967	SEPECAT Jaguar GR1 [DA]	RAF Germany
	XX968	SEPECAT Jaguar GR1 [DB]	RAF Germany
	XX969	SEPECAT Jaguar GR1 [DC]	RAF Germany
	XX970	SEPECAT Jaguar GR1 [DD]	RAF Germany
	XX974	SEPECAT Jaguar GR1 [DH]	RAF Germany
	XX975	SEPECAT Jaguar GR1 [DJ]	RAF Germany
	XX976	SEPECAT Jaguar GR1 [DK]	RAF Germany
	XX977	SEPECAT Jaguar GR1 [DL]	RAF Germany
	XX979	SEPECAT Jaguar GR1	MoD(PE) A&AEE Boscombe Down
	XZ101	SEPECAT Jaguar GR1 [EK]	RAF Germany
	XZ103	SEPECAT Jaguar GR1 [23]	RAF Germany
	XZ104	SEPECAT Jaguar GR1 [24]	RAF Germany
	XZ105	SEPECAT Jaguar GR1 [25]	RAF Germany
	XZ106	SEPECAT Jaguar GR1	RAF Germany
	XZ107	SEPECAT Jaguar GR1 [27]	RAF Germany
	XZ108	SEPECAT Jaguar GR1 [28]	RAF Germany
	XZ109	SEPECAT Jaguar GR1 [29]	RAF Germany
	XZ110	SEPECAT Jaguar GR1	RAF Germany
	XZ111	SEPECAT Jaguar GR1	RAF Germany
	XZ112	SEPECAT Jaguar GR1 [32]	RAF Germany
	XZ113	SEPECAT Jaguar GR1 [A]	RAF Strike Command, 38 Group
	XZ114	SEPECAT Jaguar GR1 [B]	RAF Strike Command, 38 Group
	XZ115	SEPECAT Jaguar GR1 [C]	RAF Strike Command, 38 Group
	XZ116	SEPECAT Jaguar GR1 [D]	RAF Strike Command, 38 Group
	XZ117	SEPECAT Jaguar GR1 [E]	RAF Strike Command, 38 Group
	XZ118	SEPECAT Jaguar GR1 [F]	RAF Strike Command, 38 Group
	XZ119	SEPECAT Jaguar GR1 [G]	RAF Strike Command, 38 Group
	XZ129	HS Harrier GR3 [29]	RAF Strike Command, No 1 Sqn
	XZ130	HS Harrier GR3 [27]	RAF Strike Command, No 1 Sqn
	XZ131	HS Harrier GR3 [M]	RAF Germany
	XZ132	HS Harrier GR3 [12]	RAF Strike Command, No 1 Sqn
	XZ133	HS Harrier GR3 [10]	RAF Strike Command, 1417 Flt
	XZ134	HS Harrier GR3 [AJ]	RAF Germany
	XZ135	HS Harrier GR3 [P]	RAF Germany
	XZ136	HS Harrier GR3	MoD(PE) A&AEE Boscombe Down
	XZ138	HS Harrier GR3 [Q]	RAF Germany
	XZ145	HS Harrier T4 [AT]	RAF Germany
	XZ146	HS Harrier T4 [Y]	RAF Germany
	XZ147	HS Harrier T4 [Z]	RAF Strike Command, 233 OCU
	XZ166	Westland Lynx HAS2 (G-1-2)	MoD(PE) RAE Farnborough
	XZ170	Westland Lynx AH1	MoD(PE) A&AEE Boscombe Down
	XZ171	Westland Lynx AH1	MoD(PE) Rolls-Royce, Filton
	XZ172	Westland Lynx AH1	AAC, ARW/LCF Middle Wallop
	XZ173	Westland Lynx AH1	AAC, BAOR
	XZ174	Westland Lynx AH1	AAC, BAOR
	XZ175	Westland Lynx AH1	AAC, ARW/LCF Middle Wallop
	XZ176	Westland Lynx AH1	AAC, ATS
	XZ177	Westland Lynx AH1	AAC, BAOR
	XZ178	Westland Lynx AH1	AAC, RNAY Fleetlands, store
	XZ179	Westland Lynx AH1	AAC, DETS Middle Wallop
	XZ180	Westland Lynx AH1	MoD(PE) Westland, Yeovil
	XZ181	Westland Lynx AH1	AAC, BAOR
	XZ182	Westland Lynx AH1	On rebuild, Fleetlands
	XZ183	Westland Lynx AH1	AAC, BAOR
	XZ184	Westland Lynx AH1	AAC, BAOR
	XZ185	Westland Lynx AH1	AAC, BAOR
	XZ186	Westland Lynx AH1	AAC, BAOR
	XZ187	Westland Lynx AH1	AAC, UK
	XZ188	Westland Lynx AH1	AAC, UK
	XZ190	Westland Lynx AH1	AAC, RNAY Wroughton, store
	XZ191	Westland Lynx AH1	AAC, BAOR
	XZ192	Westland Lynx AH1	AAC, BAOR
	XZ193	Westland Lynx AH1	AAC, BAOR
	XZ194	Westland Lynx AH1	AAC, BAOR
	XZ195	Westland Lynx AH1	AAC, BAOR
	XZ196	Westland Lynx AH1	AAC, BAOR
	XZ197	Westland Lynx AH1	AAC, BAOR
	XZ198	Westland Lynx AH1	AAC, BAOR
	XZ199	Westland Lynx AH1	AAC, BAOR

XX280 HS Hawk T1. *APM*

X2234 Westland Lynx HAS2. *PRM*

Serial	Type (alternative identity)	Owner, Operator or Location	Notes
XZ203	Westland Lynx AH1	AAC, Dem & Trials Sqn, Middle Wallop	
XZ204	Westland Lynx AH1	AAC, BAOR	
XZ205	Westland Lynx AH1	AAC, BAOR	
XZ206	Westland Lynx AH1	AAC, RNAY Wroughton, store	
XZ207	Westland Lynx AH1	AAC, BAOR	
XZ208	Westland Lynx AH1	AAC, BAOR	
XZ209	Westland Lynx AH1	AAC, BAOR	
XZ210	Westland Lynx AH1	AAC, Dem & Trials Sqn, Middle Wallop	
XZ211	Westland Lynx AH1	AAC, BAOR	
XZ212	Westland Lynx AH1	AAC, BAOR	
XZ213	Westland Lynx AH1	AAC, BAOR	
XZ214	Westland Lynx AH1	AAC, RNAY Wroughton, store	
XZ215	Westland Lynx AH1	AAC, AETW Middle Wallop	
XZ216	Westland Lynx AH1	AAC, BAOR	
XZ217	Westland Lynx AH1	AAC, BAOR	
XZ218	Westland Lynx AH1	AAC, BAOR	
XZ219	Westland Lynx AH1	AAC, BAOR	
XZ220	Westland Lynx AH1	AAC, BAOR	
XZ221	Westland Lynx AH1	AAC, Dem & Trials Sqn	
XZ222	Westland Lynx AH1	AAC, ARW/LCF Middle Wallop	
XZ227	Westland Lynx HAS2 [478/—]	RN NASU, RNAS Yeovilton	
XZ228	Westland Lynx HAS2	RN NASU, RNAS Yeovilton	
XZ229	Westland Lynx HAS2 [302/—]	RN No 815 Sqn, RNAS Portland	
XZ230	Westland Lynx HAS2 [301/PO]	RN No 815 Sqn, RNAS Portland	
XZ231	Westland Lynx HAS2 [645/PO]	RN No 702 Sqn, RNAS Portland	
XZ232	Westland Lynx HAS2 [233/BM]	RN No 815 Sqn, RNAS Portland	
XZ233	Westland Lynx HAS2	RN No 815 Sqn, RNAS Portland	
XZ234	Westland Lynx HAS2 [643/PO]	RN No 702 Sqn, RNAS Portland	
XZ235	Westland Lynx HAS2	MoD(PE) Westland, Yeovil	
XZ236	Westland Lynx HAS2 [—/AT]	MoD(PE) Westland, Yeovil	
XZ237	Westland Lynx HAS2	MoD (PE) Westland, Yeovil	
XZ238	Westland Lynx HAS2	RN No 815 Sqn, RNAS Portland	
XZ239	Westland Lynx HAS2 [322/LP]	RN No 815 Sqn, RNAS Portland	
XZ240	Westland Lynx HAS2	RN No 815 Sqn, RNAS Portland	
XZ241	Westland Lynx HAS2 [326/AW]	RN No 815 Sqn, RNAS Portland	
XZ243	Westland Lynx HAS2 [640/PO]	RN No 702 Sqn, RNAS Portland	
XZ244	Westland Lynx HAS2 [644/PO]	RN No 702 Sqn, RNAS Portland	
XZ245	Westland Lynx HAS2	RN No 815 Sqn, RNAS Portland	
XZ246	Westland Lynx HAS2 [304/PO]	RN No 815 Sqn, RNAS Portland	
XZ247	Westland Lynx HAS2 [463/CP]	RN No 815 Sqn, RNAS Portland	
XZ248	Westland Lynx HAS2	RN No 702 Sqn, RNAS Portland	
XZ249	Westland Lynx HAS2	RN No 815 Sqn, RNAS Portland	
XZ250	Westland Lynx HAS2 [305/PO]	RN No 815 Sqn, RNAS Portland	
XZ252	Westland Lynx HAS2 [—/AG]	RN No 815 Sqn, RNAS Portland	
XZ254	Westland Lynx HAS2	RN No 815 Sqn, RNAS Portland	
XZ255	Westland Lynx HAS2	RN No 815 Sqn, RNAS Portland	
XZ256	Westland Lynx HAS2	RN No 815 Sqn, RNAS Portland	
XZ257	Westland Lynx HAS2 [—/PO]	RN No 815 Sqn, RNAS Portland	
XZ280	BAe Nimrod AEW3	MoD(PE) BAe Woodford	
XZ281	BAe Nimrod AEW3	MoD(PE) BAe Woodford	
XZ282	HS Nimrod MR1	RAF Strike Command, 18 Group	
XZ283	BAe Nimrod R1	RAF Strike Command, No 51 Sqn	
XZ284	HS Nimrod MR2	RAF Strike Command, 18 Group	
XZ285	BAe Nimrod AEW3	MoD(PE) BAe Woodford	
XZ286	BAe Nimrod AEW3	MoD(PE) BAe Woodford	
XZ287	BAe Nimrod AEW3	MoD(PE) BAe Woodford	

Notes	Serial	Type (alternative identity)	Owner, Operator or Location
	XZ290	Westland Gazelle AH1	AAC, ARWS Middle Wallop
	XZ291	Westland Gazelle AH1	AAC, BAOR
	XZ292	Westland Gazelle AH1	AAC, BAOR
	XZ294	Westland Gazelle AH1	AAC, BAOR
	XZ295	Westland Gazelle AH1	AAC, BAOR
	XZ296	Westland Gazelle AH1	AAC, BAOR
	XZ297	Westland Gazelle AH1	AAC, BAOR
	XZ298	Westland Gazelle AH1	AAC, BAOR
	XZ299	Westland Gazelle AH1	AAC, UK
	XZ300	Westland Gazelle AH1	AAC, BAOR
	XZ301	Westland Gazelle AH1	AAC, BAOR
	XZ303	Westland Gazelle AH1	AAC, BAOR
	XZ304	Westland Gazelle AH1	AAC, BAOR
	XZ305	Westland Gazelle AH1	AAC, BAOR
	XZ307	Westland Gazelle AH1	AAC, BAOR
	XZ308	Westland Gazelle AH1 [L]	AAC, ARWS Middle Wallop
	XZ309	Westland Gazelle AH1	AAC, BAOR
	XZ310	Westland Gazelle AH1	AAC, BAOR
	XZ311	Westland Gazelle AH1	AAC, BAOR
	XZ312	Westland Gazelle AH1	AAC, UK
	XZ313	Westland Gazelle AH1 [N]	AAC, ARWS Middle Wallop
	XZ314	Westland Gazelle AH1	AAC, ARWS Middle Wallop
	XZ315	Westland Gazelle AH1 [P]	AAC, ARWS Middle Wallop
	XZ316	Westland Gazelle AH1 [R]	AAC, ARWS Middle Wallop
	XZ317	Westland Gazelle AH1 [Q]	AAC, ARWS Middle Wallop
	XZ318	Westland Gazelle AH1 [U]	AAC, ARWS Middle Wallop
	XZ319	Westland Gazelle AH1 [S]	AAC, ARWS Middle Wallop
	XZ320	Westland Gazelle AH1	AAC, UK
	XZ321	Westland Gazelle AH1	AAC, UK
	XZ322	Westland Gazelle AH1	AAC, UK
	XZ323	Westland Gazelle AH1	AAC, UK
	XZ324	Westland Gazelle AH1	AAC, UK
	XZ325	Westland Gazelle AH1	AAC, UK
	XZ326	Westland Gazelle AH1	AAC, UK
	XZ327	Westland Gazelle AH1	AAC, UK
	XZ328	Westland Gazelle AH1	AAC, UK
	XZ329	Westland Gazelle AH1 [J]	AAC, ARWS Middle Wallop
	XZ330	Westland Gazelle AH1	AAC, UK
	XZ331	Westland Gazelle AH1	AAC, UK
	XZ332	Westland Gazelle AH1 [O]	AAC, ARWS Middle Wallop
	XZ333	Westland Gazelle AH1 [A]	AAC, ARWS Middle Wallop
	XZ334	Westland Gazelle AH1	AAC, UK
	XZ335	Westland Gazelle AH1	AAC, UK
	XZ336	Westland Gazelle AH1	AAC, UK
	XZ337	Westland Gazelle AH1	AAC, UK
	XZ338	Westland Gazelle AH1 [X]	AAC, ARWS Middle Wallop
	XZ339	Westland Gazelle AH1	MoD(PE), A&AEE Boscombe Down
	XZ340	Westland Gazelle AH1 [T]	AAC, ARWS Middle Wallop
	XZ341	Westland Gazelle AH1	AAC, Dem & Trials Sqn, Middle Wallop
	XZ342	Westland Gazelle AH1	AAC, BAOR
	XZ344	Westland Gazelle AH1	AAC, UK
	XZ345	Westland Gazelle AH1	AAC, UK
	XZ346	Westland Gazelle AH1	AAC, UK
	XZ347	Westland Gazelle AH1	AAC, UK
	XZ348	Westland Gazelle AH1	AAC, UK
	XZ349	Westland Gazelle AH1 [M]	AAC, ARWS Middle Wallop
	XZ355	SEPECAT Jaguar GR1 [GA]	RAF Strike Command, 38 Group
	XZ356	SEPECAT Jaguar GR1 [BP]	RAF Germany
	XZ357	SEPECAT Jaguar GR1 [K]	RAF Strike Command, 38 Group
	XZ358	SEPECAT Jaguar GR1 [L]	RAF Strike Command, 38 Group
	XZ359	SEPECAT Jaguar GR1 [M]	RAF Strike Command, 38 Group
	XZ360	SEPECAT Jaguar GR1 [Y]	RAF Strike Command, 38 Group
	XZ361	SEPECAT Jaguar GR1 [20]	RAF Germany
	XZ362	SEPECAT Jaguar GR1 [19]	RAF Germany
	XZ363	SEPECAT Jaguar GR1 [Z]	RAF Strike Command, 38 Group
	XZ364	SEPECAT Jaguar GR1	RAF Germany
	XZ365	SEPECAT Jaguar GR1 [J]	RAF Strike Command, 38 Group
	XZ366	SEPECAT Jaguar GR1 [22]	RAF Germany
	XZ367	SEPECAT Jaguar GR1	RAF Strike Command, 226 OCU
	XZ368	SEPECAT Jaguar GR1 [EL]	RAF Strike Command, 38 Group
	XZ369	SEPECAT Jaguar GR1 [AP]	RAF Germany

Serial	Type (alternative identity)	Owner, Operator or Location	Notes
XZ370	SEPECAT Jaguar GR1 [BN]	RAF Germany	
XZ371	SEPECAT Jaguar GR1 [BB]	RAF Germany	
XZ372	SEPECAT Jaguar GR1 [AK]	RAF Germany	
XZ373	SEPECAT Jaguar GR1 [BG]	RAF Germany	
XZ374	SEPECAT Jaguar GR1 [CA]	RAF Germany	
XZ375	SEPECAT Jaguar GR1 [CB]	RAF Germany	
XZ376	SEPECAT Jaguar GR1 [BE]	RAF Germany	
XZ377	SEPECAT Jaguar GR1 [CF]	RAF Germany	
XZ378	SEPECAT Jaguar GR1 [CH]	RAF Germany	
XZ381	SEPECAT Jaguar GR1 [BL]	RAF Germany	
XZ382	SEPECAT Jaguar GR1 [AE]	RAF Germany	
XZ383	SEPECAT Jaguar GR1 [BC]	RAF Germany	
XZ384	SEPECAT Jaguar GR1 [CM]	RAF Germany	
XZ385	SEPECAT Jaguar GR1 [AG]	RAF Germany	
XZ386	SEPECAT Jaguar GR1 [AJ]	RAF Germany	
XZ387	SEPECAT Jaguar GR1 [DN]	RAF Germany	
XZ388	SEPECAT Jaguar GR1 [BK]	RAF Germany	
XZ389	SEPECAT Jaguar GR1 [CN]	RAF Germany	
XZ390	SEPECAT Jaguar GR1 [DM]	RAF Germany	
XZ391	SEPECAT Jaguar GR1 [DF]	RAF Germany	
XZ392	SEPECAT Jaguar GR1 [DE]	RAF Germany	
XZ393	SEPECAT Jaguar GR1 [BJ]	RAF Germany	
XZ394	SEPECAT Jaguar GR1 [CQ]	RAF Germany	
XZ395	SEPECAT Jaguar GR1 [GN]	RAF Strike Command, 38 Group	
XZ396	SEPECAT Jaguar GR1 [EM]	RAF Strike Command, 38 Group	
XZ399	SEPECAT Jaguar GR1 [EN]	RAF Strike Command, 38 Group	
XZ400	SEPECAT Jaguar GR1 [GP]	RAF Strike Command, 38 Group	
XZ430	HS Buccaneer S2B	RAF Strike Command, 1 Group	
XZ431	HS Buccaneer S2B	RAF Strike Command, 1 Group	
XZ432	HS Buccaneer S2B	RAF Strike Command, 1 Group	
XZ439	BAe Sea Harrier FRS1 [2]	RN No 899 Sqn, RNAS Yeovilton	
XZ440	BAe Sea Harrier FRS1 [40]	MoD(PE) A&AEE Boscombe Down	
XZ445	BAe Harrier T4 [Q]	RAF Strike Command, 233 OCU	
XZ451	BAe Sea Harrier FRS1 [710]	RN No 899 Sqn, RNAS Yeovilton	
XZ455	BAe Sea Harrier FRS1 [715]	RN No 899 Sqn, RNAS Yeovilton	
XZ457	BAe Sea Harrier FRS1	RN No 899 Sqn, RNAS Yeovilton	
XZ458	BAe Sea Harrier FRS1 [58]	RN No 809 Sqn, RNAS Yeovilton	
XZ459	BAe Sea Harrier FRS1 [256]	RN No 809 Sqn, RNAS Yeovilton	
XZ460	BAe Sea Harrier FRS1 [26]	RN No 800 Sqn, RNAS Yeovilton	
XZ491	BAe Sea Harrier FRS1 [002]	RN No 801 Sqn RNAS Yeovilton	
XZ492	BAe Sea Harrier FRS1 [712]	RN No 899 Sqn RNAS Yeovilton	
XZ493	BAe Sea Harrier FRS1 [123]	RN No 800 Sqn RNAS Yeovilton	
XZ494	BAe Sea Harrier FRS1 [714]	RN No 899 Sqn RNAS Yeovilton	
XZ495	BAe Sea Harrier FRS1 [003]	RN No 801 Sqn, RNAS Yeovilton	
XZ496	BAe Sea Harrier FRS1 [257]	RN No 809 Sqn, RNAS Yeovilton	
XZ497	BAe Sea Harrier FRS1 [4]	RN No 899 Sqn, RNAS Yeovilton	
XZ498	BAe Sea Harrier FRS1 [124/H]	RN No 800 Sqn, RNAS Yeovilton	
XZ499	BAe Sea Harrier FRS1 [255]	RN No 809 Sqn, RNAS Yeovilton	
XZ500	BAe Sea Harrier FRS1 [252]	RN No 809 Sqn, RNAS Yeovilton	
XZ550	Slingsby Venture T2	RAF Support Command, 642 GS	
XZ551	Slingsby Venture T2 [H]	RAF Support Command, CGS	
XZ552	Slingsby Venture T2	RAF Support Command, 632 GS	
XZ553	Slingsby Venture T2 [Q]	RAF Support Command, CGS	
XZ554	Slingsby Venture T2 [4]	RAF Support Command, 633 GS	
XZ555	Slingsby Venture T2 [A]	RAF Support Command, CGS	
XZ556	Slingsby Venture T2	RAF Support Command, 632 GS	
XZ557	Slingsby Venture T2 [7]	RAF Support Command, 633 GS	
XZ558	Slingsby Venture T2	RAF Support Command, 616 GS	
XZ559	Slingsby Venture T2	RAF Support Command, 616 GS	
XZ560	Slingsby Venture T2	RAF Support Command, CGS/611GS	
XZ561	Slingsby Venture T2	RAF Support Command, CGS/611GS	
XZ562	Slingsby Venture T2	RAF Support Command, 625 GS	
XZ563	Slingsby Venture T2	RAF Support Command, 642 GS	
XZ564	Slingsby Venture T2	RAF Support Command, 625 GS	
XZ570	Westland Sea King HAS2	MoD(PE) A&AEE Boscombe Down	
XZ571	Westland Sea King HAS5 [143/—]	RN No 826 Sqn, RNAS Culdrose	
XZ573	Westland Sea King HAS5	RN No 826 Sqn, RNAS Culdrose	
XZ574	Westland Sea King HAS5 [016/N]	RN No 820 Sqn, RNAS Culdrose	
XZ575	Westland Sea King HAS5 [595/—]	RN No 706 Sqn, RNAS Culdrose	

Notes	Serial	Type (alternative identity)	Owner, Operator or Location
	XZ576	Westland Sea King HAS5 [411/N]	RNAY Fleetlands
	XZ577	Westland Sea King HAS5 [142/—]	RN No 826 Sqn, RNAS Culdrose
	XZ578	Westland Sea King HAS5 [141/—]	RN No 826 Sqn, RNAS Culdrose
	XZ579	Westland Sea King HAS2 [271/—]	RN No 814 Sqn, RNAS Culdrose
	XZ580	Westland Sea King HAS2 [272/—]	RN No 825 Sqn, RNAS Culdrose
	XZ581	Westland Sea King HAS2 [593/CU]	RN No 814 Sqn, RNAS Culdrose
	XZ582	Westland Sea King HAS2	RN No 814 Sqn, RNAS Culdrose
	XZ585	Westland Sea King HAR3	RAF Strike Command, No 202 Sqn
	XZ586	Westland Sea King HAR3	RAF Strike Command, No 202 Sqn
	XZ587	Westland Sea King HAR3	MoD(PE) A&AEE Boscombe Down
✓	XZ588	Westland Sea King HAR3	RAF Strike Command, No 202 Sqn
✗	XZ589	Westland Sea King HAR3	RAF Strike Command, No 202 Sqn
	XZ590	Westland Sea King HAR3	RAF Strike Command, No 202 Sqn
	XZ591	Westland Sea King HAR3 [SC]	RAF Strike Command, Ascension Island
	XZ592	Westland Sea King HAR3 [SA]	RAF Strike Command, Ascension Island
	XZ593	Westland Sea King HAR3	RAF Strike Command, No 202 Sqn
	XZ594	Westland Sea King HAR3	RAFSKTF, RNAS Culdrose
	XZ595	Westland Sea King HAR3	RAFSKTF, RNAS Culdrose
	XZ596	Westland Sea King HAR3	RAF Strike Command, No 202 Sqn
	XZ597	Westland Sea King HAR3	RAF Strike Command, No 202 Sqn
	XZ598	Westland Sea King HAR3	RAF Strike Command, No 202 Sqn
	XZ599	Westland Sea King HAR3	RAF Strike Command, No 202 Sqn
	XZ605	Westland Lynx AH1	RM 3 CBAS, RNAS Yeovilton
	XZ606	Westland Lynx AH1	AAC, BAOR
	XZ607	Westland Lynx AH1	AAC, BAOR
	XZ608	Westland Lynx AH1	AAC, BAOR
	XZ609	Westland Lynx AH1	AAC, BAOR
	XZ610	Westland Lynx AH1	AAC, BAOR
	XZ611	Westland Lynx AH1 [L]	AAC, ATS Middle Wallop
	XZ612	Westland Lynx AH1	AAC, BAOR
	XZ613	Westland Lynx AH1	AAC, BAOR
	XZ614	Westland Lynx AH1	AAC, BAOR
	XZ615	Westland Lynx AH1	AAC, BAOR
	XZ616	Westland Lynx AH1	AAC, BAOR
	XZ617	Westland Lynx AH1	AAC, BAOR
	XZ630	Panavia Tornado	MoD(PE) A&AEE Boscombe Down
	XZ631	Panavia Tornado	MoD(PE) A&AEE/BAe Warton
	XZ640	Westland Lynx AH1	AAC, ATS Middle Wallop
	XZ641	Westland Lynx AH1	AAC, BAOR
	XZ642	Westland Lynx AH1	AAC, BAOR
	XZ643	Westland Lynx AH1	AAC, BAOR
	XZ644	Westland Lynx AH1	AAC, BAOR
	XZ645	Westland Lynx AH1	AAC, BAOR
	XZ646	Westland Lynx AH1	AAC, BAOR
	XZ647	Westland Lynx AH1	AAC, BAOR
	XZ648	Westland Lynx AH1	AAC, ARW/LCF Middle Wallop
	XZ649	Westland Lynx AH1	AAC, ATS Middle Wallop
	XZ650	Westland Lynx AH1	AAC, BAOR
	XZ651	Westland Lynx AH1	AAC, BAOR
	XZ652	Westland Lynx AH1	AAC, BAOR
	XZ653	Westland Lynx AH1	AAC, BAOR
	XZ654	Westland Lynx AH1	AAC, BAOR
	XZ655	Westland Lynx AH1	AAC, BAOR
	XZ661	Westland Lynx AH1	AAC, BAOR
	XZ662	Westland Lynx AH1	AAC, BAOR
	XZ663	Westland Lynx AH1	AAC, BAOR
	XZ664	Westland Lynx AH1	AAC, ATS Middle Wallop
	XZ665	Westland Lynx AH1	AAC, RNAY Wroughton, store
	XZ666	Westland Lynx AH1	AAC, RNAY Wroughton, store
	XZ667	Westland Lynx AH1	AAC, BAOR
	XZ668	Westland Lynx AH1	AAC, BAOR
	XZ669	Westland Lynx AH1	AAC, BAOR
	XZ670	Westland Lynx AH1	AAC, BAOR
	XZ671	Westland Lynx AH1	AAC, BAOR

Serial	Type (alternative identity)	Owner, Operator or Location	Notes
XZ672	Westland Lynx AH1	AAC, BAOR	
XZ673	Westland Lynx AH1	AAC, BAOR	
XZ674	Westland Lynx AH1	AAC, BAOR	
XZ675	Westland Lynx AH1	AAC, BAOR	
XZ676	Westland Lynx AH1	AAC, BAOR	
XZ677	Westland Lynx AH1	AAC, BAOR	
XZ678	Westland Lynx AH1	AAC, BAOR	
XZ679	Westland Lynx AH1	AAC, ARW/LCF Middle Wallop	
XZ680	Westland Lynx AH1	AAC, BAOR	
XZ681	Westland Lynx AH1	AAC, BAOR	
XZ689	Westland Lynx HAS2 [641/PO]	RN No 702 Sqn, RNAS Portland	
XZ690	Westland Lynx HAS2	RN No 815 Sqn, RNAS Portland	
XZ691	Westland Lynx HAS2	RN No 815 Sqn, RNAS Portland	
XZ692	Westland Lynx HAS2 [431/PO]	RN No 815 Sqn, RNAS Portland	
XZ693	Westland Lynx HAS2	RN No 815 Sqn, RNAS Portland	
XZ694	Westland Lynx HAS2 [344/GW]	RN No 815 Sqn, RNAS Portland	
XZ695	Westland Lynx HAS2	RN No 815 Sqn, RNAS Portland	
XZ696	Westland Lynx HAS2	RN No 815 Sqn, RNAS Portland	
XZ697	Westland Lynx HAS2	RN No 815 Sqn, RNAS Portland	
XZ698	Westland Lynx HAS2	RN No 815 Sqn, RNAS Portland	
XZ699	Westland Lynx HAS2 [[642/PO]	RN No 702 Sqn, RNAS Portland	
XZ719	Westland Lynx HAS2 [646/PO]	RN No 702 Sqn, RNAS Portland	
XZ720	Westland Lynx HAS2	RN No 815 Sqn, RNAS Portland	
XZ721	Westland Lynx HAS2 [323/AB]	RN No 815 Sqn, RNAS Portland	
XZ722	Westland Lynx HAS2	RN No 815 Sqn, RNAS Portland	
XZ723	Westland Lynx HAS2	RN No 815 Sqn, RNAS Portland	
XZ724	Westland Lynx HAS2	RN No 815 Sqn, RNAS Portland	
XZ725	Westland Lynx HAS2	RN SSTF, RNAS Portland	
XZ726	Westland Lynx HAS2	RN No 815 Sqn, RNAS Portland	
XZ727	Westland Lynx HAS2	RN No 815 Sqn, RNAS Portland	
XZ728	Westland Lynx HAS2 [305/—]	RN No 815 Sqn, RNAS Portland	
XZ730	Westland Lynx HAS2	RN No 815 Sqn, RNAS Portland	
XZ731	Westland Lynx HAS2 [300/—]	RN No 815 Sqn, RNAS Portland	
XZ732	Westland Lynx HAS2	RNAY Fleetlands	
XZ733	Westland Lynx HAS2	RN No 815 Sqn, RNAS Portland	
XZ734	Westland Lynx HAS2	MoD(PE) A&AEE Boscombe Down	
XZ735	Westland Lynx HAS2 [320/AZ]	RN No 815 Sqn, RNAS Portland	
XZ736	Westland Lynx HAS2	RN No 815 Sqn, RNAS Portland	
XZ916	Westland Sea King HAS5	MoD(PE) Westland, Yeovil	
XZ918	Westland Sea King HAS5 [020/N]	RN No 820 Sqn, RNAS Culdrose	
XZ919	Westland Sea King HAS5 [271/—]	RN No 826 Sqn, RNAS Culdrose	
XZ920	Westland Sea King HAS5 [010/N]	RN No 820 Sqn, RNAS Culdrose	
XZ921	Westland Sea King HAS5 [017/N]	RN No 820 Sqn, RNAS Culdrose	
XZ922	Westland Sea King HAS5 [272/—]	RN No 814 Sqn, RNAS Culdrose	
XZ930	Westland Gazelle HT2 [Q]	RAF Support Command, 2 FTS	
XZ931	Westland Gazelle HT2 [R]	RAF Support Command, 2 FTS	
XZ932	Westland Gazelle HT2 [S]	RAF Support Command, 2 FTS	
XZ933	Westland Gazelle HT2 [T]	RAF Support Command, 2 FTS	
XZ934	Westland Gazelle HT2 [U]	RAF Support Command, 2 FTS	
XZ935	Westland Gazelle HCC4	RAF Support Command, No 32 Sqn	
XZ936	Westland Gazelle HT2	MoD(PE) ETPS Boscombe Down	
XZ937	Westland Gazelle HT2 [Y]	RAF Support Command, 2 FTS	
XZ938	Westland Gazelle HT2 [545/CU]	RN No 705 Sqn, RNAS Culdrose	
XZ939	Westland Gazelle HT2 [Z]	RAF Support Command, 2 FTS	
XZ940	Westland Gazelle HT2 [O]	RAF Support Command, 2 FTS	
XZ941	Westland Gazelle HT2 [B]	RAF Support Command, 2 FTS	
XZ942	Westland Gazelle HT2 [FL]	RNAY Fleetlands	
XZ964	BAe Harrier GR3 [P]	RAF Strike Command, 233 OCU	

Notes	Serial	Type (alternative identity)	Owner, operator or location
	XZ965	BAe Harrier GR3 [AM]	RAF Germany
	XZ966	BAe Harrier GR3 [14]	RAF Strike Command, No 1 Sqn
	XZ967	BAe Harrier GR3	RAF Strike Command, 417 Flt
	XZ968	BAe Harrier GR3 [K]	RAF Germany
	XZ969	BAe Harrier GR3 [AS]	RAF Germany
	XZ970	BAe Harrier GR3 [AR]	RAF Germany
	XZ971	BAe Harrier GR3 [N]	RAF Strike Command, 233 OCU
	XZ972	BAe Harrier GR3 [33]	RAF Strike Command, No 1 Sqn
	XZ987	BAe Harrier GR3 [AX]	RAF Germany
	XZ990	BAe Harrier GR3 [H]	RAF Germany
	XZ991	BAe Harrier GR3 [AD]	RAF Germany
	XZ992	BAe Harrier GR3 [05]	RAF Strike Command, No 1 Sqn
	XZ993	BAe Harrier GR3 [E]	RAF Germany
	XZ994	BAe Harrier GR3 [I]	RAF Strike Command, 233 OCU
	XZ995	BAe Harrier GR3 [AO]	RAF Germany
	XZ996	BAe Harrier GR3 [I]	RAF Strike Command, 233 OCU
	XZ997	BAe Harrier GR3 [31]	RAF Strike Command, No 1 Sqn
	XZ998	BAe Harrier GR3 [J]	RAF Strike Command, 233 OCU
	XZ999	BAe Harrier GR3 [I]	RAF Germany
	ZA101	BAe Hawk T50 (G-HAWK)	BAe, Dunsfold
	ZA105	Westland Sea King HAR3 [SB]	RAF Strike Command, Ascension Island
	ZA110	BAe Jetstream T2 (G-AXUO) [573/—]	RN No 750 Sqn, RNAS Culdrose
	ZA111	BAe Jetstream T2 (G-AXFV) [574/CU]	RN No 750 Sqn, RNAS Culdrose
	ZA126	Westland Sea King HAS5 [012/N]	RN No 820 Sqn, RNAS Culdrose
	ZA127	Westland Sea King HAS5 [011/N]	RN No 820 Sqn, RNAS Culdrose
	ZA128	Westland Sea King HAS5 [014/N]	RN NASU RNAS Culdrose
	ZA129	Westland Sea King HAS5 [144/—]	RN No 826 Sqn, RNAS Culdrose
	ZA130	Westland Sea King HAS5 [353/—]	RN No 824 Sqn, RNAS Culdrose
	ZA131	Westland Sea King HAS5 [133/—]	RN No 826 Sqn, RNAS Culdrose
	ZA133	Westland Sea King HAS5 [135/—]	RN No 826 Sqn, RNAS Culdrose
	ZA134	Westland Sea King HAS5 [013/N]	RN No 820 Sqn, RNAS Culdrose
	ZA135	Westland Sea King HAS5 [015/N]	RN No 820 Sqn, RNAS Culdrose
	ZA136	Westland Sea King HAS5 [140/—]	RN No 826 Sqn, RNAS Culdrose
	ZA137	Westland Sea King HAS5 [146/—]	RN No 826 Sqn, RNAS Culdrose
	ZA140	BAe VC10 K2 (G-ARVL)	MoD(PE) for RAF, Filton
	ZA141	BAe VC10 K2 (G-ARVG)	MoD(PE) for RAF, Filton
	ZA142	BAe VC10 K2 (G-ARVI)	MoD(PE) for RAF, Filton
	ZA143	BAe VC10 K2 (G-ARVK)	MoD(PE) for RAF, Filton
	ZA144	BAe VC10 K2 (G-ARVC)	MoD(PE) for RAF, Filton
	ZA147	BAe VC10 K3 (5H-MMT)	MoD(PE) for RAF, Filton
	ZA148	BAe VC10 K3 (5Y-ADA)	MoD(PE) for RAF, Filton
	ZA149	BAe VC10 K3 (5X-UVJ)	MoD(PE) for RAF, Filton
	ZA150	BAe VC10 K3 (5H-MOG)	MoD(PE) for RAF, Filton
	ZA166	Westland Sea King HAS5 [352/—]	RN No 824 Sqn, RNAS Culdrose
	ZA167	Westland Sea King HAS5 [353/—]	RN No 824 Sqn, RNAS Culdrose
	ZA168	Westland Sea King HAS5 [267/—]	RN No 814 Sqn, RNAS Culdrose
	ZA169	Westland Sea King HAS5	RN NASU RNAS Culdrose
	ZA170	Westland Sea King HAS5	RN NASU RNAS Culdrose
	ZA175	BAe Sea Harrier FRS1 [125/H]	RN No 800 Sqn, RNAS Yeovilton
	ZA176	BAe Sea Harrier FRS1 [250]	RN No 809 Sqn, RNAS Yeovilton
	ZA177	BAe Sea Harrier FRS1 [711]	RN No 899 Sqn, RNAS Yeovilton
	ZA190	BAe Sea Harrier FRS1 [009]	RN No 801 Sqn, RNAS Yeovilton
	ZA191	BAe Sea Harrier FRS1 [253]	RN No 809 Sqn, RNAS Yeovilton
	ZA193	BAe Sea Harrier FRS1 [254]	RN No 809 Sqn, RNAS Yeovilton
	ZA194	BAe Sea Harrier FRS1 [251]	RN No 809 Sqn, RNAS Yeovilton

XZ294 Westland Gazelle AH1. *PRM*

ZA141 BAe VC10 K2. *APM*

Serial	Type (alternative identity)	Owner, operator or location	Notes
ZA195	BAe Sea Harrier FRS1	MoD(PE) for RN	
ZA250	BAe Harrier T52 (G-VTOL)	British Aerospace, Dunsfold	
ZA254	Panavia Tornado F2	MoD(PE) BAe Warton	
ZA267	Panavia Tornado F2	MoD(PE) BAe Warton	
ZA283	Panavia Tornado F2	MoD(PE) BAe Warton	
ZA291	Westland Sea King HC4 [VB]	RN No 846 Sqn, RNAS Yeovilton	
ZA292	Westland Sea King HC4 [VH]	RN No 846 Sqn, RNAS Yeovilton	
ZA293	Westland Sea King HC4 [VK]	RN No 846 Sqn, RNAS Yeovilton	
ZA295	Westland Sea King HC4 [VM]	RN No 846 Sqn, RNAS Yeovilton	
ZA296	Westland Sea King HC4 [VF]	RN No 846 Sqn, RNAS Yeovilton	
ZA297	Westland Sea King HC4 [VG]	RN No 846 Sqn, RNAS Yeovilton	
ZA298	Westland Sea King HC4 (G-BJNM) [VA]	RN No 846 Sqn, RNAS Yeovilton	
ZA299	Westland Sea King HC4 [VE]	RN No 846 Sqn, RNAS Yeovilton	
ZA310	Westland Sea King HC4 [VC]	RN No 846 Sqn, RNAS Yeovilton	
ZA312	Westland Sea King HC4 [VW]	RN No 846 Sqn, RNAS Yeovilton	
ZA313	Westland Sea King HC4 [VZ]	RN No 846 Sqn, RNAS Yeovilton	
ZA314	Westland Sea King HC4	RN No 846 Sqn, RNAS Yeovilton	
ZA319	Panavia Tornado GR1T (B-11)	RAF Strike Command, TTTE	
ZA320	Panavia Tornado GR1T (B-01)	RAF Strike Command, TTTE	
ZA321	Panavia Tornado GR1 (B-58)	RAF Strike Command, TTTE	
ZA322	Panavia Tornado GR1 (B-50)	RAF Strike Command, TTTE	
ZA322	Panavia Tornado GR1 replica (BAPC 155)	RAF Exhibition Flight, Abingdon	
ZA323	Panavia Tornado GR1T	MoD(PE) BAe Warton	
ZA324	Panavia Tornado GR1T (B-02)	RAF Strike Command, TTTE	
ZA325	Panavia Tornado GR1T (B-03)	RAF Strike Command, TTTE	
ZA326	Panavia Tornado GR1T	MoD(PE) BAe Warton	
ZA327	Panavia Tornado GR1 (B-51)	RAF Strike Command, TTTE	
ZA328	Panavia Tornado GR1	MoD(PE) BAe Warton	
ZA329	Panavia Tornado GR1T (B-52)	RAF Strike Command, TTTE	
ZA352	Panavia Tornado GR1 (B-04)	RAF Strike Command, TTTE	
ZA353	Panavia Tornado GR1 (B-53)	RAF Strike Command, TTTE	
ZA354	Panavia Tornado GR1	MoD(PE) BAe Warton	
ZA355	Panavia Tornado GR1 (B-54)	RAF Strike Command, TTTE	
ZA356	Panavia Tornado GR1T (B-07)	RAF Strike Command, TTTE	
ZA357	Panavia Tornado GR1T (B-05)	RAF Strike Command, TTTE	
ZA358	Panavia Tornado GR1T (B-06)	RAF Strike Command, TTTE	
ZA359	Panavia Tornado GR1 (B-55)	RAF Strike Command, TTTE	
ZA360	Panavia Tornado GR1 (B-56)	RAF Strike Command, TTTE	
ZA361	Panavia Tornado GR1 (B-57)	RAF Strike Command, TTTE	
ZA362	Panavia Tornado GR1T (B-09)	RAF Strike Command, TTTE	
ZA365	Panavia Tornado GR1T	RAF Strike Command, TWCU	
ZA366	Panavia Tornado GR1T	RAF Strike Command, TWCU	
ZA367	Panavia Tornado GR1T	RAF Strike Command, TWCU	
ZA368	Panavia Tornado GR1T	RAF Strike Command, TWCU	
ZA369	Panavia Tornado GR1	RAF Strike Command	
ZA370	Panavia Tornado GR1	RAF Strike Command	
ZA371	Panavia Tornado GR1	RAF Strike Command	
ZA372	Panavia Tornado GR1	RAF Strike Command, TWCU	
ZA373	Panavia Tornado GR1	MoD(PE) for RAF	
ZA374	Panavia Tornado GR1	MoD(PE) for RAF	
ZA375	Panavia Tornado GR1	MoD(PE) for RAF	
ZA376	Panavia Tornado GR1	MoD(PE) for RAF	
ZA392	Panavia Tornado GR1	MoD(PE) for RAF	
ZA393	Panavia Tornado GR1	MoD(PE) for RAF	
ZA394	Panavia Tornado GR1	MoD(PE) for RAF	
ZA395	Panavia Tornado GR1	MoD(PE) for RAF	
ZA396	Panavia Tornado GR1	MoD(PE) for RAF	
ZA397	Panavia Tornado GR1	MoD(PE) for RAF	
ZA398	Panavia Tornado GR1	MoD(PE) for RAF	
ZA399	Panavia Tornado GR1	MoD(PE) for RAF	
ZA400	Panavia Tornado GR1	MoD(PE) for RAF	
ZA401	Panavia Tornado GR1	MoD(PE) for RAF	
ZA402	Panavia Tornado GR1	MoD(PE) for RAF	
ZA403	Panavia Tornado GR1	MoD(PE) for RAF	
ZA404	Panavia Tornado GR1	MoD(PE) for RAF	
ZA405	Panavia Tornado GR1	MoD(PE) for RAF	
ZA406	Panavia Tornado GR1	MoD(PE) for RAF	
ZA407	Panavia Tornado GR1	MoD(PE) for RAF	
ZA408	Panavia Tornado GR1	MoD(PE) for RAF	

Notes	Serial	Type (alternative identity)	Owner, operator or location
	ZA409	Panavia Tornado GR1	MoD(PE) for RAF
	ZA410	Panavia Tornado GR1	MoD(PE) for RAF
	ZA411	Panavia Tornado GR1	MoD(PE) for RAF
	ZA412	Panavia Tornado GR1	MoD(PE) for RAF
	ZA446	Panavia Tornado GR1T	MoD(PE) for RAF
	ZA447	Panavia Tornado GR1T	MoD(PE) for RAF
	ZA448	Panavia Tornado GR1T	MoD(PE) for RAF
	ZA449	Panavia Tornado GR1T	MoD(PE) for RAF
	ZA450	Panavia Tornado GR1	MoD(PE) for RAF
	ZA451	Panavia Tornado GR1	MoD(PE) for RAF
	ZA452	Panavia Tornado GR1	MoD(PE) for RAF
	ZA453	Panavia Tornado GR1	MoD(PE) for RAF
	ZA454	Panavia Tornado GR1	MoD(PE) for RAF
	ZA455	Panavia Tornado GR1	MoD(PE) for RAF
	ZA456	Panavia Tornado GR1	MoD(PE) for RAF
	ZA457	Panavia Tornado GR1	MoD(PE) for RAF
	ZA458	Panavia Tornado GR1	MoD(PE) for RAF
	ZA459	Panavia Tornado GR1	MoD(PE) for RAF
	ZA460	Panavia Tornado GR1	MoD(PE) for RAF
	ZA461	Panavia Tornado GR1	MoD(PE) for RAF
	ZA462	Panavia Tornado GR1	MoD(PE) for RAF
	ZA463	Panavia Tornado GR1	MoD(PE) for RAF
	ZA464	Panavia Tornado GR1	MoD(PE) for RAF
	ZA465	Panavia Tornado GR1	MoD(PE) for RAF
	ZA466	Panavia Tornado GR1	MoD(PE) for RAF
	ZA467	Panavia Tornado GR1	MoD(PE) for RAF
	ZA468	Panavia Tornado GR1	MoD(PE) for RAF
	ZA469	Panavia Tornado GR1	MoD(PE) for RAF
	ZA470	Panavia Tornado GR1	MoD(PE) for RAF
	ZA471	Panavia Tornado GR1	MoD(PE) for RAF
	ZA472	Panavia Tornado GR1	MoD(PE) for RAF
	ZA473	Panavia Tornado GR1	MoD(PE) for RAF
	ZA474	Panavia Tornado GR1	MoD(PE) for RAF
	ZA475	Panavia Tornado GR1	MoD(PE) for RAF
	ZA490	Panavia Tornado GR1	MoD(PE) for RAF
	ZA491	Panavia Tornado GR1	MoD(PE) for RAF
	ZA492	Panavia Tornado GR1	MoD(PE) for RAF
	ZA493	Panavia Tornado GR1	MoD(PE) for RAF
	ZA494	Panavia Tornado GR1	MoD(PE) for RAF
	ZA540	Panavia Tornado GR1T (B-12)	RAF Strike Command, TTTE
	ZA541	Panavia Tornado GR1T	RAF Strike Command, TWCU
	ZA542	Panavia Tornado GR1	RAF Strike Command, TWCU
	ZA543	Panavia Tornado GR1 (B-59)	RAF Strike Command, TTTE
	ZA544	Panavia Tornado GR1T	RAF Strike Command, TWCU
	ZA545	Panavia Tornado GR1	RAF Strike Command, TWCU
	ZA546	Panavia Tornado GR1	RAF Strike Command, TWCU
	ZA547	Panavia Tornado GR1T	RAF Strike Command, TWCU
	ZA548	Panavia Tornado GR1T (B-10)	RAF Strike Command, TTTE
	ZA549	Panavia Tornado GR1	RAF Strike Command, TWCU
	ZA550	Panavia Tornado GR1	RAF Strike Command, TWCU
	ZA551	Panavia Tornado GR1T	RAF Strike Command, TWCU
	ZA552	Panavia Tornado GR1T	RAF Strike Command, TWCU
	ZA553	Panavia Tornado GR1T	RAF Strike Command, TWCU
	ZA554	Panavia Tornado GR1	RAF Strike Command, TWCU
	ZA555	Panavia Tornado GR1T	RAF Strike Command, TWCU
	ZA556	Panavia Tornado GR1	MoD(PE) BAe Warton/A&AEE
	ZA557	Panavia Tornado GR1	RAF Strike Command, TWCU
	ZA558	Panavia Tornado GR1	RAF Strike Command, TWCU
	ZA559	Panavia Tornado GR1	RAF Strike Command, TWCU
	ZA560	Panavia Tornado GR1	RAF Strike Command, TWCU
	ZA561	Panavia Tornado GR1	RAF Strike Command, TWCU
	ZA562	Panavia Tornado GR1T	RAF Strike Command, TWCU
	ZA563	Panavia Tornado GR1	RAF Strike Command, TWCU
	ZA564	Panavia Tornado GR1	RAF Strike Command, TWCU
	ZA585	Panavia Tornado GR1	RAF Strike Command, TWCU
	ZA586	Panavia Tornado GR1 [A]	RAF Strike Command, No 9 Sqn
	ZA587	Panavia Tornado GR1 [B]	RAF Strike Command, No 9 Sqn
	ZA588	Panavia Tornado GR1 [C]	RAF Strike Command, No 9 Sqn
	ZA589	Panavia Tornado GR1 [D]	RAF Strike Command, No 9 Sqn
	ZA590	Panavia Tornado GR1 [E]	RAF Strike Command, No 9 Sqn
	ZA591	Panavia Tornado GR1 [F]	RAF Strike Command, No 9 Sqn

ZA193 BAe Sea Harrier FRS1. *PRM*

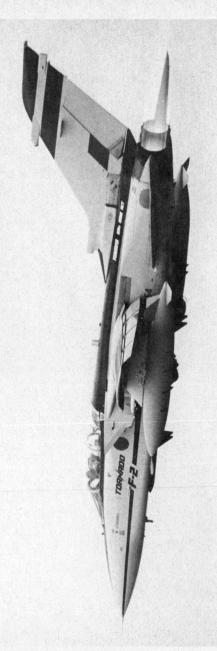

ZA254 Panavia Tornado F2. *APM*

Serial	Type (alternative identity)	Owner, operator or location	Notes
ZA592	Panavia Tornado GR1 [G]	RAF Strike Command, No 9 Sqn	
ZA593	Panavia Tornado GR1 [H]	RAF Strike Command, No 9 Sqn	
ZA594	Panavia Tornado GR1T	RAF Strike Command, TWCU	
ZA595	Panavia Tornado GR1T [K]	RAF Strike Command, No 9 Sqn	
ZA596	Panavia Tornado GR1T [L]	RAF Strike Command, No 9 Sqn	
ZA597	Panavia Tornado GR1 [M]	RAF Strike Command, No 9 Sqn	
ZA598	Panavia Tornado GR1T [N]	RAF Strike Command, No 9 Sqn	
ZA599	Panavia Tornado GR1T	RAF Strike Command, TWCU	
ZA600	Panavia Tornado GR1	RAF Strike Command, No 617 Sqn	
ZA601	Panavia Tornado GR1	RAF Strike Command, No 617 Sqn	
ZA602	Panavia Tornado GR1T [P]	RAF Strike Command, No 9 Sqn	
ZA603	Panavia Tornado GR1	RAF Strike Command, No 617 Sqn	
ZA604	Panavia Tornado GR1T	RAF Strike Command, No 617 Sqn	
ZA605	Panavia Tornado GR1	RAF Strike Command, No 617 Sqn	
ZA606	Panavia Tornado GR1	RAF Strike Command, No 617 Sqn	
ZA607	Panavia Tornado GR1	RAF Strike Command, No 617 Sqn	
ZA608	Panavia Tornado GR1	RAF Strike Command, No 617 Sqn	
ZA609	Panavia Tornado GR1	RAF Strike Command, No 617 Sqn	
ZA610	Panavia Tornado GR1	RAF Strike Command, No 617 Sqn	
ZA611	Panavia Tornado GR1	RAF Strike Command, No 617 Sqn	
ZA612	Panavia Tornado GR1T	RAF Strike Command, No 617 Sqn	
ZA613	Panavia Tornado GR1	RAF Strike Command, No 617 Sqn	
ZA614	Panavia Tornado GR1	RAF Strike Command, TSF	
ZA625	Slingsby Venture T2	RAF Support Command, 616 GS	
ZA626	Slingsby Venture T2 [C]	RAF Support Command, 632 GS	
ZA627	Slingsby Venture T2	RAF Support Command, 625 GS	
ZA628	Slingsby Venture T2	RAF Support Command, 611 GS	
ZA629	Slingsby Venture T2 [9]	RAF Support Command, 633 GS	
ZA630	Slingsby Venture T2	RAF Support Command, 642 GS	
ZA631	Slingsby Venture T2 [1]	RAF Support Command, 613 GS	
ZA632	Slingsby Venture T2 [2]	RAF Support Command, 613 GS	
ZA633	Slingsby Venture T2 [3]	RAF Support Command, 613 GS	
ZA634	Slingsby Venture T2 [C]	RAF Support Command, CGS/644 GS	
ZA652	Slingsby Venture T2	RAF Support Command, 612 GS	
ZA653	Slingsby Venture T2	RAF Support Command, 612 GS	
ZA654	Slingsby Venture T2	RAF Support Command, 612 GS	
ZA655	Slingsby Venture T2 [V]	RAF Support Command, CGS	
ZA656	Slingsby Venture T2	RAF Support Command, 642 GS	
ZA657	Slingsby Venture T2	RAF Support Command, CGS	
ZA658	Slingsby Venture T2	RAF Support Command, 633 GS	
ZA659	Slingsby Venture T2	RAF Support Command, CGS/644 GS	
ZA660	Slingsby Venture T2	RAF Support Command, 637 GS	
ZA661	Slingsby Venture T2	RAF Support Command, 637 GS	
ZA662	Slingsby Venture T2	RAF Support Command, 637 GS	
ZA663	Slingsby Venture T2	RAF Support Command, CGS	
ZA664	Slingsby Venture T2	RAF Support Command, 611 GS	
ZA665	Slingsby Venture T2	RAF Support Command, 625 GS	
ZA666	Slingsby Venture T2	RAF Support Command, 633 GS	
ZA670	B-V Chinook HC1 (N37010) [BS]	RAF Strike Command, No 18 Sqn	
ZA671	B-V Chinook HC1	MoD(PE) A&AEE Boscombe Down	
ZA672	B-V Chinook HC1 [FF]	RAF Strike Command, 240 OCU	
ZA673	B-V Chinook HC1 [FG]	RAF Strike Command, 240 OCU	
ZA674	B-V Chinook HC1 [FH]	RAF Strike Command, 240 OCU	
ZA675	B-V Chinook HC1 [FI]	RAF Strike Command, 240 OCU	
ZA676	B-V Chinook HC1 [FJ]	RAF Strike Command, 240 OCU	
ZA677	B-V Chinook HC1 [FK]	RAF Strike Command, 240 OCU	
ZA678	B-V Chinook HC1 [FL]	RAF Strike Command, 240 OCU	
ZA679	B-V Chinook HC1 [BV]	RAF Strike Command, No 18 Sqn	
ZA680	B-V Chinook HC1 [BW]	RAF Strike Command, No 18 Sqn	
ZA681	B-V Chinook HC1 [FZ]	RAF Strike Command, 240 OCU	
ZA682	B-V Chinook HC1 [BY]	RAF Strike Command, No 18 Sqn	
ZA683	B-V Chinook HC1 [BX]	RAF Strike Command, No 18 Sqn	
ZA684	B-V Chinook HC1	RAF Strike Command, RNAY Fleetlands	
ZA704	B-V Chinook HC1	MoD(PE) A&AEE Boscombe Down	
ZA705	B-V Chinook HC1 [BU]	RAF Strike Command, No 18 Sqn	
ZA707	B-V Chinook HC1 [BP]	RAF Strike Command, No 18 Sqn	
ZA708	B-V Chinook HC1 [BE]	RAF Strike Command, No 18 Sqn	
ZA709	B-V Chinook HC1 [BD]	RAF Strike Command, No 18 Sqn	
ZA710	B-V Chinook HC1 [BC]	RAF Strike Command, Nos 7/18 Sqns	
ZA711	B-V Chinook HC1 [BR]	RAF Strike Command, Nos 7/18 Sqns	

Notes	Serial	Type (alternative identity)	Owner, Operator or Location
	ZA712	B-V Chinook HC1 [BZ]	RAF Strike Command, No 18 Sqn
	ZA713	B-V Chinook HC1 [BJ]	RAF Strike Command, No 18 Sqn
	ZA714	B-V Chinook HC1 [BH]	RAF Strike Command, No 18 Sqn
	ZA715	B-V Chinook HC1 [BL]	RAF Strike Command, No 18 Sqn
	ZA717	B-V Chinook HC1 [BK]	RAF Strike Command, No 18 Sqn
	ZA718	B-V Chinook HC1 [BN]	RAF Strike Command, No 18 Sqn
	ZA720	B-V Chinook HC1 [BG]	RAF Strike Command, No 18 Sqn
	ZA721	B-V Chinook HC1 [BF]	RAF Strike Command, Nos 7/18 Sqns
	ZA726	Westland Gazelle AH1	AAC, BATUS Canada
	ZA727	Westland Gazelle AH1	AAC, BATUS Canada
	ZA728	Westland Gazelle AH1 [CA]	Royal Marines, 3 CBAS
	ZA729	Westland Gazelle AH1	AAC, BAOR
	ZA730	Westland Gazelle AH1	Royal Marines, 3 CBAS
	ZA731	Westland Gazelle AH1	AAC, BAOR
	ZA732	Westland Gazelle AH1	AAC, BAOR
	ZA733	Westland Gazelle AH1	AAC, BATUS, Alberta, Canada
	ZA734	Westland Gazelle AH1	AAC, Belize
	ZA735	Westland Gazelle AH1	AAC, Belize
	ZA736	Westland Gazelle AH1	AAC, Belize
	ZA737	Westland Gazelle AH1 [V]	AAC, ARWS Middle Wallop
	ZA765	Westland Gazelle AH1	AAC, Belize
	ZA766	Westland Gazelle AH1	AAC, BAOR
	ZA767	Westland Gazelle AH1	AAC, Belize
	ZA768	Westland Gazelle AH1 [F]	AAC, ARWS Middle Wallop
	ZA769	Westland Gazelle AH1 [K]	AAC, ARWS Middle Wallop
	ZA770	Westland Gazelle AH1	AAC, BAOR
	ZA771	Westland Gazelle AH1	AAC, BAOR
	ZA772	Westland Gazelle AH1	AAC, BAOR
	ZA773	Westland Gazelle AH1	AAC, UK
	ZA774	Westland Gazelle AH1	AAC, UK
	ZA775	Westland Gazelle AH1	AAC, BAOR
	ZA776	Westland Gazelle AH1 [H]	Royal Marines, 3 CBAS
	ZA777	Westland Gazelle AH1	AAC, BAOR
	ZA802	Westland Gazelle HT3 [W]	RAF Support Command, 2 FTS
	ZA803	Westland Gazelle HT3 [X]	RAF Support Command, 2 FTS
	ZA804	Westland Gazelle HT3 [I]	RAF Support Command, 2 FTS
	ZA934	Westland Puma HC1 [CS]	RAF Strike Command, No 33 Sqn
	ZA935	Westland Puma HC1 [CT]	RAF Strike Command, No 33 Sqn
	ZA936	Westland Puma HC1 [CU]	RAF Strike Command, No 33 Sqn
	ZA937	Westland Puma HC1 [CV]	RAF Strike Command, No 33 Sqn
	ZA938	Westland Puma HC1 [CW]	RAF Strike Command, No 33 Sqn
	ZA939	Westland Puma HC1 [CX]	RNAY Fleetlands, store
	ZA940	Westland Puma HC1 [DO]	RAF Germany, No 230 Sqn
	ZA941	Westland Puma HC1	MoD(PE) RAE Farnborough
	ZA947	Douglas Dakota C3 (KG661)	MoD(PE) RAE Farnborough
	ZB506	Westland Sea King Mk 4X	MoD(PE) Westland, Yeovil
	ZB600	BAe Harrier T4	MoD(PE) for RAF
	ZB601	BAe Harrier T4	MoD(PE) for RAF
	ZB602	BAe Harrier T4	MoD(PE) for RAF
	ZB603	BAe Harrier T4	MoD(PE) for RAF
	ZB604	BAe Harrier T4	MoD(PE) for RN
	ZB605	BAe Harrier T4	MoD(PE) for RN
	ZB606	BAe Harrier T4	MoD(PE) for RN
	ZB615	SEPECAT Jaguar T2	MoD(PE) IAM, Farnborough
	ZB625	Westland Gazelle HT3	RAF Support Command, 2 FTS
	ZB626	Westland Gazelle HT3	RAF Support Command, 2 FTS
	ZB627	Westland Gazelle HT3	RAF Support Command, 2 FTS
	ZB628	Westland Gazelle HT3	RAF Support Command, 2 FTS
	ZB646	Westland Gazelle HT2	RN No 705 Sqn, RNAS Culdrose
	ZB647	Westland Gazelle HT2	RN No 705 Sqn, RNAS Culdrose
	ZB665	Westland Gazelle AH1	MoD(PE) for AAC
	ZB666	Westland Gazelle AH1	MoD(PE) for AAC
	ZB667	Westland Gazelle AH1	MoD(PE) for AAC
	ZB668	Westland Gazelle AH1	MoD(PE) for AAC
	ZB669	Westland Gazelle AH1	MoD(PE) for AAC
	ZB670	Westland Gazelle AH1	MoD(PE) for AAC
	ZB671	Westland Gazelle AH1	MoD(PE) for AAC
	ZB672	Westland Gazelle AH1	MoD(PE) for AAC
	ZB673	Westland Gazelle AH1	MoD(PE) for AAC
	ZB674	Westland Gazelle AH1	MoD(PE) for AAC

Serial	Type (alternative identity)	Owner, Operator or Location	Notes
ZB675	Westland Gazelle AH1	MoD(PE) for AAC	
ZB676	Westland Gazelle AH1	MoD(PE) for AAC	
ZB677	Westland Gazelle AH1	MoD(PE) for AAC	
ZB678	Westland Gazelle AH1	MoD(PE) for AAC	
ZB679	Westland Gazelle AH1	MoD(PE) for AAC	
ZB680	Westland Gazelle AH1	MoD(PE) for AAC	
ZB681	Westland Gazelle AH1	MoD(PE) for AAC	
ZB682	Westland Gazelle AH1	MoD(PE) for AAC	
ZB683	Westland Gazelle AH1	MoD(PE) for AAC	
ZB684	Westland Gazelle AH1	MoD(PE) for AAC	
ZB685	Westland Gazelle AH1	MoD(PE) for AAC	
ZB686	Westland Gazelle AH1	MoD(PE) for AAC	
ZB687	Westland Gazelle AH1	MoD(PE) for AAC	
ZB688	Westland Gazelle AH1	MoD(PE) for AAC	
ZB689	Westland Gazelle AH1	MoD(PE) for AAC	
ZD230	BAC Super VC10 (G-ASGA)	RAF Abingdon, stored	
ZD231	BAC Super VC10 (G-ASGB)	RAF Abingdon, stored	
ZD232	BAC Super VC10 (G-ASGD) (8699M)	RAF Brize Norton, JATE	
ZD233	BAC Super VC10 (G-ASGE)	RAF Brize Norton	
ZD234	BAC Super VC10 (G-ASGF) (8700M)	RAF Brize Norton	
ZD235	BAC Super VC10 (G-ASGG)	RAF Abingdon, stored	
ZD236	BAC Super VC10 (G-ASGH)	RAF Abingdon, stored	
ZD237	BAC Super VC10 (G-ASGI)	RAF Abingdon, stored	
ZD238	BAC Super VC10 (G-ASGJ)	RAF Abingdon, stored	
ZD239	BAC Super VC10 (G-ASGK)	RAF Abingdon, stored	
ZD240	BAC Super VC10 (G-ASGL)	RAF Abingdon, stored	
ZD241	BAC Super VC10 (G-ASGM)	RAF Abingdon, stored	
ZD242	BAC Super VC10 (G-ASGP)	RAF Abingdon, stored	
ZD243	BAC Super VC10 (G-ASGR)	RAF Abingdon, stored	
ZD249	Westland Lynx HAS3	MoD(PE) A&AEE Boscombe Down	
ZD250	Westland Lynx HAS3 [630/PO]	RN No 702 Sqn, RNAS Portland	
ZD251	Westland Lynx HAS3 [631/PO]	RN No 702 Sqn, RNAS Portland	
ZD252	Westland Lynx HAS3	RN No 702 Sqn, RNAS Portland	
ZD253	Westland Lynx HAS3	RN NASU Yeovilton	
ZD254	Westland Lynx HAS3	RN NASU Yeovilton	
ZD485	FMA IA58 Pucara (A-515)	MoD(PE) A&AEE Boscombe Down	
ZD487	FMA IA58 Pucara	MoD(PE) A&AEE Boscombe Down	
ZD493	BAC VC10 (G-ARVJ)	RAF Brize Norton	

ZA709 B-V Chinook HC1. *PRM*

RAF Maintenance Command/Support Command 'M' number cross-reference for serials listed in Military Aircraft Markings

1746M/K4972	7616M/WW388	7869M/WK935	8043M/XF836	8160M/XD622
5377M/EP120	7618M/WW442	7874M/XR568	8044M/XP286	8161M/XE993
5405M/LF738	7621M/WV686	7887M/XD375	8046M/XL770	8162M/WM913
5466M/LF751	7622M/WV606	7890M/XD453	8049M/WE168	8163M/XP919
5690M/MK356	7625M/WD356	7891M/XM693	8050M/XG329	8169M/WH364
5713M/BM597	7630M/VZ304	7894M/XD818	8052M/WH166	8171M/XJ607
5758M/DG202	7641M/XA634	7895M/WF784	8053M/WK968	8172M/XJ609
6372M/EE549	7646M/VX461	7896M/XA900	8054AM/XM410	8173M/XN685
6490M/LA255	7648M/XF785	7898M/XP854	8054BM/XM417	8174M/WZ576
6709M/TE356	7656M/WJ573	7899M/XG540	8055AM/XM402	8175M/XE950
6850M/TE184	7688M/WW421	7900M/WA576	8055BM/XM404	8177M/WM224
6944M/RW386	7693M/WV483	7906M/WH132	8056M/XG337	8179M/XN928
6947M/RW388	7696M/WV493	7917M/WA591	8057M/XR243	8180M/XN930
6960M/MT847	7697M/WV495	7920M/WL360	8059M/XN956	8182M/XN953
7000M/TE392	7698M/WV499	7923M/XT133	8060M/WW397	8183M/XN962
7014M/N6720	7705M/WL505	7928M/XE849	8062M/XR669	8184M/WT520
7060M/VF301	7709M/WT933	7929M/XH768	8063M/WT536	8186M/WR977
7090M/EE531	7711M/PS915	7930M/WH301	8072M/PK624	8187M/WH791
7118M/LA198	7712M/WK281	7931M/RD253	8076M/XM386	8188M/XG327
7119M/LA226	7715M/XK724	7932M/WZ744	8077M/XN594	8189M/WD646
7150M/PK683	7716M/WS776	7933M/XR220	8078M/XM351	8190M/XJ918
7151M/VT229	7717M/XA549	7937M/WS843	8079M/XN492	8191M/XK862
7154M/WB188	7718M/WA577	7938M/XH903	8080M/XM480	8192M/XR658
7174M/VX272	7719M/WK277	7939M/XD596	8081M/XM468	8194M/XK862
7175M/VV106	7729M/WB758	7940M/XL764	8082M/XM409	8196M/XE920
7200M/VT812	7734M/XD536	7949M/XF974	8083M/XM367	8197M/WT346
7241M/TE311	7735M/XP812	7955M/XH767	8084M/XM369	8198M/WT339
7243M/TE462	7737M/XD602	7957M/XF545	8085M/XM467	8203M/XD377
7244M/TB382	7739M/XA801	7959M/WS774	8087M/XN925	8205M/XN819
7245M/RW382	7750M/WL168	7960M/WS726	8088M/XN602	8206M/WG419
7246M/TD248	7755M/WG760	7961M/WS739	8090M/XM698	8209M/WG418
7256M/TB752	7758M/PM651	7964M/WS760	8092M/WK654	8211M/WK570
7257M/TB252	7759M/PK664	7965M/WS792	8101M/WH984	8212M/WK587
7288M/PK724	7761M/XH318	7967M/WS788	8102M/WT486	8216M/WP927
7293M/RW393	7770M/WT746	7969M/WS840	8103M/WR985	8218M/WB645
7323M/VV217	7791M/WT778	7971M/XK699	8106M/WR982	8219M/XR455
7325M/R5868	7796M/WJ676	7972M/XH764	8108M/WV703	8221M/XP409
7421M/WT660	7805M/TW117	7973M/WS807	8113M/WV753	8222M/XJ604
7422M/WT684	7806M/TA639	7976M/XK418	8114M/WL798	8223M/XN658
7443M/WX853	7809M/XA699	7980M/XM561	8117M/WR974	8224M/XN699
7451M/TE476	7814M/XD511	7982M/XH892	8118M/WZ549	8225M/XN705
7458M/WX905	7816M/WG763	7983M/XD506	8119M/WR981	8226M/XP921
7464M/XA564	7817M/TX214	7986M/WG777	8120M/WR981	8229M/XM355
7470M/XA553	7820M/XM527	7990M/XD452	8121M/XM474	8230M/XM362
7491M/WT569	7822M/XP248	7997M/XG452	8122M/XD613	8231M/XM375
7496M/WT612	7825M/WK991	7998M/XD515	8129M/WH779	8232M/XM381
7499M/WT555	7827M/XA917	8005M/WG768	8138M/XN700	8233M/XM408
7510M/WT694	7829M/XH992	8009M/XG518	8139M/XJ582	8234M/XN458
7525M/WT619	7839M/WV781	8010M/XG547	8140M/XJ571	8235M/XN549
7532M/WT651	7840M/XK482	8011M/XV269	8141M/XN688	8236M/XP573
7533M/WT680	7841M/WV783	8012M/VS562	8142M/XJ560	8237M/XS179
7543M/WN901	7843M/WE145	8017M/XL762	8143M/XN691	8238M/XS180
7544M/WN904	7847M/WV276	8018M/XN344	8144M/XN707	8239M/XS210
7564M/XE982	7849M/XF319	8019M/WZ869	8145M/XJ526	8340M/XP341
7570M/XD674	7850M/XA923	8021M/XL824	8151M/WV795	8344M/WH960
7582M/WP190	7852M/XG506	8022M/XN341	8152M/WV794	8345M/XG540
7583M/WP185	7859M/XP283	8023M/XD463	8153M/WV903	8346M/XN734
7602M/WE600	7862M/XR246	8025M/XH124	8154M/WV908	8350M/WH840
7604M/XD542	7863M/WZ679	8027M/XM555	8155M/WV797	8352M/XN632
7605M/WS692	7865M/TX226	8033M/XD382	8156M/XE339	8355M/XN645
7606M/WV562	7866M/XH278	8034M/XL703	8157M/XE390	KG374
7607M/TJ138	7867M/XH980	8040M/XR493	8158M/XE369	8357M/WK576
7615M/WV679	7868M/WZ736	8041M/XF690	8159M/XD528	8359M/WF825

ZA594 Panavia Tornado GR1T. *APM*

8362M/WG477	8429M/XH592	8532M/XS423	8614M/XP515	8674M/XP395
8363M/WG463	8431M/XR651	8533M/XS449	8616M/XP541	8675M/WL793
8364M/WG464	8434M/XM411	8534M/XS450	8617M/XM709	8676M/XL577
8365M/XK421	8435M/XN512	8535M/XS454	8618M/XP504	8677M/XJ695
8366M/XG454	8436M/XN554	8537M/XN778	8619M/XP511	8678M/XE656
8367M/XG474	8438M/XP761	8538M/XN781	8620M/XP534	8679M/XF526
8368M/XF926	8439M/WZ849	8546M/XN720	8621M/XR538	8680M/XF527
8369M/WE139	8440M/WD935	8548M/WT507	8622M/XR980	8681M/XG164
8370M/N1671	8441M/XR107	8549M/WT534	8623M/XR998	8682M/XP404
8371M/XA847	8442M/XP411	8551M/XN774	8624M/XS102	8683M/WJ870
8372M/K8042	8444M/XP400	8554M/TG511	8625M/XS105	8684M/XJ634
8373M/P2617	8445M/XK968	8556M/XN855	8626M/XS109	8685M/XF516
8375M/NX611	8446M/XP748	8557M/XP500	8627M/XP558	8686M/XG158
8376M/RF398	8447M/XP359	8558M/XP439	8628M/XJ380	8687M/XJ639
8377M/R9125	8450M/WE145	8559M/XN467	8629M/WL801	8689M/WK144
8378M/T9707	8451M/WJ611	8560M/XR569	8630M/WG362	8691M/WT518
8379M/DG590	8452M/XK885	8561M/XS100	8631M/XR574	8694M/XH554
8382M/VR930	8453M/XP745	8562M/XS110	8632M/XP533	8695M/WJ817
8383M/K9942	8454M/XP442	8564M/XN387	8633M/MK732	8696M/WH773
8384M/A4590	8455M/XP444	8566M/XV279	8634M/WP314	8697M/WJ825
8385M/N5912	8457M/XS871	8567M/WL738	8635M/XP514	8699M/ZD232
8386M/NV778	8458M/XP672	8568M/XP503	8636M/XR540	8700M/ZD234
8387M/T6296	8459M/XR650	8569M/XR535	8637M/XR991	8701M/XP352
8388M/XL993	8460M/XR680	8570M/XR954	8638M/XS101	8702M/XG196
8389M/VX573	8463M/XP355	8571M/XR984	8639M/XS107	8703M/VW453
8390M/SL542	8465M/W1048	8572M/XM706	8640M/XR977	8704M/XN643
8391M/SL574	8467M/WP912	8573M/XM708	8641M/XR987	8705M/XT281
8392M/SL674	8473M/WP190	8575M/XP542	8642M/XR537	8706M/XF383
8393M/XK987	8488M/WL627	8576M/XP502	8643M/WJ867	8707M/XF386
8394M/WG422	8489M/XN816	8577M/XP532	8644M/XR457	8708M/XF509
8395M/WF408	8490M/WH703	8578M/XR534	8645M/XD163	8709M/XG209
8396M/XK740	8491M/WJ880	8579M/XR140	8646M/XK969	8710M/XG274
8398M/WR967	8492M/WJ872	8580M/XP516	8647M/XP338	8711M/XG290
8400M/XP583	8493M/XR571	8581M/WJ775	8648M/XK526	8712M/XF439
8401M/XP686	8494M/XP557	8582M/XE874	8649M/XP331	8713M/XG225
8402M/XN769	8495M/XR672	8585M/XE670	8650M/XP333	8714M/XK149
8403M/XK531	8497M/XM698	8586M/XE643	8651M/WG556	8715M/XG264
8405M/TG536	8498M/XR670	8590M/XM191	8652M/WH794	8716M/XV155
8406M/XP831	8501M/XP640	8592M/XM969	8653M/XS120	8718M/XX396
8407M/XP585	8502M/XP686	8595M/XH278	8654M/XL898	8719M/XT257
8408M/XS186	8503M/XS451	8598M/WP270	8655M/XN126	8720M/XP353
8409M/XS209	8506M/XR704	8601M/XL450	8656M/XP405	8721M/XP354
8410M/XR662	8507M/XS215	8602M/XR541	8657M/VZ634	8722M/WJ640
8411M/XM139	8508M/XS218	8603M/XR951	8659M/XV340	8723M/XL567
8412M/XM147	8509M/XT141	8604M/XS104	8660M/XW538	8726M/XP299
8413M/XM192	8510M/XP567	8605M/XA536	8661M/XJ727	8727M/XR486
8414M/XM173	8511M/WT305	8606M/XP530	8662M/XR458	8728M/WT532
8415M/XM181	8512M/VP973	8607M/XP538	8664M/WJ603	8729M/WJ815
8416M/XM183	8514M/XS176	8608M/XP540	8665M/WL754	8735M/WJ681
8417M/XM144	8515M/WH869	8609M/XR953	8666M/XE793	8736M/XF375
8418M/XM178	8516M/XR643	8610M/XL502	8668M/WJ821	8739M/XH170
8422M/XM169	8517M/XA932	8611M/WF128	8671M/XJ435	8742M/WH856
8427M/XM172	8530M/WD948	8612M/XD182	8672M/XP351	8747M/WJ629
8428M/XH593	8531M/XS418	8613M/XJ724	8673M/XD165	

RN engineering 'A' airframe number cross-reference for serials listed in Military Aircraft Markings

A2055/SX336	A2510/WM913	A2532/WV826	A2551/XA868	A2579/XN332
A2123/NL750	A2511/WM983	A2533/XA456	A2556/XE327	A2580/XE369
A2126/BB731	A2517/WM961	A2534/XE368	A2557/WV798	A2581/XK532
A2439/WF219	A2522/WM993	A2538/XJ393	A2571/XG577	A2596/XT448
A2459/XA523	A2525/XN334	A2539/XG831	A2572/XJ402	A2597/XS509
A2472/XA508	A2526/WV911	A2540/WN464	A2574/XD332	A2598/XJ482
A2483/WF259	A2528/XA363	A2542/XA862	A2575/XG574	A2600/XN934
A2503/WM994	A2530/WM969	A2543/XA870	A2576/WV198	A2601/XJ477
A2509/WF299	A2531/WG718	A2550/XA866	A2577/XB480	A2603/XK911

A2605/XN308	A2627/XN967	A2650/XP160	A2670/XS128	A2687/XS877
A2607/XK944	A2629/XM667	A2651/XG596	A2671/XS867	A2688/XP158
A2608/XA459	A2630/XL853	A2652/XN261	A2672/XS537	A2689/XM874
A2609/XM329	A2632/WV903	A2654/XN302	A2673/WF122	A2690/XS887
A2610/XN647	A2633/XE369	A2655/XN953	A2674/WF125	A2691/XS868
A2611/XJ575	A2634/WV794	A2658/XP984	A2675/XS881	A2692/XM917
A2613/XN706	A2635/XE339	A2659/XV669	A2676/XR572	A2693/XM843
A2614/XN314	A2636/XE390	A2660/WV908	A2677/XR993	A2694/XS865
A2615/XT256	A2637/WV797	A2661/WV795	A2678/XR955	A2695/XS876
A2616/XN651	A2639/XN650	A2662/WF299	A2679/XP535	A2696/XS882
A2618/XP116	A2642/XL836	A2663/XN309	A2680/XP157	A2697/XS870
A2619/XS695	A2643/XN311	A2664/XV644	A2681/XP117	A2698/XP105
A2621/XJ584	A2645/WF225	A2665/XL839	A2682/XM845	A2699/XS570
A2622/XJ602	A2646/XK988	A2666/XS872	A2683/XS878	A2700/XP980
A2623/XN697	A2647/XS463	A2667/XP226	A2684/XP151	A2701/XL500
A2624/XN692	A2648/XS125	A2668/XS885	A2685/XS886	A2702/XS545
A2626/XL847	A2649/XS869	A2669/XP149	A2686/XS873	

ZA110 BAe Jetstream T2. *PRM*

RN landing platform and shore station code-letters

Tail code	Name and Pennant Number	Type/task
AB	HMS *Ambuscade* (F172)	Type 21
AC	HMS *Achilles* (F12)	Leander
AE	HMS *Ariadne* (F72)	Leander
AG	HMS *Avenger* (F185)	Type 21
AJ	HMS *Ajax* (F114)	Leander
AL	HMS *Alacrity* (F174)	Type 21
AM	HMS *Andromeda* (F57)	Leander
AN	HMS *Antrim* (D18)	County
AP	HMS *Apollo* (F70)	Leander
AR	HMS *Arethusa* (F38)	Leander
AT	HMS *Argonaut* (F56)	Leander
AU	HMS *Aurora* (F10)	Leander
AV	HMS *Active* (F171)	Type 21
AW	HMS *Arrow* (F173)	Type 21
AZ	HMS *Amazon* (F169)	Type 21
BA	HMS *Bearer* (F93)	Type 22
BC	HMS *Bacchante* (F69)	Leander
BD	RFA *Sir Bedivere* (L3004)	Landing ship
BE	RFA *Blue Rover* (A270)	Fleet tanker
BK	HMS *Berwick* (F115)	Type 12
BM	HMS *Birmingham* (D86)	Type 42
BN	HMS *Brazen* (F91)	Type 22
BS	HMS *Bristol* (D23)	Type 82
BT	HMS *Brilliant* (F90)	Type 22
BV	HMS *Black Rover* (A273)	Fleet tanker
BW	HMS *Broadsword* (F88)	Type 22
BX	HMS *Battleaxe* (F89)	Type 22
CF	HMS *Cardiff* (D108)	Type 42
CP	HMS *Cleopatra* (F28)	Leander
CS	HMS *Charybdis* (F75)	Leander
CU	RNAS Culdrose (HMS *Seahawk*)	
DC	HMS *Dumbarton Castle* (P268)	Fishery protection
DM	BRNC Dartmouth	
DM	HMS *Diomede* (F16)	Leander
DN	HMS *Danae* (F47)	Leander
DO	HMS *Dido* (F104)	Leander
ED	HMS *Endurance* (F171)	Ice Patrol
EU	HMS *Euryalus* (F115)	Leander
EX	HMS *Exeter* (D89)	Type 42
FA	RFA *Fort Austin* (A386)	Support ship
FF	HMS *Fife* (D20)	County
FG	RFA *Fort Grange* (A385)	Support ship
FL	RNAY Fleetlands	
FM	HMS *Falmouth* (F113)	Type 12
FS	HMS *Fearless* (L10)	Assault
GA	HMS *Galatea* ((F18)	Leander
GL	HMS *Glamorgan* (D19)	County
GN	RFA *Green Rover* (A268)	Fleet tanker
GR	RFA *Sir Garaint* (L3027)	Landing ship
GV	RFA *Gold Rover* (A271)	Fleet tanker
GW	HMS *Glasgow* (D88)	Type 42

Tail Code	Name and Pennant Number	Type/Task
GY	RFA *Grey Rover* (A269)	Fleet tanker
H	HMS *Hermes* (R12)	Carrier
HD	HMS *Hydra* (A144)	Hecla
HE	HMS *Herald* (A138)	Hecla
HL	HMS *Hecla* (A133)	Hecla
HT	HMS *Hecate* (A137)	Hecla
ID	HMS *Intrepid* (L11)	Assault
JO	HMS *Juno* (F52)	Leander
JP	HMS *Jupiter* (F60)	Leander
L	HMS *Illustrious* (R06)	Carrier
LC	HMS *Leeds Castle* (P258)	Fishery protection
LD	HMS *Londonderry* (F108)	Type 12
LE	HMS *Leander* (F109)	Leander
LN	RFA *Sir Lancelot* (L3029)	Assault ship
LP	HMS *Liverpool* (D92)	Type 42
LS	RNAS Lee-on-Solent (HMS *Daedalus*)	
LT	HMS *Lowestoft* (F103)	Type 12
LY	HMS *Lyness* (A339)	Support ship
M	HMS *Manchester* (D95)	Type 42
MV	HMS *Minerva* (F45)	Leander
N	HMS *Invincible* (R05)	Carrier
NA	HMS *Naiad* (F39)	Leander
NC	HMS *Newcastle* (D87)	Type 42
NF	HMS *Norfolk* (D21)	County
OD	RFA *Olmeda* (A124)	Fleet tanker
ON	RFA *Olna* (A123)	Fleet tanker
OW	RFA *Olwen* (A122)	Fleet tanker
PB	HMS *Phoebe* (F42)	Leander
PL	HMS *Plymouth* (F126)	Type 12
PN	HMS *Penelope* (F127)	Leander
PO	RNAS Portland (HMS *Osprey*)	
PV	RFA *Sir Pervical* (L3036)	Landing ship
PW	Prestwick Airport (HMS *Gannet*)	
R	HMS *Ark Royal* (R09)	Carrier
RG	RFA *Regent* (A486)	Support ship
RL	HMS *Rhyl* (F129)	Type 12
RO	HMS *Rothesay* (F107)	Type 12
RS	RFA *Resource* (A480)	Support ship
SC	HMS *Scylla* (F71)	Leander
SN	HMS *Southampton* (D90)	Type 42
SS	HMS *Sirius* (F40)	Leander
ST	RFA *Stromness* (A344)	Support ship
TB	RFA *Tarbatness* (A345)	Support ship
TP	RFA *Tidepool* (A76)	Fleet tanker
TS	RFA *Tidespring* (A75)	Fleet tanker
VL	RNAS Yeovilton (HMS *Heron*)	
WU	RNAY Wroughton	
YM	HMS *Yarmouth* (F101)	Type 12

216 Fouga Super Magister. *PRM*

Military Aircraft Markings carried by Aircraft of the Irish Army Air Corps

Notes	Serial	Type (alternative identity)	Owner, Operator or Location
	34	Miles Magister	Engineering Wing, Baldonnel
	141	Avro Anson	Irish Aviation Museum, Dublin
	164	DH Chipmunk	Engineering Wing, Baldonnel
	165	DH Chipmunk	Engineering Wing, Baldonnel
	166	DH Chipmunk	Engineering Wing, Baldonnel
	167	DH Chipmunk	Engineering Wing, Baldonnel
	168	DH Chipmunk	Training Wing, Gormanston
	172	DH Chipmunk	Engineering Wing, Baldonnel
	173	DH Chipmunk	Basic Flying Training Wing, Gormanston
	176	DH Dove	Civil Defence, Phoenix Park
	181	Percival Provost T1	Fire Section, Baldonnel
	183	Percival Provost T1	Apprentice School, Baldonnel
	184	Percival Provost T1	Fire Section, Baldonnel
	191	DH Vampire T11	Irish Aviation Museum, Dublin
	192	DH Vampire T11	Bolton Street Technical College, Dublin
	195	Sud Alouette III	No 1 Support Wing, Baldonnel
	196	Sud Alouette III	No 1 Support Wing, Baldonnel
	197	Sud Alouette III	No 1 Support Wing, Baldonnel
	198	DH Vampire T11 (XE977)	On display, Casement
	199	DH Chipmunk	Training Wing, Gormanston
	202	Sud Alouette III	No 1 Support Wing, Baldonnel
	203	Cessna FR172H	No 2 Support Wing, Gormanston
	204	Cessna FR172H	Engineering Wing, Baldonnel
	205	Cessna FR172H	No 2 Support Wing, Gormanston
	206	Cessna FR172H	No 2 Support Wing, Gormanston
	207	Cessna FR172H	No 2 Support Wing, Gormanston
	208	Cessna FR172H	No 2 Support Wing, Gormanston
	209	Cessna FR172H	No 2 Support Wing, Gormanston
	210	Cessna FR172H	No 2 Support Wing, Gormanston
	211	Sud Alouette III	No 1 Support Wing, Baldonnel
	212	Sud Alouette III	No 1 Support Wing, Baldonnel
	213	Sud Alouette III	No 1 Support Wing, Baldonnel
	214	Sud Alouette III	No 1 Support Wing, Baldonnel
	215	Fouga Super Magister	No 1 Support Wing, Baldonnel
	216	Fouga Super Magister	No 1 Support Wing, Baldonnel
	217	Fouga Super Magister	No 1 Support Wing, Baldonnel
	218	Fouga Super Magister	No 1 Support Wing, Baldonnel
	219	Fouga Super Magister	No 1 Support Wing, Baldonnel
	220	Fouga Super Magister	No 1 Support Wing, Baldonnel
	221	Fouga Super Magister	Engineering Wing, Baldonnel
	222	SIAI SF-260W Warrior	Training Wing, Baldonnel
	223	SIAI SF-260W Warrior	Training Wing, Baldonnel
	225	SIAI SF-260W Warrior	Training Wing, Baldonnel
	226	SIAI SF-260W Warrior	Training Wing, Baldonnel
	227	SIAI SF-260W Warrior	Training Wing, Baldonnel
	228	SIAI SF-260W Warrior	Training Wing, Baldonnel
	229	SIAI SF-260W Warrior	Training Wing, Baldonnel
	230	SIAI SF-260W Warrior	Training Wing, Baldonnel
	231	SIAI SF-260W Warrior	Training Wing, Baldonnel
	232	Beech King Air 200 (EI-BCY)	Maritime Squadron, Baldonnel
	233	SIAI SF-260MC	Engineering Wing, Baldonnel
	234	Beech King Air 200 (EI-BFJ)	Maritime Squadron, Baldonnel
	235	SIAI SF-260W Warrior	Training Wing, Baldonnel
	237	Aerospatiale Gazelle	Advanced Flying Training School, Baldonnel
	238	HS125/700B	Transport Squadron, Baldonnel
	240	Beech King Air 200	Transport Squadron, Baldonnel
	241	Aerospatiale Gazelle	Advanced Flying Training School, Baldonnel
	242	SA330J Puma (F-BRQK)	Advanced Flying Training School, Baldonnel
	243	Cessna FR172P	No 2 support Wing, Gormanston

Historic aircraft in overseas markings

'Historic' aircraft carrying the markings of overseas air arms which can be seen in the UK, mainly preserved in museums and collections or taking part in air shows.

Serial	Type (alternative identity)	Owner, operator or location	Notes
Argentina			
A-515	FMA IA58 Pucara	MoD(PE) A&AEE Boscombe Down	
A-522	FMA IA58 Pucara	RAF St Athan	
A-528	FMA IA58 Pucara	RAF Cosford, Aerospace Museum	
A-533	FMA IA58 Pucara	MoD(PE)/RAF	
A-549	FMA IA58 Pucara	Fleet Air Arm Museum, Yeovilton	
AE-331	Agusta A109 Hirundo	Royal Marines, Middle Wallop	
AE-334	Agusta A109 Hirundo	Fleet Air Arm Museum, Yeovilton	
AE-409	Bell UH-1H	MoD(PE)/RAF	
AE-413	Bell UH-1H	MoD(PE)/RAF	
AE-422	Bell UH-1H	Fleet Air Arm Museum, Yeovilton	
AE-520	Vertol CH-47C Chinook	RNAY, Fleetlands	
PA-12	Sud SA330L Puma	RNAY, Fleetlands	
Australia			
A2-4	Supermarine Seagull V (VH-ALB)	RAF Battle of Britain Museum, Hendon	
A16-199	Lockheed Hudson IV (G-BEOX)	RAF Museum, Hendon	
Belgium			
FT-36	Lockheed T-33A	Dumfries & Galloway Av Gp	
FT-37	Lockheed T-33A	RAF Alconbury	
FU-6	Republic F-84F Thunderstreak (52-7133)	Historic Aircraft Museum	
Cambodia			
125	Morane MS733 Alcyon (G-SHOW)	Privately owned, Sutton Bridge	
Canada			
20385	CCF AT-16 Harvard IV (G-BGPB)	Privately owned, Duxford	
920	VS Stranraer (CF-BXO)	RAF Museum, Hendon	
9059	Bristol Bolingbroke IVT	Privately owned, Portsmouth	
9893	Bristol Bolingbroke IVT	Privately owned, Duxford	
9940	Bristol Bolingbroke IVT	Royal Scottish Museum, East Fortune	
10038	Bristol Bolingbroke IVT (G-MKIV)	Privately owned, Duxford	
10201	Bristol Bolingbroke IVT	Strathallan Collection	
18393	Avro Canada CF-100 (G-BCYK)	Imperial War Museum, Duxford	
Denmark			
E-402	Hawker Hunter F51	Wealden Aviation Group, Hailsham	
E-407	Hawker Hunter F51	Loughborough & Leicester Air Museum	
E-408	Hawker Hunter F51 (8565M)	RAF Brawdy main gate	
E-409	Hawker Hunter F51	Wales Air Museum, Cardiff	
E-419	Hawker Hunter F51	North-East Air Museum	
E-424	Hawker Hunter F51	Lincolnshire Aviation Museum	
E-425	Hawker Hunter F51	Midland Air Museum, Coventry	
E-427	Hawker Hunter F51	BAe Apprentice School, Brough	
ET-271	Hawker Hunter T53	Warbirds of GB, Blackbushe	
ET-273	Hawker Hunter T7	Bomber County Aviation Museum, Cleethorpes	
L866	Consolidated Catalina	Aerospace Museum, RAF Cosford	
Eire			
177	Percival Provost T1	Privately owned, Shobdon	
178	Pervical Provost T1 (G-EIRE)	Privately owned, Woodvale	
France			
19	Deperdussin Replica (BAPC136)	Leisure Sport, Thorpe Park	
25	Dassault Mystere IVA	RAF Sculthorpe, store	
45	SNCAN Stampe SV4C (G-BHFG)	Privately owned, Enstone	
50	Dassault Mystere IVA	RAF Sculthorpe, store	
57	Dassault Mystere IVA	Imperial War Museum, Duxford	
59	Dassault Mystere IVA	Wales Air Museum, Cardiff	
61	Dassault Mystere IVA	RAF Sculthorpe, store	
70	Dassault Mystere IVA	Midland Air Museum, Coventry	
75	Dassault Mystere IVA	RAF Lakenheath, BDRF	
79	Dassault Mystere IVA	Norfolk & Suffolk Air Museum, Flixton	

Historic Aircraft

Notes	Serial	Type (alternative identity)	Owner, operator or location
	83	Dassault Mystere IVA	Newark Air Museum, Winthorpe
	84	Dassault Mystere IVA	Lashenden Air Museum, Headcorn
	85	Dassault Mystere IVA	Loughborough & Leicester Air Museum
	92	MH Broussard (G-BJGW)	Privately owned, Duxford
	97	Dassault Mystere IVA	RAF Sculthorpe, store
	99	Dassault Mystere IVA	RAF Sculthorpe, store
	101	Dassault Mystere IVA	Bomber County Aviation Museum Cleethorpes
	104	Dassault Mystere IVA	RAF Sculthorpe, store
	120	Stampe SV4C (3) (G-AZGC)	Privately owned, Booker
	121	Dassault Mystere IVA	City of Norwich Aviation Museum
	126	Dassault Mystere IVA	RAF Sculthorpe, store
	129	Dassault Mystere IVA	RAF Sculthorpe, store
	131	Dassault Mystere IVA	RAF Sculthorpe, store
	146	Dassualt Mystere IVA	North East Aircraft Museum
	180	Dassault Mystere IVA	RAF Sculthorpe, store
	184	Dassault Mystere IVA	RAF Lakenheath, BDRF
	276	Dassault Mystere IVA	RAF Sculthorpe, store
	309	Dassault Mystere IVA	RAF Lakenheath, BDRF
	318	Dassault Mystere IVA	Dumfries & Galloway Aviation Museum
	319	Dassault Mystere IVA	Rebel Air Museum, Andrewsfield
	399	Dassault Mystere IVA	RAF Sculthorpe, store
	1049	Morane MS230 (G-BJCL)	Privately owned, Booker
	3398	Spad XII Replica (G-BFYO)	Leisure Sport, Thorpe Park
Germany			
	D5397/17	Albatross D.VA Replica (G-BFXL)	Leisure Sport, Thorpe Park
	AT+JX	Bucker Jungmann (G-ATJX)	Privately owned, Duxford
	AX+IH	Bucker Jungmeister (G-AXIH)	Privately owned, Booker
	N8+AA	CASA 352L (G-BFHD)	Warbirds of GB, Blackbushe
	N9+AA	CASA 352L (G-BECL)	Warbirds of GB, Blackbushe
	6J+PR	CASA 2-111 (G-AWHB)	Historic Aircraft Museum
	475081	Fieseler Fi156C Storch (VP546)	RAF St Athan Museum
	CB+VD	Fieseler Fi156C Storch (D-EKMU)	Historic Aircraft Museum
	28368	Flettner Fl282V Kolibri	Midland Air Museum
	100143	Focke-Achgelis Fa330	Imperial War Museum, Duxford
	100406	Focke-Achgelis Fa330	Institute of Technology, Cranfield
	100502	Focke-Achgelis Fa330	The Aeroplane Collection, Wigan
	100509	Focke-Achgelis Fa330	Science Museum, London
	100549	Focke-Achgelis Fa330	Merseyside Aviation Society
	160000	Focke-Achgelis Fa330 (really 100545)	Torbay Aircraft Museum
	04	Focke Wulf FW190 Replica (G-WULF)	Privately owned, Elstree
	584219/38	Focke Wulf FW190F-8/UI	RAF St Athan Museum
	733682	Focke Wulf FW190A-8/R6	Imperial War Museum, Lambeth
	5125/18	Fokker D.VII Replica (BAPC 110)	Leisure Sport, Thorpe Park
	8417/18	Fokker D.VII	RAF Museum, Hendon
	150/17	Fokker Dr.1 Driedekker Replica (BAPC 139)	Leisure Sport, Thorpe Park
	425/17	Fokker Dr.1 Driedekker Replica (G-BEFR)	Leisure Sport, Thorpe Park
	425/17	Fokker Dr.1 Driedekker Replica (BAPC 133)	Torbay Aircraft Museum
	22912	Hansa Brandenburg W.29 Replica (BAPC 138)	Leisure Sport, Thorpe Park
	701152	Heinkel He111H-23 (8471M)	Battle of Britain Museum, Hendon
	120227	Heinkel He162 Salamander (8472M)	RAF St Athan Museum
	120235	Heinkel He162 Salamander	Imperial War Museum, Lambeth
	14	Hispano HA1112 (G-BJZZ)	Privately owned, Duxford
	1Z+NK	Junkers Ju52/3m (6316)	Imperial War Museum, Duxford
	494083	Junkers Ju87 D-3 (8474M)	Battle of Britain Museum, Hendon
	360043	Junkers Ju88R-1 (PJ876)	Battle of Britain Museum, Hendon
	7198/18	LVG C.VI (G-AANJ)	Shuttleworth Collection, Old Warden
	1190	Messerschmitt Bf109E-3	Privately owned, Hurn
	4101	Messerschmitt Bf109E-4 (8477M)	Battle of Britain Museum, Hendon
	10639	Messerschmitt Bf109G-2 (RN228)	RAF Northolt
	730301	Messerschmitt Bf110C-4 (8479M)	Battle of Britain Museum, Hendon
	191316	Messerschmitt Me163B Komet	Science Museum, London

A-549 FMA IA58 Pucara. *APM*

111

463221 NA P-51D Mustang. *PRM*

Serial	Type (alternative identity)	Owner, operator or location	Notes
191614	Messerschmitt Me163B Komet	Aerospace Museum, RAF Cosford	
191659	Messerschmitt Me163B Komet	Royal Scottish Museum, East Fortune	
191660	Messerschmitt Me163B Komet	Imperial War Museum, Duxford	
191904	Messerschmitt Me163B Komet	RAF St Athan Museum	
112372	Messerschmitt Me262A-1 (8482M)	Aerospace Museum, RAF Cosford	
420430	Messerschmitt Me410A-1/U2 (8483M)	Aerospace Museum, RAF Cosford	
7A+WN	Morane 500 (G-AZMH)	Privately owned, Booker	
Fl+S	Morane 505 (G-BIRW)	Privately owned, Duxford	

Italy

Serial	Type (alternative identity)	Owner, operator or location	Notes
MM5701	Fiat CR42 (BT474)	Battle of Britain Museum, Hendon	
MM53211	Fiat G.46-4	Historic Aircraft Museum, Southend	
MM53432	NA T-6D (RM-11)	Privately owned, Staverton	
MM53664	NA T-6D (RM-9)	Privately owned, Sandown	
MM542540	Piper Super Cub	RAF Woodbridge, store	

Netherlands

Serial	Type (alternative identity)	Owner, operator or location	Notes
E-15	Fokker S11 Instructor (G-BIYU)	Privately owned, Blackbushe	
R-163	Piper Super Cub (G-BIRH)	Privately owned, Lee-on-Solent	
204/V	Lockheed SP-2H Neptune	Aerospace Museum, RAF Cosford	

Norway

Serial	Type (alternative identity)	Owner, operator or location	Notes
321	Saab Safir	Newark Air Museum, Winthorpe	

Spain

Serial	Type (alternative identity)	Owner, operator or location	Notes
T2B-272	Casa C.352L	Cosford Aerospace Museum	

Sweden

Serial	Type (alternative identity)	Owner, operator or location	Notes
35075/40	Saab J-35J Draken	Duxford Aviation Society, Duxford	
29640	Saab J-29F	Historic Aircraft Museum, Southend	
50000	Saab Safir (09) (G-BCFV)	Privately owned, Booker	

Switzerland

Serial	Type (alternative identity)	Owner, operator or location	Notes
J-108	Pilatus P-2 (G-BJAX)	Privately owned, Booker	
U-109	Pilatus P-2 (G-BJAT)	Privately owned, Booker	
U-110	Pilatus P-2 (G-PTWO)	Privately owned, Duxford	
U-125	Pilatus P-2	Privately owned, Blackbushe	
U-142	Pilatus P-2 (G-BONE)	Privately owned, Southend	
U-143	Pilatus P-2	Privately owned, Blackbushe	
J-1008	DH Vampire FB6	Mosquito Aircraft Museum	
J-1172	DH Vampire FB6	Manchester Air & Space Museum	
J-1704	DH Venom FB4	Cosford Aerospace Museum	
282	Dewoitine D.26 (G-BBMI)	Privately owned, Duxford	

USA

Serial	Type (alternative identity)	Owner, operator or location	Notes
0-17899	Convair VT-29B	Imperial War Museum, Duxford	
111989	Cessna L-19A Bird Dog (N33600)	Museum of Army Flying	
115302	Piper L-18C (G-BJTP)	Privately owned, Wellesbourne Mountford	
117445	Lockheed T-33A	RAF Sculthorpe, store	
117524	Lockheed T-33A	RAF Sculthorpe, store	
12392	NA AT-6D Harvard III (LN-BNM)	Historic Aircraft Museum, Southend	
133722	C-V F4U-7 Corsair (NX1337A)	Privately owned, Coningsby	
133854	NA Harvard (G-SUES)	Privately owned, Biggin Hill	
14060	Lockheed T-33A	USAF Lakenheath	
14286	Lockheed T-33A	Imperial War Museum, Duxford	
14419	Lockheed T-33A	Midland Air Museum, Coventry	
146289	NA T-28 Trojan (N99153)	Norfolk & Suffolk Aviation Museum, Flixton	
151632	NA TB-25N Mitchell (NL9494Z)	Privately owned, Wellesbourne Mountford	
16769	Lockheed T-33A	RAF Mildenhall, on display	
17473	Lockheed T-33A	RAF Cosford Aerospace Museum	
18752	Lockheed T-33A	RAF Sculthorpe, store	
19036	Lockheed T-33A	Newark Air Museum, Winthorpe	
19252	Lockheed T-33A	Wealden Aviation Group, Hailsham	
231938	Boeing B-17G (F-BDRS)	Imperial War Museum, Duxford	
24535	Kaman HH-43F Huskie	Midland Air Museum, Coventry	
26	Boeing Stearman (G-BAVO)	Privately owned, Liverpool	

Historic Aircraft

Notes	Serial	Type (alternative identity)	Owner, operator or location
	27767	Aeronca L-3A (G-BIHW)	Privately owned, Glasgow
	2807	NA T-6G Texan (G-BHTH)	Privately owned, Speke
	29963	Lockheed T-33A	Wales Aircraft Museum, Cardiff
	315509	Douglas C-47D (G-AGIV/G-BHUB)	Imperial War Museum, Duxford
	329417	Piper J-3C-65 Cub (G-BDHK)	Privately owned, Coleford
	329601	Piper J-3C-65 Cub (G-AXHR)	Privately owned, Old Warden
	413048	Piper J-3C-65 Cub (G-BCXJ)	Privately owned, Compton Abbas
	42157	NA F-100D Super Sabre	North East Aviation Museum
	42160	NA F-100D Super Sabre	Wales Air Museum, Cardiff
	42163	NA F-100D Super Sabre	Dumfries & Galloway Aviation Group
	42165	NA F-100D Super Sabre	Imperial War Museum, Duxford
	42174	NA F-100D Super Sabre	Midland Air Museum, Coventry
	42196	NA F-100D Super Sabre	Norfolk & Suffolk Aviation Museum
	42204	NA F-100D Super Sabre	RAF Woodbridge
	42212	NA F-100D Super Sabre	RAF Sculthorpe, on display
	42223	NA F-100D Super Sabre	Newark Air Museum, Winthorpe
	42239	NA F-100D Super Sabre	Loughborough & Leics Air Museum
	42265	NA F-100D Super Sabre	USAF, Wethersfield gate
	429366	NA TB-25N Mitchell (N9115Z)	RAF Bomber Command Museum, Hendon
	430210	NA TB-25N Mitchell (N9455Z)	Privately owned, France
	431171	NA B-25J Mitchell	Imperial War Museum, Duxford
	454537	Piper L-4J Cub (G-BFDL)	Privately owned, Prestwick
	461748	Boeing B-29A (G-BHDK)	Imperial War Museum, Duxford
	463221	NA P-51D (really 473149/N6340T)	Privately owned, Geneva
	472028	NA P-51D	Privately owned, Tees-side
	472216	NA P-51D (G-BIXL)	Privately owned, Duxford
	472258	NA P-51D (really 473979)	Imperial War Museum, Duxford
	473543	NA P-51D (PF-543)	Privately owned, Woburn Green, Bucks
	479865	Piper J-3C-65 Cub (G-BHPK)	Privately owned, Wellesbourne Mountford
	480308	Piper J-3C-65 Cub (G-BDCD)	Privately owned, Slinfold
	480594	Piper J-3C-65 Cub (G-BEDJ)	Privately owned, Ashford Hill
	483009	NA AT-6 Harvard	Privately owned, North Weald
	485784	Boeing B-17G (G-BEDF/N17TE)	Privately owned, Duxford
	540	Piper L-4 Cub (G-BCNX)	Privately owned, Monewden
	54048	NA F-100D (really 42269)	RAF Lakenheath gate
	542447	Piper PA-18-135 (G-SCUB)	Privately owned, Anwick
	54433	Lockheed T-33A	Norfolk & Suffolk Aviation Museum
	54439	Lockheed T-33A	North East Aviation Museum
	549205	Republic P-47D (N47DE)	Warbirds of GB, Blackbushe
	63935	NA F-100F Super Sabre	RAF Sculthorpe, Rescue Training
	63938	NA F-100F	Lashenden Air Warfare Museum
	7797	Aeronca L-16A (G-BFAF)	Privately owned, Finmere
	82062	DHC U-6A Beaver	Midland Air Museum, Coventry
	8810677	NA AT-6C Harvard IIA (G-VALE)	Privately owned, Shobdon

US Military Aircraft Markings

All USAF aircraft have been allocated a fiscal year (FY) number since 1921. Individual aircraft are given a serial according to the fiscal year in which they are ordered. The numbers commence at 001 and are prefixed with the year of allocation. For example F-111E 68-0001 was the first aircraft ordered in 1968. The fiscal year serial is carried on the technical bloc which is usually stencilled on the left hand side of the aircraft just below the cockpit. The number displayed on the fin is a corruption of the FY serial. Most tactical aircraft carry the fiscal year in small figures followed by the last three digits of the serial in large figures. For example F-111F 70-2362 carries 70362 on its tail. An exception to this practice is the F-5E which carries the five digits of the production serial without the fiscal year. For example the FY serial of the F-5E which displays 01532 is 74-01532. Large transport and tanker aircraft such as C-130s and KC-135s usually display a five-figure number commencing with the last digit of the appropriate fiscal year and four figures of the production number. An example of this is EC-135H 61-0282 which displays 10282 on its fin.

USN serials follow a straightforward numerical sequence which commenced, for the present series, with the allocation of 00001 to an SB2C Helldiver by the Bureau of Aeronautics in 1940. Numbers in the 160000 series are presently being issued. They are usually carried in full on the rear fuselage of the aircraft and displayed either as a five figure sequence or in full on the fin.

UK based USAF aircraft

The following aircraft are normally based in the UK. They are listed in alphabetical order of type with individual aircraft in fiscal year serial number order. The number in brackets is that carried on the aircraft fin.

Notes	Serial	Serial	Notes
	Boeing EC-135H	79-0161 (79161)	
	(513TAW/10 ACCS, Mildenhall)	79-0162 (79162)	
	61-0282 (10282)	79-0163 (79163)	
	61-0285 (10285)	79-0164 (79164)	
	61-0286 (10286)	79-0217 (79217)	
	61-0291 (10291)	79-0218 (79218)	
		79-0219 (79219)	
	Fairchild A-10A Thunderbolt II	79-0220 (79220)	
	(81TFW Woodbridge/	79-0221 (79221)	
	Bentwaters WR)	79-0222 (79222)	
	78-0596 (78596)	79-0224 (79224)	
	78-0597 (78597)	79-0225 (79225)	
	78-0600 (78600)	80-0143 (80143)	
	78-0603 (78603)	80-0144 (80144)	
	79-0109 (79109)	80-0145 (80145)	
	79-0110 (79110)	80-0146 (80146)	
	79-0111 (79111)	80-0147 (80147)	
	79-0113 (79113)	80-0148 (80148)	
	79-0114 (79114)	80-0155 (80155)	
	79-0118 (79118)	80-0156 (80156)	
	79-0124 (79124)	80-0157 (80157)	
	79-0125 (79125)	80-0158 (80158)	
	79-0126 (79126)	80-0159 (80159)	
	79-0130 (79130)	80-0160 (80160)	
	79-0131 (79131)	80-0167 (80167)	
	79-0132 (79132)	80-0168 (80168)	
	79-0133 (79133)	80-0169 (80169)	
	79-0135 (79135)	80-0170 (80170)	
	79-0140 (79140)	80-0171 (80171)	
	79-0141 (79141)	80-0172 (80172)	
	79-0157 (79157)	80-0179 (80179)	
	79-0158 (79158)	80-0180 (80180)	
	79-0159 (79159)	80-0181 (80181)	
	79-0160 (79160)	80-0183 (80183)	

Notes	Serial	Serial	Notes
	80-0184 (80184)	81-0948 (81948)	
	80-0192 (80192)	81-0949 (81949)	
	80-0193 (80193)	81-0950 (81950)	
	80-0194 (80194)	81-0951 (81951)	
	80-0195 (80195)		
	80-0196 (80196)	**General Dynamics F-111E**	
	80-0202 (80202)	(20TFW, Upper Heyford UH)	
	80-0203 (80203)	67-0119 (67119)	
	80-0204 (80204)	67-0121 (67121)	
	80-0205 (80205)	67-0122 (67122)	
	80-0206 (80206)	68-0001 (68001)	
	80-0207 (80207)	68-0002 (68002)	
	80-0208 (80208)	68-0004 (68004)	
	80-0215 (80215)	68-0005 (68005)	
	80-0216 (80216)	68-0006 (68006)	
	80-0217 (80217)	68-0007 (68007)	
	80-0218 (80218)	68-0009 (68009)	
	80-0219 (80219)	68-0010 (68010)	
	80-0220 (80220)	68-0011 (68011)	
	80-0227 (80227)	68-0013 (68013)	
	80-0228 (80228	68-0014 (68014)	
	80-0229 (80229)	68-0015 (68015)	
	80-0230 (80230)	68-0016 (68016)	
	80-0231 (80231)	68-0017 (68017)	
	80-0232 (80232)	68-0019 (68019)	
	80-0233 (80233)	68-0020 (68020)	
	80-0234 (80234)	68-0021 (68021)	
	80-0235 (80235)	68-0022 (68022)	
	80-0236 (80236)	68-0023 (68023)	
	80-0237 (80237)	68-0025 (68025)	
	80-0270 (80270)	68-0026 (68026)	
	80-0271 (80271)	68-0027 (68027)	
	80-0272 (80272)	68-0028 (68028)	
	80-0273 (80273)	68-0029 (68029)	
	80-0274 (80274)	68-0030 (68030)	
	80-0275 (80275)	68-0031 (68031)	
	80-0276 (80276)	68-0032 (68032)	
	80-0277 (80277)	68-0033 (68033)	
	80-0278 (80278)	68-0034 (68034)	
	80-0279 (80279)	68-0035 (68035)	
	80-0280 (80280)	68-0036 (68036)	
	80-0281 (80281)	68-0037 (68037)	
	81-0001 (81001)*	68-0038 (68038)	
	81-0002 (81002)*	68-0039 (68039)	
	81-0003 (81003)*	68-0040 (68040)	
	81-0004 (81004)*	68-0041 (68041)	
	81-0005 (81005)*	68-0043 (68043)	
	81-0006 (81006)*	68-0044 (68044)	
	81-0009 (81009)*	68-0046 (68046)	
	81-0010 (81010)*	68-0047 (68047)	
	81-0011 (81011)*	68-0048 (68048)	
	81-0012 (81012)*	68-0049 (68049)	
	81-0013 (81013)*	68-0050 (68050)	
	81-0952 (81952)	68-0051 (68051)	
	81-0953 (81953)	68-0052 (68052)	
	81-0954 (81954)	68-0053 (68053)	
	81-0955 (81955)	68-0054 (68054)	
	81-0956 (81956)	68-0055 (68055)	
	81-0961 (81961)	68-0056 (68056)	
		68-0059 (68059)	
	*These serials duplicate others	68-0061 (68061)	
	which have already been issued.	68-0062 (68062)	
	They are being re-serialled	68-0063 (68063)	
	respectively:	68-0064 (68064)	
		68-0065 (68065)	
	81-0939 (81939)	68-0066 (68066)	
	81-0940 (81940)	68-0067 (68067)	
	81-0941 (81941)	68-0068 (68068)	
	81-0942 (81942)	68-0069 (68069)	
	81-0943 (81943)	68-0071 (68071)	
	81-0944 (81944)	68-0072 (68072)	
	81-0947 (81947)		

Notes	Serial	Serial	Notes
	68-0073 (68073)	71-0893 (71893)	
	68-0074 (68074)	71-0894 (71894)	
	68-0075 (68075)	72-1442 (72442)	
	68-0076 (68076)	72-1443 (72443)	
	68-0077 (68077)	72-1444 (72444)	
	68-0078 (68078)	72-1445 (72445)	
	68-0079 (68079)	72-1446 (72446)	
	68-0080 (68080)	72-1448 (72448)	
	68-0083 (68083)	72-1449 (72449)	
	68-0084 (68084)	72-1450 (72450)	
		72-1451 (72451)	

General Dynamics F-111F
(48TFW, Lakenheath/LN)

70-2362 (70362)	72-1452 (72452)	
70-2363 (70363)	73-0707 (73707)	
70-2364 (70364)	73-0708 (73708)	
70-2365 (70365)	73-0710 (73710)	
70-2366 (70366)	73-0711 (73711)	
70-2368 (70368)	73-0712 (73712)	
70-2369 (70369)	73-0713 (73713)	
70-2370 (70370)	74-0177 (74177)	
70-2371 (70371)	74-0178 (74178)	
70-2372 (70372)	74-0180 (74180)	
70-2373 (70373)	74-0181 (74181)	
70-2374 (70374)	74-0182 (74182)	
70-2375 (70375)	74-0183 (74183)	
70-2376 (70376)	74-0184 (74184)	
70-2377 (70377)	74-0185 (74185)	
70-2379 (70379)	74-0188 (74188)	

70-2381 (70381)
70-2382 (70382)
70-2383 (70383)

Lockheed HC-130 Hercules
(67ARRS, Woodbridge)

70-2384 (70384)
70-2385 (70385)

66-0220 (60220)
  HC-130P
69-5820 (95820)
  HC-130N
69-5823 (95823)
  HC-130N
69-5826 (95826)
  HC-130N
69-5827 (95827)
  HC-130N

70-2386 (70386)
70-2387 (70387)
70-2389 (70389)
70-2390 (70390)
70-2391 (70391)
70-2392 (70392)
70-2394 (70394)
70-2396 (70396)
70-2397 (70397)
70-2398 (70398)

**McDonnell-Douglas RF-4C
Phantom**
(1TRS, 10TRW, Alconbury/AR)

70-2401 (70401)
70-2402 (70402)

67-0469 (67469)
68-0553 (68553)
68-0554 (68554)

70-2403 (70403)
70-2404 (70404)
70-2405 (70405)
70-2406 (70406)
70-2408 (70408)
70-2409 (70409)
70-2411 (70411)
70-2412 (70412)
70-2413 (70413)
70-2414 (70414)
70-2415 (70415)
70-2416 (70416)
70-2417 (70417)
70-2418 (70418)
70-2419 (70419)

68-0555 (68555)
68-0556 (68556)
68-0557 (68557)
68-0562 (68562)
68-0563 (68563)
68-0564 (68564)
68-0565 (68565)
68-0567 (68567)
68-0568 (68568)
68-0570 (68570)
68-0571 (68571)
68-0580 (68580)
69-0369 (69369)
69-0370 (69370)
69-0382 (69382)
69-0383 (69383)

71-0883 (71883)
71-0884 (71884)
71-0885 (71885)
71-0886 (71886)

Northrop F-5E Tiger II
(572TFTAS, 10TRW, Alconbury)

71-0887 (71887)
71-0888 (71888)
71-0889 (71889)
71-0890 (71890)
71-0891 (71891)
71-0892 (71892)

74-01532 (01532)
74-01534 (01534)
01534 Replica
Alconbury gate
74-01535 (01535)

USAF Serials

Notes	Serial	Serial	Notes
	74-01542 (01542)	74-01560 (01560)	
	74-01543 (01543)	74-01563 (01563)	
	74-01544 (01544)	74-01569 (01569)	
	74-01545 (01545)		
	74-01547 (01547)	**Sikorsky HH-53C**	
	74-01549 (01549)	(67 ARRS, Woodbridge)	
	74-01551 (01551)	68-8284 (8284)	
	74-01553 (01553)	69-5784 (5784)	
	74-01554 (01554)	69-5785 (5785)	
	74-01556 (01556)	69-5796 (5796)	
	74-01559 (01559)	69-5797 (5797)	

US Navy aircraft based in the UK

Notes	Serial
	Beech UC-12B
	(Mildenhall NAF)
	161322 (1322/8D)
	161503 (1503/8G)

61-0286 Boeing EC-135H.   *APM*

European based USAF aircraft

These aircraft are normally based in NW Europe with USAFE. They are shown in alphabetical order of type with individual aircraft in fiscal year serial number order. The five-figure serial number often carried on the aircraft, particularly transports, is shown in brackets, with unit allocation and base also provided.

Serial	Serial	Serial

Beech C-12A
(*58 MAS Ramstein
†7005ABS Stuttgart
‡HQ/USAREUR)
73-1216 (31216)*
73-22254 (22254)‡
73-22255 (22255)‡
73-22261 (22261)‡
73-22262 (22262)‡
76-0166 (60166)*
76-0169 (60169)*
76-0171 (60171)*
76-22549 (22549)†
76-22550 (22550)†
76-22557 (22557)‡
76-22558 (22558)‡
77-22931 (22931)†
77-22932 (22932)†
77-22933 (22933)†
77-22950 (22950)‡

Beech C-12C
(HQ/USAREUR)
78-23126 (23126)
78-23127 (23127)
78-23128 (23128)

Bell UH-1N
(Det 2 67ARRS
Ramstein)
69-6606 (96606)
69-6607 (96607)
69-6608 (96608)
69-6609 (96609)

**General Dynamics
F-16A**
(50TFW Hahn — HR)
(* 313TFS; † 1OTFS;
‡ 496TFs)
80-0541 (00541)*
80-0542 (00542)*
80-0543 (00543)*
80-0544 (00544)*
80-0545 (00545)*
80-0546 (00546)*
80-0555 (00555)*
80-0556 (00556)*
80-0558 (00558)*
80-0559 (00559)*
80-0560 (00560)*
80-0561 (00561)*
80-0562 (00562)*
80-0563 (00563)*
80-0564 (00564)*
80-0565 (00565)*
80-0568 (00568)*
80-0572 (00572)*
80-0574 (00574)*
80-0575 (00575)*
80-0576 (00576)*
80-0577 (00577)*
80-0585 (00585)*
80-0586 (00586)*

80-0587 (00587)†
80-0588 (00588)†
80-0589 (00589)†
80-0590 (00590)†
80-0591 (00591)†
80-0592 (00592)†
80-0601 (00601)†
80-0602 (00602)†
80-0603 (00603)†
80-0604 (00604)†
80-0605 (00605)†
80-0606 (00606)†
80-0610 (00610)†
80-0612 (00612)†
80-0613 (00613)†
80-0614 (00614)†
80-0615 (00615)†
80-0616 (00616)†
80-0617 (00617)†
80-0618 (00618)†
80-0619 (00619)†
80-0620 (00620)‡
80-0622 (00622)‡
81-0664 (10664)‡
81-0665 (10665)‡
81-0666 (10666)‡
81-0669 (10669)‡
81-0671 (10671)‡
81-0672 (10672)‡
81-0673 (10673)‡
81-0680 (10680)‡
81-0681 (10681)‡
81-0682 (10682)‡
81-0694 (10694)‡
81-0695 (10695)‡
81-0696 (10696)‡
81-0697 (10697)‡
81-0698 (10698)‡
81-0699 (10699)‡
81-0700 (10700)‡
81-0711 (10711)‡
81-0712 (10712)‡
81-0713 (10713)‡

**General Dynamics
F-16B**
(50TFW Hahn — HR)
(* 313TFS; † 1OTFS)
80-0636 (00636)*
80-0637 (00637)†

**Lockheed C-130E
Hercules**
(37TAS Rhein Main)
63-7885 (37885)
64-0527 (40527)
64-0550 (40550)
64-17681 (17681)
64-18240 (18240)
68-10935 (10935)
68-10938 (10938)
68-10943 (10943)
68-10944 (10944)
68-10947 (10947)

69-6566 (96566)
69-6582 (96582)
69-6583 (96583)
70-1260 (01260)
70-1264 (01264)
70-1271 (01271)
70-1274 (01274)

**Lockheed MC-130E
Hercules**
(7SOS Rhein Main)
64-0523 (40523)
64-0551 (40551)
64-0555 (40555)
64-0561 (40561)
64-0566 (40566)

**Lockheed VC-140B
Jetstar**
(58MAS Ramstein)
61-2489 (12489)
61-2491 (12491)
62-4198 (24198)
62-4200 (24200)
62-4201 (24201)

**McDonnell Douglas
RF-4C Phantom**
(26TRW/38TRS
Zweibrucken AB) ZR
68-0595 (80595)
68-0596 (80596)
68-0599 (80599)
68-0600 (80600)
68-0602 (80602)
68-0603 (80603)
68-0605 (80605)
69-0350 (90350)
69-0356 (90356)
69-0360 (90360)
69-0361 (90361)
69-0364 (90364)
69-0365 (90365)
69-0366 (90366)
69-0367 (90367)
69-0368 (90368)
69-0371 (90371)
69-0372 (90372)
69-0373 (90373)
69-0374 (90374)
71-0249 (10249)
71-0254 (10254)
72-0152 (20151)
72-0153 (20153)

**McDonnell Douglas
F-4D Phantom**
(SP 52TFW
  Spangdahlem,
TJ 401TFW Torrejon)
65-0716 (50716) TJ
65-0781 (50781) TJ
66-7466 (67466) TJ
66-7511 (67511) SP

Serial

66-7514 (67514) SP
66-7519 (67519) TJ
66-7520 (67520) TJ
66-7525 (67525) TJ
66-7539 (67539) TJ
66-7542 (67542) TJ
66-7551 (67551) TJ
66-7553 (67553) TJ
66-7559 (67559) SP
66-7560 (67560) TJ
66-7566 (67566) TJ
66-7575 (67575) TJ
66-7578 (67578) TJ
66-7579 (67579) TJ
66-7604 (67604) TJ
66-7605 (67605) TJ
66-7607 (67607) TJ
66-7609 (67609) SP
66-7610 (67610) TJ
66-7614 (67614) TJ
66-7615 (67615) TJ
66-7619 (67619) TJ
66-7620 (67620) TJ
66-7623 (67623) TJ
66-7629 (67629) TJ
66-7633 (67633) TJ
66-7649 (67649) TJ
66-7656 (67656) TJ
66-7662 (67662) SP
66-7664 (67664) TJ
66-7669 (67669) TJ
66-7676 (67676) TJ
66-7689 (67689) SP
66-7692 (67692) TJ
66-7694 (67694) TJ
66-7702 (67702) TJ
66-7708 (67708) TJ
66-7710 (67710) TJ
66-7711 (67711) TJ
66-7712 (67712) SP
66-7714 (67714) TJ
66-7720 (67720) TJ
66-7728 (67728) SP
66-7735 (67735) TJ
66-7738 (67738) SP
66-7747 (67747) TJ
66-7751 (67751) TJ
66-7759 (67759) TJ
66-7768 (67768) TJ
66-8689 (68689) TJ
66-8711 (68711) SP
66-8714 (68714) SP
66-8727 (68727) SP
66-8734 (68734) SP
66-8737 (68737) SP
66-8753 (68753) SP
66-8756 (68756) SP
66-8765 (68765) SP
66-8768 (68768) SP
66-8797 (68797) SP
66-8798 (68798) SP
66-8804 (68804) TJ
66-8813 (68813) SP
66-8824 (68824) TJ
66-8825 (68825) SP

**McDonnell Douglas
F-4E Phantom**
(57FIS Keflavik AB)
66-0300 (60300)
66-0304 (60304)

66-0314 (60314)
66-0323 (60323)
66-0328 (60328)
66-0330 (60330)
66-0334 (60334)
66-0336 (60336)
66-0344 (60344)
66-0345 (60345)
66-0346 (60346)
66-0370 (60370)
66-0382 (60882)
67-0224 (70224)

**McDonnell Douglas
F-4E Phantom**
(HR 50TFW Hahn;
RS 86TFW Ramstein;
SP 152TFW
   Spangdahlem AB)
67-0343 (70343) HR
68-0321 (80321) HR
68-0372 (80372) HR
68-0378 (80378) RS
68-0379 (80379) RS
68-0381 (80381) HR
68-0382 (80382) HR
68-0384 (80384) RS
68-0386 (80386) HR
68-0388 (80388) HR
68-0391 (80391) HR
68-0392 (80392) HR
68-0393 (80393) RS
68-0394 (80394) HR
68-0401 (80401) RS
68-0403 (80403) RS
68-0405 (80405) RS
68-0406 (80406) RS
68-0408 (80408) HR
68-0411 (80411) HR
68-0412 (80412) RS
68-0413 (80413) RS
68-0438 (80438) HR
68-0440 (80440) HR
68-0441 (80441) RS
68-0443 (80443) HR
68-0444 (80444) HR
68-0445 (80445) HR
68-0446 (80446) RS
68-0447 (80447) RS
68-0452 (80452) RS
68-0459 (80459) HR
68-0464 (80464) HR
68-0465 (80465) HR
68-0467 (80467) HR
68-0476 (80476) HR
68-0478 (80478) RS
68-0480 (80480) HR
68-0481 (80481) HR
68-0490 (80490) RS
68-0491 (80491) HR
68-0495 (80495) HR
68-0496 (80496) HR
68-0497 (80497) RS
68-0503 (80503) HR
68-0506 (80506) HR
68-0507 (80507) HR
68-0508 (80508) HR
68-0509 (80509) RS
68-0512 (80512) RS
68-0513 (80513) RS
68-0514 (80514) HR

68-0516 (80516) HR
68-0517 (80517) HR
68-0526 (80526) HR
68-0527 (80527) RS
68-0528 (80528) HR
68-0529 (80529) HR
68-0531 (80531) HR
68-0532 (80532) RS
68-0533 (80533) HR
68-0534 (80534) HR
68-0535 (80535) HR
68-0536 (80536) HR
68-0538 (80538) HR
69-0244 (90244) HR
69-0249 (90249) RS
69-0260 (90260) HR
69-0278 (90278) HR
71-0247 (10247) SP
71-1079 (11079) SP
72-0165 (20165) SP
72-0166 (20166) HR
72-1476 (21476) RS
72-1484 (21484) RS
72-1489 (21489) HR
74-0652 (40652) SP
74-0654 (40654) SP
74-0657 (40657) SP
74-0659 (40659) SP
74-0662 (40662) SP
74-0663 (40663) SP
74-0664 (40664) RS
74-1041 (41041) SP
74-1044 (41044) SP
74-1045 (41045) SP
74-1047 (41047) SP
74-1049 (41049) SP
74-1050 (41050) SP
74-1052 (41052) SP
74-1053 (41053) SP
74-1056 (41056) SP
74-1057 (41057) SP
74-1059 (41059) SP
74-1060 (41060) SP
74-1620 (41620) RS
74-1622 (41622) RS
74-1623 (41623) RS
74-1628 (41628) SP
74-1630 (41630) RS
74-1633 (41633) RS
74-1634 (41634) SP
74-1635 (41635) SP
74-1636 (41636) SP
74-1638 (41638) RS
74-1639 (41639) RS
74-1641 (41641) SP
74-1642 (41642) RS
74-1644 (41644) SP
74-1645 (41645) RS
74-1647 (41647) RS
74-1648 (41648) RS
74-1649 (41649) RS
74-1650 (41650) SP
74-1651 (41651) RS
74-1653 (41653) RS

**McDonnell Douglas
F-4G Phantom**
(SP 52TFW
   Spangdahlem AB)
69-0240 (90240)
69-0247 (90247)

Serial	Serial	Serial
69-0248 (90248)	79-0046 (90046) BT†	79-0007 (90007) BT‡
69-0250 (90250)	79-0047 (90047) BT†	79-0008 (90008) BT*
69-0253 (90253)	79-0048 (90048) BT†	79-0009 (90009) BT‡
69-0255 (90255)	79-0049 (90049) BT*	79-0010 (90010) BT†
69-0259 (90259)	79-0050 (90050) BT†	79-0011 (90011) BT†
69-0280 (90280)	79-0051 (90051) BT*	79-0012 (90012) BT†
69-0281 (90281)	79-0052 (90052) BT*	
69-0284 (90284)	79-0053 (90053) BT‡	
69-0285 (90285)	79-0054 (90054) BT*	**North American**
69-0286 (90286)	79-0055 (90055) BT†	**OV-10A Bronco**
69-7202 (97202)	79-0056 (90056) BT*	(601TCW Sembach)
69-7212 (97212)	79-0057 (90057) BT*	66-13553 (13553)
69-7223 (97223)	79-0058 (90058) BT†	66-13554 (13554)
69-7228 (97228)	79-0059 (90059) BT*	66-13555 (13555)
69-7256 (97256)	79-0060 (90060) BT*	66-13556 (13556)
69-7262 (97262)	79-0061 (90061) BT†	66-13559 (13559)
69-7293 (97293)	79-0062 (90062) BT†	66-13562 (13562)
69-7295 (97295)	79-0063 (90063) BT*	67-14618 (14618)
69-7300 (97300)	79-0064 (90064) BT*	67-14621 (14621)
69-7556 (97556)	79-0065 (90065) BT*	67-14623 (14623)
69-7558 (97558)	79-0066 (90066) BT‡	67-14624 (14624)
69-7566 (97566)	79-0067 (90067) BT‡	67-14625 (14625)
69-7579 (97579)	79-0068 (90068) BT‡	67-14626 (14626)
69-7588 (97588).	79-0069 (90069) BT‡	67-14630 (14630)
	79-0070 (90070) BT‡	67-14637 (14637)
	79-0071 (90071) BT‡	67-14639 (14639)
McDonnell Douglas	79-0072 (90072) BT‡	67-14641 (14641)
C-9A Nightingale	79-0073 (90073) BT‡	67-14643 (14643)
(*55AAS and	79-0074 (90074) BT‡	67-14650 (14650)
†7111OS Rhein Main)	79-0075 (90075) BT‡	67-14652 (14652)
71-0876 (10876)†	79-0076 (90076) BT‡	67-14653 (14653)
71-0879 (10879)*	79-0077 (90077) BT‡	67-14654 (14654)
71-0880 (10880)*	79-0078 (90078) BT‡	67-14666 (14666)
71-0881 (10881)*	79-0079 (90079) BT‡	67-14674 (14674)
71-0882 (10882)†	79-0080 (90080) BT‡	67-14675 (14675)
	79-0081 (90081) BT‡	67-14679 (14679)
McDonnell Douglas	80-0002 (00002) BT†	67-14681 (14681)
F-15C Eagle	80-0003 (00003) BT‡	67-14684 (14684)
(CR 32TFS Soesterberg	80-0004 (00004) BT*	67-14689 (14689)
AB;	80-0005 (00005) BT*	67-14690 (14690)
BT 36TFW Bitburg AFB)	80-0006 (00006) BT*	67-14694 (14694)
(* 22FTS; † 525TFS;	80-0008 (00008) BT‡	67-14697 (14697)
‡ 53TFS)	80-0009 (00009) BT*	67-14701 (14701)
79-0015 (90015) CR	80-0010 (00010) BT*	68-3785 (83785)
79-0016 (90016) CR	80-0011 (00011) BT†	68-3790 (83790)
79-0017 (90017) CR	80-0012 (00012) BT‡	68-3793 (83793)
79-0018 (90018) CR	80-0013 (00013) BT‡	68-3795 (83795)
79-0019 (90019) CR	80-0014 (00014) BT‡	68-3796 (83796)
79-0020 (90020) CR	80-0015 (00015) BT‡	68-3797 (83797)
79-0021 (90021) CR	80-0016 (00016) BT*	68-3799 (83799)
79-0022 (90022) BT*	80-0017 (00017) BT†	68-3805 (83805)
79-0023 (90023) CR	80-0018 (00018) BT†	68-3809 (83809)
79-0024 (90024) CR	80-0019 (00019) BT†	68-3811 (83811)
79-0025 (90025) BT†	80-0020 (00020) BT†	68-3814 (83814)
79-0027 (90027) CR	80-0021 (00021) BT*	68-3816 (83816)
79-0028 (90028) CR	80-0022 (00022) BT*	68-3825 (83825)
79-0029 (90029) CR	80-0023 (00023) BT*	68-3829 (83829)
79-0030 (90030) CR	80-0024 (00024) BT†	
79-0031 (90031) CR	80-0025 (00025) BT†	
79-0032 (90032) CR	80-0026 (00026) BT*	**North American**
79-0033 (90033) CR		**T-39A/CT-39A**
79-0034 (90034) CR		(*58MAS Ramstein;
79-0035 (90035) BT†	**McDonnell Douglas**	†1868FCS Rhein
79-0036 (90036) BT*	**F-15D Eagle**	Main
79-0037 (90037) BT†	(CR 32TFS Soesterberg	‡7005ABS Stuttgart)
79-0038 (90038) BT†	AB;	61-0651 (10651)*
79-0039 (90039) BT†	BT 36TFW Bitburg AFB)	61-0653 (10653)*
79-0041 (90041) BT†	(* 525 TFS; † 22TFS;	61-0654 (10654)*
79-0042 (90042) BT†	‡ 53TFS)	61-0677 (10677)‡
79-0043 (90043) BT†	79-0004 (90004) CR	61-0679 (10679)‡
79-0044 (90044) BT†	79-0005 (90005) CR	61-0684 (10684)‡
79-0045 (90045) BT*	79-0006 (90006) BT*	61-0685 (10685)‡
		62-4453 (24453)†

USAF Serials

Serial	Serial	Serial
62-4461 (24461)*	**Sikorsky CH-53C**	68-10932 (10932)
62-4462 (24462)*	(601TCW Sembach)	70-1625 (01625)
62-4471 (24471)*	68-10924 (10924)	70-1626 (01626)
62-4474 (24474)*	68-10928 (10928)	70-1629 (01629)
	68-10930 (10930)	70-1630 (01630)

69-7202 McD F-4G Phantom. *APM*

US Army aircraft based in Europe

Serial	Serial	Serial
Beech C-12A Super King Air (* 7th Corps; † HQ/USEUCOM; ‡ 6AvCo) 73-22253 (22253)* 73-22257 (22257)† 73-22260 (22260)‡ 76-22556 (22556)‡ 77-22944 (22944)‡	67-18537 (18537)‡ 67-18540 (18540)* 67-18548 (18548)* 68-15829 (15829)‡ 68-15838 (15838)† 68-15846 (15846)* 68-15847 (15847)† 68-15851 (15851)* 68-15856 (15856)* 68-15865 (15865)* 68-15867 (15867)*	74-22283 (22283)‡ 74-22284 (22284)‡ 74-22285 (22285)‡ 74-22286 (22286)‡ 74-22291 (22291)‡ 74-22292 (22292)‡ 74-22293 (22293)‡ 76-22677 (22677)‡ 76-22679 (22679)‡ 76-22681 (22681)* 76-22684 (22684)* 79-23394 (23394)* 79-23395 (23395)† 79-23396 (23396)* 79-23398 (23398)†
Beech U-21 King Air (* EU-21A) 66-18000 (18000)* 66-18010 (18010) 66-18013 (18013)* 66-18014 (18014) 66-18019 (18019) 66-18025 (18025) 66-18027 (18027)* 66-18037 (18037) 66-18040 (18040) 66-18048 (18048) 66-18049 (18049) 66-18050 (18050) 66-18058 (18058) 66-18078 (18078) 66-18080 (18080) 67-18116 (18116)	68-15993 (15993)* 68-15995 (15995)* 68-15997 (15997)* 68-16002 (16002)† 68-16006 (16006)* 68-16008 (16008)* 68-16009 (16009)† 68-16028 (16028)† 68-16030 (16030)† 69-17106 (17106)† 69-17114 (17114)‡ 69-17116 (17116)‡ 69-17117 (17117)‡ 69-17118 (17118)* 69-17126 (17126)†	**Grumman V-1 Mohawk** (* RV-1D; † OV-1D) 64-14239 (14239)* 64-14247 (14247)* 64-14248 (14248)* 64-14256 (14256)* 64-14258 (14258)* 64-14270 (14270)* 64-14272 (14272)* 69-17001 (17001)† 69-17004 (17004)† 69-17008 (17008)† 69-17010 (17010)† 69-17011 (17011)† 69-17014 (17014)† 69-17016 (17016)† 69-17017 (17017)† 69-17019 (17019)† 69-17020 (17020)† 69-17022 (17022)† 69-17024 (17024)†
Boeing-Vertol CH-47C Chinook (* 180AvCo; † 205AvCo; ‡ 295AvCo) 67-18509 (18509)† 67-18516 (18516)‡ 67-18528 (18528)‡	70-15002 (15002)* 70-15028 (15028)† 70-15029 (15029)† 70-15030 (15030)† 70-15032 (15032)† 71-20946 (20946)† 71-20950 (20950)† 71-20951 (20951)† 71-20952 (20952)† 71-20953 (20953)† 71-20954 (20954)‡ 74-22281 (22281)‡	

US Navy aircraft based in Europe

Serial	Serial	Serial
Beech UC-12B Super King Air ((8C) NAF Sigonella; 161206 (8C) 161323 (8C)	**Grumman C-2 Greyhound** (VR-24 Sigonella) 148148 (JM31) 152786 152791 152792 155123 (JM34) 155124	150494 (JQ25)† 150502 (JQ22)† 150503 (JQ26)† 150505 (JQ24)†
Douglas EA-3B Skywarrior (VQ-2 Rota) 144850 (JQ12) 144852 (JQ18) 146453 (JQ15)	**Lockheed C-130F Hercules** (VR-24 Rota/ Sigonella) 149790 (JM790) 149794 (JM794) 149797 (JM797) 149801 (JM801)	**NA CT-39G Sabreliner** (VR-24 Sigonella) 159361 (JM10) 159362 (JM11) 159363 (JM12)
Grumman C-1 Trader (VR-24 Sigonella) 136753 (JM44) 136756 (JM46) 136757 (JM45) 136774 146024 (JM42) 146025 (JM41) 146028	**Lockheed P-3 Orion** (VQ-2 Rota; * P-3A; † EP-3E) 148888 (JQ23)† 149668 (JQ21)† 149677 (JQ20)*	**Sikorsky RH-53D Sea Stallion** (VR-24 Sigonella) 158690 (JM50) 158691 (JM51) 158692 (JM52) **Vertol HH-46A Sea Knight** (NAF Rota) 151911 151955

US based aircraft of the USAF

The following aircraft are normally based in the USA but are likely to visit the UK. They are listed in alphabetical order of the type with individual aircraft in fiscal year serial number order. The standard five figure serial number, displayed on the tails of such aircraft as the C-5, C-141 and KC-135, is shown in brackets.

Serial	Serial	Serial
Boeing E-3A	55-0087 (50087)	56-0675 (60675)
Sentry	55-0088 (50088)	56-0676 (60676)
(552AW/CW)	55-0089 (50089)	56-0679 (60679)
71-1407 (11407)	55-0090 (50090)	56-0680 (60680)
71-1408 (11408)	55-0091 (50091)	56-0681 (60681)
73-1675 (31675)	55-0092 (50092)	56-0683 (60683)
75-0556 (50556)	55-0093 (50093)	56-0684 (60684)
75-0557 (50557)	55-0094 (50094)	56-0685 (60685)
75-0558 (50558)	55-0095 (50095)	56-0686 (60686)
75-0559 (50559)	55-0098 (50098)	56-0687 (60687)
75-0560 (50560)	55-0099 (50099)	56-0688 (60688)
76-1604 (61604)	55-0101 (50101)	56-0689 (60689)
76-1605 (61605)	55-0102 (50102)	56-0690 (60690)
76-1606 (61606)	55-0103 (50103)	56-0692 (60692)
76-1607 (61607)	55-0104 (50104)	56-0694 (60694)
77-0351 (70351)	55-0105 (50105)	56-0695 (60695)
77-0352 (70352)	55-0107 (50107)	56-0696 (60696)
77-0353 (70353)	55-0108 (50108)	56-0697 (60697)
77-0354 (70354)	55-0111 (50111)	56-0698 (60698)
77-0355 (70355)	55-0112 (50112)	
77-0356 (70356)	55-0113 (50113)	**Boeing B-52G**
78-0576 (80576)	55-0114 (50114)	**Stratofortress**
78-0577 (80577)	55-0116 (50116)	57-6468 (76468)
78-0578 (80578)	55-0673 (50673)	57-6469 (76469)
79-0001 (90001)	55-0674 (50674)	57-6470 (76470)
79-0002 (90002)	55-0675 (50675)	57-6471 (76471)
79-0003 (90003)	55-0676 (50676)	57-6472 (76472)
80-0137 (00137)	55-0677 (50677)	57-6473 (76473)
80-0138 (00138)	56-0580 (60580)	57-6474 (76474)
80-0139 (00139)	56-0585 (60585)	57-6475 (76475)
	56-0586 (60586)	57-6476 (76476)
Boeing E-4A/B*	56-0587 (60587)	57-6477 (76477)
(55SRW)	56-0588 (60588)	57-6478 (76478)
73-1676 (31676)	56-0591 (60591)	57-6479 (76479)
73-1677 (31677)	56-0593 (60593)	57-6480 (76780)
74-0787 (40787)	56-0595 (60595)	57-6482 (76482)
75-0125 (50125)*	56-0596 (60596)	57-6483 (76483)
	56-0600 (60600)	57-6484 (76484)
Boeing B-52D	56-0601 (60601)	57-6485 (76485)
Stratofortress	56-0602 (60602)	57-6486 (76486)
55-0056 (50056)	56-0605 (60605)	57-6487 (76487)
55-0057 (50057)	56-0606 (60606)	57-6488 (76468)
55-0059 (50059)	56-0607 (60607)	57-6489 (76489)
55-0060 (50060)	56-0610 (60610)	57-6490 (76490)
55-0062 (50062)	56-0612 (60612)	57-6491 (76491)
55-0063 (50063)	56-0614 (60614)	57-6492 (76492)
55-0065 (50065)	56-0617 (60617)	57-6494 (76494)
55-0066 (50066)	56-0621 (60621)	57-6495 (76495)
55-0067 (50067)	56-0627 (60627)	57-6497 (76497)
55-0068 (50068)	56-0628 (60628)	57-6499 (76499)
55-0069 (50069)	56-0629 (60629)	57-6500 (76500)
55-0070 (50070)	56-0630 (60630)	57-6501 (76501)
55-0071 (50071)	56-0657 (60657)	57-6502 (76502)
55-0073 (50073)	56-0658 (60658)	57-6503 (76503)
55-0074 (50074)	56-0659 (60659)	57-6504 (76504)
55-0075 (50075)	56-0660 (60660)	57-6505 (76505)
55-0077 (50077)	56-0662 (60662)	57-6506 (76506)
55-0079 (50079)	56-0663 (60663)	57-6507 (76507)
55-0080 (50080)	56-0665 (60665)	57-6508 (76508)
55-0082 (50082)	56-0667 (60667)	57-6509 (76509)
55-0083 (50083)	56-0668 (60668)	57-6510 (76510)
55-0084 (50084)	56-0670 (60670)	57-6511 (76511)
55-0085 (50085)	56-0671 (60671)	57-6512 (76512)
55-0086 (50086)	56-0672 (60672)	57-6513 (76513)

Serial	Serial	Serial
57-6514 (76514)	58-0230 (80230)	60-0003 (00003)
57-6515 (76515)	58-0231 (80231)	60-0004 (00004)
57-6516 (76516)	58-0232 (80232)	60-0005 (00005)
57-6517 (76517)	58-0233 (80233)	60-0007 (00007)
57-6518 (76518)	58-0234 (80234)	60-0008 (00008)
57-6519 (76519)	58-0235 (80235)	60-0009 (00009)
57-6520 (76520)	58-0236 (80236)	60-0010 (00010)
58-0158 (80158)	58-0237 (80237)	60-0011 (00011)
58-0159 (80159)	58-0238 (80238)	60-0012 (00012)
58-0160 (80160)	58-0239 (80239)	60-0013 (00013)
58-0161 (80161)	58-0240 (80240)	60-0014 (00014)
58-0162 (80162)	58-0241 (80241)	60-0015 (00015)
58-0163 (80163)	58-0242 (80242)	60-0016 (00016)
58-0164 (80164)	58-0243 (80243)	60-0017 (00017)
58-0165 (80165)	58-0244 (80244)	60-0018 (00018)
58-0166 (80166)	58-0245 (80245)	60-0019 (00019)
58-0167 (80167)	58-0247 (80247)	60-0020 (00020)
58-0168 (80168)	58-0248 (80248)	60-0021 (00021)
58-0170 (80170)	58-0249 (80249)	60-0022 (00022)
58-0171 (80171)	58-0250 (80250)	60-0023 (00023)
58-0172 (80172)	58-0251 (80251)	60-0024 (00024)
58-0173 (80173)	58-0252 (80252)	60-0025 (00025)
58-0175 (80175)	58-0253 (80253)	60-0026 (00026)
58-0176 (80176)	58-0254 (80254)	60-0027 (00027)
58-0177 (80177)	58-0255 (80255)	60-0028 (00028)
58-0178 (80178)	58-0257 (80257)	60-0029 (00029)
58-0179 (80179)	58-0258 (80258)	60-0030 (00030)
58-0180 (80180)	59-2564 (92564)	60-0031 (00031)
58-0181 (80181)	59-2565 (92565)	60-0032 (00032)
58-0182 (80182)	59-2566 (92566)	60-0033 (00033)
58-0183 (80183)	59-2567 (92567)	60-0034 (00034)
58-0184 (80184)	59-2568 (92568)	60-0035 (00035)
58-0185 (80185)	59-2569 (92569)	60-0036 (00036)
58-0186 (80186)	59-2570 (92570)	60-0037 (00037)
58-0187 (80187)	59-2571 (92571)	60-0038 (00038)
58-0188 (80188)	59-2572 (92572)	60-0040 (00040)
58-0189 (80189)	59-2573 (92573)	60-0041 (00041)
58-0190 (80190)	59-2574 (92574)	60-0042 (00042)
58-0191 (80191)	59-2575 (92575)	60-0043 (00043)
58-0192 (80192)	59-2576 (92576)	60-0044 (00044)
58-0193 (80193)	59-2577 (92577)	60-0045 (00045)
58-0194 (80194)	59-2578 (92578)	60-0046 (00046)
58-0195 (80195)	59-2579 (92579)	60-0047 (00047)
58-0196 (80196)	59-2580 (92580)	60-0048 (00048)
58-0197 (80197)	59-2581 (92581)	60-0049 (00049)
58-0199 (80199)	59-2582 (92582)	60-0050 (00050)
58-0200 (80200)	59-2583 (92583)	60-0051 (00051)
58-0201 (80201)	59-2584 (92584)	60-0052 (00052)
58-0202 (80202)	59-2585 (92585)	60-0053 (00053)
58-0203 (80203)	59-2586 (92586)	60-0054 (00054)
58-0205 (80205)	59-2587 (92587)	60-0055 (00055)
58-0206 (80206)	59-2588 (92588)	60-0056 (00056)
58-0210 (80210)	59-2589 (92589)	60-0057 (00057)
58-0211 (80211)	59-2590 (92590)	60-0058 (00058)
58-0212 (80212)	59-2591 (92591)	60-0059 (00059)
58-0213 (80213)	59-2592 (92592)	60-0060 (00060)
58-0214 (80214)	59-2593 (92593)	60-0061 (00061)
58-0215 (80215)	59-2594 (92594)	60-0062 (00062)
58-0216 (80216)	59-2595 (92595)	61-0001 (10001)
58-0217 (80217)	59-2596 (92596)	61-0002 (10002)
58-0218 (80218)	59-2597 (92597)	61-0003 (10003)
58-0219 (80219)	59-2598 (92598)	61-0004 (10004)
58-0220 (80220)	59-2599 (92599)	61-0005 (10005)
58-0221 (80221)	59-2600 (92600)	61-0006 (10006)
58-0222 (80222)	59-2601 (92601)	61-0007 (10007)
58-0223 (80223)	59-2602 (92602)	61-0008 (10008)
58-0224 (80224)		61-0009 (10009)
58-0225 (80225)	**Boeing B-52H**	61-0010 (10010)
58-0226 (80226)	**Stratofortress**	61-0011 (10011)
58-0227 (80227)	60-0001 (00001)	61-0012 (10012)
58-0228 (80228)	60-0002 (00002)	61-0013 (10013)
58-0229 (80229)		

125

Serial	Serial	Serial
61-0014 (10014)	56-3630 (63630)*	57-1469 (71469)
61-0015 (10015)	56-3631 (63631)*	57-1470 (71470)
61-0016 (10016)	56-3632 (63632)	57-1471 (71471)
61-0017 (10017)	56-3633 (63633)	57-1472 (71472)
61-0018 (10018)	56-3634 (63634)	57-1473 (71473)
61-0019 (10019)	56-3635 (63635)	57-1474 (71474)
61-0020 (10020)	56-3636 (63636)	57-1475 (71475)*
61-0021 (10021)	56-3637 (63637)	57-1476 (71476)
61-0022 (10022)	56-3638 (63638)*	57-1477 (71477)
61-0023 (10023)	56-3639 (63639)	57-1478 (71478)*
61-0024 (10024)	56-3640 (63640)*	57-1479 (71479)†
61-0025 (10025)	56-3641 (63641)*	57-1480 (71480)*
61-0026 (10026)	56-3642 (63642)	57-1481 (71481)*
61-0027 (10027)	56-3643 (63643)*	57-1482 (71482)*
61-0028 (10028)	56-3644 (63644)	57-1483 (71483)
61-0029 (10029)	56-3645 (63645)	57-1484 (71484)*
61-0030 (10030)	56-3646 (63646)	57-1485 (71485)*
61-0031 (10031)	56-3647 (63647)	57-1486 (71486)
61-0032 (10032)	56-3648 (63648)*	57-1487 (71487)
61-0034 (10034)	56-3649 (63649)	57-1488 (71488)
61-0035 (10035)	56-3650 (63650)*	57-1490 (71490)
61-0036 (10036)	56-3651 (63651)	57-1491 (71491)*
61-0037 (10037)	56-3652 (63652)	57-1492 (71492)
61-0038 (10038)	56-3653 (63653)	57-1493 (71493)
61-0039 (10039)	56-3654 (63654)*	57-1494 (71494)*
61-0040 (10040)	56-3656 (63656)	57-1495 (71495)*
	56-3658 (63658)*	57-1496 (71496)*
Boeing KC-135A	57-1418 (71418)	57-1497 (71497)
Stratotanker	57-1419 (71419)	57-1499 (71499)
(*ANG, Air National	57-1420 (71420)	57-1502 (71502)
Guard;	57-1421 (71421)	57-1503 (71503)*
†AFRES, Air Force	57-1422 (71422)†	57-1504 (71504)†
Reserve)	57-1423 (71423)*	57-1505 (71505)*
55-3130 (53130)	57-1425 (71425)*	57-1506 (71506)
55-3136 (53136)	57-1426 (71426)*	57-1507 (71507)*
55-3137 (53137)	57-1427 (71427)	57-1508 (71508)
55-3139 (53139)	57-1428 (71428)*	57-1509 (71509)*
55-3141 (53141)*	57-1429 (71429)*	57-1510 (71510)*
55-3142 (53142)	57-1430 (71430)	57-1511 (71511)†
55-3143 (53143)*	57-1431 (71431)*	57-1512 (71512)†
55-3145 (53145)	57-1432 (71432)	57-1514 (71514)
55-3146 (53146)*	57-1433 (71433)*	57-2589 (72589)
56-3591 (63591)	57-1434 (71434)*	57-2590 (72590)
56-3592 (63592)	57-1435 (71435)	57-2591 (72591)
56-3593 (63593)*	57-1436 (71436)	57-2592 (72592)
56-3594 (63594)	57-1437 (71437)	57-2593 (72593)
56-3595 (63595)	57-1438 (71438)†	57-2594 (72594)
56-3600 (63600)	57-1439 (71439)	57-2595 (72595)*
56-3601 (63601)	57-1440 (71440)	57-2596 (72596)
56-3603 (63603)	57-1441 (71441)	57-2597 (72597)
56-3604 (63604)*	57-1443 (71443)*	57-2598 (72598)†
56-3606 (63606)*	57-1445 (71445)*	57-2599 (72599)
56-3607 (63607)*	57-1447 (71447)	57-2600 (72600)*
56-3608 (63608)	57-1448 (71448)*	57-2601 (72601)
56-3609 (63609)*	57-1450 (71450)*	57-2602 (72602)
56-3610 (63610)	57-1451 (71451)	57-2603 (72603)†
56-3611 (63611)*	57-1452 (71452)*	57-2604 (72604)*
56-3612 (63612)*	57-1453 (71453)	57-2605 (72605)
56-3614 (63614)	57-1454 (71454)	57-2606 (72606)*
56-3615 (63615)	57-1455 (71455)*	57-2607 (72607)*
56-3616 (63616)	57-1456 (71456)	57-2608 (72608)*
56-3617 (63617)	57-1458 (71458)*	57-2609 (72609)
56-3619 (63619)	57-1459 (71459)	58-0001 (80001)
56-3620 (63620)	57-1460 (71460)*	58-0003 (80003)*
56-3621 (63621)	57-1461 (71461)	58-0004 (80004)
56-3622 (63622)*	57-1462 (71462)	58-0005 (80005)
56-3623 (63623)†	57-1463 (71463)*	58-0006 (80006)*
56-3624 (63624)	57-1464 (71464)	58-0008 (80008)*
56-3625 (63625)	57-1465 (71465)*	58-0009 (80009)
56-3626 (63626)*	57-1467 (71467)	58-0010 (80010)
56-3627 (63627)	57-1468 (71468)†	58-0011 (80011)

126

Serial	Serial	Serial
58-0012 (80012)*	58-0116 (80116)	59-1522 (91522)
58-0013 (80013)†	58-0118 (80118)	60-0313 (00313)
58-0014 (80014)	58-0119 (80119)	60-0314 (00314)
58-0015 (80015)	58-0120 (80120)	60-0315 (00315)
58-0016 (80016)	58-0121 (80121)	60-0316 (00316)
58-0017 (80017)*	58-0122 (80122)	60-0317 (00317)
58-0018 (80018)	58-0123 (80123)	60-0318 (00318)
58-0020 (80020)*	58-0124 (80124)	60-0319 (00319)
58-0021 (80021)	58-0126 (80126)	60-0320 (00320)
58-0023 (80023)	58-0128 (80128)	60-0321 (00321)
58-0024 (80024)*	58-0130 (80130)	60-0322 (00322)
58-0025 (80025)	59-1443 (91443)	60-0323 (00323)
58-0027 (80027)	59-1444 (91444)	60-0324 (00324)
58-0028 (80028)	59-1445 (91445)*	60-0325 (00325)
58-0029 (80029)	59-1446 (91446)	60-0326 (00326)
58-0030 (80030)	59-1447 (91447)†	60-0327 (00327)
58-0032 (80032)*	59-1448 (91448)*	60-0328 (00328)
58-0033 (80033)	59-1449 (91449)	60-0329 (00329)
58-0034 (80034)	59-1450 (91450)*	60-0330 (00330)
58-0035 (80035)	59-1451 (91451)†	60-0331 (00331)
58-0036 (80036)	59-1452 (91452)*	60-0332 (00332)
58-0037 (80037)	59-1453 (91453)	60-0333 (00333)
58-0038 (80038)	59-1454 (91454)	60-0334 (00334)
58-0040 (80040)*	59-1455 (91455)	60-0347 (00347)
58-0041 (80041)†	59-1456 (91456)*	60-0348 (00348)
58-0043 (80043)*	59-1457 (91457)*	60-0349 (00349)
58-0044 (80044)	59-1458 (91458)	60-0350 (00350)
58-0051 (80051)	59-1459 (91459)	60-0351 (00351)
58-0052 (80052)†	59-1461 (91461)	60-0353 (00353)
58-0053 (80053)†	59-1463 (91463)	60-0355 (00355)
58-0056 (80056)	59-1466 (91466)	60-0356 (00356)
58-0057 (80057)*	59-1469 (91469)	60-0357 (00357)
58-0058 (80058)†	59-1472 (91472)	60-0358 (00358)
58-0059 (80059)	59-1473 (91473)*	60-0359 (00359)
58-0063 (80063)	59-1475 (91475)	60-0360 (00360)
58-0064 (80064)†	59-1476 (91476)	60-0361 (00361)
58-0066 (80066)	59-1477 (91477)†	60-0362 (00362)
58-0067 (80067)*	59-1478 (91478)	60-0363 (00363)
58-0068 (80068)*	59-1479 (91479)*	60-0364 (00364)
58-0070 (80070)	59-1482 (91482)	60-0365 (00365)
58-0073 (80073)	59-1483 (91483)	60-0366 (00366)
58-0075 (80075)	59-1484 (91484)	60-0367 (00367)
58-0076 (80076)	59-1485 (91485)*	61-0264 (10264)
58-0078 (80078)*	59-1486 (91486)	61-0266 (10266)
58-0079 (80079)	59-1487 (91487)*	61-0267 (10267)
58-0080 (80080)*	59-1488 (91488)	61-0268 (10268)
58-0081 (80081)	59-1489 (91489)*	61-0270 (10270)
58-0082 (80082)*	59-1492 (91492)	61-0271 (10271)
58-0083 (80083)	59-1493 (91493)	61-0272 (10272)
58-0085 (80085)†	59-1494 (91494)*	61-0275 (10275)
58-0087 (80087)*	59-1495 (91495)	61-0276 (10276)
58-0090 (80090)†	59-1496 (91496)	61-0277 (10277)
58-0091 (80091)	59-1497 (91497)*	61-0280 (10280)
58-0092 (80092)	59-1498 (91498)	61-0281 (10281)
58-0093 (80093)	59-1499 (91499)*	61-0284 (10284)
58-0096 (80096)†	59-1500 (91500)	61-0288 (10288)
58-0097 (80097)	59-1501 (91501)	61-0290 (10290)
58-0098 (80098)	59-1502 (91502)	61-0292 (10292)
58-0100 (80100)	59-1503 (91503)	61-0294 (10294)
58-0102 (80102)	59-1505 (91505)*	61-0295 (10295)
58-0104 (80104)	59-1506 (91506)*	61-0298 (10298)
58-0105 (80105)	59-1507 (91507)	61-0299 (10299)
58-0106 (80106)	59-1508 (91508)	61-0300 (10300)
58-0107 (80107)*	59-1509 (91509)*	61-0302 (10302)
58-0108 (80108)†	59-1511 (91511)	61-0303 (10303)*
58-0109 (80109)	59-1514 (91514)	61-0304 (10304)
58-0110 (80110)	59-1515 (91515)	61-0305 (10305)
58-0111 (80111)*	59-1516 (91516)	61-0306 (10306)
58-0113 (80113)	59-1517 (91517)	61-0307 (10307)
58-0114 (80114)	59-1519 (91519)*	61-0308 (10308)
58-0115 (80115)*	59-1521 (91521)	61-0309 (10309)

USAF Serials

Serial	Serial	Serial
61-0311 (10311)	62-3558 (23558)	63-8028 (38028)
61-0312 (10312)	62-3559 (23559)	63-8029 (38029)
61-0313 (10313)	62-3560 (23560)	63-8030 (38030)
61-0314 (10314)	62-3561 (23561)	63-8031 (38031)
61-0315 (10315)	62-3562 (23562)	63-8032 (38032)
61-0317 (10317)	62-3563 (23563)	63-8033 (38033)
61-0318 (10318)	62-3564 (23564)	63-8034 (38034)
61-0320 (10320)	62-3565 (23565)	63-8035 (38035)
61-0321 (10321)	62-3566 (23566)	63-8036 (38036)
61-0323 (10323)	62-3567 (23567)	63-8037 (38037)
61-0324 (10324)	62-3568 (23568)	63-8038 (38038)
61-0325 (10325)	62-3569 (23569)	63-8039 (38039)
62-3497 (23497)	62-3571 (23571)	63-8040 (38040)
62-3498 (23498)	62-3572 (23572)	63-8041 (38041)
62-3499 (23499)	62-3573 (23573)	63-8043 (38043)
62-3500 (23500)	62-3574 (23574)	63-8044 (38044)
62-3501 (23501)	62-3575 (23575)	63-8045 (38045)
62-3502 (23502)	62-3576 (23576)	63-8055 (38055)
62-3503 (23503)	62-3577 (23577)	63-8871 (38871)
62-3504 (23504)	62-3578 (23578)	63-8872 (38872)
62-3505 (23505)	62-3580 (23580)	63-8873 (38873)
62-3506 (23506)	63-7976 (37976)	63-8874 (38874)
62-3507 (23507)	63-7977 (37977)	63-8875 (38875)
62-3508 (23508)	63-7978 (37978)	63-8876 (38876)
62-3509 (23509)	63-7979 (37979)	63-8877 (38877)
62-3510 (23510)	63-7980 (37980)	63-8878 (38878)
62-3511 (23511)	63-7981 (37981)	63-8879 (38879)
62-3512 (23512)	63-7982 (37982)	63-8880 (38880)
62-3513 (23513)	63-7983 (37983)	63-8881 (38881)
62-3514 (23514)	63-7984 (37984)	63-8883 (38883)
62-3515 (23515)	63-7985 (37985)	63-8884 (38884)
62-3516 (23516)	63-7986 (37986)	63-8885 (38885)
62-3517 (23517)	63-7987 (37987)	63-8886 (38886)
62-3518 (23518)	63-7988 (37988)	63-8887 (38887)
62-3519 (23519)	63-7990 (37990)	63-8888 (38888)
62-3520 (23520)	63-7991 (37991)	64-14833 (14833)
62-3521 (23521)	63-7992 (37992)	64-14834 (14834)
62-3522 (23522)	63-7993 (37993)	64-14835 (14835)
62-3523 (23523)	63-7995 (37995)	64-14836 (14836)
62-3524 (23524)	63-7996 (37996)	64-14837 (14837)
62-3525 (23525)	63-7997 (37997)	64-14838 (14838)
62-3526 (23526)	63-7998 (37998)	64-14839 (14839)
62-3527 (23527)	63-7999 (37999)	64-14840 (14840)
62-3528 (23528)	63-8000 (38000)	
62-3529 (23529)	63-8001 (38001)	**Boeing KC-135Q**
62-3530 (23530)	63-8002 (38002)	**Stratotanker**
62-3531 (23531)	63-8003 (38003)	58-0019 (80019)
62-3532 (23532)	63-8004 (38004)	58-0042 (80042)
62-3533 (23533)	63-8005 (38005)	58-0045 (80045)
62-3534 (23534)	63-8006 (38006)	58-0046 (80046)
62-3537 (23537)	63-8007 (38007)	58-0047 (80047)
62-3538 (23538)	63-8008 (38008)	58-0049 (80049)
62-3539 (23539)	63-8009 (38009)	58-0050 (80050)
62-3540 (23540)	63-8010 (38010)	58-0054 (80054)
62-3541 (23541)	63-8011 (38011)	58-0055 (80055)
62-3542 (23542)	63-8012 (38012)	58-0060 (80060)
62-3543 (23543)	63-8013 (38013)	58-0061 (80061)
62-3544 (23544)	63-8014 (38014)	58-0062 (80062)
62-3545 (23545)	63-8015 (38015)	58-0065 (80065)
62-3546 (23546)	63-8016 (38016)	58-0069 (80069)
62-3547 (23547)	63-8017 (38017)	58-0071 (80071)
62-3548 (23548)	63-8018 (38018)	58-0072 (80072)
62-3549 (23549)	63-8019 (38019)	58-0074 (80074)
62-3550 (23550)	63-8020 (38020)	58-0077 (80077)
62-3551 (23551)	63-8021 (38021)	58-0084 (80084)
62-3552 (23552)	63-8022 (38022)	58-0086 (80086)
62-3553 (23553)	63-8023 (38023)	58-0088 (80088)
62-3554 (23554)	63-8024 (38024)	58-0089 (80089)
62-3555 (23555)	63-8025 (38025)	58-0094 (80094)
62-3556 (23556)	63-8026 (38026)	58-0095 (80095)
62-3557 (23557)	63-8027 (38027)	58-0099 (80099)

Serial	Type	Serial	Type	Serial
58-0103 (80103)		61-2672 (12672)	WC-135B	**Lockheed C-5A**
58-0112 (80112)		61-2673 (12673)	WC-135B	**Galaxy**
58-0117 (80117)		61-2674 (12674)	WC-135B	(*60MAW;
58-0125 (80125)		62-3570 (23570)	EC-135G	†436MAW;
58-0129 (80129)		62-3579 (23579)	EC-135G	‡443MAW)
59-1460 (91460)		62-3581 (23581)	EC-135C	66-8304 (68304)†
59-1462 (91462)		62-3582 (23582)	EC-135C	66-8305 (68305)*
59-1464 (91464)		62-3583 (23583)	EC-135C	66-8306 (68306)*
59-1467 (91467)		62-3584 (23584)	EC-135J	66-8307 (68307)†
59-1468 (91468)		62-3585 (23585)	EC-135C	67-0167 (70167)*
59-1470 (91470)		62-4125 (24125)	VC-135B	67-0168 (70168)†
59-1471 (91471)		62-4126 (24126)	C-135B	67-0169 (70169)*
59-1474 (91474)		62-4127 (24127)	C-135B	67-0170 (70170)†
59-1480 (91480)		62-4128 (24128)	EC-135B	67-0171 (70171)*
59-1490 (91490)		62-4129 (24129)	C-135B	67-0173 (70173)*
59-1504 (91504)		62-4130 (24130)	C-135B	67-0174 (70174)†
59-1510 (91510)		62-4131 (24131)	RC-135M	68-0211 (80211)*
59-1512 (91512)		62-4132 (24132)	RC-135M	68-0212 (80212)†
59-1513 (91513)		62-4133 (24133)	EC-135B	68-0213 (80213)*
59-1520 (91520)		62-4134 (24134)	RC-135M	68-0214 (80214)†
59-1523 (91523)		62-4135 (24135)	RC-135W	68-0215 (80215)†
60-0335 (00335)		62-4138 (24138)	RC-135M	68-0216 (80216)*
60-0336 (00336)		62-4139 (24139)	RC-135M	68-0217 (80217)†
60-0337 (00337)		62-6000 (26000)	VC-137C	68-0219 (80219)*
60-0338 (00338)		63-7994 (37994)	EC-135G	68-0220 (80220)†
60-0339 (00339)		63-8001 (38001)	EC-135G	68-0221 (80221)*
60-0341 (00341)		63-8046 (38046)	EC-135C	68-0222 (80222)†
60-0342 (00342)		63-8047 (38047)	EC-135C	68-0223 (80223)*
60-0343 (00343)		63-8048 (38048)	EC-135C	68-0224 (80224)†
60-0344 (00344)		63-8049 (38049)	EC-135C	68-0225 (80225)†
60-0345 (00345)		63-8050 (38050)	EC-135C	68-0226 (80226)*
60-0346 (00346)		63-8051 (38051)	EC-135C	68-0228 (80228)*
		63-8052 (38052)	EC-135C	69-0001 (90001)‡
		63-8053 (38053)	EC-135C	69-0002 (90002)*
Boeing C-135		63-8054 (38054)	EC-135C	69-0003 (90003)†
Stratotanker variants		63-8056 (38056)	EC-135C	69-0004 (90004)†
58-0019 (80019)	EC-135P	63-8057 (38057)	EC-135C	69-0005 (90005)†
58-0022 (80022)	EC-135P	63-8058 (38058)	KC-135D	69-0006 (90006)†
58-6970 (86970)	VC-137B	63-8059 (38059)	KC-135D	69-0007 (90007)*
58-6971 (86971)	VC-137B	63-8060 (38060)	KC-135D	69-0008 (90008)†
58-6972 (86972)	VC-137B	63-8061 (38061)	KC-135D	69-0009 (90009)*
59-1518 (91518)	EC-135K	63-9792 (39792)	RC-135V	69-0010 (90010)*
60-0372 (00372)	EC-135N	64-14828 (14828)	EC-135C	69-0011 (90011)*
60-0374 (00374)	EC-135N	64-14829 (14829)	EC-135C	69-0012 (90012)*
60-0375 (00375)	EC-135N	64-14830 (14830)	EC-135C	69-0013 (90013)*
61-0261 (10261)	EC-135L	64-14831 (14831)	EC-135C	69-0014 (90014)*
61-0262 (10262)	EC-135A	64-14832 (14832)	EC-135C	69-0015 (90015)†
61-0263 (10263)	EC-135L	64-14841 (14841)	RC-135V	69-0016 (90016)†
61-0269 (10269)	EC-135L	64-14842 (14842)	RC-135V	69-0017 (90017)†
61-0274 (10274)	EC-135H	64-14843 (14843)	RC-135V	69-0018 (90018)*
61-0278 (10278)	EC-135A	64-14844 (14844)	RC-135V	69-0019 (90019)†
61-0279 (10279)	EC-135L	64-14845 (14845)	RC-135V	69-0020 (90020)*
61-0283 (10283)	EC-135L	64-14846 (14846)	RC-135V	69-0021 (90021)†
61-0287 (10287)	EC-135A	64-14847 (14847)	RC-135U	69-0022 (90022)*
61-0289 (10289)	EC-135A	64-14848 (14848)	RC-135V	69-0023 (90023)*
61-0293 (10293)	KC-135R	64-14849 (14849)	RC-135U	69-0024 (90024)*
61-0297 (10297)	EC-135A	64-27000 (27000)	VC137C	69-0025 (90025)*
61-0310 (10310)	VC-135A			69-0026 (90026)†
61-0316 (10316)	VC-135A			69-0027 (90027)†
61-0326 (10326)	EC-135N			70-0445 (00445)†
61-0327 (10327)	EC-135N			70-0446 (00446)*
61-0329 (10329)	EC-135N			70-0447 (00447)†
61-0330 (10330)	EC-135N	**Boeing C-18A**		70-0448 (00448)†
61-2662 (12662)	RC-135S	81-0891 (10891)		70-0449 (00449)*
61-2663 (12663)	RC-135S	81-0892 (10892)		70-0450 (00450)*
61-2665 (12665)	WC-135B	81-0893 (10893)		70-0451 (00451)*
61-2666 (12666)	WC-135B	81-0894 (10894)		70-0452 (00452)†
61-2667 (12667)	WC-135B	81-0895 (10895)		70-0453 (00453)†
61-2668 (12668)	C-135C	81-0896 (10896)		70-0454 (00454)†
61-2669 (12669)	C-135C	81-0897 (10897)		70-0455 (00455)†
61-2670 (12670)	WC-135B	81-0898 (10898)		70-0456 (00456)†
61-2671 (12671)	C-135C			

129

Serial	Serial	Serial
70-0457 (00457)*	62-1850 (21850)†	63-7842 (37842)
70-0458 (00458)*	62-1851 (21851)*	63-7845 (37845)
70-0459 (00459)*	62-1852 (21852)†	63-7846 (37846)
70-0460 (00460)†	62-1855 (21855)	63-7847 (37847)
70-0461 (00461)*	62-1856 (21856)*	63-7848 (37848)†
70-0462 (00462)*	62-1858 (21858)†	63-7849 (37849)
70-0463 (00463)†	62-1859 (21859)	63-7850 (37850)
70-0464 (00464)†	62-1860 (21860)†	63-7851 (37851)
70-0465 (00465)†	62-1862 (21862)*	63-7852 (37852)*
70-0466 (00466)†	62-1864 (21864)*	63-7853 (37853)†
70-0467 (00467)‡	62-1866 (21866)*	63-7854 (37854)
	62-3487 (23487)†	63-7856 (37856)*
Lockheed C-130E	63-7764 (37764)*	63-7857 (37857)
Hercules	63-7765 (37765)	63-7858 (37858)
(*ANG, Air National	63-7767 (37767)	63-7859 (37859)
Guard;	63-7768 (37768)	63-7860 (37860)
†AFRES, Air Force	63-7769 (37769)	63-7861 (37861)
Reserve)	63-7770 (37770)*	63-7863 (37863)*
61-2358 (12358)*	63-7771 (37771)	63-7864 (37864)
61-2359 (12359)*	63-7776 (37776)	63-7865 (37865)
61-2367 (12367)*	63-7777 (37777)	63-7866 (37866)
61-2368 (12368)	63-7778 (37778)	63-7867 (37867)†
61-2370 (12370)*	63-7779 (37779)	63-7868 (37868)
61-2371 (12371)	63-7781 (37781)	63-7871 (37871)
61-2372 (12372)*	63-7782 (37782)	63-7872 (37872)
61-2373 (12373)*	63-7784 (37784)	63-7874 (37874)
62-1784 (21784)*	63-7786 (37786)	63-7876 (37876)
62-1786 (21786)*	63-7788 (37788)	63-7877 (37877)
62-1787 (21787)*	63-7790 (37790)	63-7879 (37879)
62-1788 (21788)*	63-7791 (37791)	63-7880 (37880)
62-1789 (21789)†	63-7792 (37792)	63-7881 (37881)
62-1790 (21790)*	63-7793 (37793)	63-7882 (37882)*
62-1792 (21792)*	63-7794 (37794)	63-7883 (37883)†
62-1793 (21793)*	63-7795 (37795)	63-7884 (37884)
62-1794 (21794)†	63-7796 (37796)	63-7887 (37887)
62-1795 (21795)*	63-7799 (37799)	63-7888 (37888)
62-1798 (21798)*	63-7800 (37800)	63-7889 (37889)
62-1799 (21799)*	63-7803 (37803)	63-7890 (37890)
62-1801 (21801)*	63-7804 (37804)	63-7891 (37891)
62-1803 (21803)†	63-7805 (37805)*	63-7892 (37892)†
62-1804 (21804)*	63-7806 (37806)	63-7893 (37893)
62-1806 (21806)†	63-7807 (37807)	63-7894 (37894)
62-1807 (21807)†	63-7808 (37808)	63-7895 (37895)
62-1808 (21808)†	63-7809 (37809)	63-7896 (37896)
62-1810 (21810)†	63-7811 (37811)	63-7897 (37897)
62-1811 (21811)*	63-7812 (37812)	63-7898 (37898)
62-1812 (21812)*	63-7813 (37813)	63-7899 (37899)
62-1816 (21816)†	63-7814 (37814)	63-9810 (39810)
62-1817 (21817)*	63-7817 (37817)*	63-9811 (39811)
62-1819 (21819)	63-7818 (37818)	63-9812 (39812)
62-1821 (21821)	63-7819 (37819)	63-9813 (39813)†
62-1822 (21822)	63-7820 (37820)	63-9814 (39814)
62-1823 (21823)†	63-7821 (37821)	63-9815 (39815)
62-1824 (21824)*	63-7822 (37822)*	64-0495 (40495)
62-1826 (21826)*	63-7823 (37823)	64-0496 (40496)
62-1827 (21827)	63-7824 (37824)	64-0497 (40497)
62-1828 (21828)	63-7825 (37825)	64-0498 (40498)
62-1829 (21829)*	63-7826 (37826)†	64-0499 (40499)
62-1830 (21830)†	63-7829 (37829)	64-0500 (40500)
62-1833 (21833)*	63-7830 (37830)	64-0501 (40501)
62-1834 (21834)†	63-7831 (37831)	64-0502 (40502)
62-1835 (21835)†	63-7832 (37832)†	64-0503 (40503)
62-1837 (21837)*	63-7833 (37833)†	64-0504 (40504)
62-1838 (21838)†	63-7834 (37834)†	64-0510 (40510)
62-1839 (21839)	63-7835 (37835)	64-0512 (40512)
62-1842 (21842)*	63-7836 (37836)	64-0513 (40513)
62-1844 (21844)†	63-7837 (37837)	64-0514 (40514)
62-1846 (21846)*	63-7838 (37838)	64-0515 (40515)
62-1847 (21847)†	63-7839 (37839)	64-0517 (40517)
62-1848 (21848)†	63-7840 (37840)	64-0518 (40518)
62-1849 (21849)†	63-7841 (37841)	64-0519 (40519)

Serial	Serial	Serial	Wing
64-0520 (40520)	73-1584 (31584)	79-0476 (90476)*	
64-0521 (40521)	73-1585 (31585)	79-0477 (90477)*	
64-0524 (40524)	73-1586 (31586)	79-0478 (90478)*	
64-0525 (40525)	73-1587 (31587)	79-0479 (90479)*	
64-0526 (40526)	73-1588 (31588)	79-0480 (90480)*	
64-0529 (40529)	73-1590 (31590)		
64-0530 (40530)	73-1592 (31592)		
64-0531 (40531)	73-1594 (31594)	**Lockheed C-141 Starlifter**	
64-0533 (40533)	73-1595 (31595)	A, C-141A; B, C-141B	
64-0534 (40534)	73-1597 (31597)	61-2778 (12278) A	438MAW
64-0535 (40535)	73-1598 (31598)	63-8075 (38075) B	60MAW
64-0537 (40537)	74-1658 (41658)	63-8076 (38076) A	438MAW
64-0538 (40538)	74-1659 (41659)	63-8078 (38078) B	437MAW
64-0539 (40539)	74-1660 (41660)	63-8079 (38079) B	437MAW
64-0540 (40540)	74-1661 (41661)	63-8080 (38080) B	438MAW
64-0541 (40541)	74-1662 (41662)	63-8081 (38081) B	62MAW
64-0542 (40542)	74-1663 (41663)	63-8082 (38082) B	62MAW
64-0543 (40543)	74-1664 (41664)	63-8083 (38083) B	438MAW
64-0544 (40544)	74-1665 (41665)	63-8084 (38084) A	63MAW
64-0549 (40549)	74-1666 (41666)	63-8085 (38085) A	63MAW
64-0556 (40556)	74-1667 (41667)	63-8086 (38086) B	62MAW
64-0557 (40557)	74-1668 (41668)	63-8087 (38087) A	63MAW
64-0560 (40560)	74-1669 (41669)	63-8088 (38088) B	60MAW
64-0569 (40569)	74-1670 (41670)	63-8089 (38089) B	438MAW
64-0570 (40570)	74-1671 (41671)	63-8090 (38090) B	438MAW
64-17680 (17680)	74-1673 (41673)	64-0609 (40609) B	62MAW
68-10934 (10934)	74-1674 (41674)	64-0610 (40610) B	437MAW
68-10937 (10937)	74-1675 (41675)	64-0611 (40611) B	437MAW
68-10939 (10939)	74-1676 (41676)	64-0612 (40612) B	437 MAW
68-10940 (10940)	74-1677 (41677)	64-0613 (40613) B	437MAW
68-10941 (10941)	74-1679 (41679)	64-0614 (40614) A	63MAW
68-10942 (10942)	74-1680 (41680)	64-0615 (40615) B	437MAW
68-10945 (10945)	74-1681 (41681)	64-0616 (40616) A	438MAW
68-10946 (10946)	74-1682 (41682)	64-0617 (40617) A	63MAW
68-10948 (10948)	74-1684 (41684)	64-0618 (40618) A	437MAW
68-10949 (10949)	74-1685 (41685)	64-0619 (40619) A	443MAW
68-10950 (10950)	74-1686 (41686)	64-0620 (40620) B	438MAW
69-6579 (96579)	74-1687 (41687)	64-0621 (40621) B	438MAW
69-6580 (96580)	74-1688 (41688)	64-0622 (40622) B	438MAW
70-1259 (01259)	74-1689 (41689)	64-0623 (40623) B	438MAW
70-1261 (01261)	74-1690 (41690)	64-0624 (40624) A	437MAW
70-1262 (01262)	74-1691 (41691)	64-0625 (40625) B	438MAW
70-1263 (01263)	74-1692 (41692)	64-0626 (40626) B	438MAW
70-1265 (01265)	74-1693 (41693)	64-0627 (40627) B	438MAW
70-1266 (01266)	74-2061 (42061)	64-0628 (40628) B	438MAW
70-1267 (01267)	74-2062 (42062)	64-0629 (40629) B	437MAW
70-1268 (01268)	74-2063 (42063))	64-0630 (40630) A	437MAW
70-1269 (01269)	74-2065 (42065)	64-0631 (40631) B	437MAW
70-1270 (01270)	74-2066 (42066)	64-0632 (40632) A	60MAW
70-1272 (01272)	74-2067 (42067)	64-0633 (40633) A	443MAW
70-1273 (01273)	74-2068 (42068)	64-0634 (40634) A	63MAW
70-1275 (01275)	74-2069 (42069)	64-0635 (40635) B	62MAW
70-1276 (01276)	74-2070 (42070)	64-0636 (40636) B	63MAW
72-1288 (21288)	74-2071 (42071)	64-0637 (40637) A	60MAW
72-1289 (21289)	74-2072 (42072)	64-0638 (40638) A	438MAW
72-1290 (21290)	74-2130 (42130)	64-0639 (40639) B	438MAW
72-1291 (21291)	74-2131 (42131)	64-0640 (40640) B	60MAW
72-1292 (21292)	74-2132 (42132)	64-0642 (40642) A	443MAW
72-1293 (21293)	74-2133 (42133)	64-0643 (40643) B	60MAW
72-1294 (21294)	74-2134 (42134)	64-0644 (40644) B	437MAW
72-1295 (21295)	78-0806 (80806)*	64-0645 (40645) B	60MAW
72-1296 (21296)	78-0807 (80807)*	64-0646 (40646) B	437MAW
72-1298 (21298)	78-0808 (80808)*	64-0648 (40648) B	443MAW
72-1299 (21299)	78-0809 (80809)*	64-0649 (40649) B	437MAW
	78-0810 (80810)*	64-0650 (40650) B	438MAW
	78-0811 (80811)*	64-0651 (40651) A	437MAW
Lockheed C-130H	78-0812 (80812)*	64-0652 (40652) B	437MAW
Hercules	78-0813 (80813)*	64-0653 (40653) B	63MAW
73-1580 (31580)	79-0473 (90473)*	65-0216 (50216) B	63MAW
73-1581 (31581)	79-0474 (90474)*	65-0217 (50217) A	437MAW
73-1582 (31582)	79-0475 (90475)*	65-0218 (50218) B	437MAW
73-1583 (31583)			

USAF Serials

Serial	Wing	Serial	Wing	Serial	Wing
65-0219 (50219) B	443MAW	65-9408 (59408) B	437MAW	66-0191 (60191) B	60MAW
65-0220 (50220) B	437MAW	65-9409 (59409) B	438MAW	66-0192 (60192) B	62MAW
65-0221 (50221) B	438MAW	65-9410 (59410) A	62MAW	66-0193 (60193) B	63MAW
65-0222 (50222) B	437MAW	65-9411 (59411) A	438MAW	66-0194 (60194) B	437MAW
65-0223 (50223) B	438MAW	65-9412 (59412) B	438MAW	66-0195 (60195) B	437MAW
65-0224 (50224) B	438MAW	65-9413 (59413) B	438MAW	66-0196 (60196) B	437MAW
65-0225 (50225) B	63MAW	65-9414 (59414) B	63MAW	66-0197 (60197) B	62MAW
65-0226 (50226) A	60MAW	66-0126 (60126) B	438MAW	66-0198 (60198) A	63MAW
65-0227 (50227) B	62MAW	66-0128 (60128) B	63MAW	66-0199 (60199) B	443MAW
65-0228 (50228) B	62MAW	66-0129 (60129) B	62MAW	66-0200 (60200) B	63MAW
65-0229 (50229) B	62MAW	66-0130 (60130) A	63MAW	66-0201 (60201) A	63MAW
65-0230 (50230) B	60MAW	66-0131 (60131) B	437MAW	66-0202 (60202) B	437MAW
65-0231 (50231) A	60MAW	66-0132 (60132) B	438MAW	66-0203 (60203) B	437MAW
65-0232 (50232) B	62MAW	66-0133 (60133) A	438MAW	66-0204 (60204) A	438MAW
65-0233 (50233) B	60MAW	66-0134 (60134) B	443MAW	66-0205 (60205) B	63MAW
65-0234 (50234) B	60MAW	66-0135 (60135) B	437MAW	66-0206 (60206) B	62MAW
65-0235 (50235) B	62MAW	66-0136 (60136) B	63MAW	66-0207 (60207) B	438MAW
65-0236 (50236) B	443 MAW	66-0137 (60137) B	443MAW	66-0208 (60208) B	63MAW
65-0237 (50237) B	62MAW	66-0138 (60138) B	63MAW	66-0209 (60209) B	437MAW
65-0238 (50238) B	60MAW	66-0139 (60139) A	63MAW	66-7944 (67944) A	60MAW
65-0239 (50239) B	60MAW	66-0140 (60140) A	438MAW	66-7945 (67945) B	437MAW
65-0240 (50240) B	62MAW	66-0141 (60141) B	62MAW	66-7946 (67946) B	63MAW
65-0241 (50241) B	62MAW	66-0142 (60142) B	62MAW	66-7947 (67947) B	437MAW
65-0242 (50242) A	60MAW	66-0143 (60143) B	63MAW	66-7948 (67948) A	438MAW
65-0243 (50243) A	62MAW	66-0144 (60144) B	437MAW	66-7949 (67949) A	63MAW
65-0244 (50244) B	62MAW	66-0145 (60145) B	62MAW	66-7950 (67950) B	438MAW
65-0245 (50245) B	60MAW	66-0146 (60146) B	438MAW	66-7951 (67951) B	62MAW
65-0246 (50246) B	60MAW	66-0147 (60147) B	60MAW	66-7952 (67952) A	63MAW
65-0247 (50247) A	60MAW	66-0148 (60148) A	63MAW	66-7953 (67953) B	437MAW
65-0248 (50248) B	62MAW	66-0149 (60149) B	438MAW	66-7954 (67954) B	438MAW
65-0249 (50249) B	60MAW	66-0150 (60150) B	63MAW	66-7955 (67955) B	437MAW
65-0250 (50250) A	60MAW	66-0151 (60151) A	60MAW	66-7956 (67956) B	437MAW
65-0251 (50251) A	60MAW	66-0152 (60152) B	437MAW	66-7957 (67957) B	63MAW
65-0252 (50252) A	60MAW	66-0153 (60153) A	63MAW	66-7958 (67958) B	63MAW
65-0253 (50253) B	62MAW	66-0154 (60154) B	438MAW	66-7959 (67959) B	63MAW
65-0254 (50254) B	60MAW	66-0155 (60155) B	438MAW	67-0001 (70001) B	63MAW
65-0255 (50255) B	62MAW	66-0156 (60156) B	63MAW	67-0002 (70002) B	438MAW
65-0256 (50256) A	60MAW	66-0157 (60157) B	438MAW	67-0003 (70003) B	438MAW
65-0257 (50257) B	62MAW	66-0158 (60158) B	62MAW	67-0004 (70004) B	437MAW
65-0258 (50258) B	62MAW	66-0159 (60159) B	62MAW	67-0005 (70005) B	63MAW
65-0259 (50259) B	60MAW	66-0160 (60160) B	63MAW	67-0007 (70007) B	443MAW
65-0260 (50260) A	60MAW	66-0161 (60161) B	62MAW	67-0009 (70009) B	63MAW
65-0261 (50261) B	438MAW	66-0162 (60162) B	438MAW	67-0010 (70010) B	437MAW
65-0262 (50262) B	60MAW	66-0163 (60163) B	438MAW	67-0011 (70011) B	437MAW
65-0263 (50263) B	62MAW	66-0164 (60164) B	62MAW	67-0012 (70012) B	437MAW
65-0264 (50264) B	62MAW	66-0165 (60165) B	62MAW	67-0013 (70013) B	438MAW
65-0265 (50265) B	438MAW	66-0166 (60166) B	438MAW	67-0014 (70014) B	437MAW
65-0266 (50266) B	437MAW	66-0167 (60167) B	437MAW	67-0015 (70015) B	63MAW
65-0267 (50267) B	437MAW	66-0168 (60168) A	437MAW	67-0016 (70016) B	437MAW
65-0268 (50268) B	60MAW	66-0169 (60169) B	438MAW	67-0018 (70018) B	62MAW
65-0269 (50269) B	437MAW	66-0170 (60170) A	438MAW	67-0019 (70019) B	438MAW
65-0270 (50270) B	437MAW	66-0171 (60171) B	63MAW	67-0020 (70020) B	438MAW
65-0271 (50271) B	438MAW	66-0172 (60172) A	63MAW	67-0021 (70021) B	438MAW
65-0272 (50272) B	437MAW	66-0173 (60173) B	438MAW	67-0022 (70022) A	443MAW
65-0273 (50273) B	437MAW	66-0174 (60174) B	443MAW	67-0023 (70023) B	63MAW
65-0275 (50275) B	437MAW	66-0175 (60175) B	443MAW	67-0024 (70024) B	438MAW
65-0276 (50276) B	437MAW	66-0176 (60176) B	443MAW	67-0025 (70025) A	60MAW
65-0277 (50277) B	62MAW	66-0177 (60177) A	63MAW	67-0026 (70026) B	437MAW
65-0278 (50278) B	60MAW	66-0178 (60178) A	437MAW	67-0027 (70027) A	438MAW
65-0279 (50279) B	437MAW	66-0179 (60179) B	63MAW	67-0028 (70028) A	63MAW
65-0280 (50280) B	62MAW	66-0180 (60180) B	63MAW	67-0029 (70029) A	63MAW
65-9397 (59397) A	63MAW	66-0181 (60181) B	60MAW	67-0031 (70031) B	60MAW
65-9398 (59398) B	60MAW	66-0182 (60182) B	62MAW	67-0164 (70164) B	62MAW
65-9399 (59399) B	62MAW	66-0183 (60183) A	438MAW	67-0165 (70165) B	438MAW
65-9400 (59400) A	63MAW	66-0184 (60184) B	63MAW	67-0166 (70166) B	443MAW
65-9401 (59401) B	437MAW	66-0185 (60185) B	443MAW		
65-9402 (59402) B	443MAW	66-0186 (60186) B	443MAW		
65-9403 (59403) B	60MAW	66-0187 (60187) B	437MAW		
65-9404 (59404) B	63MAW	66-0188 (60188) B	443MAW		
65-9405 (59405) A	60MAW	66-0189 (60189) B	443MAW		
65-9406 (59406) B	63MAW	66-0190 (60190) B	63MAW		

Serial	Serial	Serial
Lockheed U-2R	64-17956 (17956)	**McDonnell–Douglas**
(9SRW)	64-17958 (17958)	**KC-10A Extender**
68-10329 (10329)	64-17959 (17959)	(2BW)
68-10331 (10331)	64-17960 (17960)	79-0433 (90433)
68-10332 (10332)	64-17961 (17961)	79-0434 (90434)
68-10333 (10333)	64-17962 (17962)	79-1710 (91710)
68-10335 (10335)	64-17964 (17964)	79-1711 (91711)
68-10336 (10336)	64-17967 (17967)	79-1712 (91712)
68-10337 (10337)	64-17968 (17968)	79-1713 (91713)
68-10338 (10338)	64-17969 (17969)	79-1946 (91946)
68-10339 (10339)	64-17970 (17970)	79-1947 (91947)
68-10340 (10340)	64-17971 (17971)	79-1948 (91948)
	64-17972 (17972)	79-1949 (91949)
Lockheed SR-71A	64-17974 (17974)	79-1950 (91950)
(9SRW)	64-17975 (17975)	79-1951 (91951)
64-17950 (17950)	64-17976 (17976)	82-0190 (20190)
64-17952 (17952)	64-17979 (17979)	82-0191 (20191)
64-17953 (17953)	64-17980 (17980)	82-0192 (20192)
		82-0193 (20193)

58-0192 Boeing B-52G Stratofortress. *PRM*

Overseas Military Aircraft Markings

Aircraft included in this section are a selection of those likely to be seen visiting UK civil and military airfields on transport flights, exchange visits, exercises and for air shows. It is not intended to be a comprehensive list of all aircraft operated by the air arms concerned.

Serial	Serial	Serial
AUSTRALIA	**AUSTRIA**	AT13
Royal Australian Air Force	**Oesterreichische**	AT14
	Luftstreitkrafte	AT15
Boeing 707-338C	**Saab 105ÖE**	AT16
A20-624	**(yellow)**	AT17
A20-627	1101/A	AT18
	1102/B	AT19
Lockheed	1104/D	AT20
C-130H Hercules	1105/E	AT21
A97-001	1106/F	AT22
A97-002	1107/G	AT23
A97-003	1108/H	AT24
A97-004	1109/I	AT25
A97-005	1110/J	AT26
A97-006	**Saab 105ÖE**	AT27
A97-007	**(green)**	AT28
A97-008	1111/A	AT29
A97-009	1112/B	AT30
A97-010	1114/D	AT31
A97-011	1116/F	AT32
	1117/G	AT33
Lockheed	1119/I	
C130E Hercules	1120/J	**Dassault Mirage**
A97-012	**Saab 105ÖE (red)**	**5BA**
A97-159	1122/B	BA01
A97-160	1123/C	BA02
A97-167	1124/D	BA03
A97-168	1125/E	BA05
A97-171	1126/F	BA08
A97-172	1127/G	BA10
A97-177	1128/H	BA11
A97-178	1129/I	BA13
A97-180	1130/J	BA15
A97-181	**Saab 105ÖE (blue)**	BA16
A97-189	1131/A	BA17
A97-190	1132/B	BA18
	1133/C	BA19
Lockheed	1134/D	BA20
P-3B Orion	1135/E	BA21
A9-291	1136/F	BA22
A9-292	1137/G	BA23
A9-293	1139/I	BA26
A9-294	1140/J	BA27
A9-295	**Short SC7**	BA29
A9-296	**Skyvan 3M**	BA30
A9-297	5S-TA	BA31
A9-298	5S-TB	BA33
A9-299		BA35
A9-300		BA37
	BELGIUM	BA39
	Force Aerienne Belge/	BA41
Lockheed	**Belgische Luchtmacht**	BA42
P-3C Orion	**D-BD Alpha Jet**	BA43
A9-605	AT01	BA44
A9-751	AT02	BA45
A9-752	AT03	BA46
A9-753	AT05	BA48
A9-754	AT06	BA50
A9-755	AT07	BA51
A9-756	AT08	BA52
A9-757	AT09	BA53
A9-758	AT10	BA54
A9-759	AT11	BA55
A9-760	AT12	BA56
		BA57

Serial	Serial	Serial
BA59	**Hawker–Siddeley**	FA70
BA60	**HS748 srs 2A**	FA71
BA62	CS01	FA72
BA63	CS02	FA73
Dassault Mirage	CS03	FA74
5BD	**General Dynamics**	FA75
BD01	**F–16A**	FA76
BD03	FA01	FA77
BD04	FA02	FA78
BD05	FA03	FA79
BD06	FA04	FA80
BD07	FA05	FA81
BD09	FA06	FA82
BD10	FA07	FA83
BD11	FA09	FA84
BD12	FA10	FA85
BD13	FA12	FA86
BD14	FA13	FA87
BD15	FA15	FA88
	FA16	FA89
Dassault Mirage	FA17	FA90
5BR	FA18	FA91
BR03	FA19	FA92
BR04	FA20	FA93
BR07	FA21	FA94
BR08	FA22	**General Dynamics**
BR09	FA23	**F–16B**
BR10	FA24	FB01
BR12	FA25	FB02
BR13	FA26	FB03
BR14	FA27	FB04
BR15	FA28	FB05
BR17	FA30	FB06
BR18	FA31	FB07
BR19	FA32	FB08
BR20	FA33	FB09
BR21	FA34	FB10
BR22	FA36	FB11
BR23	FA37	FB12
BR24	FA38	FB13
BR25	FA39	FB14
BR26	FA40	FB15
BR27	FA41	FB16
Boeing 727-29C	FA42	FB17
CB01	FA43	FB18
CB02	FA44	FB19
Swearingen	FA45	FB20
Merlin IIIA	FA46	**Westland Sea**
CF01	FA47	**King Mk48**
CF02	FA48	RS01
CF04	FA49	RS02
CF05	FA50	RS04
CF06	FA51	RS05
Lockheed	FA52	**Siai Marchetti**
C-130H Hercules	FA53	**SF.26OMB**
CH01	FA54	ST02
CH02	FA55	ST03
CH03	FA56	ST04
CH04	FA57	ST07
CH05	FA58	ST08
CH06	FA59	ST09
CH07	FA60	ST11
CH08	FA61	ST12
CH09	FA62	ST14
CH10	FA63	ST15
CH11	FA64	ST16
CH12	FA65	ST17
	FA66	ST18
Dassault	FA67	ST19
Mystere 20	FA68	ST20
CM01	FA69	ST21
CM02		

Overseas Serials

Serial	Serial	Serial
ST22	104646	104799
ST23	104647	104804
ST24	104648	104805
ST25	104650	104806
ST26	104652	104807
ST27	104653	104808
ST28	104658	104810
ST29	104661	104813
ST30	104663	104815
ST31	104665	104821
ST32	104668	104822
ST33	**Canadair CF-104**	104823
ST34	**Starfighter**	104824
ST35	104701	104826
ST36	104702	104827
	104704	104828
	104705	104829
Belgische Landmacht	104706	104830
Britten-Norman BN-2A	104709	104834
Islander	104710	104835
B01/LA	104711	104837
B02/LB	104713	104838
B03/LC	104714	104839
B04/LD	104715	104840
B05/LE	104716	104841
B06/LF	104718	104843
B07/LG	104720	104845
B08/LH	104721	104847
B09/LI	104722	104848
B10/LJ	104723	104854
B11/LK	104731	104857
B12/LL	104732	104861
	104733	104862
	104735	104863
BRAZIL	104737	104864
Forca Aerea Brazileira	104739	104865
Lockheed	104743	104866
C-130E Hercules	104744	104868
C-130 2451	104747	104869
C-130 2454	104749	104872
C-130 2455	104750	104873
C-130 2456	104751	104877
C-130 2457	104753	104880
C-130 2458	104754	104883
C-130 2459	104756	104891
C-130 2460	104760	104892
Lockheed	104761	104893
KC-130H Hercules	104762	104895
C-130 2461	104763	104899
C-130 2462	104768	**DHC CC-115**
Lockheed	104769	**Buffalo**
C-130H Hercules	104770	115451
C-130 2463	104772	115452
C-130 2464	104773	115453
C-130 2465	104774	115454
	104775	115455
	104776	115456
CANADA	104779	115457
Canadian Armed Forces	104780	115458
Canadair CF104D	104781	115459
Starfighter	104783	115460
104631	104784	115461
104634	104785	115463
104636	104786	115464
104638	104787	115465
104639	104788	**Lockheed**
104640	104789	**C-130E Hercules**
104641	104790	130305
104642	104792	130306
104643	104795	130307
104644	104796	130308
104645		

Serial	Serial	Serial
130309	140116	T402
130310	140117	T403
130311	140118	T404
130313		T405
130314	**CHILE**	T406
130315	**Fuerza Aérea de Chile**	T407
130316	**Lockheed**	T408
130317	**C-130H Hercules**	T409
130318	995	T410
130319	996	T411
130320		T412
130321	**DENMARK**	T413
130322	**Kongelige Danske**	T414
130323	**Flyvevaabnet**	T415
130324	**Saab A-35XD**	T417
130325	**Draken**	T418
130326	A001	T419
130327	A002	T420
130328	A004	T421
Lockheed	A005	T422
C-130H Hercules	A006	T423
130329	A007	T424
130330	A008	T425
130331	A009	T426
130332	A010	T427
130333	A011	T428
DHC CC-132	A012	T429
Dash 7	A014	T430
132001	A017	T431
132002	A018	T432
Canadair CT-133	A019	**Grumman**
Silver Star	A020	**Gulfstream III**
133026	**Saab S-35XD**	F249
133052	**Draken**	F313
133069	AR102	F330
133094	AR104	**General Dynamics**
133345	AR105	**F-16A**
133393	AR106	E174
133402	AR107	E175
133405	AR108	E176
133435	AR109	E177
133442	AR110	E178
133450	AR111	E179
133542	AR112	E180
133564	AR113	E181
133581	AR114	E182
133613	AR115	E183
Boeing CC-137	AR116	E184
(B.707-374C)	AR117	E185
13701	AR118	E186
13702	AR119	E187
13703	AR120	E188
13704	**Saab Sk-35XD**	E189
13705	**Draken**	E190
Lockheed	AT151	E191
CP-140 Aurora	AT152	E192
140101	AT153	E193
140102	AT154	E194
140103	AT155	E195
140104	AT156	E196
140105	AT157	E197
140106	AT158	E198
140107	AT160	E199
140108	**Lockheed**	E200
140109	**C-130H Hercules**	E201
140110	B678	E202
140111	B679	E203
140112	B680	E596
140113	**Saab 17**	E597
140114	**Supporter**	E598
140115	T401	E599

Overseas Serials

Serial	Serial	Serial
E600	H209	**Cessna 411**
E601	H210	185 AC
E602	H211	248 AB
E603	H213	F006 AD
E604	H244	F008 AE
E605	H245	**D-BD Alpha Jet**
E606	H246	* Patrouille de France
E607		01
E608	**EGYPT**	02
E609	**Al Quwwat al-Jawwiya**	E1
E610	**Ilmisriya**	E3 118-BR
E611	**Lockheed**	E4 118-BS
General Dynamics	**C-130H Hercules**	E5 118-BU
F-16B	1271/SU-BAB	E6 314-LA
ET204	1272/SU-BAC	E7 314-LB
ET205	1273/SU-BAD	E8 314-LC
ET206	1274/SU-BAE	E9 314-LD
ET207	1275/SU-BAF	E10 314-LE
ET208	1277/SU-BAI	E11 314-LF
ET209	1278/SU-BAJ	E12 314-LG
ET210	1279/SU-BAK	E13 314-LH
ET211	1280/SU-BAL	E14 314-LI
ET612	1281/SU-BAM	E15 314-LJ
ET613	1282/SU-BAN	E16 314-LK
ET614	1283/SU-BAP	E17 314-LL
ET615	1284/SU-BAQ	E18 314-LM
Sikorsky S-61A	1285/SU-BAR	E19 314-LN
U240	1286/SU-BAS	E20 314-LO
U275	1287/SU-BAT	E21 314-LP
U276	1288/SU-BAU	E22 314-LQ
U277	1289/SU-BAV	E23 8-MQ
U278		E24 8-MA
U279	**FRANCE**	E25 314-LT
U280	**Armee de l'Air**	E26 314-TK
U301	**Aerospatiale TB-30**	E27 8-MD
U481	**Epsilon**	E28 314-TL
	01 VO	E29 314-LV
Sovaernets Flyvetjaeneste	02 VJ	E30 314-LW
(Navy)	**Boeing KC-135F**	E31 314-LX
Sud Alouette III	38470/CA	E32 314-LY
M019	38471/CB	E33 314-TA
M030	38472/CC	E34 314-LZ
M070	38474/CE	E35 314-TB
M071	38475/CF	E36 314-TC
M072	312735/CG	E37 314-TD
M388	312736/CH	E38 314-TE
M438	312737/CI	E39 314-TF
M439	312738/CJ	E40 314-TG
Westland Lynx	312739/CK	E41 314-TH
HAS80	312740/CL	E42 314-TI
S134	**Caarp CAP-20**	E43 314-TJ
S142	01 VU	E44 314-TN
S170	02 VV	E45 314-TM
S175	03 VW	E46 314-TO
S181	04 VX	E47 314-TP
S187	05 VY	E48 314-TQ
S191	06 VZ	E49 314-TR
S196	**Cessna 310**	E50 314-TS
	045 AU	E51 F-TERA* (4)
Haerens	046 AV	E52 F-TERB* (6)
Flyvetjaeneste	185 AC	E53 F-TERC*
(Army)	186 BI	E55 F-TERE*
Hughes 500M	187 BJ	E56 F-TERF*
H201	188 BK	E57 F-TERG* (2)
H202	190 BL	E58 F-TERH* (7)
H203	192 BM	E59 F-TERI* (5)
H204	193 BG	E60
H205	194 BH	E61 F-TERJ* (8)
H206	242 BW	E63 F-TERL* (1)
H207	244 AX	E64 314-TT
H208	820 CL	E65 314-TU

E105 D-BD Alpha Jet. *APM*

118 Dassault Etendard IVP. *PRM*

Serial		Serial		Serial	
E66	314-TV	260	A	77	30-MN
E67	314-TW	268	K	78	30-FG
E68	314-TX	291	P	79	10-SK
E69	314-TZ	463	339-WM	80	12-ZM
E70	314-TY	**Dassault Falcon 50**		81	12-YN
E72	314-UA	5	F-RAFI	82	12-YB
E73	314-UB	**Dassault**		83	12-KD
E74	314-UC	**Mirage F.1C**		84	30-MP
E75	314-UD	2	118-AK	85	12-ZN
E76	314-UE	3		87	10-SL
E77	314-UF	4	118-AM	90	12-ZO
E78	314-UG	5		100	30-FK
E79	314-UH	6	30-MA	101	
E81	314-UI	8	5-OK	102	12-KM
E82	314-UK	9	12-KB	103	12-KN
E83	314-UJ	10	5-OF	201	118-AZ
E84	314-UL	12		202	5-OR
E85	314-UM	13	12-YA	203	30-MJ
E86	314-UN	14	30-ME	204	5-OH
E87	314-UO	15	30-MS	205	30-FI
E88	314-UP	16	12-ZA	206	5-OA
E89	314-UQ	17	30-MD	207	30-FE
E90	314-UR	18	12-KG	208	5-OJ
E91	314-US	19	12-ZB	210	30-FN
E92		20		211	5-NH
E93		21	5-NG	213	30-MG
E94		22	118-AN	214	5-OG
E95	8-MI	23		216	5-OL
E96	8-MZ	24	5-OD	217	30-MK
E97	314-UW	25	10-SA	218	5-OM
E98		26	5-NF	219	5-NL
E99		27	10-SQ	220	5-OE
E100		29	30-FF	221	12-YT
E101		30	12-YC	223	5-NM
E102		31	12-ZC	224	5-OI
E103		32	30-FJ	225	
E104	314-UZ	33	30-FK	226	12-YO
E105	314-VA	34	30-FL	227	12-KP
E106	314-VB	35	12-ZD	228	12-ZR
E107	F-TERK* (3)	36	12-YE	229	5-ND
E108	314-VC	37	30-FO	230	118-AP
E109	314-VD	38	12-KL	231	12-YH
E110		39	10-SB	232	30-MT
E111		40	5-OO	233	12-KA
E112		41	30-FB	234	5-OC
E113		42	10-SD	235	30-FP
E114		43	10-SJ	236	5-OP
E115		44	30-FM	237	12-YI
E116		45	12-ZE	238	5-NR
E117		46	12-ZF	239	5-NJ
E118		47	30-SO	240	5-NA
E119		48	30-MF	241	5-NE
E120		49		242	12-YJ
E121		50	12-ZH	243	5-NO
E122		52	12-YG	244	5-OQ
E123		54	30-FC	245	5-NI
E124		55	30-MI	246	5-NC
E125		60	12-ZI	247	30-FR
Dassault		62	30-MC	248	12-YP
Falcon 20C		63	12-YK	249	12-ZS
22	CS	64		250	12-KQ
49	J	67	12-KI	251	
79	CT	68	12-KF	252	5-ON
86	CG	69	12-ZJ	253	10-SP
93	N	70	30-FD	254	12-ZT
115	339-WL	71	12-YM	255	5-NQ
124	CC	72	12-KK	256	
131	CD	73	12-YD	257	12-KO
138	CR	74	30-FQ	258	12-YL
167	L	75	12-2K	259	30-FA
238	M	76	12-KJ	260	5-OB

Overseas Serials

Serial		Serial		Serial	
261	5-NF	82	CM	F53/61-MY	
262	30-MU	83	NC	F54/61-MZ	
263	5-NP	91		F55/61-ZC	
264		92	CP	F86/61-ZD	
265		93		F87/61-ZE	
266	12-ZW	94	118-DA	F88/61-ZF	
267		96	LU	F89/61-ZG	
268		97	43-BA	F90/61-ZH	
269		100	NG	F91/61-ZI	
270	12-KE	113	NI	F92/61-ZJ	
271		114	NJ	F93/61-ZK	
272-5-AU		115		F94/61-ZL	
273	5-AV	116	ON	F95/61-ZM	
274	5-AW	117	AZ	F96/61-ZN	
275	5-NH	118	NQ	F97/61-ZO	
DHC6 Twin Otter		119	NL	F98/61-ZP	
292	OW	**Nord 262 Fregate**		F99/61-ZQ	
298	OY	3	OH	F100/61-ZR	
300	OZ	28		F153/61-ZS	
603	82-PU	51		F154/61-ZT	
730	52-LF	55	MH	F155/61-ZU	
742	52-LG	58	MJ	F156/61-ZV	
743	63-VX	64	AA	F157/61-ZW	
745	63-VY	66	AB	F158/61-ZY	
		67	MI	F159/61-ZZ	
Douglas DC8F		68	AC	**SEPECAT**	
45570	F-RAFE	76	AD	**Jaguar A**	
45692	F-RAFB	77		A1	
45819	F-RAFC	78	AF	A2	118-AE
45820	F-RAFA	80	AW	A3	
46043	F-RAFD	81	AH	A4	
46130	F-RAFF	83	AI	A5	7-PQ
		86	AJ	A6	3-XH
Morane Saulnier		87	AN	A7	3-XF
Paris		88		A8	3-XJ
1	118-DB	89	AM	A9	3-XK
14	070-MD	91	AT	A10	3-XE
19		92	AO	A11	
20		93	AP	A12	
23		94	MB	A13	3-XD
24	LW	95	AR	A14	
25	118-D1	105		A15	
26		106	AY	A16	7-II
27	41-AS	107		A17	
29	43-BB	108	AG	A19	
34		109		A20	3-XM
35	DD	110	MA	A21	7-IN
36	43-BD	**C-160A Transall**		A22	
38	41-AT	A02/61-MI		A23	3-XL
44	44-CN	A04/61-BI		A24	
45	41-AR	A06/61-ZB		A25	7-IO
51		F1/61-MA		A26	7-HI
53	41-AN	F2/61-MB		A27	7-PE
54		F3/61-MC		A28	7-HB
56		F4/61-MD		A29	7-HJ
57		F5/61-ME		A30	3-XP
58		F11/61-MF		A31	7-HE
59	070-MC	F12/61-MG		A32	7-IL
60	LO	F13/61-MH		A33	7-IM
61		F14/61-MI		A34	7-HM
62		F15/61-MJ		A35	7-HA
65		F17/61-ML		A36	7-IA
68		F18/61-MM		A37	7-PE
70	LT	F42/61-MN		A38	3-XG
71		F43/61-MO		A39	11-EI
73		F44/61-MP		A40	3-XC
75		F45/61-MQ		A41	7-IP
77		F46/61-MR		A42	7-HC
78		F48/61-MT		A43	7-PI
79		F51/61-MW		A44	
80	LM	F52/61-MX		A46	7-HH
81					

Serial		Serial		Serial	
A47	7-IB	A121	11-RW	E32	
A48	7-IG	A122	11-RN	E33	
A49	11-RM	A123	11-RO	E34	
A50	11-EC	A124	11-YL	E35	11-RC
A51	3-XI	A125	11-YM	E36	11-YZ
A52		A126	11-YH	E37	
A53	11-RS	A127	11-YI	E38	7-NN
A54	11-RT	A128	11-YJ	E39	7-NO
A55		A129	11-YN	E40	7-PN
A56		A130	11-MK		
A57	7-PG	A131	7-NA	**Aeronavale/Marine**	
A58		A132	11-MO	**Morane Saulnier**	
A59	7-IC	A133	7-NB	**Paris**	
A60		A134		32	
A61		A135	7-NC	33	
A63	11-RO	A136	7-ND	40	
A64	11-RE	A137	7-NK	41	
A65		A138	7-NG	42	
A66	3-XM	A139		46	
A67	3-XN	A140	7-NH	47	
A68		A141		48	
A69	11-RX	A142		85	
A70	11-ED	A143	7-NM	87	
A72		A144	11-EL	88	
A73		A145			
A74		A146		**Nord 262 Fregate**	
A75		A147		28	
A76	3-XB	A148		43	
A77		A149	11-YB	45	
A78	3-XD	A150	11-RT	46	
A79	7-HN	A151	7-NE	51	
A80	11-EH	A152	11-RG	52	
A81	11-MA	A153	11-MB	53	
A82	11-RB	A154	11-MP	59	
A83	11-MC	A155	11-EM	60	
A84	11-MD	A156		61	
A85	11-MF	A157		62	
A86	11-MG	A158	11-MW	63	
A87	11-MH	A159	11-RS	65	
A88	11-MM	A160		70	
A89				71	
A90	118-AI	**SEPECAT Jaguar E**		72	
A91	11-MQ	E1		73	
A92		E2		75	
A93		E3		79	
A94	11-ED	E4		85	
A95	11-EG	E5		104	
A96		E6			
A97	11-RH	E7	7-PA	**SA.321G Super**	
A98	11-EB	E8	118-AB	**Frelon**	
A99		E9		101	
A100	11-ED	E10		102	
A101	11-EJ	E11		105	
A102		E12	7-PF	106	
A103	118-AH	E13		112	
A104		E14		114	
A105	11-EV	E15		118	
A107	11-MW	E16	11-RF	120	
A108	11-ES	E17	7-PQ	122	
A109		E18	11-YY	134	
A110	118-AG	E19	7-PM	137	
A111		E20	7-IJ	141	
A112	11-RV	E21	11-EA	144	
A113	11-YA	E22	11-ME	148	
A114	11-YB	E23	118-AD	149	
A115	11-ES	E24	7-PC	159	
A116	11-YD	E25	7-PL	160	
A117	11-YE	E27		162	
A118	11-YF	E28		163	
A119	11-YG	E29	7-PA	164	
A120	11-ER	E30	7-PL	165	
		E31			

Overseas Serials

Serial	Serial	Serial
Breguet 1050	47	12
Alizé	48	13
1	49	14
5	50	15
9	51	16
11	52	17
12	53	18
13	54	19
16	66	20
17	67	21
25	68	22
26	**Dassault**	23
27	**Etendard IVM**	25
28	2	26
30	3	27
31	4	28
33	5	29
34	6	30
36	7	31
37	9	32
41	11	33
42	15	34
43	16	37
45	21	38
47	22	39
48	29	40
49	30	41
50	32	42
51	33	43
52	34	44
53	36	45
55	37	46
56	40	47
59	41	48
61	42	49
65	51	50
68	52	51
69	53	52
72	56	53
73	57	54
75	59	55
76	60	57
80	62	58
87	63	59
Breguet 1150	66	60
Atlantic	**Dassault**	61
1	**Etendard IVP**	62
3	101	63
5	103	64
7	107	65
9	108	66
11	109	67
13	114	68
15	115	69
17	116	70
19	117	71
21	118	**Dassault Falcon**
23	120	**10(MER)**
25	**Dassault Super**	32
27	**Etendard**	101
31	1	129
32	2	133
33	3	**LTV F–8E (FN)**
35	4	**Crusader**
37	5	1
38	6	2
40	7	3
41	8	4
44	9	6
45	10	7
46	11	8

Serial	Serial	Serial
10	XZ274	MM61990/46-04
11	XZ275	MM61991/46-05
12	XZ276	MM61992/46-06
14	XZ277	MM61993/46-07
16	XZ278	MM61994/46-08
17	XZ620	MM61995/46-09
18	XZ621	MM61997/46-11
19	XZ622	MM61998/46-12
20	XZ623	MM61999/46-13
22	XZ624	MM62000/46-14
23	XZ625	MM62001/46-15
24	XZ626	**Panavia Tornado**
25	XZ627	TTTE Cottesmore
26		MM55000/I-42
27	**GREECE**	MM55001/I-40
29	**Elliniki Aeroporia**	MM55002/I-41
30	**Lockheed**	MM55003/I-43
31	**C-130H Hercules**	MM55004/I-44
32	741	MM7002/I-92
33	742	MM7004/I-90
34	743	MM7005/I-91
35	744	
37	745	**JORDAN**
39	746	**Al Quwwat Al–Jawwiya**
40	747	**Alamalakiya Al-Urduniya**
41	748	**Lockheed**
42	749	**C-130B Hercules**
Lockheed	750	340
Neptune	751	**Lockheed**
146432	752	**C-130H Hercules**
146433		344
147563	**ISRAEL**	345
147564	**Heyl ha'avir**	
147566	**Lockheed**	**KUWAIT**
147567	**C-130H Hercules**	**Kuwait Air Force**
147568	4X-FBA/102	**Lockheed**
147569	4X-FBB/106	**L100-20 Hercules**
147570	4X-FBC/009	KAF 318
148330	**Lockheed**	
148331	**C-130E Hercules**	**LUXEMBOURG**
148333	4X-FBE/304	**NATO — Geilenkirchen**
148334	4X-FBF/301	**Boeing E-3A**
148335	4X-FBG	LX-N90442
148336	4X-FBH/312	LX-N90443
Piper Navajo	4X-FBI/002	LX-N90444
227	4X-FBK/318	LX-N90445
232	4X-FBL/313	
903	4X-FBM/316	**NETHERLANDS**
904	4X-FBN/307	**Koninklijke Luchmacht**
906	4X-FBO/203	**Fokker F-27-100**
912	4X-FBP/208	**Friendship**
914	**Lockeed**	C-1
916	**C-130H Hercules**	C-2
925	4X-FBQ/420	C-3
927	4X-FBS/427	**Fokker F-27-300M**
929	4X-FBT/435	**Troopship**
931	4X-FBU/448	C-4
Westland Lynx	4X-FBW/436	C-5
XZ260	4X-FBX/428	C-6
XZ261	**Lockheed**	C-7
XZ262	**KC-130H Hercules**	C-8
XZ263	4X-FBY/522	C-9
XZ264	4X-FBZ/545	C-10
XZ265		C-11
XZ266	**ITALY**	C-12
XZ267	**Aeronautica Militare**	**F-27-200MPA**
XZ269	**Italiano**	M-1
XZ270	**Lockheed**	M-2
XZ271	**C-130H Hercules**	**General Dynamics**
XZ272	MM61988/46-02	**F-16A**
XZ273	MM61989/46-03	J212

Overseas Serials

Serial	Serial	Serial
J213	J645	K3049
J214	J646	K3050
J215	J647	K3051
J218	J648	K3052
J219	**General Dynamics**	K3054
J220	**F-16B**	K3055
J221	J259	K3056
J222	J260	K3057
J223	J261	K3058
J224	J262	K3060
J225	J263	K3061
J226	J264	K3062
J227	J265	K3063
J228	J266	K3065
J229	J267	K3066
J230	J268	K3067
J231	J269	K3068
J232	J270	K3069
J234	J271	K3070
J235	J649	K3072
J236	J650	K3073
J238	J651	**Northrop NF-5B**
J239	J652	K4001
J240	J653	K4002
J241	J654	K4003
J242	J655	K4005
J243	J656	K4006
J244	J657	K4007
J245	**Northrop NF-5A**	K4008
J246	K3001	K4009
J247	K3003	K4010
J248	K3004	K4011
J249	K3005	K4012
J250	K3007	K4013
J251	K3008	K4014
J252	K3011	K4015
J253	K3012	K4016
J254	K3013	K4017
J255	K3014	K4018
J256	K3015	K4019
J257	K3016	K4020
J258	K3017	K4021
J616	K3018	K4023
J617	K3019	K4024
J618	K3020	K4025
J619	K3021	K4026
J620	K3022	K4027
J621	K3023	K4028
J622	K3024	K4029
J623	K3025	K4030
J624	K3026	
J625	K3027	**Marine Luchtvaartdienst**
J626	K3028	**Breguet Atlantic**
J627	K3030	250
J628	K3031	251
J629	K3032	252
J630	K3033	254
J631	K3034	256
J632	K3035	258
J633	K3036	**Lockheed**
J634	K3038	**P-3C Orion**
J635	K3039	300
J636	K3040	301
J637	K3041	302
J638	K3042	303
J639	K3043	304
J640	K3044	305
J641	K3045	306
J642	K3046	307
J643	K3047	308
J644	K3048	309

C-12 Fokker F-27-300M Troopship. *PRM*

275 General Dynamics F-16A. *APM*

Serial	Serial	Serial
310	277	953
311	278	954
312	279	955
Westland Lynx	281	956
260 UH14A	282	957
261 UH14A	283	**Lockheed**
262 UH14A	284	**P-3B Orion**
264 UH14A	285	576
265 UH14A	286	583
266 SH14B	287	599
267 SH14B	288	600
268 SH14B	289	601
269 SH14B	290	602
270 SH14B	291	603
271 SH14B	292	**Northrop F-5A**
272 SH14B	293	125
273 SH14B	294	128
274 SH14B	295	129
276 SH14C	296	130
277 SH14C	297	131
278 SH14C	298	132
279 SH14C	299	133
280 SH14C	300	134
281 SH14C	658	156
282 SH14C	659	164
283 SH14C	660	165
	661	207
NEW ZEALAND	662	208
Royal New Zealand Air Force	663	209
Lockheed	664	210
C-130H Hercules	665	211
NZ7001	666	212
NZ7002	667	214
NZ7003	668	215
NZ7004	669	219
NZ7005	670	220
Lockheed	671	224
P-3B Orion	672	227
NZ4201	673	228
NZ4202	674	229
NZ4203	675	368
NZ4204	676	369
NZ4205	677	370
	678	371
NIGERIA	679	372
Federal Nigerian Air Force	680	373
Lockheed	681	374
C-130H Hercules	682	375
NAF-910	683	376
NAF-911	684	562
NAF-912	685	563
NAF-913	686	565
NAF-914	687	566
NAF-915	688	567
	General Dynamics	568
NORWAY	**F-16B**	569
Kongelige Norske	301	570
Luftforsvaret	302	571
Dassault	303	573
Falcon 20	304	574
041	305	575
053	306	576
125	307	577
151	689	578
General Dynamics	690	579
F-16A	691	580
272	692	895
273	693	896
274	**Lockheed**	897
275	**C-130H Hercules**	898
276	952	901

Overseas Serials

Serial	Serial	Serial
902	907	1617
904	908	1620
905	910	1621
Northrop RF-5A	911	
100	912	
101	913	**SINGAPORE**
102	914	**Republic of Singapore Air**
103	915	**Force**
104	916	**Lockheed**
105		**C-130B Hercules**
106	**PORTUGAL**	720
107	**Forca Aerea Portuguesa**	721
108	**Lockheed**	**Lockheed**
109	**C-130H Hercules**	**C-130H Hercules**
110	6801	724
112	6802	725
113	6803	730
489	6804	731
490	6805	732
Northrop F-5B		733
135	**SAUDI ARABIA**	
136	**Al Quwwat Al-Jawwiya**	
241	**as Sa' udiya**	**SPAIN**
242	**Lockheed**	**Ejercito del Aire**
243	**C-130E Hercules**	**Fokker F.27M**
244	451	**Friendship**
387	452	**400MPA**
595	453	D.2-01
906	455	D.2-02
907	**Lockheed**	D.2-03
908	**KC-130H Hercules**	**Lockheed**
909	456	**C-130H Hercules**
Westland	457	T.10-2/312-02
Sea King Mk43	458	T.10-3/311-03
060	459	T.10-4/311-04
062	**Lockheed**	T.10-8/311-05
066	**C-130H Hercules**	T.10-9/311-06
068	460	T.10-10/312-04
069	461	**Lockheed**
070	462	**KC-130H Hercules**
071	463	TK.10-5
072	464	TK.10-6
073	465	TK.10-7
074	466	TK.10-11
189	467	TK.10-12
Westland Lynx	468	
Mk86	469	
207	470	**SWEDEN**
216	1601	**Kungl Svenska Flygvapnet**
228	1602	**Lockheed**
232	1603	**C-130E Hercules**
235	1604	84001/841
237	1605	84002/842
	Lockheed	**Lockheed**
OMAN	**C-130E Hercules**	**C-130H Hercules**
Al Quwwat al Jawwiya al	1606	84003/843
Saltanat Oman	1607	84004/844
BAC 1-11	1608	84005/845
srs 485GD	1609	84006/846
551	1610	84007/847
552	1611	84008/848
553	**Lockheed**	
Lockheed	**C-130H Hercules**	
C-130H Hercules	1612	**SWITZERLAND**
501	1614	**Schweizerische Flugwaffe**
Short Skyvan 3M	1615	**Beech E-50**
901	1618	**Twin Bonanza**
902	1619	A-711
903	**Lockheed**	A-712
904	**KC-130H Hercules**	A-713
906	1616	

Serial	Serial	Serial
TURKEY	20+77	21+85
Turk Hava Kuvvetleri	20+81	21+86
Lockheed	20+91	21+87
C-130E Hercules	20+93	21+88
ETI-00991	20+94	21+90
ETI-01468	20+96	21+91
ETI-01947	21+00	21+92
ETI-13186	21+01	21+93
ETI-13187	21+02	21+94
ETI-13188	21+03*	21+95
ETI-13189	21+06	21+96*
	21+07*	21+97
UNITED ARAB EMIRATES	21+09*	21+98
United Arab Emirates Air	21+11*	21+99
Force	21+13*	22+00
Lockheed	21+14*	22+01
C-130H Hercules	21+15*	22+03
1211	21+16*	22+04
1212	21+17*	22+05
1213	21+18*	22+06
1214	21+19*	22+07
	21+20*	22+08
WEST GERMANY	21+21*	22+10
Luftwaffe (Marinesflieger —	21+22*	22+11*
shown by*)	21+23*	22+12*
Boeing 707-307C	21+24*	22+13*
10+01	21+25*	22+14*
10+02	21+26*	22+15*
10+03	21+27*	22+16*
10+04	21+29*	22+17*
VFW 614	21+30*	22+18*
17+01	21+31*	22+19*
17+02	21+32*	22+20*
17+03	21+34	22+21*
Lockheed	21+35	22+22*
F-104G Starfighter	21+36	22+26*
20+01	21+37	22+28*
20+02	21+38	22+29*
20+04	21+40	22+31
20+05	21+42	22+32
20+06	21+44	22+33
20+07	21+45	22+35
20+08	21+49	22+36
20+09	21+50	22+37
20+13	21+52	22+38
20+36	21+53	22+39
20+37	21+55	22+40
20+38	21+56	22+41
20+39	21+57	22+42
20+42	21+58	22+43
20+43	21+60	22+44
20+46	21+61	22+45
20+47	21+62	22+46
20+49	21+63	22+47
20+50	21+64	22+48
20+53	21+65	22+49
20+56	21+67	22+50
20+57	21+68	22+54
20+59	21+69	22+55
20+61	21+71	22+56
20+62	21+72	22+57
20+64	21+74	22+58
20+67	21+75	22+59
20+68	21+77	22+60
20+69	21+78	22+61
20+70	21+79	22+62
20+71	21+80	22+63
20+72	21+81	22+64
20+74	21+82	22+65
20+75	21+83	22+67
20+76	21+84	22+68

Overseas Serials

Serial	Serial	Serial
22+69	23+62	24+85
22+70*	23+65	24+87
22+71*	23+74	24+88
22+72*	23+75	24+89
22+73*	23+82	24+90
22+74*	23+83	24+92
22+75*	23+84	24+95
22+76*	23+87	24+96
22+77*	23+88	24+97
22+78*	23+89	24+98
22+79*	23+90	24+99
22+80*	23+92	25+02
22+81*	23+94	25+03*
22+82*	23+95	25+04
22+83*	23+98	25+05
22+84*	23+99	25+06
22+85*	24+00	25+08
22+86*	24+01	25+09
22+87*	24+02	25+10
22+88*	24+03	25+11
22+89*	24+05	25+12
22+90	24+06	25+13
22+91	24+07	25+14
22+92	24+08	25+15
22+93*	24+09	25+16
22+95*	24+10	25+17
22+96*	24+11	25+18
22+97*	24+12	25+19
22+98*	24+13	25+22
22+99*	24+14	25+23
23+00*	24+17	25+24
23+01	24+19	25+25
23+02*	24+21	25+26
23+05*	24+22	25+27
23+06*	24+23	25+28
23+07*	24+24	25+29
23+08*	24+25	25+30
23+09*	24+26	25+31
23+11*	24+27	25+32
23+12*	24+28	25+33
23+13*	24+29	25+34
23+14*	24+31	25+35
23+15*	24+32	25+36
23+16*	24+34	25+37
23+17*	24+35	25+40
23+18*	24+37	25+41
23+19*	24+38	25+42
23+20*	24+39	25+43
23+22*	24+41	25+44
23+23*	24+42	25+45
23+24	24+43	25+46
23+25*	24+44	25+47
23+27	24+46	25+48
23+29	24+49	25+49
23+30	24+51	25+50
23+31	24+53	25+51
23+32	24+54	25+52
23+36	24+57	25+53
23+38	24+58	25+54
23+39	24+59	25+55
23+40	24+60	25+59
23+44	24+61	25+61
23+45	24+62	25+62
23+48	24+65	25+64
23+49	24+66	25+65
23+50	24+68	25+70
23+51	24+74	25+72
23+52	24+77	25+73
23+54	24+79	25+74
23+55	24+83	25+77
23+61	24+84	25+78

22+29 Lockheed F-104G Starfighter. *APM*

Overseas Serials

Serial	Serial	Serial
25+79	26+72*	35+60
25+80	26+73*	35+61
25+81	26+74*	35+62
25+82	26+75*	35+63
25+83	26+76*	35+64
25+84	26+78*	35+65
25+86	26+79*	35+66
25+87	26+80*	35+67
25+88	26+81*	35+68
25+92	26+82*	35+69
25+97	26+83*	35+71
25+99	26+85*	35+72
26+03	26+86*	35+73
26+04	26+87*	35+74
26+05	26+88*	35+75
26+06	26+89*	35+76
26+07	26+90*	35+77
26+08	**McD RF-4E**	35+78
26+09	**Phantom**	35+79
26+11	35+01	35+80
26+12	35+02	35+81
26+13	35+03	35+82
26+15	35+04	35+83
26+16	35+05	35+84
26+17	35+06	35+85
26+18	35+07	35+86
26+19	35+08	35+87
26+20	35+09	35+88
26+23	35+10	**McD F-4F**
26+24	35+11	**Phantom**
26+25	35+12	37+01
26+26	35+13	37+03
26+27	35+14	37+04
26+28	35+17	37+05
26+29	35+18	37+06
26+30	35+19	37+07
26+31	35+20	37+08
26+32	35+21	37+09
26+33	35+22	37+10
26+34	35+24	37+11
26+36	35+25	37+12
26+37	35+26	37+13
26+38	35+27	37+14
26+39	35+28	37+15
26+40	35+29	37+16
26+41	35+31	37+17
26+42	35+32	37+18
26+43	35+33	37+19
26+44	35+34	37+20
26+45	35+35	37+21
26+47	35+36	37+22
26+48	35+37	37+23
26+49	35+38	37+24
26+51	35+39	37+25
26+52	35+40	37+26
26+53	35+41	37+27
26+54	35+42	37+28
26+55*	35+43	37+29
26+56*	35+44	37+30
26+57*	35+46	37+31
26+58*	35+48	37+32
26+60*	35+49	37+33
26+61*	35+50	37+34
26+62*	35+51	37+35
26+63*	35+52	37+36
26+65*	35+53	37+37
26+66*	35+54	37+38
26+67*	35+56	37+39
26+68*	35+57	37+40
26+69*	35+58	37+41
26+70*	35+59	37+42

Serial	Serial	Serial
37+43	38+21	40+21
37+44	38+24	40+22
37+45	38+25	40+23
37+46	38+26	40+24
37+47	38+27	40+25
37+48	38+28	40+26
37+49	38+29	40+27
37+50	38+30	40+28
37+51	38+31	40+29
37+52	38+32	40+30
37+53	38+33	40+31
37+54	38+34	40+32
37+55	38+36	40+33
37+56	38+37	40+34
37+57	38+38	40+35
37+58	38+39	40+36
37+59	38+40	40+37
37+60	38+41	40+38
37+61	38+42	40+39
37+63	38+43	40+40
37+64	38+44	40+41
37+66	38+45	40+42
37+67	38+46	40+43
37+69	38+47	40+44
37+70	38+48	40+45
37+71	38+49	40+46
37+73	38+50	40+47
37+74	38+51	40+48
37+76	38+52	40+49
37+77	38+53	40+50
37+78	38+54	40+51
37+79	38+55	40+52
37+80	38+56	40+53
37+81	38+57	40+54
37+82	38+58	40+55
37+83	38+59	40+56
37+84	38+60	40+57
37+85	38+61	40+58
37+86	38+62	40+59
37+88	38+63	40+60
37+89	38+64	40+61
37+90	38+66	40+62
37+91	38+67	40+63
37+92	38+68	40+64
37+93	38+69	40+65
37+94	38+70	40+66
37+95	38+72	40+67
37+96	38+73	40+68
37+97	38+74	40+69
37+98	38+75	40+70
37+99	**D-BD Alpha Jet**	40+71
38+00	40+01	40+72
38+01	40+02	40+73
38+02	40+03	40+74
38+03	40+04	40+75
38+04	40+05	40+76
38+05	40+06	40+77
38+06	40+07	40+78
38+07	40+08	40+79
38+08	40+09	40+80
38+09	40+10	40+81
38+10	40+11	40+82
38+11	40+12	40+83
38+12	40+13	40+84
38+13	40+14	40+85
38+14	40+15	40+86
38+15	40+16	40+87
38+16	40+17	40+88
38+17	40+18	40+89
38+18	40+19	40+90
38+20	40+20	40+91

Serial	Serial	Serial
40+92	41+63	**Transall C-160**
40+93	41+64	50+01
40+94	41+66	50+05
40+95	41+66	50+06
40+96	41+67	50+07
40+97	41+68	50+08
40+98	41+69	50+09
40+99	41+70	50+10
41+00	41+71	50+17
41+01	41+72	50+29
41+02	41+73	50+33
41+03	41+74	50+34
41+04	41+75	50+35
41+05		50+36
41+06	**Panavia Tornado**	50+37
41+07	* Est-61 Ingolstadt	50+38
41+08	‡ LVR-1 Erding	50+39
41+09	(†TTTE Cottesmore)	50+40
41+10	(S) Strike	50+41
41+11	(T) Trainer	50+42
41+12	(T)43+01/G-20†	50+43
41+13	(T)43+02/G-21†	50+44
41+14	(T)43+03/G-22†	50+45
41+15	(T)43+04/G-23†	50+46
41+16	(T)43+05/G-24†	50+47
41+17	(T)43+06/G-25†	50+48
41+18	(T)43+07/G-26†	50+49
41+19	(T)43+08/G-27†	50+50
41+20	(T)43+09/G-28†	50+51
41+21	(T)43+10/G-29†	50+52
41+22	(T)43+11/G-30†	50+53
41+23	(S)43+12/G-70†	50+54
41+24	(S)43+13/G-71†	50+55
41+25	(S)43+14/G-72†	50+56
41+26	(T)43+15/G-31†	50+57
41+27	(T)43+16/G-32†	50+58
41+28	(T)43+17/G-33†	50+59
41+29	(S)43+18	50+60
41+30	(S)43+19*	50+61
41+31	(S)43+20/G-73†	50+62
41+32	(T)43+21	50+64
41+33	(T)43+22	50+65
41+34	(T)43+23/G-34†	50+66
41+35	(S)43+24/G-74†	50+67
41+36	(S)43+25/G-75†	50+68
41+37	(S)43+26/G-76†	50+69
41+38	(S)43+27*	50+70
41+39	(S)43+28‡	50+71
41+40	(T)43+29‡	50+72
41+41	(S)43+30‡	50+73
41+42	(T)43+31‡	50+74
41+43	(S)43+32‡	50+75
41+44	(T)43+33‡	50+76
41+45	(S)43+34‡	50+77
41+46	(T)43+35‡	50+78
41+47	(S)43+36‡	50+79
41+48	(T)43+37‡	50+80
41+49	(S)43+38‡	50+81
41+50	(S)43+39‡	50+82
41+51	(S)43+40‡	50+83
41+52	(S)43+41‡	50+84
41+53	(T)43+42 MFG-1	50+85
41+54	(T)43+43*	50+86
41+55	(T)43+44*	50+87
41+56	(T)43+45 MFG-1	50+88
41+57	(S)43+46*	50+89
41+58	(S)43+47 MFG-1	50+90
41+59	(S)43+48 MFG-1	50+91
41+60	(S)43+49 MFG-1	50+92
41+61	(S)43+50 MFG-1	50+93
41+62	(S)43+51 MFG-1	50+94

Overseas Serials

Serial	Serial	Serial
50+95	58+49	59+17*
50+96	58+50	59+18*
50+97	58+51	59+19*
50+98	58+52	59+20*
50+99	58+53	59+21*
51+00	58+54	59+22*
51+01	58+55	59+23*
51+02	58+56	59+24*
51+03	58+57	59+25*
51+04	58+58	
51+05	58+59	**Breguet**
51+06	58+60	**1151 Atlantic**
51+07	58+61	61+01*
51+08	58+62	61+02*
51+09	58+63	61+03*
51+10	58+64	61+04*
51+11	58+65	61+05*
51+12	58+66	61+06*
51+13	58+67	61+07*
51+14	58+68	61+08*
51+15	58+69	61+09*
Dornier Do.28D-2	58+70	61+10*
Skyservant	58+71	61+11*
58+05	58+72	61+12*
58+06	58+73	61+13*
58+07	58+74	61+14*
58+08	58+75	61+15*
58+09	58+76	61+16*
58+10	58+77	61+17*
58+11	58+78	61+19*
58+12	58+79	61+20*
58+13	58+80	
58+14	58+81	**Westland**
58+15	58+82	**Lynx Mk88**
58+16	58+83	83+01*
58+17	58+84	83+02*
58+18	58+85	83+03*
58+19	58+86	83+04*
58+20	58+87	83+05*
58+21	58+89	83+06*
58+22	58+90	83+07*
58+23	58+91	83+08*
58+24	58+92	83+09*
58+25	58+93	83+10*
58+26	58+94	83+11*
58+27	58+95	83+12*
58+28	58+96	
58+29	58+97	**Westland Sea**
58+30	58+98	**King HAS.41***
58+31	58+99	89+50*
58+32	59+00	89+51*
58+33	59+01	89+53*
58+34	59+02	89+54*
58+35	59+03	89+55*
58+36	59+04	89+56*
58+37	59+05	89+57*
58+38	59+06*	89+59*
58+39	59+07*	89+60*
58+40	59+08*	89+61*
58+41	59+09*	89+62*
58+42	59+10*	89+63*
58+43	59+11*	89+65*
58+44	59+12*	89+66*
58+45	59+13*	89+67*
58+46	59+14*	89+68*
58+47	59+15*	89+69*
58+48	59+16*	89+70*
		89+71*

Addenda

ADDITIONS

Serial	Type (alternative identity)	Owner, operator or location
TW641	Auster AOP6 (G-ATDN)	Privately owned, Biggin Hill
ZD255	Westland Lynx HAS3	RN NASU, RNAS Yeovilton

Argentina

AE-406	Bell UH-1N	Royal Navy, Fleetlands

Denmark

ET-272	Hunter T7	Privately owned, Hurn
K-683	Douglas C-47A (N3239W)	Aces High, Duxford
K-684	Douglas C-47A	Aces High, Duxford

Germany

BA+AY	Valtion Viima II (G-BAAY)	Privately owned, White Waltham

USAF

Fairchild A-10A (81TFW)
81-0957, 81-0962, 81-0963, 81-0964, 81-0966, 81-0967

*General Dynamics F-16A (50TFW: *10TFS, †496TFS)*
80-0607*, 80-0608*, 81-0674†, 81-0683†, 81-0686†, 81-0707†, 81-0709†, 81-0710†, 81-0721†, 81-0722†, 81-0723†

DELETIONS
WT702, XD184, XE546, XE582, XF376, XF442, XF445, XG291, XJ437, XJ686, XJ687, XJ688, XK137, XK138, XK141, XK896, XK970, XK986, XL387, XL444, XM646, XP329, XP345, XP346, XP361, XP398, XS543, XW767, XX400, XZ247, ZA177.

Fairchild A-10A
79-0124, 79-0125, 80-0148

General Dynamics F-111F
70-2377

McDonnell Douglas F-4E Phantom
68-0321, 68-0382, 68-0391, 68-0412, 68-0443, 68-0444, 68-0447, 68-0452, 68-0478, 68-0490, 68-0495, 68-0497, 68-0503, 68-0514, 68-0536, 72-1476
Note: The 50th TFW gave up its last F-4Es during 1982, replacing them by F-16As. Aircraft listed above have returned to the USA, others have been allocated to the 52nd TFW and 86th TFW.

Boeing B-52G
57-6483

DON'T MISS **Civil Aircraft Markings** — *THE* GUIDE TO
AIRLINER REGISTRATIONS AND MOVEMENTS

LAAS-Europe's Largest Aviation Society

Are you an aviation person?

An enthusiast, commercial operator, pilot, historian, or just interested?

If so, LAAS Aviation News and Review is for you. Published monthly and mailed direct to you, LAAS Aviation News and Review is full of the very latest news:- ● Airline and operators news, sales, purchases, routes, worldwide ● Aircraft production, commercial and general ● Comprehensive register review, UK and European ● Aircraft deliveries **PLUS** ● Aircraft movements review ● Aerodrome news ● Special features ● Travel home and abroad.

LAAS also publish specialist aviation books, all at discounted members prices.

For just **£6.00** we will mail you Aviation News and Review every month for a whole year.

Send £6.00 or for a sample copy 60p to:
**LAAS Aviation News and Review, Dept MAM, 83
10 Devon Road, Luton, Beds. LU2 0RH.
Don't delay - join today.**